RIGHT FROM THE START

Right from the Start

The Memoirs
of Sir Wyn Roberts

The Rt. Hon. Lord Roberts of Conwy

UNIVERSITY OF WALES PRESS
CARDIFF
2006

British Library Cataloguing in Publication Data
A catalogue record for this book is available from the British Library.

ISBN-10   0-7083-1962-9
ISBN-13-07083-1962-8

Printed in Wales by Dinefwr Press, Llandybïe

Contents

Preface   vii

In the Beginning . . .   1

A Child's War   6

Chance of a Lifetime   12

London, Spring 1944   16

Four Years On   21

A Very Cold War   28

Vienna, 1949   32

Oxford Blues   39

Mersey Beat   46

The Beeb   53

Tele Wele Wales   59

The Switch   74

To Westminster, 1970   79

Noise of Battle   86

Aftertime   96

Child Harold and Sunny Jim   107

The 1979 Election   119

Sea of Troubles   127

Pussyfooting   139

Contents

Walking the Plank   146

A Friend Falls   162

Devils Rampant   174

Pot-Pourri   181

Home and Abroad   189

Towards a Third Term   200

Walker's Way   213

Around the World   224

Open Road   231

A Funny Old World   241

Major in Charge   252

Black and White Wednesday   264

East and West   278

Going, Going . . .   288

Summer Clouds   302

The Sleazy Life   309

Time for Change   316

Issues Revisited   329

Loose Ends   337

Index   342

Preface

Some men have only one book in them; others a library. So the witty Sydney Smith, canon of St Paul's, told his daughter, Saba, who published his words in her *Memoir* (1855). If I ever had a library in me, it has appeared publicly over the years in articles, speeches and broadcasts, but some of my writings, my personal diaries, have not appeared at all until now. This is my only book. It is the story of my life as lived against the scenario of our times.

Of course, it touches other people's lives, people of my generation and others who came before and after. Some of my living contemporaries may feel that I have not shown them in as favourable a light as they would have wished. All I can say is that I have portrayed them as they appeared to me at the time, in the context of events in which they participated. If they are offended, I too am hurt. I would ask each of them to salve his or her real or imagined wound with the affection and respect they know I have for them. I hope too that the funny side of things shines through the sombreness that pervades so much of everyday life.

The book is as accurate in its dating of events as I have been able to make it with the help of my diaries and available sources and it should be useful to those interested in 'the facts'. What people thought at the time, often so very different from their subsequent thinking, is also recorded. But I make no claim to infallibility, especially in the matter of other people's views. I accept all blame for any errors of fact, judgement or opinion. I thank all who have helped me throughout my life whether mentioned in the book or not and especially my wife and family without whose support and tolerance I could not have functioned at all. Sadly, my eldest son Rhys died on 20 February 2004 at the age of forty-seven. This book is dedicated to his memory.

In the Beginning . . .

I have a fuzzy, sensory recollection in the deepest vaults of my memory of nuzzling in the exquisite warmth of mother's bosom. It was a heavenly experience, which embraced every need of my young life. There was soft comfort and complete security in her arms, copious sustenance and somniferous heat in her breast; her left, with me lying on my right, is the one I particularly cherished. I wanted no more from the world than the continued enjoyment of this eximious existence – not that I knew any other. Of course, I appreciate your doubt about my ability to recall that paradisal state but not my fall from it when the world inflicted its first, truly nasty shock upon me.

Mother must have been tiring under the strain of giving constant succour to the ravenous incubus at her bosom and, unknown to me, had decided it was time to wean her debilitating suckler. In the 1930s the recommended medical practice was to smear the nipples with asafoetida, a brown, resinous liquid with a strong, alliaceous odour and an equally foul taste of raw garlic and onions. It was guaranteed to repel the most voracious infant from the succulent paps that sustained him and make him reach avidly, angrily, for the bottled substitute offered to his limpet lips. I can personally vouch for the devastating efficacy of this dastardly procedure.

Even the horrendous shock of finding my sweetest heaven suddenly transformed into the bitterest hell was catered for. Asafoetida was reputed to have anti-spasmodic properties and, however much I raged and howled against my enforced change of circumstances and shattered lifestyle, I was unlikely to suffer gross, immediate, physical or mental damage. The longer-term consequences of this horrid experience were not much thought about at the time and can only now be guessed at.

For me, this abrupt weaning proved an eye-opener to awareness of the world. I began to notice contrasting things beyond my

1

mother's arms – my father's reverend white dog collar resting on the black apron at his neck and, outdoors, the intriguing darkness of a farmhouse cellar beyond its bright, sunlit entrance. There were contrasting smells too; my mother's always richly fertile but fragrant with eau de cologne when she wore her fox-fur stole and father's always predominantly tobacco flavoured – his clothes, his breath. I became aware of the differences between sounds; a jolly but hypnotic Welsh lullaby mother sang down to a whisper as I dozed off – 'Gee ceffyl bach, yn cario ni'n dau' ('Gee little horse, bearing us both') – and occasional raised voices below stairs at night, which roused me from my slumbers and made me cry to silence them. And touch? That fox-fur stole was a perpetually intriguing toy, especially the beady eyes that I could never dislodge, and while I clung to the brown fur no harm could possibly come to me. I would never fall in the glowing red coal fire I was constantly being warned against from the day I began to crawl.

Family life in the 1930s demanded a large measure of love and unstinting devotion. Making ends meet and properly feeding and clothing the children was a continual challenge, even to the lower echelons of the professional middle class to which we belonged. Many working-class families lived in poverty and when there was no work the children's bellies were filled with bread soaked in tea. Dole money would not extend to much else. A snared rabbit was a treat.

My parents made love according to the book, as you would expect a very practical former school teacher and her other-worldly Methodist minister husband to do. I know because, a few years on, I found the book, neatly tucked away from prurient eyes among endless volumes of J. H. Newman's *Parochial and Plain Sermons*. It was brown covered, just like the sermons, but the title was *Married Love* by Dr Marie Stopes, the canny botanist who devoted herself to sex education and family planning in the 1920s and 1930s. Her books were the bedroom bibles of the middle class. She taught them how to make love and douse the consequences. Father bought the book – I feel sure because he was the bibliophile of the family – but it was Mother who absorbed its contents. They were happy enough and close, especially when he called her 'Honey'. They had two children, my older brother and myself.

My mother was a stern matriarch and controlled the family finances and her children's education rather as Japanese house-wives do. My brother, her first-born, bore the brunt of her teaching and I was left to pick up the gist of things as my brother's learning progressed. The village school was next door to our home and I was taken there at the abominably early age of two and a half. I objected in the strongest possible terms, not so much to the prospect of being taught, as to the itchy, clinging, teletubby, woollen pantaloons I had been dressed in for my classroom debut. My altercation with Mother degenerated into a physical struggle as we entered the school building. When I was presented to the head-mistress at an inner door in a pine and glass partition beyond which I glimpsed her rows of pupils, trapped in their desks, my rebellious nature exploded. I seized the brass door handle in the partition and howled the place down. But my epic struggle was of no avail. The two women prized my fingers from the brass while they maintained a genteel conversation about how normally well behaved I was and how I would soon settle down in my new environment. I still hate the tang of pine.

My father read, wrote and thought all day in what we called the dining room, apart from meal times when he would join us in the living room-kitchen, often still deep in thought as he ate. We boys were obliged to be quiet when he was so engrossed in his room – an obligation mother rigorously enforced with the injunction: 'Your father's thinking!' And think he did unceasingly about spiritual things and with evident concentration. He rubbed his hands gently when his relished thoughts flowed smoothly and shook with sup-pressed anger when he was disturbed. He wrote out his sermons in full and more than once because he seldom corrected a word or phrase. He simply rewrote, with a uniquely delicate hand and a split nib pen he dipped periodically in a bottle of blue-black Stephen's ink. He also wrote a weekly column for his denomination's news-paper (Y *Goleuad*) and when this composition was underway, the spittle would boil in the bowl of his pipe or overflow from his lips and down the stem but never onto the sacred, lined, writing paper. At night, he worked under the white light of an Aladdin lamp whose mantle burned black if it was turned too high. I sat alone watching him in fascinated silence many times while my brother talked to Mam in the kitchen. Welsh was our first language and everything – our speaking, writing, thinking – was done in Welsh. We learnt English at school.

Father once gave me a spare pen as well as the usual sheet of blank paper but I must have pressed the nib too hard: it broke and shot into my eye. All hell was let loose for a time, until father nudged out the metal with a corner of his handkerchief. I am tearful still with the memory of his tenderness.

Father was a short, portly man and his right leg was an inch and a half shorter than his left. Mother told me that his deformity was due to a bad bone-set after he broke his leg in childhood. He never spoke about it and always walked with a stick out of doors. He could never play games with us but I remember him lifting me bodily to the top of a high cupboard once when I was in a tantrum and teasing the temper out of me. 'You little ogre,' he said again and again until I laughed. I must have been very small for him to lift me so high.

He always had a motor car, which was unusual in those distant days; a solid spoke-wheeled Rover when I came into the world in July 1930, which was replaced by a brand new Austin Seven in 1936 at a cost of £130. Mother's prudent management of our finances must have been severely stretched. Occasionally, the car became the village ambulance as Father took to hospital people too ill to go by bus. He did the rounds of his chapel members regularly but reluctantly, I sensed, because he regarded visiting as a distraction from his real work. He cared more for people's souls than their bodies and often said so.

Father never talked politics – he was more interested in the next world than in this – but the horrors of the war in Abyssinia and the bombing of innocent tribesmen to further the imperial ambitions of Italian Fascists deeply affected us all. I was five at the time and Mother had no difficulty in persuading my brother and me to add the unfortunate people of that country to our nightly prayers. Their diminutive emperor, Haile Selassie, the Lion of Judah as he called himself, was also commended to the mercy of the Almighty. He lived to a ripe old age. I remember my fifth birthday on 10 July 1935 and the shapely, quivering jellies Mother made in an aluminium mould. I was king of all I surveyed that day. But I was troubled by warts on my hands. One Saturday morning, my brother took me across the field behind our house to William Thomas's smithy to dip my hands in the water tub where he cooled his irons. The smith was as fierce as his trade, with arms thick as stanchions and a temper as hot as his metal. We watched him lean on the bull-horn-tipped arm of his bellows and fan the smithy fire until the horseshoe was white hot, hammer the shoe on the anvil – we blinked as the hot sparks flew – and then rush out to the stable next door to fit the shoe to the hoof. That was the moment we were waiting for. My brother ushered me to the tub and I washed my hands in the tepid, iron-laden water. The warts disappeared in days and I never suffered from them again.

Severe as she was on occasion, Mother had a heart of gold, soft and sensitive. She could also be very informative, as when Mrs Lloyd George came to see us one afternoon to talk to Mother about one of her charities. I listened quietly. After she had gone, I told Mother that our visitor had seemed very sad. Mother pondered briefly on my comment before delivering her own: 'The wives of famous men are often sad; they have a lot to worry about.' I did not know then about the legendary vagaries of LG's love life but Mother clearly had an inkling if not more.

Mother read me Welsh poems that plucked my heartstrings and brought tears to my eyes. My favourite was about a little orphaned girl who found solace in her Bible. It was deplorable, sentimental stuff by today's standards but I lapped it up. On my sixth birthday, Mother presented me with the soft, brown-cover volume of poetry from which she read (Ceiriog) and I can still see in my mind her bold, handwritten dedication on the frontispiece even though the book has long gone.

It was the year when King George V died and his son, the Prince of Wales, whom Mother had lifted me up to see when he rode in an open car through Bangor, succeeded as Edward VIII. 'Something must be done,' said the king when he saw the poverty of the unemployed in the Rhondda. He could have said the same to the Jarrow marchers. People were moved to hope against hope.

The dictators abroad were certainly doing something. Mussolini won his war in Abyssinia and proclaimed that Italy at last had an empire. The Nazis reoccupied the Rhineland and a bloody, atrocious civil war erupted in Spain. Franco was no better than Mussolini and the ex-painter, Hitler. They were all in cahoots with one another. 'Cain and Abel, brother against brother,' my father muttered over breakfast and some dreadful news from Spain. I looked suspiciously at my own brother. He was always taking my things. We were always at war one way or another.

A Child's War

That first fateful Sunday in September 1939 was a day of sunshine and Mother and I were in our front garden when a fourteen-year-old boy called Alfred came along with an empty bucket on the crook of his arm. He was going to fetch drinking water from the newly installed village pump twenty yards from our front gate. Before the new pump, we had all drawn our water from an earthen pipe where excess water from a distant well flowed freely and copiously, except in the dry summer season when the flow was reduced to a trickle.

'We've declared war on Germany,' Alfred said.

'No!' exclaimed Mother in disbelief.

'It was on the wireless,' Alfred affirmed.

Mother was upset and ordered me indoors as if I had done some something wrong. She had lost a brother, my Uncle Willie, in the Great War – he died of pneumonia in France – and another brother, my Uncle John, had lost his right arm in the Dardanelles. His empty sleeve, when he was not dressed up and wearing his artificial arm, had been a forceful reminder to us over the years of the dreadful personal cost of war to members of Mother's family. Not surprisingly, she was a pacifist at heart. I remembered her recoiling at the sudden sight of soldiers and artillery on the quay at Caernarfon when we went there to see the magical Lloyd George addressing the National Eisteddfod. Her grip on my hand had tightened unforgettably at the sight of soldiers.

The declaration of war came as no surprise. On the preceding Wednesday, my father had been visited by a gentle, quiet-spoken giant of a man in khaki uniform with a rifle slung over his shoulder. He was a near neighbour and the father of four ginger-haired children, three boys and a girl. As a member of the Territorial Army, he had been one of the first to be called up. His wife was crying on his shoulder and Mother took her to the kitchen while her husband,

Robert Roberts, and my father talked in our best, front room. While I eyed the heavy .303 rifle resting against the sofa, he told Father that he would shortly be going to France and he solemnly commended his wife and family to Father's care although he was not a member of our chapel. Father nodded agreement and gave such consolation as he could. Shortly after, Mr Roberts picked up his rifle and left. In a matter of weeks, he had embarked for France along with thousands of others in the British Expeditionary Force and within months he had been killed by mortar fire. A friend saw him die and confirmed it personally to his wife after being miraculously rescued himself from the hellish beaches at Dunkirk. Mrs Roberts gave birth to a daughter in the spring of 1940 and named her Frances in her father's memory.

This was a time of intensive preparation. Not only were all school children supplied with gas masks, which we trundled around in cardboard boxes with weatherproof canvas holders, but there were constant evacuation drills in case the execrable Hitler bombed our school. (I had moved at the age of seven from our village school to another at Menai Bridge, four miles and a 4d return bus ride away.)

All road direction signs had already been removed. Now, holes were dug in main roads ready for mining in the event of an invasion and breezeblock machine-gun posts and concrete tank barriers were built at strategic locations. Thousands of acres of sandy beaches were planted at intervals with large wooden poles to stop hostile landing craft and to buttress Churchill's courageous claim that we would fight the enemy on the beaches as well as on land and in the air. Every able-bodied person was involved in the war effort and even my one-armed Uncle John – no friend of Churchill, the planner of the Dardanelles fiasco – took a job as a factory hand at the Daimler works in Bangor.

Occasionally, late at night behind our blackout curtains and in the safety of our beds, we heard the drone of heavily loaded German bombers crossing Anglesey to raid Liverpool docks. We would hear about it on the wireless news the next day. (We had bought a wireless at the beginning of hostilities and listening to the nine o'clock news in hushed silence had become part of our daily routine.)

After one such raid, the village was agog with the surprising intelligence that a returning German bomber had dumped its remaining bombs into the sea at Red Wharf Bay where, incidentally, the submarine *Thetis* had sunk during trials just before the war. The turbulence caused by the bombs killed a shoal of herrings, which were now being washed ashore in waves. Doctors pronounced the fish wholesome and local people filled buckets, baskets and even casks. Fresh herring was a welcome change from a diminishing hoard of tinned salmon, which a select few had had the money and the foresight to buy before the war dried up supplies of such delicacies.

Some time before the blitz on Liverpool began in earnest, our one-shop village had experienced an invasion of children, evacuated from Merseyside to the comparative safety of our rural community. More than a dozen of them arrived one day at the church hall at the gentrified, more Anglicized, lower end of the village where the majority of churchgoers lived and worked as gardeners, stable hands and the like. The church had owned some farms in that neighbourhood before Lloyd George disestablished it and church attendance had been a condition of tenancy. Chapel people occupied the upper end of the village where farmland was not so encumbered. The church end, with its brace of great houses – Treffos and Gadlys – was alien territory to us chapel folk and we seldom ventured there without a trace of anxiety in our hearts.

But the country was at war, chapelgoers included, and we were not to be outdone in patriotism or humanity. Mother led the way to the church hall and returned with two boys, Frank who was my brother's age and a pale six-year-old called Jimmy. When I first saw Jimmy, he was standing stark naked in a wash tub in our back garden and Mother was scrubbing him from head to foot. I was told to keep my distance. Poor Jimmy was covered with the largest lice Mother had ever seen and every one jack of them had to be combed from his hair and out of every crevice in his little body. He was given some of my clothes; his own infested garments had to be burnt. Father too took a close interest in Jimmy because he was a Roman Catholic and his faith and his rosary, odious as they might be, had to be fully respected in our very Protestant household. Jimmy was as happy as a six-year-old from Scotland Road could be in his clean, new surroundings but he missed his mother and she him. He did not stay with us for long and returned to the bombs.

There were three girls in one of the grand houses at the church end of the village, staying with Mrs Morgan and her rich archdeacon husband with a booming voice and a patch over his right eye. It was said he owned half the town of Aberystwyth. He certainly had a string of smart horses – hunters mainly – before the war took its toll on them. He also employed a fierce, monoglot English gamekeeper who jealously guarded his shooting rights over the entire village, including chapel people's land. Pheasants were not God's creatures; they were the archdeacon's. His shotgun was specially made and had a curved stock so that he could tuck the butt in his right shoulder and still aim with his good left eye. His ecclesiastical office was attached to the church at nearby Beaumaris. He was a power in the land and so was his wife.

Rumour had it among my older friends that the jolly girls at Gadlys, the Morgans' mansion, were fond of sweets and were prepared to give something in return. Len, the eldest of us, had proved it with Joyce, the eldest of them, and had had a very enjoyable kiss. Little Owie, who always stank of urine, claimed to have had a similar experience with Olive, the next junior. There remained the youngest, Rita, who was my age. I gave her a sweet over the school wall but the wall was too high for a kiss. In any case, at the age of ten, I was not that interested. Yet, the boys kept on talking about making an assignation and we planned a daring expedition to meet the girls in a field behind the church hall. It was not far from their home ground. I took a rabbit net with me, partly as an alibi to explain my presence in this alien territory and partly in case the girls failed to turn up.

They were certainly not there at the appointed time and so I set the rabbit net over a hole in the hedge. And then we heard the exciting sound of girlish laughter. 'They're coming! They're coming!' we whispered loudly to each other, hardly believing our luck. We quickly paired off and went to our own secluded spots. Rita was very talkative and soon told me how Mrs Morgan had instructed them on menstruation and warned of the pregnant consequences of coition with a male thereafter. Rita had seen signs of bleeding in herself, she told me with great seriousness.

To pass the time, Rita agreed to lie back on the grass to let me view her lovely, endearing expanse of tummy and the curvaceous swell of her Venus mound. I did not touch her cleft, as I had done with other girls, after what she had said about the blood. She in turn had a reassuring look at my limpid, immature little member and flicked her fingers over it, fearfully and all too briefly. We both realized that this was doctors-and-nurses stuff and we were getting beyond that kind of childish curiosity. But where? Nothing was happening: nothing could happen; nothing did.

We waited for a decent interval of time to pass but were the first to rise from our lair. As soon as we did so, the others rose too. I guessed they had been waiting for us as we had for them. When the girls had gone, we compared notes. Owie claimed to have gone 'all the way', but we did not believe him. Len was quietly thoughtful. Perhaps he too had been handicapped in his seduction by Mrs Morgan's lecture to the girls on teenage pregnancy.

Three days later, Mother, seething with suppressed rage, tackled me head on.

'Were you at church hall on Saturday? I want the truth.'

It was clear she knew something. Had the girls blabbed to Mrs Morgan?

'Yes. Why do you ask?'

'Never you mind,' she said, her voice full of menace.

'We were looking for rabbits. My net is still there,' I muttered.

Mother was not to be diverted so easily.

'Did you see those Gadlys girls?'

'Who?'

'Those girls staying with that dreadful Mrs Morgan.' She was spluttering with impatience at my prevarication.

'They were around,' I said as nonchalantly as I could. Mother watched the guilt curdle in my eyes under her glare.

'How dare you disgrace me in the eyes of that woman! Go upstairs and get into your pyjamas. I'm going to beat the devil out of you.'

I did as I was told, not really believing that she would carry out her threat. She had never laid a hand on me before. But her firm, determined step on the stairs filled me with foreboding and when she appeared in the room with some kind of birch, I knew that my punishment was premeditated. I howled as she rained her blows on my bottom but, somehow, I sensed her restraint. She was not quite as mad as she pretended to be and her fear that she might do me harm was real enough.

After the beating was over, I cried myself to sleep and vowed to get my own back on Mother, which I did a few days later by taking her with me to recover the rabbit net, still in place in the hedge where I had set it. She grew pensive on our return journey, possibly impressed by the evidence I had provided of my claim to innocence and her own folly in believing Mrs Morgan's sensational account of our orgy.

'Never tangle with those church people' she said. 'They're not like us.'

I had been a casualty of the perennial war between church and chapel.

Our local newspaper, the *Liverpool Daily Post*, carried a war picture daily on its front page and I cut them out and pasted them in a book I had titled 'The War 1939 –'. It began with a picture of the battleship *Royal Oak*, sunk by a German torpedo in her home base of Scapa Flow in October 1939. I was particularly interested in the war at sea because I intended joining the Navy when I grew up and I followed every move in the chase of the German battleship, the *Graf Spee*, by the immortal British cruisers – *Ajax*, *Achilles* and *Exeter* – to its final scuttling in Montevideo harbour.

My friend Len's craggy faced uncle, Tommy, had been a seaman all his life. When he was home on leave, he taught us how to climb a rope and make fast by tucking the rope under the shoulder and, more engrossing still, he showed us a string of unarmed combat tricks, never to be forgotten. We became walking manuals on commando tactics and practised in the art of depriving an attacker of his knife, dislocating his shoulder or putting a heel in his chin depending on his approach. We learnt how to deal with an armlock around the neck, inflicted from behind, by grabbing the attacker's 'goolies' as Tommy called them; how to fall backwards before a frontal assault, grip the assailant at the chest and lever him up with a boot in the stomach before hurling him to kingdom come. Tommy was an encyclopaedia of such knowledge and expert at imparting it. None of us was ever seriously hurt on the mattress in the shed where we practised. The one secret Tommy knew but would never tell was how to kill a man with one's bare hands. 'It's too easily done,' said the unsmiling Tommy. We had no reason to doubt his word.

I spent the summer holidays with my cousins at Malltraeth, near Bodorgan. There were hundreds of Italian prisoners of war there, helping to drain the marshes, and my cousins were so familiar with them that any qualms I had about visiting the cruel oppressors of Abyssinia soon evaporated. 'They'll make you a cigarette case for sixpence,' one of my cousins said, rehearsing his *buon giorno* and sundry Italian phrases he had found useful.

When I met these young men, who totally disarmed me with a mug of superb, hot coffee and a ham-bacon sandwich so tasty that I have never found its equal, it was hard to believe that they could have played any part in the atrocities perpetrated in Abyssinia. They were kind men with soft brown eyes, brothers, lovers and young fathers who, left to themselves, would not have harmed a soul. It was dawning on me that it was misguided nationalism and evil-minded leaders that corrupted decent, civilized peoples and induced them to perpetrate barbaric acts against others over whom they had power.

Chance of a Lifetime

In the summer of 1943, Allied Forces gained their first foothold in mainland Europe with the Sicily landings. The Russians broke the backbone of their German invaders in a massive and decisive tank battle at Kursk. Alas, my brother contracted scarlet fever and was taken away to an isolation hospital. I was kept home from school and told to keep away from other children. I was determined not to suffer the same fate as my brother and spent as much time as I could outdoors. When I had to go indoors, I went about the house holding my breath to avoid infection. A week went by and my skin was still clear of the reddish, tell-tale spots that heralded the dreaded disease.

One morning, Mother, holding an open letter in her hand, asked me, 'Would you like to go to the school that Churchill went to?' I answered 'Yes' immediately. I would have gone anywhere to escape the scourge that had placed my brother virtually behind bars. I had seen him through the hospital window, smiling bravely but deeply unhappy. Mother soon disillusioned me. I was not going anywhere now or even when my quarantine ended. I would have to meet people who would judge my suitability for the new school. The first, who had dandled me on his knee years before, was our local councillor, Sir Harry Verney, who was coming to see us that afternoon. Sir Harry, a stocky, jovial man, bubbling with conversation, duly arrived accompanied by his son, Lawrence John, spick and span in a sub-altern's uniform complete with peaked cap, kid gloves and a walking stick. He had just been commissioned in the Grenadier Guards and was fit as a fiddle from his Sandhurst training. They could not come inside the house because of my brother's contagious fever and so the interview, for such it was, took place in our back yard.

'We can't have you going to fight with little red spots, can we LJ?' joked Sir Harry, using his son's initials as a form of endearment. He turned to me.

'Do you know any Latin?'

'Yes.'

'What's the Latin for as fast as possible?'

'Quam celerrime.'

'Good. Do you know the Gospels?'

'Mathew, Mark, Luke and John?'

'Excellent. They're very keen on the Scriptures at Harrow. Have you read any Dickens?'

'Yes. *Oliver Twist*.'

'And the *Tale of Two Cities*?'

I nodded, more in approval than in affirmation that I had read that too, which I had not.

'Which were the two cities?'

I was stumped, clean bowled. But the ever-ebullient Sir Harry dug me out of my difficulty by giving a synopsis of the story with LJ supplementing his memory with odd details. We were getting on well. I reminded him of the story he had told me years before of his ancestor, Sir Edmund Verney, who had been killed at the Battle of Edgehill in the Civil War, clutching the king's standard so firmly that his ring had to be cut from his finger. Sir Harry was impressed.

'Wonderful!' he pronounced as the interview drew to a close.

'I would like you to meet a master from Harrow who is coming to stay with us shortly. Will you do that? He's a splendid man, Mr Plumptre, isn't he LJ?'

'Absolutely splendid,' said LJ emphatically. 'You will like him enormously.'

Wern y Wylan (gull's cove) was a very select Verney family development and comprised a hotel, objet d'art shop, a croquet lawn, with a very accurate sundial at the edge, and some spacious bungalows, all located halfway down the steep hill to Llanddona beach. I went there on my bicycle and met Mr Plumptre, a slim bespectacled man who tittered and chuckled as if he was on the verge of a loud guffaw which never came. He taught classics. We went for a walk down to the beach.

Mr Plumptre knew how to judge boys. He let me prattle on endlessly about the sinking of the submarine *Thetis*; the captain's surprising escape with the Davis apparatus while ninety-eight others perished. Then, I regaled him with the story of the German bomber that had dropped its load among the herrings. I do not know what he made of my discourse but at least I kept him amused.

My parents bought me *The Little Bible* for Christmas and I read it from cover to cover in preparation for the common entrance examination and then the much tougher scholarship papers that followed. Exceptionally, because of the difficulties of wartime travel, I was allowed to sit both exams in my own secondary school at Beaumaris where I had been transferred after passing the infamous Eleven Plus. In due course, news came that I had been awarded a scholarship on my English and history and that I would be expected to join the Head Master's House at Harrow for the start of the summer term of 1944.

I was about to enter a different and wider world, totally strange to me. I would have to give up smoking, which was threatening to get a grip on me despite the fact that cigarettes were in short supply, and that other unmentionable, compulsive but exquisite sensual delight all growing boys indulge in.

My knowledge and experience had been greatly extended by the war. Grown men not in the forces were few and far between and able-bodied boys were often called on to do men's work. I put up the pheasants for Canon Morgan (recently promoted) to shoot at for 7s 6d a day; shot rabbits myself with a borrowed shotgun and sold them to shops before going to school. On Saturdays and holidays, I worked on a farm and built up strong muscles which stood me in good stead later on.

We were sheltering from the rain in a haybarn one day when a pack of photographs of the beach at Dunkirk was handed round. The photographs had been left for safe keeping by a Canadian sailor related to the farming family we were helping out. They had clearly been taken by a German soldier because there were shots of his friends, bare headed and smiling in a machine-gun emplacement, and of hundreds of captive British soldiers marching off somewhere under armed guard. The most haunting and grotesque was a picture of a fully clad French soldier – his helmet was different from a British Tommy's – lying dead on the foreshore, his facial flesh eaten down to the bone by the sea and its creatures. This was the grim reality of war, the reality we never saw on cinema newsreels.

I was not averse to leaving my old school. The headmaster was a sadistic character and ruled by terror. I once saw him clout a boy to the ground for not having the correct amount of money to pay for his midday meals. He despised his pupils and wielded the cane in his study on the slightest provocation. Some tried to excuse his vile temper and cruel behaviour by saying that he had shrapnel in his back from the First World War. I was glad to escape his bullying, barbaric regime. But there were some excellent, dedicated teachers at Beaumaris too: Mr Griffiths, nicknamed 'Winks', the chemistry teacher, chain-smoking Miss Davies, who taught Latin, and another Miss Davies who taught Welsh. They inculcated an enduring love of their subjects and I shall be ever grateful to them.

Meanwhile, advised and generously helped by the sweet Lady Rachel, Sir Harry's 'little wife', titled in her own right as a scion of the Elgin family, mother collected the dozen pairs of socks, handkerchiefs, shirts and the rest I would need – all with my name tag sewn on them – for my first three-month sojourn at Harrow on the Hill. One of LJ's worsted suits, which he had grown out of, fitted me perfectly. I felt a proper little gent.

London, Spring 1944

My one-armed Uncle John had worked as a draper in Dickens and Jones in Regent Street before the First World War and could still wrap and tie up a parcel with one hand more deftly and neatly than any other person I have ever known. He had lived in London for some years after the Great War until he lost his job in the Depression and had to retire to live with his two surviving brothers on the farm at Newborough. But he had kept in touch with his London friends and visited them from time to time. Uncle John had 'the knowledge' as London cab drivers say. He knew the city like the back of his hand. He therefore took charge of the operation of getting me to Harrow. He booked Mother and myself in for a couple of nights at Browns Hotel, a traditional, slightly grand, family establishment, just off Baker Street.

The experience of travelling by train to London was a complete novelty to me. Few civilians travelled long distances except to take up work. The furthest I had been was Liverpool and that was a recent one-day visit. 'Is your journey really necessary?' was a slogan question plastered on hoardings throughout the war and as common as 'Careless talk costs lives' (a warning against spies). But the real eye-opener was London's West End, full of young American servicemen on leave and aware that they would shortly be invading Europe. Some looked very serious. Others carried half-bottles of Scotch in their hip pockets and I was not surprised to see a drunken brawl on an Underground station platform. The military police soon put an end to it. Hundreds of families slept on these platforms in certain stations for fear of the bombing. High-heeled girls with ankle straps stood chatting on street corners accosting male passers-by. 'All I want you to do is f**k me,' I overheard a blonde girl say to a young GI, his hands deep in his pockets and swaying slightly. But he refused to be drawn; his mind was on other things. It was the first time I had heard the four-letter word used by a woman.

The day when I was to start at my new school came all too soon and Uncle John, Mother and I took the Underground from Baker Street to Harrow on the Hill. We bundled my trunk into a taxi and were soon taking tea at the Head Master's House. I had never seen a grand piano before, certainly not used as a parking place for an empty teacup and saucer. I hung on to mine until a small plateful of delicately cut cucumber sandwiches was proffered to me. I was ravenous and there was nothing for it but to desecrate the beautifully polished black lid of the piano with my cup and saucer to free my hands for the morsels. Mercifully, another boy beat me to the piano lid and so my act was not as outlandish as I had feared.

It was a motley gathering of parents and boys. The headmaster, I guessed, was the dark-suited, smooth man with the moustache and his wife the lovely lady whose dark beauty outshone the Matisse picture of a woman above the fireplace. The matron in a dark blue uniform and the genial house master, 'Pip' Boas, were also there. I learnt who was who from a clever Adonis of a boy with very pale skin and a golden crop of curls.

'Where are you from?' he asked.

'Anglesey, north Wales. And you?'

'Manchester, Taff. My name's Colin, Colin McEvedy.'

Although he was confident as hell – just short of arrogant – I sensed he was looking for a pal. Colin said he had been beaten at his preparatory school.

'They don't beat boys here, do they?' I said incredulously – it was inconceivable amidst all that fragile china.

'Good God, yes. The older boys do it.'

I did not believe him. But I had other concerns. How was I to live in this space of unbreakable things and minute food rations?

Out of the corner of my eye, I could see Uncle John giving an ultra-graphic account to Mrs Moore, the head's wife, of how he had heard an enemy aircraft overhead during the night. His account became a performance as he demonstrated how he had dived under the bed by lowering his head to the level of Mrs Moore's dimpled knees. Losing his arm had loosened his mind, we knew. He was a volatile character, my Uncle John.

'We were bombed on the Hill last term,' Mrs Moore told him softly, no doubt hoping to quell his excitement.

'Were you indeed!' he shouted – as if he was calling chickens to their feed on the farm at home.

'Yes, incendiaries fell on Speech Room but no one was hurt.'

I was glad in a boyish way when the moment came for him to leave. Mother and I skipped the embarrassing goodbye kiss and she contented herself with her inimitable, firm grip around my shoulders, which told me everything I needed to know.

'You will now be shown to your rooms,' an authoritative voice said after the parents had gone and we boys – twelve in all – were taken along a carpeted corridor to a broad, light blue door. It opened onto a different world, with concrete-floored passages, iron-railed stairways and rushing, breathless boys of all shapes and sizes. 'Easy now!' Pip's voice commanded and the boys slowed down momentarily in their headlong gallop down the passage. I was relieved. I could survive in this rough-and-tumble world with no grand piano in sight. The boys did not look as if they were starving either.

I was introduced to my roommate, Richard Long, who had been at the school for a year. His father, the viscount, had brought his brother John, a new boy like me, up from Wiltshire that day. The viscount was the last person I saw wearing grey galoshes over his footwear. (I did not know then that he was to be given the freedom of Athens in honour of his brother, Walter, who was killed there in 1941. Walter Long's name was added to the plinth of his ancestor George Canning's statue in Athens. Both had fought for the freedom of Greece.) Richard Long was a helpful soul, later erroneously described by Alan Clark in the first edition of his diary as 'a tart at Eton'. He was neither. He was a friend for life to me as school friends are.

The novelties of my new school life kept me fully occupied for some weeks. As a scholar, I was in the alpha stream with the best of my contemporaries and I soon realized how advanced they were, especially in the classics and maths. I had no Greek so I took science which I knew something about. While they grappled with calculus, I tried to bridge the chasm between my mathematical skills and theirs, not that maths were my strong point anyway. My history and English were good. 'Odd that you can write English so well but can't speak it,' Colin mused.

We ate every meal in the house hall where the names of our predecessors, carved in gold on long, brown wood panels, looked down on our antics. W. L. Spencer Churchill was there and so was I. O. Liddell who had won the Victoria Cross. We were a multinational crowd, about seventy in all – French, Dutch and even German, many being sons of refugees from Hitler's Europe. But the major difference between us was in age. We ranged from 13/14 to

17/18. Those who had come to the school in the same year were taught together and played games together (at various levels of ability) and the whole system of fagging, privileges and responsibilities was geared to this age differential.

It was a cocky little Canadian I disliked called Hodgson who was the first to utter:

> Taffy was a Welshman
> Taffy was a thief

He got no further with his insulting doggerel. I picked him up bodily and threw him through the air into a corner of his room. He crumbled in shocked silence. News of my incredible feat of strength buzzed round the house like wildfire. It gained me a bonanza of respect at all levels and a host of friends who felt in need of a protector. One or two who fancied their chances engaged me in friendly wrestling matches, only to find their limbs at breaking point in an unarmed combat grip learnt from Tommy, the commando.

Everything was going well until a bout of homesickness struck me. Then the Samson of the new boys cried his eyes out on the pillow, night after heart-rending night. I was saved by a curious turn in the war. I was walking along the pavement in front of the Head Master's House one fine July afternoon when I heard the drone of what sounded like a mighty, spluttering motor cycle, but this heavy, intermittent roar was coming from the sky. I stopped, looked up and there, 500 feet or so above our chapel steeple, was a flying bomb, the infamous doodlebug as cockneys were now calling the V-1. It was Hitler's latest secret weapon. The spluttering, faltering noise came from its jet engine, which spat a bluish-red flame from the rear of the pilotless, sinisterly menacing plane.

I knew that when the engine stopped the aircraft would crash to the ground and explode but as it was now over the church on the very top of the Hill, it was unlikely to fall on me. I raced up the Hill to the old school yard, just in time to see the explosion and the smoke rising from the endless sea of suburban houses filling my entire vista of north-west London. I watched the pall hover in the haze of this quiet, sunny day and wondered how many people had been killed or injured beneath it. When the smoke had drifted clear, the sea of houses was much as before, vast and unchanged. I could not even detect with the naked eye where the bomb had fallen and I said to myself that Hitler would have to do worse than this to bring Britain to its knees.

Most of the doodlebugs fell on south-east London – the one I saw above the Hill, so far to the north-west, must have been a stray – but the school authorities were nervous. There were rumours that the V-1 was the first of a series of devastating devices and that there were more horrendous weapons to come as indeed proved to be the case when the invisible V-2 rocketed into London. The boys who had homes outside the metropolis were invited to return there to safety. They jumped for joy. As for me, when my homesickness was at its most acute, I had firmly resolved that, come what may, I would endure one term at Harrow if no more, rather than face the ignominy of a cowardly return home. Hitler could do his worst but he was not going to change my mind and, when I was asked whether I would like to go home, I said no.

My friends, who had not experienced my homesickness problem, thought I was a fool to refuse a holiday and escaped from the Hill as fast as they could. Our class numbers fell and my knowledge gap closed rapidly over the weeks that followed with the near one-to-one tuition given by my dedicated teachers. We slept in bunks in underground passages rather than in our rooms. A new intimacy developed in our diminished community and I began to love the school and its people.

I hated cricket because I was no good at it; I never scored more than ten runs and could not bowl for toffee. But gentle hints were dropped that cricket was not the be-all and end-all of existence – important though it was that we should beat Eton at Lords. It was 'Pip' who suggested that I might be considered for a minor part in the school play. This I knew would carry the incidental benefit of taking me off cricket every Tuesday and Thursday afternoon. I leapt at the prospect.

Four Years On

One must learn something in four years at school, something apart from the considerable intake of factual knowledge and the proper way of handling it for one's own or others' delight and benefit; something over and above the appreciation of other peoples' history, their errors and successes. I mean that special something that makes us grow from boy to young man, girl to young woman: the ambient stuff that suffuses the mind, injects itself into the spirit and develops traits in the budding personality; those things that provide a foundation for our character and makes us what we are at eighteen. Most of us do not change much after that.

One lesson I learnt in my school days was not in the classroom but in the boxing ring. Evan, who had entered the Head Master's House the same term as me, had a fine scholarly mind and was also a clever boxer. He could literally run rings round an opponent, jab away with his left and score points galore. He always won the three-round amateur contests that were our standard routine. He boxed for the school as a junior and captained the house team. I took up boxing and received some basic instruction down at the gym where the dominant theme was provided by the very apposite verse from Ecclesiastes that ran the length of the panels fronting the spectators' gallery: 'Whatever thy hand findeth to do, do it with all thy might.' But my interest in the noble art was not progressing, as it should have done. I did not have that playful, feline approach that natural boxers have or the quickness of eye that sees an opening for a lightning punch, once, twice in rapid succession with the left and then, when the opponent is off balance, a crushing right that sends him reeling.

It did not take me long to realize that I did not have the makings of a Tommy Farr, the Welsh heavyweight and one of my childhood heroes who went the distance with world champion, Joe Louis, the Brown Bomber, at Madison Square Garden in 1937. So I gravitated towards gymnastics, climbing ropes and wall bars, leaping over boxes and hanging by my toes from the bar. We had a coolly superb, ex-navy instructor, who reminded me of commando Tommy and I was drawn to him for that reason. He too knew far more than he could properly teach us.

Came the day when Evan asked me if I would box for the Head Master's House against Elmfield, a house with a fearsome reputation. I protested that I was out of training, which was true. But Evan was in a fix, he said: he did not have many to choose from; boxing was not a popular sport like squash or fives. He paced up and down my room, parrying my excuses as I made them.

'If you win, we get three points but even if you lose we get a very useful one and a half.'

Evan was a south Walian and there was a mystical Celtic bond between us. I had to support him if possible and the house, of course. We had both fought fiercely together, shoulder to shoulder, on the rugby field many times for the honour of the house. But there was an air of shrewd cunning about Evan, which I could never quite bring myself to trust.

'Who would I have to fight?' I asked.

'Findlay.'

'But there are three of them. Which one?'

'The smallest.'

I swallowed his bait, hook, line and sinker.

'See you at the ringside tomorrow then – at four sharp,' he said.

There was no time for training, hardly time to clear my lungs of smoke inhaled during the holidays. But there was no going back now. Besides, my opponent was the smallest of the Findlay brothers. He could hardly kill me. Was he really my weight? The thought crossed my mind and I put it to Evan as he tied my gloves in the dressing room.

'Just go in there fighting. Go for him right from the start,' he told me as the butterflies began to whirl in my stomach. Evan did a bit of shadow-boxing himself, the usual huffing and puffing, to rouse some viciousness, I suppose, in the yawning lump of lethargy he saw before him.

I was first in the ring and seated on my stool when the ropes at the opposite corner parted and the biggest of the Findlay brothers stepped in, tall as a lamp post and with a reach as long as the Mississippi. He could have put a hand on the crown of my head, held me there and I could not have kicked him, let alone laid a glove on him.

'There's been a mistake,' I said to Evan in a shocked whisper. But he was mucking about below the ring somewhere with the sponge and bucket. The referee, the Reverend Christie Murray, a Cambridge boxing blue, was looking at his watch.

'Seconds out! Round One,' he said, beckoning us out to touch gloves. The bell sounded and there was nothing for it but to fight, fight for dear life, fight as I had never fought before. I got inside that long reach and pummelled away at Findlay's lower chest and abdomen while his arms dangled uselessly over my shoulders. When the referee parted us, I was an easy target for those slim, steely, piston-like arms that delivered punches with a force and accuracy that surprised me. So I danced, ducked and weaved until I could get inside those flailing arms again to thump him at close quarters anywhere, everywhere. The bell rang for the end of the round.

'You won that one! You're winning!' said Evan encouragingly as he drenched my face with a flood of sponge water.

'You bas * * * d!' I muttered but never got the word out. He stuffed the water bottle in my mouth.

'Get into a clinch. Hit him where it hurts.'

'Seconds out! Round two!'

The bell rang eerily, like the prison bell in the mist at Dartmoor in the Dickens film, and we were at it again, circling each other. Findlay had been well advised by his corner to keep me at bay and constantly on the move. He was fit as a hunting dog that harries and tires its prey before leaping for its windpipe and a kill. Flagging a little, I dodged under his left but he was waiting for me with a right straight from the shoulder to the chin. It lifted, no, rocketed, me to the stars and then dropped me into the gaping depths of a black hole whose bottom looked suspiciously like the canvas I was kneeling on.

'One! Two!'

It was at that precise moment at the start of the count that I had a wicked run of thoughts. If I stay on my knee like this, I shall be counted out. But I am not on my back on the canvas, laid out by the unlucky punch I walked into from this gangly Olive Oil of a lad who has eaten Popeye spinach for breakfast. Besides, it would not look right that I should stay on my knee when I can, with a super-human effort, get up. The story of my knockout will be round the school in no time and that will be the end of my reputation as a strongman, fast disappearing anyway as other fellows develop their arm muscles in the gym. So what the hell? I feel distinctly weary. If I get up, I can probably live through this round and possibly the next

23

and if the situation looks bad, the reverend referee will surely stop the fight? He is a Christian after all; he will surely have mercy on me if the worst comes to the worst?

'Four!' – the shadow of the ref's descending arm fell across my face.

I was up on my feet, able to defend myself and Findlay was waiting for the kill as eagerly as the Brown Bomber from Detroit.

'Box on!' said the reverend and we did, except that I now lurched rather than danced, swayed rather than weaved and panted like a frog. I bore the brunt of a few punches and then the round came to an end.

'You lost that one,' said Evan in my corner as he drowned me again in a torrent of ice-cold water.

'This'll give you strength,' he said, shoving the water bottle down my throat. It was only when he took it away that I tasted the gin.

'Seconds out! Round three!'

This time the ringside bell sounded muffled, as if it was buried in the depths of the ocean. I heaved myself forward, to be greeted by a salvo of well-aimed blows to the head. I clung to the now flushed and sweaty body of my opponent, my only refuge from the red terror of his gloves.

'Break!' cried the bloody Christian, rejecting outright the plea for mercy in the look I gave him.

'Box on!'

I thought it would never end, blow after blow, straight lefts and rights, spinning at me like cricket balls from all directions. The gin or maybe the hammering I was having, or my growing certainty that the Christian gentleman was on the side of the lions in my particular arena, activated something in what was left of my brain. I began to hit back, with a dark resolve to remove that glint of triumph from Findlay's eyes, even if it meant gouging it out or a knee-jerk in the groin. I tried both just before the bell and he tottered groggily to his corner. He had won on points, of course.

'I didn't know you were such a dirty fighter,' said Evan, 'but well done, you've got us one and a half points.'

'*Stet fortuna domus*, my foot! Is my nose still in my face?'

Later, as I surveyed my battered visage alone in the washroom at the house, I vowed never again to think of taking a dive and being beaten at anything, anywhere, if I could possibly avoid it. To win may be a painful struggle but to lose is far worse. My trust in others took a hard knock too: better my own fallible judgement in future, so that any error is at least my own. In retrospect, it was a very formative afternoon. I had learnt some lessons that would last a lifetime.

The entire school assembled in speech room for special occasions such as the prime minister Winston Churchill's annual summer visit to hear the boys sing a selection of school songs. 'Speecher's', as we called it, was shaped like a Greek amphitheatre where the audience was seated in a rising semicircle of seats – tier on tier of chairs in our case – and everyone could see and hear clearly what was happening on the slightly raised, central stage below. The stage entrances were from left and right but it was the right that was most frequently used at Harrow.

It was through this entrance that Churchill came and it was during his walk to centre-stage that all eyes gained their first impression of the great man. Small in stature, like Lloyd George, and portly, in black coat, waistcoat and pinstripe trousers, he walked briskly – dramatically so – to the ample, cushioned armchair set centre-stage for him. There was not a moment's hesitation. The dark and comely Mrs Moore, feet and legs together, sat to his right with her blue-covered songbook on her lap, and the headmaster to his left. The school orchestra struck up and 300 boys launched into a jolly, welcoming song that swept the great man straight back to his own schooldays. He remained impressively immobile through-out the hour-long performance. Mrs Moore turned the pages of her songbook for each item and handed it to him but he never looked down at the words. He just listened, impassive as Rodin's thinker, and left us to guess his feelings, his memories and his thoughts. Did he recall his time in the fourth form, the dullards' reservation, or the time he pushed the head boy, Leo Amery, fully dressed into the pool at Ducker? Or was he preoccupied with some grand strategy for the peace after the war? We never knew. We always belted out 'Forty Years On' as a finale but if the old man had a tear in his eye – he was not afraid of weeping – it was well hidden by the black, horn-rimmed glasses perched on the tip of his nose.

He did not formally address the school on these occasions and left as quickly as he had come – usually to sip a whisky at the head-master's before leaving the Hill. But I did hear him begin a speech once with 'Doctor Moore' when we all knew that, while the head had many attributes, a doctorate was not one of them. Churchill soon put that right as vice-chancellor of Bristol University when he personally bestowed a doctorate on the man he had once wrongly described.

'History will record . . .' he famously said in the House of Commons and, when asked how he knew, he replied:

'I shall write it myself.'

Even in silence, he had the aura of unfathomable greatness about him. Here was a man who was master of countless other people's destinies. He had shaped my own family history, touched my destiny, more than once. He was not a man to be loved or feared. He was beyond both; he was part of oneself, one's life story.

There were other distinguished visitors in my time to select gatherings. Leo Amery, formerly secretary of state for India, came to address the essay club of which I was secretary. I wrote to invite him and was worried when he replied that he would gladly give a talk but did not have the time to write a paper. I consulted the head-master who thought it would be all right. I was asked to dine with the two of them before Amery delivered his talk. Realizing that I was not participating in their conversation, mainly about the Greek classics, Amery switched the chat very deftly to cowboys and Indians, doubtless for my benefit. He was omniscient on the Wild West too – even the headmaster was out of his depth – but that was nothing compared with the hour's erudite and flawless talk on the history of the Empire and the Commonwealth he gave to the club after dinner.

A wayward son of his was executed for treason at the end of the war. Like Lord Haw Haw, he had broadcast from Hitler's Germany. I met his brother Julian, the MP, years later but never talked about this excruciating family tragedy.

Labour's R. H. S Crossman we knew as the author of one of our textbooks, *Government and the Governed*. With his powerful boom-ing voice, he was a compelling lecturer and his theme was equally riveting. He described the US as an octopus wrapped around the immovable pillar of the Communist USSR (or was it the other way round?) and Europe as a 'no man's land' in between. This was novel stuff in the immediate post-war period.

'Does that shock you?' he asked a boy questioner during the session afterwards.

'No. No more than anything else you've said this evening.'

Even Crossman had to laugh at the lad's audacity.

Every year Speech Room was transformed into Shakespeare's Globe, when one of the Bard's plays was presented much as it might have been in his own time. It was all thanks to the genius of an inspired scholar, teacher and producer, Ronald Watkins, whose tall, lanky and endearing figure was familiar to generations of boys on the Hill.

Those of us who took part in his productions knew that we were in for many hours of meticulous rehearsals during the summer term, culminating in three nights of performance, in full costume and make-up, before our fascinated colleagues and sundry guests. Boys, as in Shakespeare's day, played female roles. (Some were so stunning in their make-up that they would have put Hollywood starlets out of business.) Props were minimal because they had to be shifted by the players and all the action took place on an open, apron stage without the aid of a proscenium arch and curtain as in normal theatres. The performance of the play was by my time a major event – not to be missed – in the school calendar.

I played Flute in *A Midsummer Night's Dream* in 1945 and a soldier and a citizen in *Julius Caesar* the following year. I had grown to admire the tall perfectionist who leapt about and instructed us in every step and utterance. He showed us how to say 'Hush!', not quietly as one normally would but loudly so that those at the very top of the auditorium could hear. He never lost his temper although he must have been frustrated to the point of implosion many times by our persistent clumsiness, obduracy and inadequacies.

It was a big deal for both of us when he asked me to play Falstaff in his forthcoming production of *Henry the Fourth, Part One*. I learnt the lines during the Easter holiday and had to unlearn them – or learn them afresh – during rehearsals with Ronnie Watkins.

'You dance the lines,' he said, demonstrating how I should move in the tavern scene with: 'Peace good pint-pot! Peace good tickle-brain.'

The performances were a great success; there was an appreciative review in *The Times*. Desmond MacCarthy – no less – wrote a kindly piece for the *New Statesman* where he compared my performance with that of the old comedian, George Robey, and commended my 'quite admirable variety and gusto' in the delivery of certain speeches.

I enjoyed the roars of laughter from my schoolmates and brought the house down some months later in a reading competition with a comical rendering of a piece by Dickens I had not previously seen. It was titled 'A murderer reveals himself'. I was the only contestant who saw the funny side of the piece but all the boys did and collapsed in paroxysms of laughter. I won the top prize.

A Very Cold War

The Ministry of Defence should have called me up for National Service early in August 1948 so that I could complete it in time to start at Oxford in the autumn of the following year. But the ministry was dilatory and I had to remind them of my existence. I had decided to do my service before going to university, partly because I felt in desperate need of a break from the stress of study and partly because that wise old bird, Sir Harry Verney, had said that the later one went to Oxford the more benefit one derived from it. I had also decided not to go for an officer's commission – that too would have been stressful – but to rough it and relax in the anonymity of the ranks.

When my call-up papers finally arrived, they ordered me to join the King's Royal Rifle Corps at Barton Stacey near Winchester, whither I went clutching a copy of *The Times*. I also had with me the second volume of the American theologian Reinhold Niebuhr's *The Nature and Destiny of Man*. The deep-red-faced corporal in charge of the billet (an intriguing character of whom more anon) asked me bluntly whether the book was pornographic or subversive and when I said neither, though the latter was questionable, his diffidence showed in his face. So I sent the book home for safekeeping and got down to polishing my boots. The King's Royal Rifle Corps was reputed to be a London regiment. But the raw young men I was with were all Geordies (Tynesiders) bar one – a very pale chap, thin as a rake, just down from Eton called Birley who muttered 'Gawd!' at every turn. I hardly understood a word uttered by the Geordies, except the four-letter one, which they used with truly astonishing frequency. They met their match in our physical training instructor who shouted at one of them:

'You're like the effing hunchback of Notre effing Dame!'

Early one morning, a couple of days into our basic training, the corporal called me out of the ranks. His crimson face matched the colour of his paratrooper's beret; his eyes were puffs of bloodshot gun smoke.

'You bin a cadet, done some training. You march these pongoes to breakfast – 120 paces to the minute mind. I'll be watching you.'

I called the squad to attention and marched them to the cookhouse at the light infantry's break-neck speed. We nearly passed it before I could halt them.

The corporal seldom turned up for breakfast parade after that. He was spending most of his nights with a girl from the NAAFI (Navy, Army and Air Force Institutes, which ran the camp canteen). He returned to the hut in the early hours to chain-smoke cigarettes on his bed. He had not slept, he told me, ever since he had been parachuted down to capture the bridge over the Rhine at Arnhem in September 1944.

'It was eight days in hell . . . only two out of ten of us got out alive, I was one of the lucky buggers.'

His mumbled reliving of the horrors cured my own insomnia brought on by excessive study. I fell asleep across the foot of his bed. He must have lugged me back to my own.

Old Etonian Birley was distinctly out of sorts. He had drawn a very good likeness of me and, in return, I had put a shine on his toecaps. He was allergic to boot polish, he said. His father was a portrait painter – 'royals mainly'.

'They say I'm too light for the Light Infantry. Have you ever heard such rot?' We were on our way to the NAAFI to sort out his problems.

'I'm being posted to the Signals in Catterick tomorrow . . . It's so far from London . . . it's nearer the Arctic Circle. I'm going to ring Mama to get Monty to cancel the posting.'

And he did phone Mama from the kiosk outside the NAAFI and Mama did call back to say that the field marshal was at a reception in Whitehall. He would return her call in the morning.

'But Mummy darling. Don't you realize I shall be half way to the North Pole by then?'

And he was. But he had not gone out of my life forever, not by a long chalk. When I next saw him, he was wearing a private's uniform cut and fitted by his tailor in Savile Row.

Soon afterwards, I was posted to a camp at Maresfield near Uckfield, Sussex. This was the training base of the Intelligence Corps. I had planned the move in my last days at Harrow with my house master, by then Major Dahl, a former member of the corps. He had promised to put in a word for me and I had repeated my wish to join the corps at every military interview since. There was a lot of formal instruction on information-gathering in the field and the current state of play in the Cold War but the drilling on the parade ground continued, albeit at a slower pace than in the light infantry. The drill sergeant major with a Dali moustache had us in stitches demonstrating the 'about turn'.

'Put some beef into it! You won't lose your wedding tackle!'

And at church parade:

'Church of England and Protestants. Atten . . . wait for it . . . Shun! Roman Catholics, Muslims, Atheists, Agnostics . . . Fall Out.'

It was a freezing cold, rainy night in January 1949 when we crossed by troopship from Harwich to the Hook of Holland and from the rail I watched dawn break over the dark waters and shore lights of Europe. How lucky I was to be making the crossing now rather than five years earlier. I was making it in safety and was out to enjoy the fruits of other men's victories. A Dutch band singing 'Buttons and Bows' – it sounded like 'Bols' – greeted us inside the enormous NAAFI at the Hook where our shipload of soldiers breakfasted. Then we boarded a troop train for Villach on the Austro–Italian border and clattered along the Rhine through a still shockingly devastated Cologne and ever onwards. There was a soldier on duty at the end of our carriage making a note of the stations we passed through.

'There are a hell of a lot of places called Herren and Damen,' he said. I put him right on that one.

The train wound its way through Alpine gorges where the mountain sides rose sheer to our right and villages nestled in the snow miles below to our left. Finally, we reached Villach at night and stepped off the train on to crisp snow that sparkled under the lights. I had the bed next to the door of the Nissen hut and every time someone opened it an icy blast bit my feet. Next day, two of us boarded a train for Vienna, the other being a prognathous-jawed, ginger-haired character from the Wirral, nicknamed 'Squib'. He soon had me worried. He said we might be popped behind the Russian lines straight away to gather information.

'So soon?'

He thought yes. We were new to the scene and had the advantage of being unknown.

'And what if we're caught?'

'They'll probably shoot you,' he said, 'but I'll get them first.' He drew a small pistol from under his breast jacket, an Italian Beretta which was hardly standard British Army issue. He had bought it from someone at the NAAFI in Villach.

'I'm taking no chances,' he said.

There were Russian soldiers on the track when the train stopped at the Enns Bridge – the start of the Russian-occupied sector – but they did not come on board, thank God. Squib frightened the life out of me with that pistol – not for the last time.

We were met at Vienna's Central Bahnhof by the strangest sergeant I had ever seen, a flaxen-haired young man with a copy of *The Complete Works of Oscar Wilde* under his arm and a handkerchief tucked flamboyantly into his battledress cuff.

'My name's Tony,' he said, leading us to the 15 cwt. truck with a civilian driver that was to take us to Number 7 Ziehrer Platz, the home of 291 Field Security Section (FSS) and mine too for the next nine months. The nature of man, if not his destiny, was about to be revealed to me.

Vienna, 1949

Austria had been divided after the war between the four victorious powers and the same fate had befallen the capital. The Russians, Americans, French and British each occupied their separate sectors but the centre of the city around Stephanskirche, the First District, was jointly controlled by all four. Visible symbols of this joint domination were the Russian soldier with a Tommy gun at the entrance to the Imperial Hotel on the Ring Strasse and the smart American rifleman outside the Hotel Bristol almost opposite. The British and the French also had their national hostelries; Sacher's Hotel being the haunt of the British.

Every evening, four well-turned-out military policemen, one from each army, patrolled the First District in a jeep. Nominally, their job was to pick up troublesome soldiers from the *weinkellers* but, in reality, it was to impress the Viennese as they drank their mocca or sipped Gumpoldskirchner on café terraces. The Viennese were not resentful or belligerent. They won over their conquerors with a distinctive, disarming smile that somehow also expressed their confidence in their own inherent superiority. And it paid off. The Americans had recently restored the roof of the Stephanskirche, used by the Nazis as a petrol dump in the war and therefore a legitimate target for American bombers.

The Ziehrer Platz, named after a musician, was just off the Land Strasse and comprised a green plot surrounded by grandly imperial blocks of flats, seven stories high. Number 7 was one of them. There was a tall, Gothic, double-door entrance to the hallway and a wrought-iron gated lift with a stone stairway winding round it to the very spacious floors above. The 291 FSS offices and accommodation were mainly on the third and fourth floors but we also had part of the fifth, once occupied by a Gestapo officer called Schmidt. His swastika badge, along with his name, was irremovably glued to the black door of his flat. The legend below the badge read: *Ich erfulle meine Pflicht 1943* (I fulfil my duty 1943). I often wondered what monstrous crimes Herr Schmidt had committed (if any) and what had happened to him. His flat was still intact; his glass cabinets of porcelain pieces and objects d'art were kept locked. I slept on his gold velvet chaise longue at one stage and a sergeant, a friend of Tony's, occupied his bed.

Seven of us lived on the premises; others were in married quarters or domiciled elsewhere like our captain, Ham-Longman. He was short, with the forward-leaning torso of Groucho Marx and bulging eyes on the point of popping out of his head. He had a mad, resonant laugh and was always being held in check by our senior regular sergeant, a tall, hardy Scot called 'Mack'. One of the section's tasks was to interview ex-prisoners of war, now streaming home from Russia and calling in to see us. These *Heimkehrer* were full of militarily useful information about where they had been and what they had seen. Mack's reports in Scots' English must have been a good read for some boffin in Whitehall.

We were breakfasting a few days after my arrival and talking about Oxbridge where most of us were going after our service when our Austrian cook, a large, middle-aged lady, sailed in with an agitated, pained look on her face. There was a wounded man in the hall, she said, shot while crossing the Czechoslovak frontier the night before.

'Ask him to wait till I've finished my corn flakes,' said Dearlove, a talkative nineteen-year-old, keen on writing comedy. I was inwardly shocked that he had become so hardened and heartless in such a short time away from humane studies and customary British civility. I had come a long way myself from home and Harrow and was now in a strange world with very different values.

While I familiarized myself with spoken German and the Viennese dialect, I was put in charge of the truck that made a weekly trek to Schönbrunn Barracks to fetch the section's NAAFI supplies – the usual personal requisites such as soap, shaving cream and toothpaste plus the all important, weekly ration of 200 cigarettes and a bottle of Scotch per man. There was no restriction on purchases of any other liquor. Having completed my shopping successfully on my second visit, I went for a coffee in the vast Schonbrunn canteen – resplendent in its Butlin's holiday-camp decor – and there, draped languidly over a chair was Birley in his slightly odd Savile Row uniform. He had done his training as a signalman at Catterick and was now stationed at the barracks.

'What are you doing for money?' he asked.

'I sell my cigarettes and whisky for Austrian schillings like everyone else.'

'Gawd! That's hardly enough for a taxi to the trotting races at the Kriau.'

One thing led to another. We agreed that he would scout the garrison at the barracks for clients who would like us to dispose of their whisky on the black market in return for a modest commission, while I would test the market outside and find out where the best prices could be got. The Kursalon in the Stadt Park, with its thousands of customers, appeared promising as did the entire joint venture.

Our trade prospered remarkably and was soon beyond our initial, ambitious dreams. Birley collected the bottles for my weekly visit and I took them away in the back of the truck to dispose of them later in the city where I could travel freely, in my civvies in off-duty hours. We had incredible luck too in the shape of a Bulgarian student who wanted a large consignment of Bols gin, which we could buy very cheaply and in abundance. I had a smart, tailored suit made with my share of the proceeds. Birley had ten days' local leave and told me he was going to visit his sister in Paris.

'But you're not supposed to go more than fifty miles from here.'

'Who's to know where I've gone?' And he went, not only to Paris but also to the Derby in England where he backed the winner, Nimbus, at seven to one.

We branched out into currency exchange on his return and regularly met the Schönbrunn commanding officer's requirements through his batman, a salacious character called Hawkes. Birley was seen once too often in his company and was hauled before a junior officer, who tried to scold him in an over familiar way:

'Look here Birley! Is Private Hawkes the sort of chappie you would take home to introduce to your mother?'

'Naaw,' drawled Birley, 'but neither are you for that matter.'

When I heard the story, I told Birley not to make enemies who might endanger our operations.

'I choose my enemies with the utmost care,' he answered. 'That twit is the most unpopular man in the Barracks.'

Even the words 'top secret' were said in a hushed whisper when the captain took some of us aside on his return from a rare visit to the UK. He outlined a madcap scheme to tap a Russian telephone cable, which ran from their Imperial Hotel headquarters in the First

District, through the British Sector and out to the east. He gave us the impression that the plan was his own and I looked around for Mack to tell him how preposterous it all was, but it soon became clear that there were bigger brains behind it at the embassy and in London.

'Engineers will be brought from England to dig under the road here' – he pointed to a detailed map of the city with his cane – 'from the cellar of a garage we've bought there. We shall open up the cable' – his eyes opened to their widest, most alarming extent – 'and link it to our own switchboard on the garage premises. Dearlove and Strickman will take it in turns with you and you' – the cane pointing at Squib and myself – 'to man the location. I am sure there are many questions but just wait and see how things develop.'

The sergeant major, a neat little man who normally confined himself to admin matters, in person took the four of us in the section truck to the so-called garage, which already had a board outside denoting it as the property of 'British Armed Forces-Austria'. The Aspangstrasse was in a fairly deserted, run-down area of the city and the garage, if that is what it had been, had no frontage at all. The sergeant major unlocked a battered metal door and disappeared down some steps to the cellar floor where the lights were. We followed him into what might once conceivably have been a workshop reception area: it was dark, dank and airless. A wooden partition at the bottom of the stairs concealed most of the interior.

'Your orders are pinned there on the partition. Read them carefully,' said the sergeant major.

I glanced at them and was surprised to read: 'Challenge ONCE only, then fire.'

The army's usual was three challenges to an intruder.

'What do we shoot with, Sergeant Major?' I asked, half-jokingly.

'A Sten gun automatic. It will have a full magazine in it at all times.' The little man with the crown on his sleeve was deadly serious. He took us behind the partition to the large, dimly lit space beyond, containing lots of empty wooden boxes that looked like rough coffins. One underground wall ran parallel with the street above and we could hear the traffic galloping noisily over the set stones.

'This is where the engineers will dig,' said the sergeant major, indicating an area about six feet below street level.

'The cable is about six yards in . . . under the road. The engineers will arrive tomorrow. You will take it in turns to guard them at Ziehrer Platz. They must not go out on the town on their own.'

Strickman, whose mouth curled automatically, giving him a cruel, disdainful look he thought women liked, threw back his forelock and laughed his suggestive, guttural laugh.

'No laughing matter, corporal,' said the sergeant major sternly. 'If they get drunk, they'll give the game away.'

He then showed us our sleeping quarters, a separate room, which might have been an office at one time, also having a wall running parallel to the street above. There were two beds already in place. Fresh air and traffic fumes came from vents that opened at pavement level.

The engineers turned out to be mainly brawny pioneers apart from a couple of specialists, but the team was directed by a mature, knowledgeable grey-haired man in a badly fitting major's field uniform. His webbing belt sagged around his midriff and one knew at once that Major Denman was no major at all but a civilian boffin in disguise (see reference to him in Peter Wright's *Spycatcher*). The lads got down to their tunnelling straight away and were soon sweating their guts out under the road, buttressing and installing thick, overhead beams as they went. One of them, 'Yorkie', christened the tunnel 'Smokeys' – a name that, curiously, became official in no time. A few days later, I saw the cable laid bare and marvelled at the telephone engineer who attached a Y junction to each of the worm-like strands of wire. He then channelled the stems of the Ys to our switchboard and put a lead seal with a blowlamp on the entire breach – to prevent moisture creeping in – and all without disturbing a single telephone call running through the system.

A lean corporal whom we knew only as Eric arrived from the UK with a Russian keyboard to his typewriter and a cylinder-disk, recording machine the like of which I have never seen since – not even at the Imperial War Museum. His uniform too was a bad fit, like the major's. Eric tested the switchboard and pronounced that the lines used by the Russian military were labelled 28 and 29 on our board. He set up his recording device, the cylinder turned and a needle scratched its surface. We heard the voices clearly on the playback machine's headphones. We were in business. Dearlove and Strickman would listen alternately for twenty-four hours and then Squib and I would relieve them. Eric would transcribe the conversations *in situ* during the day and send the stuff off to London via the embassy. The Russians always began their conversations with 'Slushyetye!' (Listen!) So it was not difficult to know when to switch on the recorder.

The entire operation ran smoothly for several weeks. A third pair of twenty-four-hour operators were brought in to lighten the burden on the original four as spring turned to summer and the weather became hot. I was sleeping stark naked in bed one hot July night when I woke to find the room full of fumes and Squib, who had been on the switchboard, whispering at my bedside:

'There's somebody at the door!'

And indeed there was somebody hammering the metal door hard and persistently with his fist. Whoever was there was not going to go away. I picked up the Sten gun at my bedside and told Squib to open the door while I covered him with the gun, naked as I was, from behind the coffin boxes the engineers had now filled with earth from the tunnel. For once, Squib did not argue. To my horror, when I looked through the rounded rear sight of the Sten, I could see Squib and the entire doorframe. If I fired, he might cop it too. I released the safety catch – never reliable on the Sten – with more trepidation than I had ever known, just as Squib opened the door. I expected a grenade to be thrown in or a gang of Russian commandos to rush in with guns blazing. Instead, a voice shouted in English:

'Are you on fire?'

There was some dialogue between Squib and the stranger and then, after an eternity of waiting, the door slammed shut again. I was breathless as the long Austrian Post bus and trailer that had exuded all the exhaust fumes into our sleeping quarters, moved off with our mysterious visitor. There was method somewhere in this late-night madness. But what was it? Perhaps the Russians were trying to find out whether Smokeys was manned at night, by how many and why?

Shortly afterwards, a man in a dark, double-breasted suit, a top-dog intelligence boffin from London, visited Smokeys and complimented each of us personally on the grand job we were doing. He obviously knew the major and Eric.

'What will you do after your National Service?' he asked me. I told him that I would head for Oxford.

'If you ever feel like working for us, let me know.' He gave me the name of B. M. Diwaker and a London address. I kept it at home for years but lost it after my mother's death. I thought no more about our London visitor except what a refined, open-faced and understanding man he was.

I went to the State Opera House on an off-duty night – as soldiers, we had free seats in the stalls – and shamefully dozed off to the sweet sound of the young Elizabeth Schwarzkopf singing in *Rigoletto*. The people in the gods liked her so much they applauded non-stop until she sang her aria again. Was it our visitor to Smokeys I glimpsed at the bar in the interval? I thought so.

A fortnight or so later, I arrived at Smokeys one morning to find the street chalk-marked for digging, precisely where we had tapped the cable. A pneumatic drill was being connected to a generator. The men were from the Austrian Post and Telephone service. I told them:

'Graben verboten!' (Digging forbidden!)

I indicated our sign above the premises. They seemed to accept my instruction and the drill was silent while I made an urgent call to the office. Our chaps moved fast. The dig was called off. Later in the day, our man at the embassy came into Smokeys accompanied by the city's chief telephone engineer. He had clearly been taken into our confidence and been put fully in the picture. He was shown the technical side of the whole operation. That night, lines 28 and 29 went dead. The Russians had stopped all calls. We had been well and truly rumbled.

The Russians raised the matter of interference with their telephone lines in the fringes of the next Four Power meeting at First District level and then inquiries began in earnest about how they had found out about Smokeys. Major Denman and Eric had been quickly recalled to the UK. An unlikeable, intellectually inferior captain from the Ministry of Defence took their place. Although the Russians returned to chatting on certain lines, the new captain – it soon became obvious – was more interested in us and in finding a culprit for the leak than he was in the Russians on the telephone. To tease him, we all became Communist sympathizers overnight, clutching copies of Karl Marx's *Das Kapital* and anything else subversive we could find. We led him a merry dance. Captain Ham-Longman had already grilled us and satisfied himself that none of us was responsible for divulging the top-secret operation. He laughed his mad laugh when we told him of our mischievous treatment of his fellow officer. No one dreamed that the real traitor might be the smooth, top dog from London in the dark, double-breasted suit. Like Caesar's wife, he was above suspicion.

Oxford Blues

It was difficult to settle down at Oxford to the venerable Bede and his history of the church in his own time – late seventh and early eighth century. I had nothing against the saintly scholar himself – he was very like my father in spirit – but he was desperately remote in time and place and completely irrelevant to my recent experience of life.

In the short interval between my return from Vienna and taking up my scholarship, I had begun writing a novel and I told Father that I wished to pursue a career in writing rather than go to university. He would surely understand, I thought. He did not. He was visibly agitated, disturbed and annoyed. Mother too was upset. It was unheard of for someone like me, who had successfully striven to win a scholarship to Oxford, to turn his back on such an opportunity. What would people think – all those who had helped me – Sir Harry, Uncle John, my teachers et al.? Did I not understand that writing was a subsidiary occupation and that one could not be certain of making a living by writing alone.

Secretly, I knew what was at stake. I could either subject myself to the arid, masochistic discipline of academic life or enjoy my innate, creative freedom and allow its spirit to lead me whither it might. Reluctantly, I conceded victory in this argument to my parents and betters.

'Do what you can do best which is not necessarily the same as what you want to do,' Charlie Lillingston, my history master at Harrow, had advised. He was on the side of my parents; I have never been certain whether he was right or wrong. There is an element of boredom in doing what comes easily and joy in striving to do things you love but lack talent for.

I had more empathy with Goethe and his *Poetry and Truth*, which was also part of my set course for the preliminary examinations two terms into my university career. I relished his account of his relationships with young women, especially with Fredrika, the parson's daughter at Sesenheim and even *The Sorrows of the Young Werther*, a best-seller in its day about a young man who fell in love with a married woman and shot himself in despair. Thackeray derided it as the soppy stuff it is by the best English standards:

> Werther had a love for Charlotte
> Such as words could never utter:
> Would you know how first he met her?
> She was cutting bread and butter.
>
> Charlotte having seen his body,
> Borne before her on a shutter,
> Like a well conducted person
> Went on cutting bread and butter.

It was a harsh comment on the early work of a great man whom I found very appealing. 'A man may wander where he will, do what he may but he will always return to the path nature has marked out for him,' Goethe wrote.

I had one close friend, Christopher Elrington, at my own university college. He had spent his National Service with the paratroopers and had the inherent toughness of the wiry man he was. He had a true scholar's turn of mind, was meticulously correct and deeply committed to historical studies. He had a long-standing girlfriend, a trainee architect, whom he married in his last year. I admired his simple, straightforward dedication to scholarship and his equally uncomplicated devotion to his girlfriend, Jean. He was a steadying influence upon me in periods of mental turbulence.

We attended the best, most popular lectures together, by star performers such as Christopher Hawkes at the Ashmolean Museum on the archaeology of early Britain, Hugh Trevor-Roper (of *The Last Days of Hitler* fame) on Cromwell and the Puritans and Lord David Cecil on Restoration drama. The last spoke as fast as his neuroses would allow him and began, with his thumbs spinning like a jenny in his cupped hands:

'Restoration dramatists were interested in two subjects – religion and sex.' (He pronounced it 'thexth'.)

The pretty young nuns at the front of the lecture hall speeded up their bead count to match the spin of his thumbs. Christopher told me that a child of Cecil's was asked what he would like to be when he grew up: 'A neurotic, like daddy,' he said.

We also listened, with a very select few, to Canon Claud Jenkins at Christ Church on 'The Theodosian Code'. He set an alarm clock on the bare table before him, closed his eyes and spoke non-stop until the alarm went off an hour later. By then there was no one left listening to him, except Chris and me and a charwoman leaning on her mop. Abstruse in the extreme though the canon was, he gave us a tip we should have heeded: 'To get a First Class degree at Oxford you should be able to write four *Times* first leaders in three hours.' It was a sound recipe for academic success.

Colin McEvedy, my Adonis of Harrow days, was at Magdalen reading medicine, with an admiring coterie of friends. It included his soulmate, Jenny, a disturbingly attractive, dark-haired, tomboy of a girl from Lady Margaret Hall. Colin gave sherry parties – always Harvey's South African – at Sunday lunchtime and kept pythons in his room. The snakes multiplied when he moved out from college into a flat on the High Street. A couple of live laboratory rats in a cage adorned the mantelpiece waiting to be fed to the pythons, which were kept warm in blanket-covered boxes. The smell, mixed with cigarette smoke, was abominable but no one seemed to mind. I got used to handling the pythons but never the rats, and to the sight of Colin with a python coiled around his arm and its head hovering over a tame rat on the carpet. The python struck with lightning speed, coiled itself around the rodent, slowly constricted it and then devoured it whole. The last thing we would see was the rat's tail disappearing between its jaws. When it was particularly cold, Colin would guide a python under his pullover to wrap itself around his armpit for extra warmth. One of his sherry party girls fainted when a reptile's head suddenly appeared from his sleeve as he greeted her.

At the beginning of my second year, when I knew that my old friend Birley was coming up to Oxford after military service, I went looking for him at Christ Church, much favoured by Old Etonians. But he was not there. I had given up the search when, one evening at dinner in my own college, I turned round and there he was sitting at the long table next to mine. He invited me to his rooms, close to the drowned Shelley's naked statue, for a silver goblet of champagne. He was his same old self but with a newly found friend from his schooldays, Spencer le Marchant, as tall as he was and joyously brandishing a coffee percolator he had just bought with the day's winnings at Sandown racecourse. When Spencer had gone, Birley told me he was £500 in debt.

'What are you doing for money?' he asked.

I told him I was living on my scholarship, which drew the familiar response:

'Oh Gawd!'

I agreed to join him and Spencer for breakfast at the Mitre Hotel next day where I found them deep in study of the *Sporting Chronicle*. Breakfast cost me 15s (as well as the 7s 6d college breakfast I had forgone) and then we ambled back to college at about ten o'clock to lay our bets by phone on the day's chosen nags. We gathered in Birley's room again at about six o'clock to celebrate one's winnings and commiserate with another's losses. I sensed it would be the same monotonous routine day after day, relieved perhaps by a visit to Sandown or Epsom. I quickly decided that it was not the life for me and I tried to warn Birley that it was not the life for him either, especially with his preliminary exams coming up fast on the rails. I left him, preferring to starve in my garret.

The college dean, Giles Alington, himself the son of an Eton headmaster, told me privately that he feared for Birley's future at the college after the prelims disclosed his laziness. I tried to intercede on his behalf with a forlorn declaration of faith in Birley's essential goodness and high quality. But Giles shook his head till his long churchwarden's pipe swivelled dangerously between his teeth. He knocked the pipe bowl on the nearest wall, dropped the subject and said as we walked towards the high railings in Logic Lane,

'If there's any justice in the world, I shall catch someone climbing in tonight.'

Birley was duly sent down from the college to seek his fortune very successfully elsewhere: he founded the exquisite nightspot, Annabel's, in Berkeley Square.

Giles invited Christopher and myself to accompany him in early January 1951 'on a not so grand tour of Holland', as he put it. He had the money to pay for all three of us but his foreign allowance had run out. (In those days, you could spend only £150 per person per year abroad.) We readily agreed to share our allowances, met him – clad in a long duffle coat and muffler – at Victoria Station and, for a second time in five years, I made the North Sea crossing from Harwich, this time to The Hague.

The Hague was full of busy people on bicycles. As we crossed a particularly hazardous street, Giles declared it to be 'the city of the quick and the dead'. With the aid of a 'Guide Bleu' and a map, which Chris read expertly, we visited picture galleries, museums and churches at The Hague, Delft, Gouda, Utrecht, Amsterdam and Haarlem. All the great Dutch pictures were there from

Rembrandt's *Night Watch* (before it was slashed by a maniac and had to be protected by glass) to Vermeer's incomparable *View of Delft*. But the painter who caught my mood was the cynical Jan Steen, with his wine-bibbing children in drunken family scenes; the travelling dentist flourishing an extracted tooth before a cheering crowd while the unfortunate victim howled in agony on his stool. Giles and Christopher thought my taste was poor but I was right in that Steen's rating as a painter and his popularity rose appreciably in subsequent years. His cynicism appealed to the rising generation.

Giles had to rest and take a day off in bed, a harbinger perhaps of a serious illness yet to come. I too felt low in spirits as a result of a leaking shoe, which took in snowy slush from the streets at every squelching step. Chris and I spent time in a tavern talking to some jovial girls in clogs. We counted fifty-four pairs of clogs in Amsterdam that day; secretly, I yearned for a pair of my own to replace my worn out footwear.

Giles recovered sufficiently to venture out to dinner. On our return walk to our obscure, side-street hotel, I confessed that my marker for the turn was a women's lingerie shop on the corner. 'And that is my marker,' said Giles, grandly indicating a towering church opposite, which I had completely missed. I was glad to go home even though it meant crossing the North Sea in a blizzard. We played cards desultorily on the deserted ship but I soon had to retire, sick as a dog, to the bilges.

Giles remained a bachelor all his life but would borrow a colleague's photograph of a lovely girl to place on the mantelpiece whenever his mother came to visit. He wanted her to believe that he had some-one and marriage in mind. He was a great wit, loved and lived the nineteenth century on which he was very knowledgeable. Some thought him pompous; if he was, it was to hide his own shyness and preserve a proper distance between his generous self and his invasive student charges. He died prematurely at the age of thirty-nine. His sister, Elizabeth, was the wife of Sir Alec Douglas-Home, prime minister 1963–4. I got to know them both.

I was reading Morley's *Life of Gladstone* one afternoon when the staircase scout came to my room to say that there was a telephone message for me at the porter's lodge. We did not have such luxuries as mobile phones or even telephone extensions and I hurried across the two quadrangles that separated me from the lodge. I knew some sudden calamity had occurred, possibly involving Mother who was seldom in good health.

I rang our village post office as the message requested. My father had passed away, quietly in his chair, Mr Owen, the postmaster, said. I rushed off to the Codrington Library at All Souls where I knew my brother would be poring over his law books. He had come up to Exeter College the previous year after gaining his first degree at Aberystwyth. I beckoned him out of the silent enclave of the law section and told him the sad news. We clearly had to drop everything and go home. I scribbled Father's obituary on Banbury station where we had a lengthy wait as we changed trains.

I had heard my father preach a few weeks earlier and had been deeply moved because I recognized that the sermon was his own spiritual biography. His text was St Paul's description in his letter to the Philippians of the little Greek, Epaphroditus, he was returning to them as 'our brother . . . my fellow worker and comrade whom you commissioned to minister to my needs' (2: 25). Father spoke about the man under the three headings of brother, fellow worker and comrade and, of course, the man he described was himself and his Christian ministry throughout his life.

Father's analysis of humility was profound and had a powerful effect upon me. It led me to a fuller appreciation of this concept and its practical application in mediaeval times by Bernard of Clairvaux, founder of the Cistercian Order and chief inspirer of the Second Crusade. Humility, coupled with service, was a potential source of immense power and influence – a fact forgotten in our modern times. The intense, thrusting and selfish egotism that had replaced it irked and riled me as I grew older, especially when I became involved in politics twenty years later.

Father had indeed died in his upright chair at his writing table while Mother had gone to the shop to buy some tobacco for him. He had fallen badly some weeks before and the injury had resulted in thrombosis. His death had been without pain. He now lay in his lace-sided coffin in the best room, looking slightly ridiculous with his head bound in one of his own white handkerchiefs to keep his lower jaw from sagging. His body without his soul, without life, was vacant and aroused no feeling in me apart from the dull grief that grips us all when a loving parent dies.

He had a public funeral and people came in their hundreds to pay tribute to him – not their last tribute either, because people talked to me about him for years afterwards. He enjoyed earthly immortality of a kind, the kind that belongs to every good man who has rendered selfless service to his fellow human beings. After the funeral, when we began to relax a little, Mother asked me to lay out the table for tea. I lay places for four people – as I had always done – and Mother said:

'We are now only three.'

'No,' I said, 'we shall always be four.'

It helped me overcome my grief to think that Father was still with us in spirit. I have taken a similar, pragmatic view of the death of close friends.

I did not do as well in my final examinations as I had hoped. I had not fully absorbed Canon Jenkins's sound advice. I scored well on the subjects I knew least about, like political philosophy, because I had to think before I answered, and less well on the subjects I thought I knew best but had not really digested. Repetition of facts is never a substitute for thought. I deluded myself that it was, but alas not my examiners. Giles used to quip that the Day of Judgement could not possibly be as bad as the day of publication of the Oxford Schools examination results. He was right in that the day changed the course of many lives, including my own. I decided that, as I had not gained the highest academic accolade, I would broach the wider world outside the constricting boundaries of Academe. But the world did not welcome me with open arms. I was not God's gift to mankind, albeit Oxford educated.

Mersey Beat

The interval after leaving university and before taking up employment is always awkward for impoverished graduates. I spent my time job-seeking and was finally invited to join my regional newspaper, the *Liverpool Daily Post*, as a trainee journalist at eight guineas a week. I was on the first rung of the writer's ladder.

The topmost room at the Manx Hotel on Mount Pleasant, Liverpool, became my abode and a galleon of a woman, Mrs Brown, my landlady. Her ambition in life was to reduce her hips to forty-four inches, she told me, with a breathless guffaw, as she swayed and swung under full sail into the small dining room with my first bacon-and-egg breakfast. Mrs Brown was a widow. She had one doe-eyed daughter, Monica, who had married a seaman rather older than herself. He had given up the sea (and alcohol) for his young wife and did the cooking in his vest in the 'galley' – as he called the kitchen. There were seldom more than two or three guests.

The *Post* and its more profitable sister, the *Echo*, an evening paper, were based in Victoria Street and were owned and controlled by the Jeans family, then represented by Alec Jeans, a hard-nosed businessman with a Dickensian mien. Like me, he attended the office daily. He was mad about trains and it was my report of an imaginary rail crash in Stephenson's tubular bridge over the Menai Straits that had secured me my first job with his newspapers. He was seldom openly critical but he did not encourage or inspire either; his tactic was always to question his subordinates closely and this induced apprehension and uncertainty on their part.

The city and its docks were going through hard times in the early 1950s. The port had been valuable during the war when shipping that had risked U-boats and raiders in the Atlantic was spared the further hazards of the English Channel if the ships landed their cargo in Liverpool. Now, in peacetime, London was stealing Liverpool's trade and the docks were often idle. The city had been frequently bombed in the war and in the post-war years the slum, predominantly Catholic, population of Scotland Road had been decanted to outlying new estates where they were said to keep their coals in the bath. The large Victorian houses at the heart of the city had also been abandoned by their middle-class owners in favour of Crosby and the Wirral. Crime was on the rampage in the shadows of the two glorious but rival new cathedrals – Lutyens's Roman Catholic masterpiece, still unfinished, and Sir Giles Gilbert Scott's magnificent Anglican edifice of dressed red stone, with its soaring Vestey tower. Nearly half the drug offences in Britain were committed in Liverpool, which some linked to the substantial Chinese population, some of whom were addicted to opium. Cannabis was grown on the bomb-sites.

One of my regular duties as a cub reporter was to attend the stipen-diary magistrate's court where summary justice was dispensed to those who opted for it rather than trial by jury which might result in a longer sentence. A docker who had breakfasted on a tin of pineapple – fallen from a crane onto the dockside, he would say – would find himself in court by ten that morning; so would the blushing maid who had pinched her mistress's silver teapot. There were dozens of cases of indecent exposure, which our paper never reported. One offender pleaded quite unnecessarily for us not to publish his name whereupon the 'Stip', as we called him, told the miscreant:

'If you had your wits about you, you would have noticed that the gentlemen of the Press are not scribbling.'

A remarkable young man came down to breakfast at Mrs Brown's one morning. He was dressed in a smart suit and waistcoat, with his shirt collar pinned under his tie knot. He introduced himself as Mr Hennesy from London and told me he was a civil servant. I asked him which grade he belonged to, administrative, executive or clerical. He replied that there were no such divisions in his section of the Inland Revenue. He was pursuing tax-dodgers, of whom there were many, very many, on Merseyside, he hinted darkly. He asked what I was doing. I told him and how much I was earning too. He inspired confidence.

'Tut, tut! It's a shame how little some employers pay graduates like you. I get a thousand a year. It's not much but I survive.'

It was more than twice my salary. I felt peeved as I walked down to the courtroom to listen to the usual batch of offences. I should be earning more than I was. A man, accused of stealing a bicycle, had brought his horde of children to corroborate his highly dubious innocence. It was criminal culture in the making.

Towards the end of the morning, as I wrote up the story, I heard a vaguely familiar voice in the dock. I looked up and there was Hennesy, minus his tie. (The police always took your tie and shoe-laces after arrest to prevent any attempt at suicide.) Hennesy's confidence had deserted him and no wonder. His name was not Hennesy but Jones. He was not an Inland Revenue officer but a deserter from the Pioneer Corps. He was not from London but from Wrexham. I gaped with astonishment as his story of confidence trickery, mainly perpetrated against gullible landladies, unfolded in evidence presented to the court. He looked down at me as the Stip passed judgement and sentenced him for a string of previous offences, also taken into account. I do not know to this day what he was trying to tell me with that strange look of his; that it had all been fun and worthwhile and that it had been a particular pleasure to con an educated idiot like me?

Liverpool had been plagued by gang warfare, which led to a series of killings known as the Wavertree murders, but this had been stamped out by a tough police chief named Balmer who enjoyed his high reputation with the press. I went to see him to talk about drugs after getting a lead from a man in a pub who spoke familiarly about hashish and marijuana. The favourite brands had the intriguing, enticing names of Congo Matady and Rangoon Brown. They were sold by the tola, my informant said.

'We're only interested when the stuff comes through in pounds,' said Balmer. 'We arrested a chap the other day carrying enough hemp to put the whole country into delirium. Why don't you write about the boys growing hemp on the bombsites, mixing it with dried grass and selling it as marijuana? That might put some of the customers off their reefers.'

We got no further. A bell sounded fiercely in the building, the phone whirred and Balmer snatched it:

'Smash and grab? . . . Jewellers . . . London Road. I'll be there.' Balmer reached for his cap on the hat stand and he was off, with me running behind him. We dived into a car and shot to the scene of the crime. I heard the jeweller's shocked account of the hold-up and of the robbers' getaway by car.

'They won't get far,' said Balmer, with a confident laugh.

I dashed to the nearest telephone kiosk to catch the last edition of the *Echo*. When I returned to the shop, Balmer had gone. I was chuffed with my scoop. It had all happened in minutes.

I had bought a new, light blue suit, much too light and much too blue for my liking outside the artificial light of the shop. On a fine, mild Saturday evening, I gave the new suit an airing with a walk along Rodney Street – Gladstone's birthplace and the poet, Arthur Clough's – and then on to the Philharmonic Hall at the very top of Mount Pleasant. On my return journey to the hotel, I noticed a group of youths sitting on the pavement at the junction of Mount Pleasant with Myrtle Street. My solitary prominence in the new suit clearly occasioned some comment among them. One got up and came towards me and another followed close on his heels.

I foresaw exactly what was going to happen. The first would bump me on my shoulder as he passed; I would then turn to remonstrate with him and the second would jump me from behind. I quickly decided to upset their plan and when the first came within range, I hit him square on the jaw. He reeled back into the arms of his mate, surprise written all over his face. The whole gang leapt to their feet; bicycle chains appeared and knife blades flashed. I ran pell-mell down the street with the gang in hot pursuit. People stopped to look and gasp as I dodged screeching traffic to increase the distance between my pursuers and myself. I reached the door of the hotel, mercifully open, and safety.

That night, I put the blue suit away in the wardrobe for another place, another time and it was just as well that I did so. Not long afterwards, this infamous Myrtle Street gang stabbed a young man who had gone to the rescue of a girl they were raping. He died of his wounds, in the gutter.

Frankie too was chased breathless and nerve shattered into the hotel one night by a rich, young Chinese restaurateur who had taken a fancy to her and refused to take no for an answer. Frankie was a Marilyn Monroe lookalike from St Albans who had come up to Lewis's store to demonstrate a new 'wonder mop'. She stayed with Mrs Brown and I met this shapely vision over breakfast. She had gloried on the front page of *Reveille*, then the equivalent of Page 3 of the *Sun*. She invited me to see the demo and I went. Of course, she demonstrated her glamorous, titillating figure and coquettish personality as well as the mop and gathered a crowd with her sales patter, many of them young males of all nationalities.

'No more getting down on your knees on cold floors, ladies!' she lisped in her overalls, bending floorwards to reveal a pair of perfect buttocks atop exquisitely long legs. 'Clean your floors with Wonder Mop, the new, wet and dry sponge that makes cleaning a pleasure.' She paused just long enough to suggest that she knew a thing or two about pleasure. 'Just dip your mop in a bucket of soapy water – no special soap required, madam – and move the Wonder Mop up and down, up and down, the area to be cleaned.' Her motion was hypnotic. 'Notice the upright position of the body [and my super bosom, she might have added]; no bending, no backache.' She adopted her classical pose – tummy in, bosom right out. Then, she slowly relaxed her entire body.

'Simple, isn't it? Return the mop to the bucket, squeeze the liquid from the sponge so, then wipe the floor dry.' Her voice had become husky as the demo progressed, as if she had been thinking all along of something else, which she might well have done since she gave her demo many times a day.

My happy days as a cub reporter came to an end and I was drawn onto the sub-editors' table to work from 5 p.m. till midnight and beyond. This was the work that trainees were ultimately pre-destined for and this was the job that might be offered to me at the end of my training. It did not take me long to realize that I was no good at devising snappy headlines. I had a moment of pride when I thought I had the perfect fourteen-point headline for a story:

Schoolmaster
Dies
Suddenly

until the chief sub, Howard Channon, pointed out that the opening words of the copy were: 'After a long illness . . .' 'I suppose you can die suddenly after a long illness,' he said, reaching for his dyspepsia pills. Channon wrote a gardening column in his spare time. It was always devoted to killing caterpillars, greenflies, slugs, insects and all sorts of other pests – never to the beauty of flowers.

Pipe-smoking Mr Morris, our leader writer, hovered unceasingly over our shoulders, tasting our copy and commenting on it, until he retired somewhere at about eight o'clock to write his own pieces. An hour later, he would be up on the stone putting his leaders to bed. He never had to add or subtract a single word. His leaders always fitted the column. If by some mischance they were short of a line or two, he would tell the man on the stone to 'space it out' and blank lead blades would be inserted between the lines of print. Mr Morris was fond of referring to a *Punch* cartoon he once showed me of a large, whiskered newspaper proprietor in plus fours behind his desk addressing a cowering figure, not unlike Mr Morris himself. The caption read: 'We want our leader writers to be brave, Mr Bloggs – brave enough to say what the proprietors think.' It summed up Mr Morris's existence and amused him no end.

The city pages were a complete mystery to most of us. They were handled exclusively by a club-footed, white-haired little man, Mr Harris, who hardly spoke to anyone. One night, he fell downstairs and I was asked to take over his work. Mercifully, most of it had been done before Mr Harris's fall, except a small table showing New York cotton prices today and yesterday. I had today's prices all right on a bit of tape from Reuters but where were yesterday's?

'In today's paper, you fool,' someone said.

In my haste to get them before the page was cast, I wrongly turned to the previous day's edition. My prices were therefore a day out. The error caused consternation in the cotton market, Mr Jeans told me glumly the following day. After that faux pas, I had a recurrent nightmare about large empty spaces on the paper's city pages that I could not fill.

I grew pale and plaintive as all sub-editors do after a while. We drank tea or coffee all evening to stimulate our minds in the wearisome ask of rewriting copy and capping it with a headline that met the requirements of the type. When I got to bed, I could not sleep for hours and so I took to visiting the late night shebeens and gambling spots around Upper Parliament Street. I persuaded myself that I was looking for a story, rather than killing time. I fell ill with tonsillitis and Dr Curran, a friend of Mrs Brown, climbed up three flights of stairs to see me.

'I shall not do that again in a hurry,' he said, gasping for breath as he examined my throat. 'I think it's tonsillitis but on the other hand, it could be diphtheria, you know. Better safe than sorry. In any case, you'll be better off in a hospital than in this mildewed garret and I shall be spared those dreadful stairs and so will Mrs Brown. You get my drift?'

Mrs Brown howled with laughter as I departed by ambulance for Fazakerley Hospital where a nursing sister with her hands firmly planted on her hips, watched me descend the ambulance steps.

'Huh!' she said. 'You're the first case of diphtheria that's ever come walking into this hospital.'

Of course, she was right. It was only tonsillitis after all.

My hospital stay gave me time to think. I had learnt a great deal about the basics of journalism with the *Daily Post* and *Echo*, what I liked and what I did not. I had also learnt a lot about life, other, poorer people's mainly, but I had also learnt something about my superiors and my relationships with them. Once, during my fortnight at Mersey House in London, I had returned to the office to file a report on a Mansion House dinner I had attended. My boss, Alec

Jeans, also in a dinner jacket, turned up and asked me where I had been. I told him.

'What a waste of a good dinner!' he muttered under his breath. I turned on him there and then.

'You should never have said that to an employee. Withdraw that remark here and now!'

To his credit, he did, but I decided there and then that I would not stay in his employment for long.

It was during that fortnight in the capital that I first met Archbishop Makarios, the Cypriot Greek leader. He had come to London to plead for the independence of Cyprus. His Beatitude, as he liked to be addressed, met the press over tea at a Park Lane hotel. With his tall, Orthodox priest's hat, black cassock and a large cross dangling over his beard, he did not strike us as a dangerous revolutionary. He was unlikely to be taken seriously by the British government. His quiet demeanour confirmed it and the reporters slipped away. But I was intrigued by this man of God and his implausible mission and I hovered about after most of the others had left, apart from a *Daily Express* photographer who tucked into the sandwiches as if he had not eaten for days. The archbishop himself, I noticed, was eyeing a plateful of very enticing cream cornets but not reaching for them, possibly for fear of being photographed. I had a word with the photographer and then the archbishop.

'If you fancy a cream cornet, my friend will not take a picture,' I said.

He was not sure whether to believe me. He abstained from the cakes – at least while I was there. I met him again in Cyprus in the 1970s, shortly before the Turkish invasion. He had had his chance to rule and had failed.

The Beeb

The BBC filled a great gap in the economic and cultural life of Wales after the chapels declined and the pulpit lost its attraction as a vocation. The talented sons of the manse who might have followed in their fathers' footsteps – as many did before the war – were now predestined for the corporation. Radio became their pulpit and they its priests. The broadcaster's pay was better than the pittance that religious denominations could afford and the prospects were excellent. Wynford Vaughan Thomas had achieved immortality overnight with his live commentary from a bombing raid over Berlin and there were others, like Huw Wheldon, who became household names along with their programmes.

The BBC in Wales as elsewhere in the United Kingdom was still in the shadow of its dour, founding father, Lord Reith, although he had long ago abandoned the corporation (after a great storm about his dictatorial attitude). His insistence that education, religion and culture should have their proper place in broadcasting, along with news and entertainment, lived after him and so did the aspiration to make the British broadcasting system the best in the world. The integrity of the BBC's war reporting had enhanced its public stature as had the tall men – in his own image – Reith had steered towards key posts. A story, which gives the flavour of Reith, relates to an announcer who was caught kissing a girl in the corridor. Reith wanted to fire the man but was prevailed upon not to do so because the kissing couple were about to marry. 'Very well. But make sure he never reads the epilogue,' was Reith's final verdict.

I was invited to the BBC station at Bangor to meet the legendary Sam Jones, a former *Western Mail* reporter, shrewd, kindly and deeply devoted to Welsh culture. His name was synonymous with the BBC in north Wales. He wanted to know about Harrow and judge for himself the effect it had had upon me. His only son was approaching the age at which he might go there. He was also aware that I was a budding journalist so he sent me by car to the snowdrifts then accumulating on the fringes of the Clwydian Hills for a 'story', which I would broadcast in Welsh over the coming weekend.

'And what if there is no story?'

'Use your imagination, dear boy . . . a colour piece we used to call it.'

Sam was a strange radio producer: he was almost stone deaf. But he was a warm-hearted enthusiast and he gave me my first chance to broadcast. Other opportunities followed, first in Swansea and then in Cardiff, the BBC's centre in Wales. I was the first news reporter to be appointed in the principality and radio was my *métier*. I travelled about in a powerful recording car, driven by an engineer, with equipment to cut discs at the back. Interviews completed, we would rush back to the studio or, if we were too distant, we could feed the discs down the line from a telephone exchange. Tape was not yet in use and the interviews had to be tight because editing a disc could be tricky.

A cargo ship, the *Tresilian*, broke in half in a storm in the Irish Sea. The crew was saved and landed at RAF Brawdy, Pembrokeshire. Rivers had flooded the roads but we got there. I spoke to the survivors hurriedly as they scoffed their first meal ashore.

'The ship's lights had gone out. We were in total darkness. We could hear our mates calling us and their voices getting further and further away. That's how we knew the ship had broken in two . . . the stern and the bows were drifting apart.'

'You dived into the sea?'

'No. We walked in. The sea was coming up the deck as the ship went down.'

It was a graphic account. One sailor had held on to his unconscious young mate in the sea, though there was no rescue vessel in sight.

'I held on to him for company,' he told me.

'I wouldn't be here if it wasn't for him,' his young mate said.

We raced in driving rain to the telephone exchange at Haverfordwest and fed the stuff through to the Light Programme's *Radio Newsreel*. It came back to us over the airwaves while we were still feeding the tail end of our recordings. There were some very fast operators in those days at Egton House, the BBC news centre in Langham Place, London.

There was a unique camaraderie too among Betty Fitch's boys. Editors might come and go but our mistress, Betty, was always there. She was a queen among the Beeb's news organizers. She invited me up for a few days familiarization with their working methods – she liked my voice, she said. I stood in for the Court reporter, Godfrey Talbot, on the night in October 1955 when Princess Margaret split from Group Captain Townsend and nervous petals drifted down from the Queen's bouquet as she stood for the anthem in the royal box at the theatre. I never mentioned the falling petals; it was not the kind of thing we reported. I attended a gala performance where there were eighteen British and Hollywood stars. Glittering Diana Dors outshone them all with her all-conquering smile and cheeky, cockney vivacity.

Betty wanted me in London on a more permanent basis but our controller in Wales, Alun Oldfield Davies, one of Reith's giants, got wind of it. He shook his head in the clouds above me when I confessed that I might be tempted to go to London if invited: 'If you went, the BBC would lose the use of your Welsh and that would not represent the best use of our resources.' I knew that was the end of that little secret ambition.

Jacob Epstein, the sculptor, came to Cardiff for the dedication of his statue of *Christ in Majesty* at Llandaff Cathedral. There was to be a live television programme about it (videotape was not yet available) with commentary by our own redoubtable deputy head of programmes, Hywel Davies, another son of the manse. But Epstein refused to take part in the television programme and had thrown a chisel at the BBC emissary sent to his studio. So, there was no point in anyone trying to pursue him further, Hywel said. But Betty Fitch wanted an interview with the sculptor for *Radio Newsreel*. I found out that Epstein was staying at the Churchill Hotel, not far from the cathedral, and I consulted our news editor, Tom Richards, about the propriety of making an approach. 'You get the interview, boy,' said Tom, with his usual boisterousness at the whiff of a scoop. 'I'll watch your back with Hywel.'

Getting an interview seemed worth the risk of displeasure at the top. Besides, I had been to the Battersea Park exhibition some years before and admired Epstein's work. I wanted to see the great man. I drove up to the hotel with my tape recorder, the new device now in vogue. As luck would have it, Epstein was pacing about on the gravel outside, waiting for a hired car to take him and his lady to the cathedral. The car was late and the sculptor fuming. I offered to take them myself and they accepted. In the car, I told him who I was and expressed my hope that he would grant me an interview. He said he would but first he had to see his statue. We walked together down the central aisle to within about thirty feet of the *Maiestas*, set at the crown of an elliptical arch spanning the nave.

Epstein sat down and looked up at his work. I plugged the microphone into my tape recorder, switched on and talked with him as he viewed his great work for the first time in place rather than in the studio. He never took his eyes off the statue and was never aware of the microphone just below his chin. He answered my questions freely and frankly.

'Is this the most controversial piece you've ever done?'

'I've never believed in doing crazy woiks [his Brooklyn accent came to the fore]. I was trained in the classical tradition and that's where all my work belongs . . .'

He told me how he had seen the roofless church after it had been bombed and conceived the idea of Christ rising from the debris. His Christ looked remarkably like his lady. Later, over tea and sandwiches, he asked me when we were going to do the interview he had promised. I told him we had already done it while he sat in the aisle. He was incredulous but content.

On my return to the studio, our head of programmes, Watkin Jones, listened with intense interest to the ten minutes or so that we had recorded. 'Do you realize,' he said 'that this is as if you had been with Michelangelo when he first saw his *Pietà* at St Peter's?' The BBC broadcast the interview in its entirety on one of its most prestigious programmes on the Home Service that night. It has been broadcast many times since – with other interviewers putting the questions!

John Ormond was a poet from Swansea, a friend of Dylan Thomas and Vernon Watkins. When Dylan died in strange circumstances in New York, he left a draft of one of John's poems on his writing table in the boathouse at Laugharne. You could see it through the window. John was working for the *Swansea Evening Post* at the time but he refused to write the hurried obituary requested by his editor: he was too upset by his friend Dylan's unexpected death.

John joined BBC News at Cardiff as a television reporter but poetry remained his true love. He had worked on captions for Hulton's popular *Picture Post* – television's precursor, along with the cinema newsreels, in the visual presentation of events – but John had little time for the rough and tumble of hard news. He was a stickler for quality in pictures and words and he drifted towards the high-class documentary where he eventually made his mark. Meanwhile, we contributed from Wales to the national bi-weekly television newsreel, synonymous with John Cotter who did for television what Betty Fitch had done for radio. He too was a topical news gatherer par excellence.

It was soon decided that we should have a regular monthly topical survey in Welsh, partly on film, supplemented by live studio interviews. John would shoot the film around Wales and edit the items at Alexandra Palace where all the facilities were and I would go up to London to record the commentary. We would then return to Cardiff and transmit at Sunday lunchtime from a chapel in Sapphire Street, Splott, where we had a solitary television camera to present live my introduction to the film and the interviews that followed. Rolling the film at Alexandra Palace on a five-second cue given down the telephone was not made any easier by the fact that John had no Welsh and did not understand what I was saying. We found the solution to that problem when I described a beautiful girl as the Gina Lollobrigida of Wales. It was the kind of cue word that could not easily be missed. 'Give me a Gina,' John would say as we prepared later editions. He did not enjoy robust health and was a testy character to work with. In spite of our disagreements, we were great friends.

The BBC was a job for life in those days provided you did not disgrace yourself too badly; even then they tried to look after you. On the strength of this conviction, I got married on 24 March 1956, the day ESB won the Grand National. My landlady's son got married the same day and his initials formed the name of the horse.

I first noticed my future wife as a little girl with spindly legs in a gymslip. She was the youngest child on the family farm where I helped out early in the war. I knew her older sisters, brothers and parents well but Enid was too young to be noticed – unless she was in the way. When she developed into a full-blown girl at the end of my Harrow days, I could never take my eyes off her. I would drop my books and hurry across fields to intercept her on her way home from the shop and to fight for a kiss. I thought of her when I was away and felt jealous pangs when I heard she had a relationship with someone else. I said nothing to her until married life became a real possibility. I then acted decisively and have never regretted it. Our first wonderful son was born on Christmas Eve and two more boys followed as quickly as we could make them. All three have brought joy to our lives.

The advent of commercial television to south Wales and the west country in 1958 offered a challenging, creative opportunity to those of us still stuck in radio who felt they were being by-passed in the BBC's slow and ponderous television development. That fireball, Donald Baverstock, was having trouble in London with his enterprising programme *Tonight* and his uphill battle with his superiors seemed typical of the BBC at that stage.

The commercial company that had won the franchise, Television Wales and the West, had successfully raised the half a million pounds necessary to build a studio and was committed to producing twice as many programmes in both Welsh and English as its local BBC rivals. I went to see its managing director, Mark Chapman Walker, in the crummy, dilapidated office of the *News of the World* in Caroline Street, Cardiff. He was impressive in his shirtsleeves and red braces. He offered me a job at £35 a year more than I was getting at the time.

'You'll double your salary in a year,' he said.

I did not believe him but I accepted.

Tele Wele Wales

About ninety of us in all worked like fiends to get the new commercial television station on air by December 1957, only to be told at the last minute by the Independent Television Authority that their transmitter would not be ready for another month. There was consternation all round. The studios, a converted farmhouse on the edge of Poncanna Fields, near the centre of Cardiff, were ready – the milk stains were still on the walls when I moved in – and we were as fully staffed as we were going to be until advertisers' money rolled in. Few of the major companies operating the commercial network were in profit as yet and our money was exceptionally tight. The delayed start was a serious threat and our 5s shares were unofficially traded at 4s.

Alec Jeans of the *Liverpool Post* was a founder shareholder, along with the odd group of fortune hunters who had formed the company. He took an interest in the news-gathering operation I had set up.

'You will have to lay off staff?' he suggested.

'No, sir. The news operation is based on freelances. We don't pay them until they contribute.'

'How do you know it will work?'

'I'm here to see that it does.'

That shut him up. I did not tell him that we had one news camera-man on the staff who shot, processed and edited his own film. Without him, we would be lost. Neither did I mention my indispensable right-hand man, Mike Towers, who had joined us from the *Bristol Evening Post*.

I was also responsible for Welsh-language programmes and had poached two very able young women, Dorothy Williams from the BBC and Eleanor Mathias who had worked with me in BBC news. I had a third area in my charge – special events – but they were not of immediate concern although the Commonwealth Games in Cardiff were looming. The lost month passed quickly and we were on air on 14 January 1958.

My task on the very first programme was to regulate the sound emanating from the smaller of our two studios: we had no one else who knew how to do it and I had mastered the control panel there. My colleague, Meurig Jones, who handled the pictures, uttered a short, personal prayer in the last few seconds before we went on air. 'It doesn't matter how much you pray, you won't be able to mix between pictures unless you press that button "A",' I told him. He muttered his thanks and TWW was on air – and not to come off for a decade. Every night was a first night in television.

Mark Chapman Walker was full of bright ideas for attracting public attention to the station's output. Billy Smart's circus came to Sophia Gardens and Mark persuaded Smart to walk his elephants up Pontcanna Fields so that they could be seen in the background while the news was transmitted from our studio lawn. The elephants came closer and closer and the newscaster was lucky not to be trampled. Mark wanted a black woman to read the news – unheard of then – and he got his way, once. The woman was simply not up to it and black-and-white pictures did not help. But the station's novel approach was talked about and the viewers converted to the new commercial channel with amazing speed. When Mark had worked for the great Lord Woolton at Conservative Central Office after the war, Woolton was alleged to have told him: 'You have come here with a new idea every day and none of them has been any good.' Perhaps this was why he never forced his more daring ideas and always put them forward shyly but temptingly. I turned down the more outrageous.

The Torrington by-election in north Devon in March 1958 was a different matter. It was on the southernmost edge of our transmission area and a potential battleground for viewers with Westward TV. Mark had persuaded Randolph Churchill to visit Cardiff on his way to cover the declaration of the result for the *Evening Standard*. A chartered plane would take him from Cardiff to the west country next day in time for the declaration. I met Randolph off the train about nine o'clock and took him to the Royal Hotel for a late dinner. Randolph had set his heart on a hot potato but there was none available. The chef had gone home. 'Do you have a pressure cooker?' he asked the waiter. He got his potato after that threat to invade the kitchen. We headed for the studios and a late live interview conducted by myself. It all went reasonably well except that on air Randolph prefaced most of his replies with 'As I told you at dinner . . .' He was oblivious of the viewers. After the programme, Randolph was in no hurry to leave the ample supply of Scotch provided for him by our station manager, Walter Kemp. Our late night ended with Randolph cursing the American police for their abominable treatment of his sister, Sarah. But his night did not end at the studios; he fell among a bunch of barristers at the hotel and talked with them till dawn.

Next morning was foggy and I wondered whether Randolph's plane had taken off. My worst fear was soon confirmed: the plane could not fly and Randolph was at the studios. The by-election result was expected at noon. There was no way he was going to get to Torrington for the *Evening Standard*. I confronted him: 'It's all my fault,' I said. He brushed my apologies aside. Over a long, well-watered glass of whisky – such as his father used to have mid-morning, he said – we plotted his coverage of the result. Everyone who came out of the count at Torrington was called to the telephone to speak to Mr Churchill and everyone did. He called the *Evening Standard* with the result before it appeared on the tapes. A substantial article followed, attributing Mark Bonham Carter's Liberal victory to his mother, the formidable Lady Violet, Asquith's daughter, who had visited the constituency a few days before. Then came his abject apology for absence to the editor and my heart went out to him.

Randolph rested in the afternoon before taking part in a novel programme format – another of Mark's ideas – where the camera crew put questions to a distinguished guest. The guest on this occasion was Nye Bevan in a London studio but there was a surprise questioner among the Cardiff crew – Randolph Churchill. It was rather like Dr Johnson meeting John Wilkes; full of banter but nothing memorable. I was to meet Nye later at his own General Election count in Tredegar in 1959 when Gaitskell, the 'desiccated calculating machine', conceded victory early, long before Nye's own result had been declared. 'I shall not concede victory until the last ballot box is opened,' said Nye from the town hall balcony. It was meaningless but magnificent. It had been a hectic couple of days looking after Randolph. Randolph sent me a copy of his book *What I said about the Press* as a memento of his visit. He sent one to Barbara, the make-up girl too.

'You call this work?' said Roy Thomson, chairman of Scottish Television when he came to visit us. 'I used to sell radios from door to door in Canada. That was real work, I can tell you.' He gained a costly immortality when he described commercial television as 'a licence to print money', but he was right in that our profit in the first year was not far short of double our capital outlay and remained at that sort of level to the end. Our shares soared on the stock market and Mark saw to it that his forecast of my increase in earnings came true as well.

The company directors were a motley band. Mark represented the interests of the *News of the World* and its owner, Sir William Carr, a pale, ashen-faced man whom I hardly ever saw without a whisky before him. There was a story circulating that he had once caught a licensee giving him a short measure. Sir William told him: 'If you ever do that again, I'll buy the pub to have the pleasure of firing you.' When he came under take-over pressure from the odious but powerful Robert Maxwell and Pergamon Press, Bill Carr was impressed by a young Aussie named Murdoch who put all his resources at Bill's disposal. In return, he was given a slip of paper promising him a share of the *News of the World*. Maxwell was beaten off. Murdoch raised money on the strength of the paper slip promise and ousted his erstwhile friend. It was nothing new in the newspaper world.

My immediate boss was an outsized man named Bryan Michie, who had compèred a talent show for the BBC and discovered Morecambe and Wise, and was a close friend of Godfrey Winn, the highly talented wartime writer for the *Daily Mirror*. Bryan was now Jack Hylton's man, Hylton being a director of TWW. Hylton had won fame as a dance bandleader and theatre impresario. At one time, Jack had as many as five shows running simultaneously in the West End. He still had an interest in the Crazy Gang and their long-running show at the Victoria Palace. He knew everyone in show business, was quietly spoken and never drank. Although ageing, he had a lively Italian mistress, Rosalina Neri, and when she faded to his villa near Cannes, he married a very lovely Australian girl, Beverley Prowse, a friend of the cricketer, Keith Miller. As someone said, 'Jack always had the best.' Once, in the early 1960s, when we were thirteen sitting down for lunch in a Sloane Street restaurant, Jack asked me, the youngest, to get up and phone Rosa to add to our unfortunate number. She flounced in, scattering kisses all round. After lunch, Jack and Rosa left together; his new wife, Beverley was away. He died a few weeks later. Rosa was distraught – and pregnant.

The American National Broadcasting Corporation also had an interest in the company and was represented by Herbert Agar. He came from an old New England family and was as ruggedly handsome as the actor, Gary Cooper. He had married Billy Wallace's mother. Billy was an old flame of Princess Margaret, or so the tabloids rumoured. Herbert's claim to fame was that he had visited Roosevelt in 1940 and waxed eloquent about the strength of Britain's will to resist the Nazis. The president had answered:

'But that is not what my ambassador (Kennedy Senior) tells me!'

'What else would you expect, Mr President, from a bloody Irishman!' replied Herbert to his eternal credit. He introduced me to the Savile Club. NBC had loaned us a benign general manager, Bob Myers, who saw to it that we kept down our costs.

The Welsh component of the board also comprised men of stature: Sir Grismond Philipps, lord lieutenant of Carmarthenshire and a personal guardian of the royal family in the war. Sir Ifan ab Owen Edwards, the Baden-Powell of the Urdd, the Welsh League of Youth, was a veteran of the trenches in the First World War and so was Huw T. Edwards, a trade unionist who had become 'the un-official Prime Minister of Wales' in the years immediately after the Second World War.

The chairman of the company was Lord Cilcennin, first lord of the Admiralty in the early 1950s, and a smart man in every sense, who could outwit them all. He was writing a book about Admiralty House and told me he would include pictures of the Earl of Sandwich, five times first lord in the eighteenth century and his mistress, Martha Ray. I encouraged him to include the infamous exchange between Sandwich and Wilkes, which occasioned one of the best repartees in English history. Sandwich told Wilkes he would either die of the pox or on the gallows and Wilkes replied: 'That depends, my Lord, on whether I embrace your mistress or your principles.' Cilcennin relished the story but resisted the temptation to include it in his volume. He died in 1960 and was succeeded in the chair by the Earl of Derby, best known to the public as a race-horse owner and to his friends as a gambling aristocrat in the eighteenth-century tradition. He was to learn 'a short sharp lesson', as he called it, in London shortly and lose a great deal of money; some said a quarter of a million pounds. 'All he has to do is walk down the hall, choose a picture, sell it and his debts are cleared,' bookmaker William Hill is supposed to have said at the time. He would have been right too. John Derby had a gallery of Old Masters.

Having launched the company successfully, Mark withdrew to the *News of the World* and was succeeded by Alfred Francis who had made a name for himself as financial director of the Old Vic Theatre. He brought in his own producer, Michael Frostick, and a swathe of high-faluting ideas intended to improve our standing with the Independent Television Authority. There was method in his madness.

The pianist, Joseph Cooper, was engaged to present our new daily topical programme *Here To-day* when I wanted the comedian, Des O'Connor. I had my own way up to a point and got Cardiff-born Shirley Bassey (now Dame) to sing 'Stormy Weather' and a couple of other numbers on videotape for our first week's editions. Her professionalism shone through when our fog machine failed as she sang 'Foggy Day in London Town'. A flood of liquid from the machine reached her feet but Shirley never stopped singing.

There was conflict in the air. Theatre people and newsmen were always at war in television. If we were philistines in their eyes, they were misplaced cultural buffs in ours. Bryan kindly told me I could not win and that I should sit back, relax and watch developments. The West Country had to be looked after as well as Wales or we might lose it to Westward Television, so the Bath Festival had to be nourished, along with Yehudi Menuhin, even if the ratings dived to zero. I had to agree. The American college lecturer Tom Lehrer's advent to the studios and his rendering at the piano of 'We'll all go together when we go' and 'Poisoning pigeons in the park' expressed not only the dire mood of the nuclear-bomb-fearing sixties but my personal disillusionment too. But I was too young to be downcast for long.

Alfred was mad about opera but whenever we put opera on air our viewership plummeted. I thought a great deal about the problem and devised a short series titled *Share my Music*. That supremely talented singer, Gwyneth Jones (now Dame), originally from Pontypool, gave me the idea. Gwyneth told me how she learnt her operatic parts as she washed the dishes in the kitchen. Why not make opera more homely and get the beautiful Gwyneth to introduce a scene from *Cosi fan Tutte* at the kitchen sink? The recipe worked and we kept half the audience of the top-rating *Wagon Train*, which preceded us on air. Alfred was impressed and friendly relationships between us were restored. I began to appreciate his favourite lines: 'The best committee is a committee of two – with one away sick' and 'People say they know what they like; what they mean is they like what they know.'

One of the *Share my Music* programmes nearly came to grief. It featured another very attractive and shapely singer, Joan Carlisle. The programme was being produced in our Bristol studio. I was not there but I could see the rehearsals on closed circuit from Cardiff. I watched Miss Carlisle take the floor and please the eye of every cameraman and studio hand present. Everything appeared to be going smoothly and I turned my mind to other things. In a matter of minutes, the producer, Chris Mercer, telephoned me to say that the singer had retired to her dressing room and would not emerge in spite of all his pleading.

'She knows the orchestra is waiting and that we've only got them for a limited time?'

'Yes,' said Chris, 'she knows all that. She's emotionally disturbed for some reason. Her journey from Austria can't have helped . . .'

I recalled her walk on to the studio floor and the admiring glances no woman could fail to appreciate. I had a desperate idea.

'Look, Chris. Get a bottle of champagne and get the floor manager to present it to her with the compliments of the crew who want to see her back in the studio.'

The ruse worked and she gave the performance of her life. We recorded her aria – as Desdemona in *Othello* – twice: in the first, she cried real tears, then she composed herself and sang with feigned tears but real artistry. There was no doubt in my mind that the second was the better. Art is always an improvement on reality, or should be.

Chris Mercer had the genius to make a mountain out of a molehill. He produced our monthly networked Welsh programme, *Land of Song*, with the charismatic Ivor Emanuel as lead singer, a host of children and a string of female stars. We supplemented traditional Welsh folk music with numbers like Ivor Novello's 'Some Enchanted Evening' and the Crazy Gang's 'Any Old Iron' sung in Welsh to the great delight of English viewers. I asked Chris to produce a small-scale, visual, music programme based on the pop discs that were flooding the market. The idea grew in his mind and in no time our big studio was heaving with teenagers writhing to the songs and electric performance of Tom Jones. *Discs a'Gogo* ran for years and climbed the charts with the Beatles.

My opportunities to produce programmes of my own grew rarer as our volume of productions increased but the chance to do something with Richard Burton was irresistible. I wanted to record him delivering some of the great English literary masterpieces about Wales for a programme to be transmitted on St David's Day under the title *This World of Wales* – part of a poetic line by Gerald Manley Hopkins. Richard was filming *VIPs* with Elizabeth Taylor in London. He agreed to give me a Saturday afternoon at the Granville Theatre for a token fee of £250 to be donated to the Invalid Tricycle

Association – Port Talbot Branch. Port Talbot was his birthplace and his sister and his brother, Graham, were still living there.

My first significant meeting with Richard was at the Oliver Messel suite at the Dorchester Hotel where he and Elizabeth were ensconced, along with her two children by Michael Wilding, a daughter by Mike Todd and a disabled little girl she had adopted. The first thing I noticed about Elizabeth was the perfect elliptical line from the tip of her nose to the extremity of her eyebrow and my own reaction to the fact that I was face to face with one of the most beautiful women in the world. Richard's brusquely macho treatment of her in conversation and her robust responses assured me that she was all woman and not a Hollywood version of a Vestal virgin to be placed on a pedestal and adored. It was as if they were continuing their aggressive dialogue in *Who's Afraid of Virginia Woolf?*.

I told Richard of the difficulty I had had in persuading his fellow actor, Emlyn Williams, to allow him to read Dylan Thomas's description of his hangover after his first Saturday night out in Swansea. Emlyn had bought up the exclusive reading rights of *Portrait of the Artist as a Young Dog*, where the description occurs, and had told me: 'Tell Richard he can do it this once and no more.' I relayed the message. Richard laughed, 'Emlyn doesn't like competition.'

My friend Rhydwen, a poet preacher, who had known Richard from earlier days, tripped as he crossed the carpet to get a signed photograph from Elizabeth. I too had a signed photograph. 'Would you boys like to eat?' Richard asked. We had had a fair amount to drink. We moved into the suite dining room and pondered over the Dorchester menu, beginning with Whitstable Natives (oysters) and ending with God knows what. 'It's bangers and mash for me. What's for you?' said Richard. And we all had bangers and mash, Elizabeth included, and the finest Burgundy the Dorchester could provide.

'Why is she worth £35,000 a week and I'm only worth seventeen?' he asked.

'She gets more publicity' I said.

'Even when we get the same publicity as with *Cleopatra*, the fees remain the same. The truth is more people are interested in what happens to her – even on film. She is box office and I am not.'

He brought Elizabeth down to south Wales to see an international rugby match at Cardiff. Richard got lost in the crowd at the Royal Hotel before the match and I ran with Elizabeth across Westgate Street to our seats in the Arms Park. Later they went to meet his family at Port Talbot. On another occasion, he came down without her and with his brother Will to see another match at the

Arms Park. That night, he got kicked in the eye by some yobbos outside the Load of Hay pub at Paddington. The white of his eye was the colour of ruby and filming of *VIPs* had to be suspended. Elizabeth reckoned it would cost the studio a million.

Our promised day at the Granville was also twice postponed but it finally arrived and we foregathered at lunchtime at a bar in the Dorchester. The Bloody Marys were already flowing when I arrived and I soon began to despair of ever reaching the theatre where the cameras and the autocue were waiting. Eventually, we set off. Unknown to me, Richard was sick as a dog when he arrived and had to fortify himself with brandy to make a start. He was in prime condition when he came to deliver the Dylan Thomas description of a hangover. He needed no make-up. He sat at a round bar table with the dregs of a pint of beer before him and acted the words as only a great actor can. As the afternoon wore on, his confidence grew just as our nervous energies flagged. After the set pieces I wanted, he recorded more poetry, unscripted and from memory. Herrick, Hopkins, Byron, Keats – all poured from his lips – and we cheered him on until we lost the recording line and could record no more.

I had arranged for that incomparable wordsmith, Gwyn Thomas, to write the introductions to the different pieces and to record them separately at Bristol a week later. We were on our way there by train when my director, Mike Towers, noticed that Gwyn's introduction to Shakespeare's Owen Glendower speech did not really say who Owen Glendower was. He had a point; it needed something like 'Owen Glendower, our national hero' because the programme might be seen in the US. Just at that point, the train plunged into the Severn Tunnel and darkness. There was nothing but the clickety clack of the train. When we emerged on the far side, Gwyn said: 'Shall we say: Owen Glendower, the nearest we ever came to Davy Crocket, give or take a few fur caps?' Only Gwyn could have produced such a line.

The programme won great acclaim in Wales – a BBC producer, Lorraine Davies, told me it was the best of its kind she had ever seen – and the Dylan scene was shown on the *Ed Sullivan Show*, coast to coast in the US. When I negotiated with Ed Sullivan's people in New York I named my price as £4,000 – the total cost of the programme. They said they could film Burton at Acapulco for that sort of money. 'He was in prime condition,' I said. 'You'll never get him in quite that condition again.' They agreed and the deal was done.

Gwyn Thomas, who had written a number of humorous, affectionate books about Wales as well as articles for *Punch* and other periodicals, should cast his Welsh eye on pastures new I felt and he agreed. As an experiment, I took him to the Cannes Film Festival. The gigantic American aircraft-carrier anchored in the bay, with its enormous destructive potential, caught his imagination and we quickly concocted a plan for a film contrasting the horrendous threat of nuclear weapons with the peaceful, beautiful humanity on the beach. The cameraman had a ball with the G-string beauties that the film editor mingled with mushroom cloud explosions. *Hotspot*, as we titled the film, won an award at the Prague Film Festival.

I took Gwyn on his first visit to New York. He knew all the mobsters' haunts in the 1920s from reading Damon Runyon and we filmed a good many of them for his film portrait of the Big Apple. He saw it as a contrast between wealth and poverty. Spain he also knew from teaching Spanish at school and close study of the country's history from the arrival of the Moors in the seventh century to the Civil War in the twentieth. He was primarily a paragraphic writer and his commentary had to be hewn to fit the pictures. The outcome was a lovely film history of Spain shown on cinema screens as well as television.

Our most adventurous journey was to Breznyev and Kosygin's Moscow in 1965 when the thaw in the Cold War was beginning to set in. Wales was playing soccer against the Moscow Dynamos and it seemed a good opportunity to find out what was going on. I spoke directly with a man at the State Committee for Radio and Television, a Mr Viertyperog, and yes, I would be welcome to bring my camera team to the match, together with the author, Gwyn Thomas, some of whose books had been translated and published in Russia. I played down the idea of a documentary: all we wanted were some street scenes.

We boarded the Aeroflot plane at Heathrow and were soon sipping generous measures of vodka. An elderly Canadian who was returning to his birthplace in Russia, and sat between Gwyn and myself, had forgotten the name of his native village by the time we arrived. We were met at the airport by a young embassy official who said nervously: 'Here come the sharks' as three or four Russians in trench coats and grey hats descended on our luggage. They were helpful as it turned out.

There were seven of us in all including our sports editor, Lloyd Lewis, and we stayed at the Ukraina Hotel overlooking the Moskva River. It was one of Stalin's grand skyscraper buildings, raised in the 1930s to show that the USSR was on its way. The sharp-eyed receptionist with an abacus allocated Gwyn and me to the same room. We did not dispute her decision. Then we had our first shock. My man at the State Committee said that the assistant he wanted to look after us was not available for a day or two:

'He is doing . . . what do you call them . . . examinations? There is another problem . . . he speaks only German.' He sounded gruff and certainly less friendly than he had when I spoke to him from Wales.

'I can get by in German,' I said weakly, convinced that there was something sinister afoot. Perhaps I had dispensed with the services of the Intourist guide too abruptly and she had reported back that something was amiss? Did they still want me after my Vienna phone tapping? Perhaps I should not have come. I told the film crew to stay put and on no account to take out the camera. (Of course, they did and filmed an exquisite sunrise over the Moskva River from their hotel room.)

'We are on thin ice,' I said. 'Don't make any wrong moves.'

Barely an hour had gone by before they came back to me, whispering that there was a false floor in the hotel. They had run downstairs from our floor 32 and up from the ground floor. Floor 19 was missing, blocked both ways. That was where the bugging devices were listened to, I guessed. Gwyn and I addressed songs of praise to Communist Russia that night, to her dynamic heroes and superlative achievements.

Two days later, when we were at our wits end with enforced idleness and suspicion, a beetle-browed stranger of about thirty walked, without so much as a knock, into my room, made a beeline for my bedside table and turned over the British coins I had left there. 'Ich bin ein Numismatist,' he said and then introduced himself as our long-awaited escort. I got the entire crew to produce their coins and he took what he wanted.

He had a very distinctive badge on his lapel that commanded a deal of respect from all and sundry. He got the policeman to hold up the traffic outside the Bolshoi so that our cameraman could get his desired shots. He took us to the furthest point of the German advance on Moscow, to the onion-domed precincts of the Kremlin and to film the crocodiles of children visiting Red Square. At the end of the day, he took our film for processing and a security check.

We got to know our escort, Vitaly Seferiantz, very well that week as he took us filming wherever we wanted. I met his boss, Viertyperog, at the Moscow Radio office. 'I drink mineral not criminal water,' Viertyperog joked. I sensed that Vitaly, as a political apparatchik, was his superior in some peculiar hierarchical line-up. Vitaly and his wife accompanied us to the Bolshoi and we chatted on the steps of the great theatre after the performance – it was opera, *The Marriage of Figaro*, rather than ballet that night. He gave me a new geographical perspective.

'Over there to our right is European Russia and barely a thousand miles away is Berlin. Over here to our left, there are two thousand miles between us and Vladivostok where I come from. That is where the new Russia will develop.'

On the eve of the soccer match, our sports reporter, Lloyd Lewis, broadcast a radio preview and was overheard to say to a colleague in the studio: 'And after this, Dennis, I'm off to look for a bint in Red Square.' Everyone between Moscow and Cardiff seemed to have over-heard it. The Russians laughed whenever his name was mentioned.

On the day itself, there was a torrential downpour on the Lenin Stadium and its 100,000 crowd. Vitaly, who had come with us in ordinary clothes, suddenly appeared at my side in full army officer's uniform under his cape. The crowd had become restless in the storm and the party was taking no chances. There was obviously a military store at the stadium. We had a small celebration in the hotel afterwards and I noticed that Vitaly always moved to the window whenever he had anything confidential to say. It was the only part of the room out of the bug's reach. He gave me a nice volume of pictures from the Hermitage at Leningrad and, when pressed, he asked for a copy of *The Rise and Fall of the Third Reich* in German. There would be no problem if I sent it to him by post, he assured me, which confirmed my well-established suspicion that he belonged to the KGB.

'You must come again,' he said. 'To Leningrad next time.'

'Why Leningrad?'

'We're much better organized there.'

When it was time for us to leave Moscow, he handed me the rolls of film. They had not been processed. 'How am I going to get this lot through your customs?' I asked. He handed me an authorizing letter on State Committee notepaper.

I leapt up the steps of the British plane taking us home only to find a soldier with a sub-machine gun just inside the door. The Russians were taking no chances. I have never been so glad to hear a British voice as I was to hear the steward, asking: 'Gin and tonic, sir?' It was only later that I found I had been the first person to take a British film crew to Communist Russia; they normally insisted on their own film crews. And it was years later that I discovered that my lads had been right about the missing floor at the Ukraina: a foreign corres-pondent, who had lived there, confirmed it on his return to the UK.

We called our documentary *The Growing People* and it won an award but it did not contain Gwyn's best line, delivered to me personally as we walked down Gorky Street after dinner one night: 'These people are just finding out that when you divide everything equally there isn't much for anybody.' When he got back to the UK and was asked how he felt about the visit, he said he thought his teeth had been bugged and he was so tired he wanted Lenin to move aside in the tomb.

I was going to take a belated holiday on Friday, 21 October 1966 and was hoping to make an early departure from the studios. I began my tour shortly before ten and called in at the newsroom. A story was breaking about a coal tip that had moved and was threatening a primary school at Aberfan near Merthyr. Just at that moment, a former teacher at the school, who was rehearsing for *Land of Song* in the main studio downstairs, burst in: 'It couldn't happen,' he said, 'the tip is three-quarters of a mile away from the school.' But it had happened. The monstrous tip, swollen with water, had tumbled like a black avalanche onto the school shortly after prayers. A desperate, frantic search began for survivors and the world's media descended upon us.

Over that weekend, we transmitted more than fifty reports on the tragedy, including complete national news programmes, with very little help from outside. The studio corridor floors turned black from the tramp of cameramen and reporters who had visited the scene. Among them was a young man named John Humphrys, later to win fame as the BBC's *Today* presenter. I was glued to my desk and the studios making the detailed arrangements for our extensive coverage 'après le deluge', as a French lady reporter put it. Gradually, it became clear that the ugly lava had taken the lives of 116 children and 32 adults. The mental strain and anguish were devastating.

We were to transmit a special programme for the ITV network on the Sunday evening. The producer, an ex-tabloid newspaperman, appeared from time to time over the weekend asking me for a suitable person to introduce it. I gave him several names but on Sunday he was still without a presenter and he suggested that I do it – not for the first time. I refused yet again. I had been under too much stress over the last couple of days. But I was fighting a losing battle – he had no one else – and by six o'clock it was too late. We were due on air in an hour. Besides, his film was still being edited.

The film was still not available for me to rehearse the commentary when we went on air – the editor ran with the reel through the studio as the opening captions appeared. My first task was to read a simple list of names of some of the children who had perished. It was heart-rending and I only just managed it without being stifled by tears. But the real shock-horror of the film was an interview with a very pretty little girl survivor, who said she would now have to look for new friends. All the gruesome ugliness of the event was encapsulated in that scene of Beauty and the Beast and the studio phones never stopped ringing. The viewers were disturbed. I knew we had crossed the boundary of 'good taste'. My only consolation was our cleaner at home, Mrs Evans, who had lost many of her family at the Senghenydd pit disaster years earlier. When I asked her views on the programme, she told me: 'It opened the eyes of a lot of people to things they did not want to know.' Armed by Mrs Evans, I was ready to face the mob of armchair critics.

We won the majority of the *Western Mail*'s television awards in 1967. There had been no formal complaints from the Independent Television Authority against our performance as a company over the years and so we expected to have our franchise renewed. But in the final weeks there was a flurry of activity to set up a rival consortium. I was aware of it because two people I knew well – Wynford Vaughan Thomas and the political correspondent, W. John Morgan – were in the thick of it. They had clearly been tipped off by someone in high places to put in a credible rival bid and they were hard at work from April onwards, collecting the names of prominent people from south Wales and the West Country. But, at the end of the day, they could only make promises while we had substantial achievements to our credit. Would promises outweigh achievements?

We had after all saved the ITA's face when a previous rival company, Wales West and North, favoured by the ITA with a franchise, had gone bankrupt in 1964. We had stepped in with a generous settlement for their shareholders and a takeover of the company's programme commitments. But there is no such thing as gratitude in television politics, any more than in any other kind of politics. Besides, there were little people at work, exploiting the Welsh nationalist undercurrent which was antipathetic to the company whatever it did to support the Welsh language and Wales.

The company was not Welsh or West Country in origin. There had been no body of people in Wales or the west country a decade earlier with the courage to put up the money required to start a commercial television operation, but there were plenty who kicked themselves afterwards when they saw the money pouring into the company's coffers. The ITA wanted these people who had missed out to have an interest rather than the venture capitalists who had had the courage to establish the business in the first place. TWW was London based and that was a damning indictment in the ITA's eyes: they wanted people from the region to have the franchise.

Personalities also crept into the equation. Lord Hill, the chairman of the ITA who had first made his name during the war with his rich voice as the radio doctor, wanted to show that his authority had teeth. He had no affection for our chairman, Lord Derby, or for our clever solicitor, Arnold Goodman. 'You here again?' was his throaty greeting to Goodman, who acted for a number of TV companies, as we trooped in for our interview with the authority. The scene was set for change. My guess is that Roy Thomson and Scottish Television were Charles Hill's first target after Roy's remark about ITV being a licence to print money, but Roy got wind of it and remonstrated with the prime minister, Harold Wilson. Roy was by then the proprietor of *The Times* and a stack of other newspapers. The ITA had to look for other targets although Scottish Television did not escape their lash either.

I accompanied John Derby on the Sunday morning when he was told at the ITA headquarters in Brompton Road that his company would have only a minority interest in the operation of the new franchise. Never have I seen a man so bereft, so desolate and deeply hurt. The prime minister, Harold Wilson, whose constituency of Huyton bordered on Derby's estate at Knowsley, had recently asked him to be lord lieutenant of Lancashire. Now he was being struck across the face. He could not understand the prime minister's cavalier treatment of him. The company consulted a top QC, Sir Andrew Clark, but he advised against legal action against the ITA. Some said Sir Andrew had given us the wrong advice. He retired shortly afterwards.

I was invited to stay with the new company, Harlech Television, and I did so for a year while they got their feet under the table. But they were a different breed of go-getters, tight-fisted, arrogant and crudely aggressive, with none of the joyful bonhomie of their predecessors. I had seen the best, most adventurous years in television and it was time to look for fresh fields and pastures new.

The Switch

Changing careers was a risky business, especially for a family man with a wife and three small boys, but not to change was equally risky. My disillusionment with television deepened over the year or so that I spent with 'The Men of Harlech'. I had no creative role to goad and inspire me and was always regarded as a suspicious survivor from the old regime. There was no future for me there.

Tony Gorard, the managing director, who had himself experienced the cruel, personal effects of takeovers in his previous business life, and Patrick Dromgoole whom I had known at Oxford, were my best friends in retrospect rather than my Welsh colleagues, W. John Morgan and Aled Vaughan. Wynford Vaughan Thomas was more sensitive and sympathetic but made no secret of the fact that his prime concern was to restore his personal fortunes after his post-war years of comparative obscurity.

Tony Gorard gave me a watching brief over a drama production featuring the actor Stanley Baker, who had made his name (and fortune) with the film *Zulu*. It was based on the incredible action at Rorke's Drift where no fewer than twenty-two soldiers of the South Wales Borderers won the Victoria Cross in a fierce battle with the Zulus. Ivor Emanuel had a cameo part and Michael Caine a great one. Stanley was now a director of the new Harlech company and I had no real control over his project. I had worked with Stanley before, on a programme I had titled *Return to the Rhondda* where I took him and the immortal Tommy Farr back to their roots. I knew only too well how Stanley had to be held in check if the production was to run smoothly. The budget rose dramatically when the production became a feature film to be shot at Twickenham Studios. The director, John Nelson Burton, had never directed a feature film before and took a gulp from a paint pot instead of his coffee cup as he answered the telephone on the set. The film was completed but

Fade Out, as it was titled, was just that as far as viewers were concerned.

Quietly, I began to think of alternative career possibilities. Politics had always attracted me. They were always there on the fringes of radio and television and I had my contacts in all parties in Wales, but I had realized, like Nye Bevan, that ultimate power lay not in Wales but at Westminster. It was there that the decision had been taken to oust TWW from its franchise, irrespective of the company's performance (and my own), and the decision, although directly attributable to a former Conservative minister, Charles Hill, must have had the endorsement of the Labour government.

Curiously, I never thought of joining the Labour Party although I had interviewed Gaitskell – a cold, imperturbable fish if ever there was one – and listened spellbound to Nye Bevan on a number of occasions. 'Now that we've lowered the cost of living, we can lower the cost of loving,' Nye told a shocked audience under his breath in Cardiff. When he was under attack from Herbert Morrison for opposing German rearmament and stood accused of being in 'curious company' for so doing, I heard him tell the miners and their families as they sat in the sun in Sophia Gardens, in his sharp, sing-song voice:

'Let us look at those who want Germany rearmed. There are the Nazis who want Germany rearmed . . . that's very curious company indeed for my Labour comrades. Then there are the Tories who want Germany rearmed . . . whatever you may say about me I have never been with them.' And then came the crack of his verbal whip: 'If we are to judge each other by the company we keep, my reputation is almost im . . . maculate.' The last word began with a stutter and then shot out like a bullet. He took a swipe too at the *Western Mail*, the national daily of Wales, on that glorious Saturday afternoon. Will Paynter, the miners' leader, complained at length of the paper's treatment of him. Nye took up the cudgels: 'Personally,' he confided, 'I have never understood why such a wonderful nation should be represented by so mis . . . erable a newspaper.' And, when his audience tittered, he added: 'You won't read that in Monday's paper!' Nye was a brilliant orator and could use words with incredible skill and relish but he was an individualist, not a proselytizer.

I knew from private correspondence between Nye and Huw Edwards that both were concerned about the overweening power of the trade unions in the Labour movement. The unions were the party's paymasters and intent on controlling its policies in their own sectional interest. Nye never faced the issue openly as far as I am aware. The net result was that there were deep and disturbing divisions between the pseudo-Communist left and the moderate right within the Labour Party and the right was always on the defensive. I distrusted the party's pro-Communist thrust which I felt at the time would eventually succeed. I knew from my Russian visit the kind of slavish society that Communism produced and I had no wish to see it in my own country. I cherished our free society and our libertarian approach.

I was much more comfortable with the Conservatives, their cavalier humour, and their devotion to British traditions and individualistic, anti-state ethos. 'That made me hot around the collar,' joked Gwilym Lloyd George when he emerged for a breath of fresh air after winding up a debate on capital punishment at the Conservative Party conference at Llandudno in 1962.

I had interviewed Harold Macmillan too when he was prime minister, at Bowood House, Wiltshire, on the day we landed troops in Kuwait in 1961. I had prepared a list of questions in advance and submitted them to the prime minister's office as the custom was. If he had answered them in the order I had arranged them, the interview would have presented my policy for the country rather than his. 'Mack' was too sharp to fall for that kind of ruse. He entered the library where we had set up our film cameras and said: 'I like your questions very much. Shall we start with question 8, go on to question 3 and answer question 1 if there's time? I'm ready, are you?' He sat down. I was disoriented. He spoke about Britain's role in Europe and the world and 'the forceful action' – landing troops in Kuwait – we had taken that morning. Afterwards, I watched him browse among the books, a strangely youthful and relaxed figure considering the magnitude of his problems. I admired his cool. He never flapped.

Lord 'Viv' Brecon, the first ever minister of state for Wales, was called to the job by Harold Macmillan from a rugby match at Twickenham. Viv was a friend and supporter to me and so was David Gibson-Watt, MP for Hereford and the Conservative spokesman on Welsh affairs in the House of Commons in the late 1960s. I had met Ted Heath in my TWW days and slipped him a bottle of his favourite Glenfiddich as he was driven away from the studios.

In those days, no one who worked in the media was permitted to reveal his political leanings – we all had to be impartial and seen to be so. Some friends in the Labour Party and Plaid Cymru were surprised when I declared myself a Conservative contender for the recently vacated candidacy at Conwy. I was a patriot but I had considered the Welsh nationalist position some years before and written articles anonymously for the Welsh periodical *Baner ac Amserau Cymru*, then owned by my friend Tom Hooson, later Conservative MP for Brecon and Radnor. If we Welsh really wished to secure independence, I argued, we would have to declare it and set up a rival state, much as Rhodesia did under Ian Smith. But it was clear that the majority of Welsh people would neither endorse such a declaration nor demonstrate their allegiance to it by tacit or open resistance to the British state and its governmental system. Wales did not have the resources to govern itself independently: it was highly subsidized by the rest of the UK. Independence could therefore only be achieved at the cost of immense sacrifices, including a lower standard of living. There was little appetite for such sacrifice except among isolated extremists who never gained much popular support. Independence was a non-starter in my view and Welsh interests were best served through the major political parties. This might involve a degree of subservience but that was inevitable. In population, Wales was only half the size of the west Midlands and there had to be a limit to our expectations.

Labour claimed to be the more caring and generous of the two major parties and held the majority of Welsh parliamentary seats. But its MPs also tended to take the loyalty of their electors for granted, to act against their best interests at times and to use their strong Welsh majorities simply as stepping stones for their personal ambitions. Many people in Wales in the late 1960s shared this antipathy towards Labour and viewed the prospect of a Conservative government with genuine hope that it might bring better things. My prospective constituency of Conwy included many hoteliers who had been antagonized by the government's introduction of selective employment tax, which penalized their industry along with other service industries.

The Conwy constituency had returned the Conservative, Peter Thomas, for fifteen years but he had lost the seat in 1966 by a narrow margin (581). I was sufficiently convinced that it could be won back to move my family to the constituency and make my home there as soon as I was officially adopted as a prospective candidate. My confidence and will to win inspired the party's voluntary workers who galvanized themselves to fight. When I began to work in the constituency in the autumn of 1969 the key question was the timing of the general election. It could be as late as 1971 in which case my personal resources, an ex-gratia payment from Harlech, would be severely stretched, but I was lucky. Harold Wilson called the election for 19 June 1970.

I campaigned hard and won over the Bangor end of the constituency when some Maoist students physically attacked a television programme I was to take part in, along with John Biffen, MP for Oswestry (now Lord). The scene was the Pritchard-Jones Hall at the University College. As the programme was about to be recorded, half a dozen students, who appeared to be high on drugs, invaded the stage and a violent young woman drew blood from the floor manager's forehead when she struck him with a microphone. Another shinned up a tall window curtain monkey fashion and harangued the well-behaved student audience below who recognized him immediately as a student who had been expelled from the college some months before. The BBC kept the cameras rolling throughout the mêlée and showed the taped pictures on the news afterwards. The city folk rose as one in my support. It was town versus gown with a vengeance.

George Brown came to support the sitting Labour member. It rained and they retired to a pub on the quay at Conwy. George lived up to his devilish reputation under the influence of alcohol. There were some lady tourists at the bar and George's amatory advances were reported verbatim by a redoubtable local journalist, Ivor Wynne Jones, much to the disadvantage of my opponent.

The Town Hall at Llandudno was packed for my last, eve-of-poll meeting. Selwyn Lloyd, MP for the Wirral and a politician of great experience, spoke before me in a fairly subdued style, which encouraged me to pull out all the stops. I was elated by my performance and rushed to the exit to shake hands with people as they left. I nearly perished at that door as person after person told me: 'Wonderful speech. Wish I could vote for you but I'm here on holiday from the Midlands,' and every other part of the UK, it seemed. I won by a majority of 903 votes. Had I lost, the rest of my life would have been very different. Ted Heath and the party won too and Harold Wilson had lost his franchise. We were going to govern the country.

To Westminster, 1970

The train journey to Westminster was a significant occasion for Welsh MPs because it gave them a chance to meet, talk and share confidences. This happened on the Swansea to Paddington run in the south and on the Holyhead to Euston journey from the north. I looked forward to my first journey on the north-south run – from Llandudno Junction in my case. I knew that an entire Welsh day debate in the 1950s had been concocted on one of these journeys by a Cardiff MP, David Llewelyn (brother of Sir Harry of 'Foxhunter' fame). He planned to make a speech attacking the BBC in Wales for its nationalist bias and told his fellow members of all parties on the train that he intended doing so. They all chipped in with their criticisms of the BBC when they arrived for the debate and vied with each other in exaggeration to grab the next day's headlines. There was corruption in the BBC 'beside which Crichel Down paled into insignificance', David Llewelyn said, and that was only the beginning. I almost fell from the press gallery as I listened. It was a day's moaning for them and a year's groaning for us who worked for the BBC at the time. We were put in cold storage for a year while an official inquiry dissected our activities. The charges, mainly related to a period before my time, were not proven.

It was important that, as the newly elected MP for Conwy, I establish good personal relationships with my neighbouring MPs although they belonged to the Labour party. The MP for Caernarfon, Goronwy Roberts, I had first heard addressing a mass meeting of quarrymen on the quay below the town's magnificent Edwardian castle in 1945. Wearing a trench raincoat, he had climbed from the crowd on to a railway wagon and fired a salvo of red-hot socialism at his audience. He attacked the local gentry and the shire stallions they kept at stud to serve the mares on neighbouring farms. 'We need a Stalin not a stallion!' he cried with a fervour worthy of Lenin talking to a collective of starving peasants.

Since those days, Goronwy had abandoned his cloth cap for a bowler hat and become a minister of state at the Foreign Office but the intensity was still there in his personality. Cledwyn Hughes, the Labour MP for Anglesey and a former Cabinet minister, was also on the train. Both our fathers had been Presbyterian ministers in Anglesey and lifelong friends. When Cledwyn was elected in 1951, my father, who seldom passed political judgement, said, 'He will be in Parliament now for twenty-five years or more', and he was right. Cledwyn, a shrewd and sensitive man, was respected and loved by everyone, apart from his political opponents who dubbed him 'Cledwyn Ice Cream'. (As minister for food and agriculture, he had promoted that industry, possibly at the expense of dairy farmers.) I knew him from my television days. The three of us chatted all the way to Euston and agreed to make common cause where local interests were concerned. They were as good as their word in the months and years to come. I was part of the Welsh Mafia – the Taffia as English colleagues called us.

David Gibson-Watt (Con., Hereford) met me at the members' entrance to the House of Commons. He had won the Military Cross and double Bar. Every inch of his towering frame spelt Eton and the Guards but David also had a softer, humorous, humane side. He lived on the Wye in mid Wales. Someone had told me that he used to go looking for the enemy in the war as if he was going to shoot pheasants, with his gamekeeper-turned-batman at his side. I could well believe it. He had been a whip and knew the House, its personalities and ways. Some weeks later when we were returning to the House after dinner at Boodle's, he paused in the members' cloakroom, just inside the entrance, sniffed the air and said: 'The House is empty – they've all gone home.' I asked him how he could tell. 'There's no smell,' he said. The House had indeed risen early.

In the Welsh Grand Committee when the opposition were in full cry only to find their quarry baring its teeth and turning on them, David summed up the situation perfectly: 'They can give it but they can't take it.' With his wartime experience of soldiering, he represented the stiff backbone of the party in the Commons and in the early 1970s there were many like him. Their gradual disappearance over time was a great loss to the party: they were a noble bunch of people. The new Conservative members had a talk from the chief whip, Francis Pym, and his deputy, Humphrey Atkins, about the 'do's and don'ts' of parliamentary life. Humphrey's final words were: 'If there's anything you don't know, ask one of the older members.' There was something – I can't remember what

– and so I asked Ernest Marples whom I had got to know in his glory days as a very innovative minister of transport. 'How should I know,' he said, 'I've only been here twenty five years!' I never asked a fellow member anything after that; the Commons staff were much more helpful.

The Conservative tables in the tea room were the places of greatest intimacy between members. It was there that genuine discussion flourished as well as gossip exchanged. Neil Marten (Con., Banbury and ex-RAF) was always there smoking his own brand of brown-papered cigarettes. He was firmly anti-Common Market and so was voluble, industrious Teddy Taylor (now Sir), who then represented Glasgow Cathcart. Marten told me that Harold Macmillan had always encouraged ministers to make an appearance in the smoking room but for Marten, an hour in the tea room after Questions was a much better use of ministerial time. People tended to express their confidence over a drink in the smoking room; doubts and worries were reserved for the tea room.

Pensive, quiet-spoken Airey Neave (Con., Abingdon), the man who had walked out of Colditz in a German officer's uniform, was also a regular at the tea room along with Maurice Macmillan (Con., Farnham), Harold Macmillan's chain-smoking son. Maurice had had a problem with alcohol but he had now given it up completely. He still looked ravaged by his earlier dissipation. The talk was all of politics but when stories were told they were usually amazing. Maurice once recalled a plane journey in India when a man appeared from the cockpit with a pale, jaundiced look and came down the aisle asking the passengers: 'Can you drive an aeroplane?' The pilot and co-pilot had had an argument and had knocked each other out. The plane was on automatic pilot. Fortunately, Maurice's travelling companion was a flier and he landed the plane safely.

An occasional visitor to our table was the Lord Chancellor, Quintin Hailsham. He described how he made porridge for himself in what was left of the Lord Chancellor's apartments, then largely taken up as offices. 'My greatest difficulty is getting in over the weekend,' said Quintin, 'but I have my keys.' He drew a huge bunch from his waistcoat pocket and swore that he used them all to gain entry. He listened sympathetically as someone highlighted a legal anomaly until the critic said: 'You have to admit, Lord Chancellor, the law is an ass.' Quintin changed abruptly: 'Yes, but it is the law. Never forget that.'

There was a Welsh table in the tea room, constantly occupied by Labour members. Gwynfor Evans, the Plaid Cymru leader, never sat there in the preceding Parliament, they told me. I did so occasionally.

I did not wish to spoil their talk, often as hushed and conspiratorial as ours. 'This House is a very difficult place to find your feet in,' Leo Abse (Lab., Pontypool) told me very soon after my arrival. He was right. Grandly intellectual Roy Jenkins (Lab., Stetchford) was later invited to join that table as a potential source of solid support for his bid for the Labour leadership after Wilson but, I am told, neither he nor his fellow Welshmen found much to say to each other. I wish I had been there to overhear the silence.

The only Tory often to be seen gossiping at the Welsh table was the bouncy, busy member for Barry, Raymond Gower. First elected to represent the seat in 1951, Raymond had held on to it through thick and thin and enjoyed the reputation of being unrivalled as an assiduous constituency member. He sent his congratulations to every child who passed his or her school certificate and his condolences to all touched by tragedy. He visited constituents at home in between elections and always peddled the popular line, irrespective of party policy. Whenever there was a scandal, Raymond would joke: 'I see that your agent has issued a statement denying your involvement.' Another favourite story of his was of the gentrified candidate who was asked by a Conservative Association if he was prepared to live in the constituency if adopted. The candidate replied after some deliberation, 'No. But I'm prepared to hunt over it.'

Sir Anthony Meyer (Con., Flint West) periodically reminded the public that he had been picked up by a KGB lady agent while serving as a diplomat in the Foreign Service in Moscow. There were other confessions later of a lengthy, sado-masochistic relationship with a black lady. It hardly seemed possible because his ever-watchful wife, Barbadee, was always in the public gallery for hours on end. He was to achieve notoriety twenty years later as Margaret Thatcher's first challenger for the leadership – the stalking-horse candidate. Geraint Morgan (Con., Denbigh) was a sour man with a chip on his shoulder. He was able enough but totally unsociable and in a permanent state of pique. Although he had been a member since 1959, he was almost unknown at the House and often referred to as 'the absent member for Denbigh'. But he always turned up on Welsh occasions to make substantial speeches on agriculture. He practised at the Liverpool Bar.

Among the newcomers like myself was John Stradling Thomas (Con., Monmouth), a former vet and farmer, who had participated in political discussion programmes in my television days. John could talk the hind legs off a donkey, especially in the early hours, and was soon made an assistant whip. Then there was Michael

Roberts (Con., Cardiff North West), who brought with him the infinite tolerance of a former headmaster. He never failed to see the funny side of things and reduced most problems to laughter. He loved his pint of beer at the strangers' bar. A close drinking companion was Ray Mawby (Con., Totnes) a former assistant postmaster general and earthy, trade union shop steward. He once said of a constituent's letter of which he disapproved: 'I wanted to reply "Dear Madam, Your letter is before me. Very shortly it will be behind me." But my secretary refused to type it.'

Peter Thomas, my Conservative predecessor in Conwy, had been returned as the member for Hendon South and made secretary of state for Wales and party chairman. His participation in government had begun in 1954 and he had risen through the Ministry of Labour to be minister of state at the Foreign Office in 1963. He knew the prime minister well and had won his trust. He had a fine legal and political mind.

Peter and I were in the smoking room one evening talking to the formidable battleaxe from Tynemouth, Dame Irene Ward, when Ted Heath joined us. He told Irene to stop 'charming these young men' and, nodding in Peter's direction, told me 'I suppose you're now paying his bills.' It was the kind of banter that presumed familiarity and friendship. Peter told me that he was minded to make me his parliamentary private secretary and that I should therefore make my maiden speech as soon as possible because after my appointment I would not be able to speak about matters that came within his sphere of responsibility. I took his advice and soon became his 'eyes and ears' in the Commons.

There are other, less benign descriptions of a PPS. George Thomas (Lab., Cardiff West) who led the Welsh opposition, occasionally referred to me as 'the Trappist Member for Conwy' because I could not speak in Welsh debates and had to content myself with supporting ministers in silence from the bench behind them. George, later Speaker, was notoriously vicious towards his own colleagues too and it was common knowledge that he had stabbed Cledwyn in the back when Cledwyn was secretary of state and George served under him. As George himself told me later: 'I only became a minister at the Welsh Office so that I could take Mam around Cardiff in the official car with the flag flying. When Cledwyn said the flag could only be flown when he, the secretary of state was in it, I promised myself he would not be secretary of state for long. And he wasn't.' George succeeded Cledwyn as secretary of state for Wales in 1968.

Each member had a place to hang his sword (a red cotton loop on his coat hanger) but not an office. I therefore found myself a chair at a table in the library. The place opposite me was usually occupied by Enoch Powell, the moustachioed Conservative member for Wolverhampton South East, dismissed from Ted Heath's shadow cabinet for his 'rivers of blood' speech in 1968. Enoch never chatted with people when he was working and he did work with the total concentration of a powerful and scholarly mind. Occasionally, he would have a conversation with someone who shared his views – John Biffen usually – but it was never trivial and always to the point.

Over lunch in the dining room, Enoch Powell could be very jovial. He once told me an Enoch and Eli joke – the standard joke figures in the Black Country as Dai and Ianto are in Wales. Enoch had a friend who had always wanted to be buried in a blue suit but only had a brown one when he died. Eli commiserated and said he too had a friend who had died and he wanted to be buried in a brown suit but only had a blue one. 'Ah well!' said Enoch, 'all we have to do then is change the heads.' It was macabre but it clearly appealed to E. Powell.

Enoch Powell wrote a great deal but he hardly ever used a note when speaking. His strong, disciplined intellect shaped and ordered the arguments in his mind beforehand and his speeches always had a logical, persuasive progression. You had to read them afterwards to find out where he had gone wrong, if indeed he had. Like Tommy Farr, he seemed to be made of sterner stuff than the rest of us. He never grew tired or slept in one of the easy chairs in the library. I saw him, after an active all-night session in the chamber, draw his hands down the length of his face and pronounce: 'The start of another day,' and set off vigorously for a fresh engagement.

There was a long table for ministers and their acolytes at the Conservative end of the dining room. The chancellor, Iain Macleod, was there: 'We are in for two terms,' he said gleefully. 'No government since the war has failed to get a second chance.' Alas, Iain died in July 1970 leaving a substantial legacy of tax reforms for his successor, Tony Barber, to implement. Had Iain survived, the story of the 1970–4 government might have had a different ending.

Harold Wilson had not been expected to lose the election but, having done so, he wasted no time in getting down to his autobiography. He wandered the corridors with a far-away look, a sure sign that his mind was elsewhere. We both had University College, Oxford in common; he had been a don there before I was a student. Another Univ. man who had come to the House with me in 1970, as the member for High Peak, was Spencer le Marchant, Mark Birley's racing friend. Alas, Spencer died prematurely in the 1980s – of a surfeit of champagne, they said.

I had begun my parliamentary life staying at the Savile Club in Brook Street and I enjoyed my morning pot of tea (with a cosy) and biscuits and having my bath run for me. The silent breakfasts were also to my liking, but not so my late-night returns to the club where there was always a bunch of inebriates ready to rubbish the Heath government's every move. It was a relief when I chanced on my old school friend, John Lotery, a member of Lloyds, who invited me to stay with him at Duchess of Bedford's Walk on Campden Hill. His parents had lived there but had now left for a villa in Ventimiglia, just over the border from Menton on the French Riviera. John was on his own and wanted company. I joined him before Christmas 1970.

There was another innovative change in my life at that time. I began to keep a diary. The first entry was made on Wednesday, 4 November 1970. It reads:

> The idea of keeping this diary came to me the night before last, at the beginning of this second week of the present session when I thought I should chronicle the progress of the quiet revolution which Mr Heath and the Conservative Party are pledged to carry out.

Dennis Skinner (Lab., Bolsover) is mentioned on the first page for his attack on the chancellor, Tony Barber, whom he accused of changing the official record. It was typical of many subsequent Skinner forays. The charge was shown to be false but Skinner refused to withdraw and there were cries of 'Name him!' from the government benches. Already there were cries against the Industrial Relations Bill – not yet published – as an attack on the workers' Magna Carta. I concluded that there was a formidable commitment to socialism 'which inspires anti-government action and supports all manner of strikes, demonstrations and protest with a moral smokescreen that misleads people into acting against their own best interests in the long term'.

The diary was never intended for publication but as a forum for my thinking about events. Naturally, I recorded other people's views when they impressed me. I found the diary a help in digesting my experience of events as they happened and in forming my own judgement upon them. It was a kind of therapy and I kept it up throughout my life in the House of Commons.

Noise of Battle

Dedicated to the principle that 'to govern is to serve', Ted Heath was a man after my own heart. I supported him throughout his period as prime minister. He was a determined leader of great ability, knowledge and experience; his inner strength and integrity, rooted in his culture and upbringing, were impregnable. The difficulties of his premiership would have overwhelmed a lesser man.

First, he had a very poor inheritance. It is difficult now to comprehend the extent to which the trade unions had Harold Wilson's government and the country in their power as the 1960s drew to a close. The trade unions ruled supreme. The more they got, the more they wanted. They were a new breed of Vikings who cared for no other interests but their own. It is difficult to justify their conduct except in terms of class warfare, which was the dominant theme in their minds. They talked a great deal about industrial democracy by which they meant the supremacy of the workers represented by the trade unions. Wilson always reminded me of a ping-pong ball dancing on top of a fairground fountain, eye-catching but powerless. He had tried to put a rein on the trade unions in the interests of the country as a whole but he had not succeeded. His prices and incomes policy had created an artificial dam and when it broke, there was nothing to stop a flood of wage claims, pushing up prices, discouraging investment and debilitating the economy. Government could do little to prevent it or ameliorate its effects and the unions knew this.

The advent of a Conservative government they regarded as a provocative challenge to their supremacy and some were determined to do their worst. Others, especially their leaders in the Trades Union Congress, were under constant pressure from their membership and were content to stand by on the sidelines as extortionate demands were forced through to the detriment of the majority of ordinary people.

Heath had to reconcile the dreadful legacy of a weak style of government and its economic consequences with his own inheritance of high principles represented by the 1970 election manifesto, *A Better Tomorrow*. The manifesto had been firmly based on the outcome of the Selsden conference prior to the election. Some on his own side were determined that he should stand by its principles – no further nationalization, no compulsory wage control – come hell or high water. Such uncompromising commitment was not helpful when Rolls Royce, the flagship of British industry, threatened to crash with the loss of thousands of jobs. Heath chose to rescue the company through partial nationalization rather than allow it to go to the wall. The purists regarded this as the first U-turn. A similar fate befell Upper Clyde Shipbuilders, threatening to put an additional 15,000 out of work in an unemployment black spot, and again the government performed a rescue operation.

Tony Benn, as a minister in the previous government, had had a hand in the making of both catastrophes but he escaped the castigation he deserved. Indeed, his reputation as a demagogue was enhanced in some quarters when he encouraged the workers sit-in at UCS. I had known him since his days as a 'reluctant peer' when he had fought for the right to sit in the House of Commons in spite of his peerage. I admired his ability but his judgement was erratic. He had a reputation as a maverick in the Labour Party, a latter-day Lord George Gordon. He has never quite overcome this handicap after a lifetime in politics.

The government was crucified on the accusation that its rescue packages represented a weakening of its resolve to stick to its principles. The charge stuck and festered because the right wing of the Conservative Party regarded it as a deliberate betrayal rather than a pragmatic reaction to events. Quite what they would have done in the circumstances was not clear, although Nicholas Ridley (Con., Cirencester and Tewkesbury) had urged the withdrawal of support from UCS in 1969 in a paper mischievously released by Tony Benn to the *Guardian*. It lent credibility to the left's view that the government was prepared to use unemployment as a means of bringing the workers to heel. Still, the general feeling in the party was fairly represented by the member who told me: 'If you had asked me to lay odds on a Conservative government nationalizing Rolls Royce, I would have given you 10,000 to one against.' Personally, I summed up the situation by saying that Ted was so far ahead of his troops that he was in danger of being mistaken for the enemy while Wilson was so far behind his followers that he was in danger of being trampled by them.

The opposition within the Conservative Party to the government's actions was as nothing compared with the belligerence of the Labour left to trade union reform. While their leaders, Harold Wilson and Barbara Castle, tried their best to forget their own failed efforts to achieve reform 'In Place of Strife', the left had a field day with the government's Industrial Relations Bill. Many MPs, sponsored by the trade unions, swore that even if the Bill was passed by Parliament, they would continue their resistance in the country. About forty of them, led by Eric Heffer (Lab., Liverpool, Walton) and Stan Orme (Lab., Salford West, late Lord) interrupted Robert Carr's closing speech on the Bill and protested in front of the Mace before the guillotine motion was put to the vote. They called endless divisions during committee stage and ended up singing the 'Red Flag' in the chamber – 'the funeral dirge of a stale herring', as George Bernard Shaw called it.

The Bill was symbolic to both sides. To the government it represented its democratic right to regulate the trade unions and bring them under the law. To the left wing of the Labour Party, it was an attack on the liberties of industrial democracy. The left's suspicions of their own leadership increased when it emerged that the government had an average majority of 67 in the division lobbies during committee stage – far more than their normal expectation of 29. There were mutterings that James Callaghan (Lab., Cardiff South East) might soon replace Wilson as leader, a forecast that eventually came true in 1976.

The economy remained stubborn over the first two years of the Heath government. Although unemployment was rising, this did not moderate wage demands as much as the government was entitled to expect. For the trade union militants, inflation was an instrument to bring down the government. Ted Heath kept his nerve and good humour. One night in the smoking room he told me how, during the Macmillan era when he was minister of labour, he had settled a wage claim half a point above the level agreed with his cabinet colleagues and in spite of Macmillan's instruction never to agree to an inflationary wage settlement. He thought his career was at an end and told Churchill so. Churchill, who had his own revered place in the smoking room, had said: 'Really, my dear? I thought my career had ended many times.'

The level of claims rose to a peak in 1971 with the National Union of Mineworkers' claim for a 45 per cent increase. Although

Joe Gormley, the miners' leader, was the moderate public face of the union, it was well known that there were reckless Communist members behind him like Mick McGahey, whom I had seen in the Kremlin (strangers' bar) with his shirt hanging out the front of his trousers. It was his associate, Arthur Scargill, who organized the flying pickets that besieged Saltley coke depot in the west Midlands and overwhelmed the police. The scenes shocked the nation. 'It was the most vivid, direct and terrifying challenge to the rule of law that I could ever recall emerging from our own country,' wrote Ted Heath later. But there were not many on the Conservative benches who would have sent in the cavalry to dent miners' skulls as had happened to Walter Padley, the Independent Labour MP for Ogmore. In Annie's Bar, he let us and members of the press lobby feel the egg-sized dent in his head made by a mounted policeman's baton in the 1920s. Conservatives had a soft spot for the miners, as did the entire country. Lord Wilberforce's final award of 20 per cent to the miners (in February 1972) was way above other wage settlements at the time. Ted Heath later described it as 'a grim day for the country and the Government'.

The budget in March 1971 had begun to fulfil some of our election promises – selective employment tax was halved, corporation tax cut and tax allowances and pensions raised – but it was not sufficient to increase levels of demand. By June, I was writing in my diary: 'Economically, the country is stagnant; gone is the budget euphoria. Demand is low and producers are braying like starved sheep. The Stock Market is at its wit's end.' The relentless rise in unemployment also demanded reflationary action. I had had dinner with the chief whip, Francis Pym (now Lord), in March and he had talked about 'the point at which the social fabric breaks down . . . we cannot go beyond that point . . . we must take action'.

By the summer the government felt that a modest reflation to stimulate growth was justified. There had been some moderation in wage increases and there was a CBI pledge to keep down prices over the coming year. So Tony Barber introduced his mini budget in July without increasing the money supply. Still, there were voices against reflation. There was a danger that it might stimulate inflation again. Ideally, it would have been better to stamp out domestic inflation once and for all but time was not on the government's side.

The prospect of joining the Common Market and division within the party worried Francis Pym. There were some on our side like John

Farr (Con., Harborough) who were implacably opposed to joining. They were less vociferous than some but equally determined in their opposition and prepared to bring down the government. Their opposition was rooted in their sense of British history and tradition and the very high value set on national independence and sovereignty. I was open minded on the issue but prepared to support British entry if it was clearly in our interests. My immediate concern was the state of our economy and our ability as a country to withstand the competitive strains and stresses of entry when it came about as, appeared increasingly likely from the summer of 1971 onwards. I had been to Paris in May with Norman St John Stevas (Con., Chelmsford, now Lord) and listened to our ambassador, Christopher Soames, wax eloquent over lunch on the case for joining. Curiously, although there was a butter mountain in Europe, there was no butter on the table.

Another refusal of entry, another 'Non!' would have sentenced us to economic isolation in a permanently slow-growth environment. That was how it appeared to me at the time. I had learnt early in the year from friends in Wales that the TUC was likely to be against joining and that Wilson might threaten to take us out if Heath took us in. And so the issue was to be decided – as far as they were concerned – by sectional and party-political interests. The question of joining the Common Market or not thus became another facet of the industrial struggle within the UK itself and, just below the surface, there was the simmering antipathy and activity of the Communist sympathizers within the trade unions and the Labour left. I visited some of the European regions in July – the Mezzogiorno, Bavaria and Brittany – to see what the Commission had done to revive them. John Hill (Con., Norfolk South) accompanied me with his pair Will Edwards (Lab., Merionethshire) and John Mackintosh (Lab., Berwick and East Lothian). We called briefly in Rome, Munich and Paris for preliminary briefings.

My colleagues were all in favour of joining for different reasons. Will was close to Roy Jenkins and unwaveringly pro-Europe. John Mackintosh was an academic and had weighed up the arguments. John Hill was a Norfolk farmer who had fought in the war. (He walked twice through the metal-detector booth at Heathrow and pronounced it useless because it failed to detect the shrapnel in his back.) Future peace and the prosperity of agriculture were major considerations in his mind.

I thought the situation was promising for Welsh agriculture. We had green pastures to rear our livestock in the open for much of the year and our farms were on average larger than the European. But what really impressed me was the generally high level of prosperity the Common Market had brought to the poorer areas of southern Italy, eastern Bavaria and Brittany. There was a will to raise living standards further in these areas with resources from the richer regions of the Community. I was also attracted by the German desire for British leadership in Europe. They needed us as a counter-balance to the French, the Bavarians told me. I regarded joining as a venture in the British imperial tradition. I was all for seeking a new direction for our energies.

The parliamentary session ran into the first week in August and all the leaders made their position clear on the issue. Harold Wilson completed his volte-face and declared himself against the terms of entry, although he had sought entry in 1967, while his deputy, Roy Jenkins, declared himself in favour. The stage was set for the crucial vote on principle on our return after the summer recess. The outcome on Thursday, 28 October 1971 was a turning point in Britain's history. On a free vote on the government side and a three-line whip against by Labour, the government won approval for the principle of entry on the terms negotiated by a majority of 112 votes. I sat in the members' lobby and watched Roy Jenkins emerge from the 'Aye' lobby; it had taken real courage on his part and 68 others to defy a three-line whip. Someone told me: 'Little do they know but they have divided themselves for ten years.'

That was indeed true: the split in the Labour Party over Europe led to the formation of the Social Democratic Party. But the 39 Tories who had supported the opposition had also divided the Conservative Party – a division that was to last even longer but that did not concern us at the time. 'Our European involvement is the last fling of a defunct Empire,' I noted privately.

In spite of the overwhelming vote in favour of entry, there was no guarantee that the necessary legislation would be equally well supported. Party loyalty is a powerful magnet when it comes to divisions. Our majority on the second reading of the European Bill fell to 8 on 17 February 1972 and I saw Bill Rodgers (Lab., Stockton on Tees, now Lord), a fervent pro-European, being dragged in tears through the opposition lobby. (Bill had come closest to guessing the majority on 28 October and had deservedly won the jackpot among the betting fraternity.) Cledwyn Hughes, another pro-European, was drawn to support his party in that division: 'I didn't vote against Europe. I voted for the miners,' he told me.

While we fought in the Commons to secure the passage of the European Communities Bill prior to accession on 1 January 1973, Ted engaged the CBI and the TUC in a series of tripartite talks to find common ground for the development of the economy. Unemployment had reached one million in January 1972 and something had to be done. The way forward was prepared by the reflationary Budget of March 1972 and John Davies's interventionist White Paper on industry and regional development. This was all anathema to the Selsden purists on the right. As *The Times* said after John Davies's speech at the second reading of the Industry Bill that followed the White Paper, 'Lame ducks never looked healthier'. There were cheers from the Labour benches and almost total silence on the Conservative side. Some like myself were relieved that something positive was being done but the right wing could scarcely conceal their horror.

As the CBI's year of price restraint approached its end (in October 1972) there was still no clear substitute or remedy emerging from the tripartite talks that the TUC would put its name to. All were agreed on the ends but not the means. The government then proceeded unilaterally with a ninety-day freeze on wages, prices, rents and dividends. There had been a similar freeze in the US in 1971 with no obvious, disadvantageous consequences, but I knew that Ted was worried. I had seen him very pensive in the smoking room. He knew that the freeze would inevitably develop into a longer-term statutory prices and wages policy, the very thing we had forsworn in our manifesto. It could only be justified on pragmatic grounds. Before long, Enoch Powell was asking on the floor of the House whether the prime minister had 'taken leave of his senses'. As it turned out, stage two of the policy was a success; export figures and the balance of trade improved and unemployment started to fall. The March 1973 Budget was neutral but it was clearly time to rein back public expenditure and this was done in May.

The opposition got some wind in their sails when Ted described the goings on at Lonrho as 'the unpleasant and unacceptable face of capitalism'. 'That's not the last you've heard of that,' a Labour MP told me behind the speaker's chair that day. But this was the fluff rather than the stuff of politics and the government might have prospered were it not for the two clouds that darkened the horizon in the later months of 1973 – the miners' wage claim and the steep rise in oil prices that accompanied the Arab–Israeli war.

Ted was triumphant at the party conference in October. He summed up the government's achievements: living standards rising twice as fast as they had during Labour's period in office; the massive increase in exports; unemployment down and falling further; entry into the European Community from a position of strength. Had Ted gone for an election in October, he could well have won but Parliament still had eighteen months to run and there was no immediate reason to go to the country. A prominent Labour figure (Cledwyn) told me afterwards that once the government had missed this opportunity, the Labour party knew that they had us beaten. I can only assume that they were aware of the growing determination of the trade unions to engineer the downfall of the government.

As we were on the verge of entering stage three of the prices and incomes policy, the price of oil rose sky-high. The miners began their overtime ban in November and a month later the train drivers' union, ASLEF, joined them. Although coal stocks were high, supplies had to be conserved. The country was faced with the prospect of a three-day week in the New Year and an immediate television blackout at 10.30 p.m. to save electricity. The miners' wage claim amounted to 50 per cent increases for some workers and was clearly in breach of stage three. But Ted Heath had met Joe Gormley in the garden at No. 10 and believed that there was a way out of the impending impasse because of the widespread recognition that the miners were a special case. The trouble was that Joe Gormley could not deliver the miners' acceptance of whatever offer was made to them. McGahey, Daly and the rest had not changed their spots. They were determined to take every possible advantage of the oil crisis and to bring the government down.

In January 1974, when the negotiations were at a critical stage, I met some moderate miners in south Wales who warned me that a strike was inevitable because some of the Wilberforce recommendations that had brought the 1972 strike to an end had still not been implemented. On my return to the House, I met Ted and reported what I had heard. I referred particularly to the Wilberforce recommendation that pay should be related to productivity. 'But the NUM won't have it,' he said. 'That's why it hasn't been implemented.'

He was right but the rank-and-file membership of the NUM were unaware of their union's opposition to the recommendation. They may well have been deliberately misled. Ted spoke nostalgically about the time when Roy Jenkins's father, a miners' leader, used to take them for a meal when they were students at Oxford.

'He was a man you could talk to,' said Ted. 'Even Willie Whitelaw has to admit that he never encountered anyone like Daly or McGahey during his spell in Northern Ireland. There's no humanity in these people.'

Ted was certainly not lacking in humanity himself. When we met again, he expressed his strongest reluctance to deprive striking miners of social security benefits and tax rebates as advocated by some right-wingers on our side. 'It would set us back thirty years,' he said. He paused and added, 'We are a peculiar nation.' It sounded very much like Margaret Thatcher's dictum, after her fall in 1990: 'It's a funny old world.'

On 3 February 1974, the miners gave notice that they would go on strike on 10 February against the statutory pay policy and in outright defiance of the law. Ted Heath called the election three days before the strike was due to begin and, for most, the issue was clear. It was who governs – the democratically elected government or the NUM. But the talk among the wiser heads in the smoking room was rather different. They thought it was best to go to the country now before the gathering whirlwind of inflation blew the government to kingdom come later in the year.

The election campaign began on the theme of 'Who governs' but in the second week Harold Wilson raised the issue of inflation. Enoch Powell had already announced that he would not be standing – he called it a 'fraudulent election' – and over the weekend before polling he advised people to vote Labour so that there could be a referendum on Britain's membership of the European Economic Community. The final week of the campaign was a media ragbag of issues. It was said that the government had got its figures wrong and the miners could have had a bigger pay award. The government failed to rebut the charge adequately and everyone concluded that there was some truth in it. Campbell Adamson, director general of the CBI, sided with Labour and called for the repeal of the Industrial Relations Act to which the trade unions had been implacably opposed.

The British electorate does not like a government that has reached the end of its tether and does not know what to do next. It was not surprising therefore that Labour won the election, but without an overall majority. There was some discussion about the possibility of a Conservative–Liberal alliance to form a new government but nothing came of it. Although the Conservative Party lost 33 seats, I not only held on to Conwy but increased my share of the vote and my majority to 4,549. It was a minor miracle.

Ted Heath will go down in history as the prime minister who took Britain into the EEC. Britain had been trying to join for a decade. When Harold Macmillan tried in 1963, he had been faced with de Gaulle's firm 'Non'. What was not fully realized at the time was that the German chancellor, Konrad Adenauer, did not favour British entry either. Willy Brandt, later chancellor himself, describes in his memoirs how he tried to persuade Adenauer to get de Gaulle to change his mind. Adenauer refused on the grounds that two's company, three's none. 'Look, what is Europe?' he told Brandt. 'First and foremost, it is France and ourselves. If the British make a third, you will always have to allow for the possibility that two will gang up and I'm afraid we'll be the odd man out.'

Germany and France had signed a treaty in 1962 and in the same year the Americans had agreed to equip the British navy with Polaris submarines. The same offer was not extended to France and the obvious closeness of Anglo-Saxon relationships and American distrust of France irritated de Gaulle. His retirement in 1969 and replacement by the much more amenable President Pompidou, coupled with Ted Heath's impeccable credentials as a strongly committed European, opened the way for Britain to join at last.

The 1970–4 Parliament, with its many long nights and endless divisions, must have been one of the most arduous and exacting on record. When it began, the prime minister said that there would always be a Cabinet minister in the smoking room to keep members informed of government thinking but, as the committee stage of the Industrial Relations Bill sapped ministers' energies, they were hardly to be seen outside their offices. There were constant complaints too that ministers were not adequately presenting the government's views to the country.

Could the Heath government have stuck to its manifesto commitments and the Selsden principles? I do not think so. They were unprepared for the ferocity of the trade unions' onslaught and their defiant, ruthless disregard for the national interest – the interests of ordinary people. Pragmatism became the order of the day. Greater strength, grit and determination in maintaining the supreme authority of government were necessary and these qualities were personified by Margaret Thatcher who succeeded Ted Heath as leader of the Conservative Party in 1975. Her attitude was summed up in a re-markable speech at a party conference early on in her premiership (Friday, 10 October 1980):

> To those waiting with bated breath for that favourite media catch phrase, the U-turn, I have only one thing to say. You turn if you want to. The lady's not for turning. I say that not only to you but to friends overseas – and also to those who are not our friends.

There was to be no compromise, no surrender, next time round.

Aftertime

A lfred, Lord Tennyson describes the traumatic period after King Arthur's last battle and before his departure for the 'island valley of Avilion' as 'aftertime'. Since so much happened after Ted Heath's defeat in February 1974 and before Margaret Thatcher's election to the leadership of the Conservative Party in February 1975, the word is apposite to that momentous period too.

Ted's account to the 1922 Committee of his approach to the Liberals over the weekend after the February election was not very satisfactory. Of course, we did not know then about the Liberal leader, Jeremy Thorpe's impending embarrassments. Ted did know but could not tell us. Talking to Thorpe in these circumstances must have been very distasteful to him. I wrote in my diary:

> He does not seem to have tried very hard with the Liberals or indeed the Ulster Unionists who have finally accepted the whip. [With them and the Liberals, the government would have had a majority big enough to carry on.] And so it seems that Ted Heath was not really unwilling to give up office.

Bernard Levin in *The Times* (5 March) thought the Liberals had missed a great opportunity. Of course, now that we know Thorpe had specifically requested for himself the position of home secretary – a sensitive post bearing in mind that he was about to face serious criminal charges – and that Ted should cease to be prime minister, the coalition proposal was a non-starter. Thorpe's demands were totally unacceptable, even grotesque in the circumstances. A Conservative–Liberal coalition could never have succeeded in any case. The Liberals were our keenest rivals in many constituencies. Peter Emery (Con., Honiton, late Sir) told me that of the 141 seats where the Liberals had come second, 123 of them were Tory and only 18 Labour. They were our enemies, not our friends.

Talk of a coalition persisted over the following months and developed into a call for a national government. This was the situation just before the Whitsun recess when there was a great deal of muckraking over Harold Wilson's relationship with the mistress of the kitchen cabinet, Marcia Williams (later Lady Falkender). The nurses were going on strike, Northern Ireland was in rebellion and an inflation rate of 20 per cent was widely expected. There was another fear lurking in some minds – the fear of a dictatorship. Sir Michael Havers, former Solicitor-General, told me one evening that Italy was likely to go for a dictatorship and that an industrialist friend was taking bets on which country would follow suit first, Germany or Britain. I did not take the threat seriously but others did.

Cledwyn Hughes (Ynys Môn), later to become chairman of the Parliamentary Labour Party, gave me a practical, party-political objection to the coalition idea. He could foresee a unanimous demand for it from the Tories but the Labour Party would be split and, after the coalition had outlived its usefulness, there would be a new three-party line-up – Tories, Liberals with right-wing Labour and a Marxist left. Such a development would clearly not be in the Labour Party's best interests. Nevertheless, a government of national unity, after consultation between parties and key economic interests, featured in the Conservative election manifesto, which appeared prematurely in September, but, desirable as it might be, it was not a credible solution if Ted was to lead it. Harold Wilson would never serve under him; neither would he serve under Harold.

It had been clear from the outset that there would be another general election in the near future and Harold Wilson had quickly set about creating a favourable scenario with talk of a social compact with the trade unions. He was about to prove the truth of Sir Frederic Bennett's (Con., Torbay) remark that if Wilson swallowed a nail he would pass out a corkscrew. The mood in the country was: 'Give Labour a chance'. The new government's honeymoon continued until the Budget in late March.

Ted Heath vigorously opposed the measure to appease the trade unions by repaying the fines imposed for refusing to register under the Industrial Relations Act. But he could not oppose other measures designed to restore the economy for fear of losing support in the country. The impression given by the Conservatives was of continuing weakness and drift. We had no new ideas and were guilty of Lord Salisbury's commonest error of 'sticking to the carcasses of dead policies'. Admittedly, the monetarists were now coming to the fore but they were unhelpful and critical of our own past rather than constructive about the future.

I thought Wilson might go to the country again in June but he bided his time and we had another, more favourable Budget in July. VAT was reduced. There was a partial lifting of dividend restraint, further food subsidies, help with domestic rates and a doubling of Regional Employment Premium to combat unemployment. 'That was a straight left to the chops for you lads,' said the government chief whip, Bob Mellish (Lab., Bermondsey), when he entered the tea room and saw our glum faces at the Tory tables.

The budget was a scene-setter for an election. But when? Harold would keep us guessing until the last moment. I began a new volume of my diary in September with the words:

> The General election will be upon us next month and we are ill prepared. Ted Heath seems a defeated man. He is not liked either in the party or the country. As things stand, we are due for a shattering defeat for lack of leadership.'

My entry for Sunday, 8 September reads: 'Last week, Sir Keith Joseph made a highly significant speech at Preston – "a post mortem repentance" Enoch called it – confessing that the last Tory government was wrong to have reflated from 1972 onwards. We had abandoned sound money policies for electoral gain.'

As the election approached on 10 October, my main worry was that hundreds of my supporters in the Conwy Constituency, having been engaged in the tourist trade all summer, would themselves be away on holiday. My diary entries tell the rest of the story.

Sunday, 6 October 1974

It is anybody's election on Thursday. Labour's Social Compact has been exploded as a myth and Ted Heath's proposal for an anti-inflation coalition can either gather strength or dissipate itself completely. In the latter event, we shall end up in much the same position as before, with a minority government of some kind.

Sunday, 13 October 1974

My darkest foreboding of last Sunday has not been justified. The Socialists have a majority of three and a very disjointed opposition facing them. It will be a long time before the opposition combines in sufficient strength to defeat the government.

Throughout the campaign, I felt Ted Heath's inadequacy as a communicator. During the first week, he allowed Labour and Liberals to make the running and he himself only came to the fore with his national unity proposals in the last week or so.

This may have been our election strategy but, even so, Ted hardly gave the impression of wanting to win. Considering that he played the defeated man and has done so ever since February, we were lucky not to be trounced more soundly.

I held on to my seat with a majority of 2,806.

Quite apart from winning two elections, this was an important period for me personally. I made my first appearance on the front bench at Welsh Questions on Monday, 6 May. I found it a lonely place. When one rises, the despatch box looms like a treasure chest. Instead of opening it, you clasp the brass corners – worn white as old gold by the sweat of many hands. You open your mouth and hope to God the right words come to frame your thoughts.

I had been a regular performer at Prime Minister's Questions since Ted Heath's time and belonged to a small group, chaired by the veteran Gilbert Longden (Con., Hertfordshire South West), who discussed possible lines of approach to the questions on the order paper and topical issues that might arise. I had some success with a question to Harold Wilson tempting him to play a leading part in Europe (16 May). Prime Minister's Questions were a pleasant diversion from Welsh affairs and a way of getting oneself noticed by the House as a whole.

Ted saw all Welsh Conservative members on Wednesday, 12 June, in preparation for our annual conference at Llandrindod the following weekend. He was relaxed and in a listening mood. I had been wrestling with a conference speech that I intended to make about devolution and I conveyed some of my doubts about the proposals to him. I noted them in my diary along with Tim Kitson, his PPS's account of Ted's recent visit to China.

The following Wednesday, Ted asked to see me in his office at the House. I recorded the event.

I went along to find Lord St Oswald and Christopher Tugendhat [Con., Cities of London and Westminster, now Lord] waiting to see him. I guessed from the latter's presence that some offer of a shadow office was about to be made to each of us. (There was a bad report in *Crossbencher* last Sunday on my chances compared with Nick Edwards, Con., Pembrokeshire.) When I went in, Ted was sitting at the far end of his leather sofa; I sat at the other end. He asked me my impression of last Saturday's conference at Llandrindod. I commented on the good attendance; he had clearly been impressed.

Then he said he had been talking to Peter Thomas and had decided to appoint both Nick and myself to the Front Bench. We were to divide the portfolio of responsibilities between us and conduct a pretty active campaign throughout August and September. It would mean hard work; I said I was used to that. To be an opposition spokesman carries no right to office, he said, but office comes to those who work and his face lit up in a smile.

We should be a good team! We certainly have an incentive now.

I had known Nick Edwards (now Lord Crickhowell) since he first stood for Pembrokeshire in 1970 and he had impressed me with his strong voice and all-conquering style. He had won the seat and held it with an increased majority in the February election. Pembrokeshire was known as 'Little England beyond Wales' and Nick fitted it perfectly.

We visited the Welsh Office on Thursday, 30 July to talk to the secretary of state, John Morris (now Lord), about the Kilbrandon Report and its proposals for devolution. I was against devolution because it would mean that Wales would lose influence and power in Whitehall and Westminster and ultimately resources. Nick, I thought, put too English a slant on our arguments – not that it would have made a blind bit of difference to John Morris, already deeply committed to the devolution principle. It is strange to read now that I recorded then:

> Nick Edwards has overtaken me in the office stakes. He is more English than I am and more to be trusted on that account. But he is a good man and I am very proud of him. He has character and strength of personality, which come out in his voice and manner. He is human and liable to err because of his strong feelings. I would be a reasonable complement to him in office.

About this time, I was invited to join fellow Conservatives in 'The Club of Twelve'. The key members were Jerry Wiggin (Weston Super Mare), Winston Churchill (Stretford), John Hannam (Exeter), John Nott (St Ives), Norman Tebbit (Chingford, now Lord), Teddy

Taylor (Cathcart) and David Walder (Clitheroe). We met at the Farmers Club once or twice and then at Jerry's home in 17 Cowley Street where Mrs Wiggin provided us with homemade cottage pie of superb quality. The club was an excellent sounding-board and occasionally invited a guest. The most memorable, apart from my old ally Arnold Goodman, was Godfrey Chandler of Cazenove who lunched with us on Tuesday, 3 December. He put paid to any thought we might have had of supporting Edward du Cann for the leadership.

After our second electoral defeat, it was only a matter of time – it seemed to me – before Ted Heath ceased to be leader. On 15 October, I wrote to Keith Joseph saying that, if he were to stand, I would support him. I admired Keith for his intellectual stamina and I was aware of the new thinking and research that he had been engaged in since the February election and, of course, the resulting string of speeches.

On the night of the State opening of the new Parliament, I was late entering the Commons dining room and Ted beckoned me over to the chief whip's table. His PPS, Kenneth Baker (Con., Cities of London and Westminster, now Lord) and Hugh Dykes (Con., Harrow East, also Lord) were there. Kenneth reported that the *Evening News* had every entrance and exit covered of a secret meeting of the 1922 Committee executive outside the House – the Mafia he called them – and it was clear that the leadership issue was sizzling behind the scenes.

Ted was very proud of having been asked to the Llanelli Rugby Club dinner. The club had been criticized for having allowed players to go to South Africa. But Ted supported their decision. Then our talk drifted to China. I was struck by how formidable and impressive Ted was at close quarters. Michael Heseltine (Con., Henley, now Lord) came up and called him 'Sir', I noticed. I noted in my diary: 'There is something about Ted that calls for such a title; he stands head and shoulders above all of us. He has a "knight in shining armour" quality which women, strangely, appreciate but it does not come over on television except in big close-up.'

The following night, Ted appeared on the small screen and implied that his leadership responsibility extended beyond the parliamentary party to the 11 million who had voted Conservative at the last election. Airey Neave, who had been pictured leaving the secret meeting of the 1922 executive, reported this next morning in the tea room. The Tory Mafia story had been fed to the press by sources close to Ted, said Airey. Airey went on to say that Ted's point about his having a wider responsibility to Conservative voters raised a constitutional issue. Was he trying to ignore the fact that any leader of the Conservative Party had to command the parliamentary party's support? The 'Ted must go' brigade were already threatening to withdraw their backing. Ted opened the 1922 Committee meeting on 14 November with a promise of a review of the leadership election procedure, a broader choice of front bench speakers and the inclusion of party committee officers in policy working-groups. These were sound, pragmatic changes.

Then we had the usual mental striptease display by those who always felt compelled to bare their innermost thoughts at the 1922. Some counselled caution on the leadership issue. Rumour had it that the Powellites wanted to delay a leadership election until Enoch was back in the fold. By the end of November, I was noting that:

> Margaret Thatcher seems to be putting herself up for the leadership and I am not surprised since the other candidates have faded. Edward du Cann regards himself as a non-combatant because of his chairmanship of the 1922. Willie is put out because he is not universally acclaimed as the heir apparent and Keith has thrust greatness away by his brilliant but erratic speeches.

The chancellor, Denis Healey, was never averse to hitting below the belt. I remembered his rabbit punch to Ted over the sale of arms to South Africa in March 1971 when he spoke of Ted's 'neurotic obsession to prove himself a man'. Ted had looked pained after that bit of goring from the Andalucian bull. Now, in December on the eve of the Christmas recess, Healey described Ted as the 'Beelzebub of Bexley'. Both were Balliol men but there was no love lost between them.

The new rules for the leadership election were duly produced by Alec Douglas-Home's committee and speculation about the likely outcome began in earnest. Before Christmas, it was reported that Ted Heath would have 130 votes, Margaret Thatcher 90 and A. N. Other 30. By January 1975, the leadership issue had become seriously entangled with the referendum on our continued membership of the European Community. We were opposed in principle to the referendum proposal. Yet, it looked as if the government might well recommend a 'Yes' vote and, with Ted leading us, there was no doubt that we would support them. But the electorate might well vote 'No'. Francis Pym agreed with my analysis and understood my concern about our inability to perform our constitutional duty to oppose.

There was some discreet canvassing. Ted lunched some of us at Buck's on 16 January but there was no attempt to grasp the realities of our situation as a party or Ted's own difficulties as our leader. Ted appeared alone in the smoking room on Monday, 20 January. He was a very lonely figure at the bar, waiting for the barman, Richard's attention. I was with Norman Lamont (Con., Kingston upon Thames, now Lord). 'Poor Ted,' he said 'buying drinks all round!' He was doing no such thing – there was hardly anyone in his vicinity – but it was an appropriate comment. Ted was no longer *primus inter pares* – just *inter pares* – and his forlorn position must have dawned on him. I expected a rally within the parliamentary party in his favour but it never came.

I spoke twice on the Finance Bill on which Margaret was leading us on the floor of the House and by Wednesday I was commenting in my diary on her improving chances of winning the leadership:

> The last possibility has suddenly become a reality, possibly owing to the canvassing of Jill Knight [Con., Edgbaston, now Baroness] and other ardents, Airey 'Colditz' Neave [Con., Abingdon] and Billy 'One Armed Bandit' Rees-Davies [Con., Thanet West]. She is also a stern mother figure to the younger Members and attracting more of the anti-Ted votes than I would have believed possible.

I took the view that the leadership election should be postponed until after the European referendum, which I was convinced would be lost. This would not suit Harold Wilson because his most rabid anti-Market members were left-wingers and, although it had become known that he would not resign in the event of a referendum defeat, he would have been embarrassed by such a victory for the left. He would also have had the very tricky task of taking us out of Europe. Ted too would obviously be gravely embarrassed. Margaret, on the other hand, was in a position to carry on, whatever the outcome of the referendum. She was assumed to be pro-Europe but she had wisely said very little on the issue.

But there was to be no postponement of the leadership election and we had the result of the first ballot on Tuesday, 4 February. It was a complete reversal of the original speculation when the new rules were announced: Margaret Thatcher 130 votes, Ted Heath 119 and Hugh Fraser 16. The same night Ted announced that he would not stand in the second ballot. The explanation given for the surprise result was that Ted's supporters had mistakenly thought he was in the lead and had concentrated on gaining the support of the

National Union and the House of Lords. They were not entitled to vote and would have had limited influence on Conservative members. At the end of the day, the truth was that no one canvassed for Ted as hard as her supporters did for Margaret. So the Grocer was out and the Grocer's Daughter was in. I concluded that day: 'We are beginning a new era in Tory history. Margaret will I am sure be its best exponent. We shall win with her if we can win with anybody.'

Margaret still had to face a second ballot. On 5 February, I lunched with Paul Channon (Con., Southend West, now Lord) and Sir Geoffrey Howe (Con., Reigate, now Lord). Geoffrey had just returned from the US and said he was being urged by friends to stand. Paul and I tried to dissuade him but to no purpose. We figured that the outcome of the second ballot would still leave Margaret without an overall majority and that the third ballot might see Willie Whitelaw triumphant.

Graham Page (Con., Crosby), who, like myself, had voted for Ted in the first ballot, told me he was transferring to Margaret and I guessed that the general shift to her had already begun. Interest in the outcome of the second ballot quickened when *The Times* pictured 'Willie washing up' – as Francis Pym put it – to match Margaret picking up the doorstep pinta. The contest threatened to become a joke within the party and outside. All we needed was a glamorous leg shot of Margaret but she avoided that. 'Margaret will lead us well,' I wrote, 'we need to be on our best behaviour and we shall be – with a lady in charge. We need to consolidate the striving classes.'

The *Daily Mail* published a poll on Monday, 10 February showing Margaret with 78 votes compared with Willie's 40, but I thought there would be a last minute reaction in favour of Willie. In the event, it did not materialize and Margaret cleared the overall majority requirement with 146 votes compared with Willie's 78. I actually voted for Willie at the last moment although I had promised my vote to Margaret. All the women I knew were against her.

That night, I dropped into one or two places where I was un-known and listened to people talking. The Conservative Party had become interesting again; the excitement was due to Margaret's star quality. Her first party political broadcast ended: 'To yesterday's men, tomorrow's woman says Hello!' Next day, I went down with a very heavy cold.

There had been a lot of talk about my joining the Conservative Group in the European Parliament. It began shortly before the 1974 Christmas recess when Peter Kirk (Con., Saffron Walden) who led the group, pressed me to join. Wales needed a representative in

Europe but could I hold on to my Westminster seat and attend the European Parliament at the same time? Much as I might like to venture to fresh woods, I realized that if I were to do so I would probably be finished at Westminster, certainly as a shadow spokesman on the front bench. It was a risky proposition and I was not at all keen but I did not give a firm refusal either. I tried to keep my options open as long as possible.

Nick Edwards got to hear of the invitation and told Welsh Conservative MPs in January with a laugh that Europe was all mine. The chief whip, Humphrey Atkins, spoke to me on 17 February and formally offered me a place in the European Group. I firmly declined his offer. Curiously, Nick also spoke to me about Europe that evening and was wrongly under the impression that I had agreed to go. I obviously did not want to take a final decision until I knew Margaret's wishes about the leadership of the Conservative Party in Wales. But I had made no approach to her. I was also reluctant to go before the referendum had taken place and our future in or out of Europe had been decided.

George Thomas (deputy speaker) had urged me to make a bid for the Welsh leadership and I had written to a few influential friends as George had suggested. But it was all too late. The following day it was announced that Nick Edwards was to be shadow secretary of state. Peter Kirk was still hopeful of winning me over to his group and that night I was sorely tempted to grasp his offer but I did not do so. 'A very sad day, savouring personal defeat,' I noted. Rejection would have been a better word.

After a night's sleep I was more convinced than ever that I should not go to Europe and told the chief whip that I would issue a statement to that effect since the story of my going had somehow been leaked to the press. To my surprise, I discovered that it was Margaret herself who had said at her press conference that I was Europe bound! I wondered who had planted the thought in her mind. That Wednesday evening (19 February) Nick came to see me in my room. It was Kenneth Baker who had told him I was going to Europe and the same message had been conveyed to Margaret. She had interviewed Nick on Monday evening for the shadow secretary of state post. Dark forces had clearly outflanked me!

Nick said that if I was not going to Europe, he would ask Margaret if he could have an extra spokesman on the front bench and would I support him. I readily agreed. On Friday, the chief whip telephoned me at home: 'Quite understand about Europe, old boy. Would you join the Front Bench team if asked?'

By now, I knew that not only had Nick asked for me but the whips, John Stradling Thomas (Monmouth) and Michael Roberts (Cardiff North West) had also been pressing for me. On Monday, 24 February I was asked to see Margaret. She invited me to sit on the long settee in the leader of the opposition's room.

'Will you' – she asked with great emphasis – 'help with front bench work on the Welsh side?'

'Of course,' I said, and we moved on to talk of prospects for the European referendum. I liked her personally as a woman and always treated her as such. At the end of that day, I noted: 'Last week was shattering. I was on antibiotics (my cold had gone to my chest) and this, coupled with the blow to my ego, was devastating. Only the pressure of work kept me sane and comparatively sensible.'

My friend John Lotery had been like a brother to me. I had seen him married to a lively and clever girl, Peta Hitchmough, and shared their joy when their son, Adam, was born. Typically, John had arranged for me to remain at Campden Hill when Peta returned with her baby. I stayed with an attractive, talkative widow, Mrs Hue-Williams, who lived on the floor below the Lotery flat. In December 1974, I was shocked to hear that John was in hospital. When I visited John at St Bartholomew's Hospital on 17 December, I learnt that he was suffering from leukaemia. The news depressed me all day. My colleague, Dr Gerry Vaughan (Con., Reading South) said the chance of a complete recovery was one in a million but the progress of the disease might be arrested. I told him that John was remarkably cheerful. Gerry said that this was typical of the disease and that sufferers never abandoned hope. John died at Barts on Saturday, 25 January 1975. He was forty-seven. I wrote on Monday:

> He will live on in my mind as my father has done, as a benign and calm spirit, willing good. John liked our occasional lunches together at the House. I used to pay for the meal and the wine, he for the port and cigars. I think he enjoyed these get-togethers because, as he used to say;
> 'When you and I are together, everything is simple, isn't it?'
> London will be poorer for me without him.

His death hurt me more than I thought at the time.

Child Harold and Sunny Jim

I was coughing in the gents just off the library corridor in the House of Commons when I heard Harold Wilson's unmistakable voice close behind me. 'That sounds bad!' he said. It might have been the start of an interesting exchange with the prime minister but it was not. I was accustomed to bowling googlies at him from the backbenches during Prime Minister's Questions but not standing beside him at a urinal. His presence arrested my flow and I could not for the life of me restart it. Harold had that kind of disconcerting effect on people. He had an isolated, dark-tower quality and you could never tell what he was really thinking.

My enduring impression of Harold Wilson towards the end of his short and difficult second premiership is of him surfing the tsunami of barracking put up by the opposition as he faced questions for fifteen minutes on Tuesdays and Thursdays. He knew that the opposition was consuming time with their raucous bawling and he turned it to his advantage as consummately as he countered an awkward question on television with a puff of pipe smoke. He was adept at subtly playing the victim and attracting the sympathy of his audience. But gone were the sparkling days of witty repartees by a thrusting premier, strongly supported by his backbenchers and anxious to increase his majority (1964–6). His performances in the 1970s were lacklustre and even a very lengthy analytical speech on Northern Ireland was hardly worthy of his intellect at its best. Perhaps he already sensed the onset of the illness which eventually deprived him of his astonishingly sharp memory – especially about his own past dicta. Harold's claim to fame was that he kept his party together – no mean achievement considering the fractious elements that comprised it – and that he kept Britain in Europe by securing the endorsement of the British electorate in the referendum on 5 June 1975.

I lunched with Margaret Thatcher on the day in 1976 when he surprised us all by announcing his resignation. It was five days after his sixtieth birthday (11 March) and the morning after we had had a vote of confidence debate following the government's defeat on its White Paper on public expenditure. The chancellor, Denis Healey, flayed the Tribune Group for their abstention in the public expenditure debate with such ferocity that even I felt a twinge of pity for them. Never had I seen the Labour Party so viciously and pathetically divided. My diary entry ran as follows:

Tuesday, 16 March 1976

A day to remember! Wilson's resignation! I was in Standing Committee on the Rating (Caravans) Bill when David Mudd (Con., Falmouth and Camborne) passed me a note on the front bench saying 'Wilson has resigned'. I thought he had got it wrong and that it should have read 'Thorpe has resigned'. I checked back with David who was as nonplussed as I was and then passed the note to Michael Morris (Con., Northampton South, now Lord) who was leading for us on the bill and was on his feet at the time. He asked for an immediate adjournment but the acting chairman, Harry Gourlay (Lab., Kirk-caldy), said the resignation was only a rumour and that he had no power to adjourn in any event. Gordon Oakes, the minister in charge of the bill, had slipped out some moments before – presumably to take a warning call from his office – and so we carried on discussing the bill all morning.

I rushed off shortly before 1 p.m. to have lunch at Jerry's with Margaret as our guest. I thought she would never turn up but she arrived at 1.20 p.m. Jerry had met some of us the night before to agree an agenda which he now tried to introduce. Margaret would have none of it. She was supremely aware of the uniqueness of the occasion of the prime minister's resignation. She wanted her reaction to be absolutely right.

She curled up on the sofa – very feminine, very feline – and her eyes became sharp as a vixen's as we discussed the future. Her real fear was that Roy Jenkins might become leader and angle for a coalition with Ted Heath. That prospect sent shivers down her spine. I had to leave at 2.15 p.m. because I had the second question to Michael Foot. Then at 3.15 p.m. we had Questions to the Prime Minister. He answered the first from Peter Blaker (Con., Blackpool South, now Lord) about the submission of evidence to the Royal Commission on the Press and then Margaret weighed in with a supplementary question, which began innocuously enough and ended with a demand for a general election. After an outlandish question from Thorpe, Ted Heath pressed for his coalition but Enoch would have none of it. If anything, he was for the Labour government continuing. Wilson parried all comers with the resigned air appropriate to the occasion.

As to why he has chosen to announce his resignation at this moment, opinion varies but a consensus is developing that the Budget due on 6 April is diabolically tough and could restore Healey to the good graces of the left. Wilson does not want Healey to succeed him and would therefore like the leadership election to take place while Healey is still in the doghouse with the left.

Jim Callaghan is the current favourite to succeed but, supposing Roy Jenkins, Tony Crosland and other right-wing candidates oppose him, the Labour moderate vote would be split. The left, if they have a modicum of wisdom, will put forward one candidate only; Tony Benn perhaps or Michael Foot. Today's betting is heavily on Callaghan who performs well at the despatch box and has the respect of the House but he is older than Harold himself. Will they acknowledge him as the heir apparent? I doubt it.

Margaret's demand for a General Election may well be right and the only realistic solution.

Thursday, 18 March 1976

There are now five candidates in the field: Callaghan, Jenkins, Crosland, Foot and Benn. Healey will, I am almost certain, be in the running by Monday.

I succumbed to the temptation of a heavy dinner with the roads lobby last night and sat near Gordon Bagier (Lab., Sunderland South). Bagier, who is no fool, gave Foot about 70 votes compared with Benn's 20. Sir Stephen McAdden (Con., Southend East) at lunch also thought Foot's following should not be discounted.

Tonight, I dropped into a West End pub after dinner and over-heard a couple of chaps arguing in favour of Healey. They were fairly knowledgeable as chaps go and appreciative of Wilson's talent for keeping the party together. They thought Callaghan too old at sixty-four.

Monday, 22 March 1976

Cledwyn Hughes told me on the train on Friday how, as chairman of the Parliamentary Labour Party, he had drafted the rules for the leadership election last Tuesday afternoon. Harold had told him of his resignation at 11.35 a.m.

According to the PM, when he had told George Thomas in 1974 that he might be retiring in the course of the next year or so, George's selfless reaction was: 'For heaven's sake, Prime Minister, don't go before I've got the Speaker's chair!'

Today, Foot is in the ascendant while Jim Callaghan is on a downward slope. The situation will change, I am sure, before the final choice is made. There will be a rush to Callaghan to stop Foot and the left and all the rest of the moderate candidates will suffer in consequence. We might have Foot, Jenkins and Callaghan in that order in the first ballot.

Tuesday, 30 March 1976

The first ballot did not turn out quite as I expected. Foot topped the poll with 90 votes, Callaghan had 86, Jenkins 56, Healey 30, Benn 37, Crosland 17. The last two fell out and Jenkins withdrew, leaving Foot, Callaghan and Healey for the second ballot today. The result was a triumph for Callaghan with 141 votes to Foot's 133 and Healey's 38. It was as predictable as the coming Saturday's Grand National! (I have a £1 on Foot to win, through Sir Stephen McAdden, immortalized by his quick reply to George Thomas who once addressed him in the chair of the Welsh Grand Committee as 'Saint Stephen'. 'I would remind the Rt. Hon Gentleman that Saint Stephen was stoned to death,' said Stephen who was known to be partial to champagne, always from a silver tankard.) Clearly the Jenkinsites had gone over to Callaghan en masse.

On our twentieth wedding anniversary last week, I bought Enid a lovely antique diamond ring from a Mr Joseph at Hatton Garden. He gave us an hour of his time and I learnt more about diamonds than I had ever known. One should hold them up to natural light to judge their quality. 'A real diamond should scream at you,' he said. He sorted diamonds for de Beers. Buying from him was a unique experience; one actually felt better after parting with one's money.

Thursday, 1 April 1976

Although I have backed Foot to win the premiership – Ladbroke's odds on him are four to one – because he would make a better leader for the Labour Party than Callaghan, who will be a short-term premier in view of his age, it certainly looks as if Sunny Jim will win on Monday.

Monday, 5 April 1976

Rag Trade won the Grand National on Saturday and Callaghan the premiership today. He appeared on television this evening and impressed my landlady, Mrs Hue-Williams. He said the government could go on until October 1979 and so it does not look as if he is going to rush to the country as many expected him to do.

James Callaghan – he preferred to be called James – was as good as his word about the timing of the election. He battled on, as you would expect of a man whose university was the Inland Revenue and who had served in the war as a chief petty officer in the Royal Navy. He neither smoked nor drank and was a devoted family man. He had been MP for Cardiff South since 1945 and quickly rose to office in Attlee's first government. He had held the key offices of state in Wilson's administrations – chancellor of the exchequer 1964–7, home secretary 1967–70 and foreign and Commonwealth secretary 1974–6. He therefore had considerable experience and a personal aura of authority about him.

Attempts to denigrate him for his close association with Sir Julian Hodge, the south Wales financier, and his appointment of his son-in-law, Peter Jay, as ambassador to Washington never succeeded in sapping his reputation for integrity. Having been a trade union official himself, it was natural that he should have some faith in the ultimate good sense of trade union leaders and their ability to put the interests of the nation above their own. But those leaders were changing and it was the extremism of the new generation of trade union leaders, including Arthur Scargill, during the 'Winter of Discontent' (1978–9) that finally brought about his electoral downfall.

To have survived as prime minister from April 1976 to May 1979 without a clear Labour majority necessitated a pact with the Liberals and a piecemeal deal with the Welsh nationalists (Plaid Cymru). It was an exercise in self-preservation which only a man with Jim Callaghan's legitimate pride and strong belief in himself could have conducted for so long and with a credible measure of grace. He never got the break he so desperately wanted from the bonds of dependence on minor parties. *Time and Chance* – the title of his autobiography – were in short supply during his premiership.

Much as I enjoyed my morning journeys by the 159 bus from Hamilton Terrace whither I had moved with Mrs Hue-Williams, the return journey from Westminster, often late at night, was not to my liking. I therefore moved back into the Savile Club. Among those who held court there was an eighty-two-year-old, wizened, little American from Kentucky, Ben Lucien Burman. As a soldier in the First World War, he had been injured at Beaumel Woods in 1918 and had settled down to write in New York in the 1920s. 'We lived on lentil soup,' he said, 'until I sold the story of *Steamboat round the Bend* to Will Rogers who made a film of it in 1925.' He had written a number of books about the Mississippi since then. Ben had also been a regular contributor to *Reader's Digest* for half a century and claimed to have spotted Robert Best as 'white trash' when Best was a correspondent in Berlin in the 1930s. Best became one of three American traitors to be convicted after the war. 'White trash', Ben thought, were descendants of the English convicts exported from Newgate prison to settle in Virginia.

It was during Callaghan's administration that the policy of devolving powers and responsibility to Scotland and Wales reached its first apogee. As a Welsh MP, I was fundamentally opposed to any policy that smacked of separatism because I was fearful that Wales would lose a great deal by weakening its connections with the rest of the United Kingdom.

The point had first been brought home to me in the early 1950s by none other than Jim Griffiths, the MP for Llanelli who later became the first secretary of state for Wales. I heard him addressing a Welsh Labour Party conference at Porthcawl, which I was reporting for the BBC. Jim described very forcibly how Wales benefited financially from the English connection; even in terms of pension contributions and receipts, the Welsh were net gainers. The message was clear. Cultural and sporting nationalism was fine but economic and political nationalism was anathema. We needed more power and influence at Westminster, not less.

Among those present were Labour MPs from the Welsh-speaking heartlands – Lady Megan Lloyd George (Carmarthenshire), Cledwyn Hughes, Goronwy Roberts, Tudor Watkins (Brecon and Radnor) and Tom Idwal Jones (Wrexham). They felt threatened in their constituencies by the growing power of the nationalist party, Plaid Cymru, barking incessantly at their heels and locally highlighting the ineffectiveness of remote 'London government'. These MPs had tried to outflank the nationalists by campaigning for a Parliament for Wales. Their very real concerns were not shared by Labour stalwarts like Nye Bevan but in time they won the day in the upper ranks of the Labour Party.

Harold Macmillan had already appointed a minister of state for Wales in 1958 – Vivian Lewis, created Lord Brecon – and in 1964 Wilson went a step further and appointed a secretary of state with a seat in the Cabinet. An embryonic Welsh Office, a pale reflection of the long-established Scottish Office, began to develop in Cardiff. The process of administrative devolution had begun in earnest.

It was a strong and heady aperitif for Plaid Cymru, the youthful, enthusiastic party of self-government for Wales, now threatening to become the major opposition party and to push Lloyd George's Liberal remnants and the Conservatives to the fringes of politics. Their president, Gwynfor Evans, crowned years of effort by taking Carmarthenshire by storm in a by-election in 1966 and the triumph became a televisual epic to be repeated ad nauseam by a sympathetic media. The threat was now keenly felt in Whitehall and dreaded in Transport House, not least because Scotland and Wales between them returned over sixty Labour MPs. Something more than administrative devolution was required to stem the nationalist tide in both countries.

Willie Hamilton, the forthright member for Fife Central, told the Scottish Labour Party conference at Troon in early April 1976 that legislative devolution was to be granted to Scotland as part of the party's policy of appeasement towards the nationalists. It was as bitter to his taste as it was to mine. While the Labour leadership struggle was still in progress, I wrote in my diary:

> The Government's fate is tied to devolution in Scotland. If they do not grant a devolved Parliament, they will lose seats there and consequently power at Westminster. I suspect they will lose seats there anyway because any concession to nationalism is a blow to Socialism, an acknowledgement that Socialism has failed to deliver the goods.

Kingsley Martin had told me at the Savile Club earlier in the decade that the world would be astonished by the persistent power of nationalism in the late twentieth century. His dictum haunted my mind.

The Conservatives were as ambivalent about devolution as the Labour Party. Ted Heath had declared himself in favour of devolution for Scotland at Perth in May 1968 and had set up a committee under the chairmanship of Sir Alec Douglas-Home. This led to a commitment to Scotland but not to Wales in the 1970 election manifesto.

No real action followed but, after the Kilbrandon Royal Commission reported favourably in 1973, Alick Buchanan-Smith (Con., Angus North and Mearns) was asked to work on the detailed application of the recommendations to Scotland and there were further commitments in the February and October 1974 manifestos.

Margaret Thatcher too had made a speech at Dundee in May 1975 repeating the commitment to a directly elected Scottish Assembly 'as briefly as I decently could' (*The Path to Power*, Harper Collins, 1995, p. 323). Despite her mounting scepticism, support for the principle was still being expressed from the front bench when we debated the government's White Paper in January 1976. All this led to an almighty row at the parliamentary party's constitutional committee on Thursday, 13 May, when Willie Whitelaw, our shadow spokesman on devolution, outlined what was to be said at the Scottish party conference at Perth the next day. There was to be yet another reaffirmation of the commitment in spite of the fact that the parliamentary party was desperately anxious to get itself and the leader off the hook. Speaker after speaker rose to say that the shadow cabinet decision to reaffirm the commitment was wrong. The argument spilled over into the 1922 Committee later that evening and the officers were deputed to urge the leader to tone down any commitment that might be made. I too was against devolution of the kind proposed for Scotland because it would only make our position more difficult, if not untenable, in Wales.

When the government introduced its Scotland and Wales Bill, there were casualties on all sides. Alick Buchanan-Smith and Malcolm Rifkind (Edinburgh, Pentlands, now Sir) resigned from their shadow posts and voted with the government at second reading, as did others. Ten Labour members voted with us. Twenty-seven Conservatives, including Ted Heath and Peter Walker, abstained but there were also 29 Labour abstentions. It was clear that the bill had no real friends in the House, as David Wood wrote in *The Times*. This dissatisfaction surfaced early in the committee stage when Labour critics of the bill took up more time than the official opposition. The Labour member for Bedwellty, Neil Kinnock (now Lord), was particularly prominent. It all came to a head when the government introduced a guillotine motion. It was defeated (on 22 February) by a majority of 29, of whom 22 were Labour members. The bill was now dead in the water.

While the government, abandoned by the nationalist parties and sustained only by their pact with the Liberals, drafted fresh legislation to provide devolution, I attended the Commonwealth parliamentary conference in Canada and had the opportunity to visit some of their provincial parliaments. The enormous distances between the provincial centres of government, the geophysical barriers between them and the sheer size of the country explained a great deal about their development and their comparatively slender relationship with the federal government in Ottawa.

Although it had its own parliament and representative in London, Quebec province, led by Rene Leveque, was demanding further acknowledgement of its sovereignty and a federal commission was beginning to examine the whole issue on an all-Canada basis. The sensitivities of the French-speaking majority in Quebec, stirred up by de Gaulle in the 1960s, accounted for much of the recent violent past of the province. It seemed to me that the crux of the argument lay in the ability or otherwise of the different provinces to sustain themselves independently and I was astonished by the contradictory replies I received when I questioned people about their province's economic and financial strength. Quebec thought it contributed more to the rest of Canada than it received in return but this was denied in Ontario. British Columbia looked south to Seattle and west to the Pacific; Quebec was over 2,000 miles away and seldom in their thoughts. 'There are two kinds of Canadians,' a British Colombian told me, 'those who live in British Columbia and those who wish they did.'

The visit confirmed my view that devolving power and responsibility was hardly a recipe for political contentment, let alone success in great enterprises requiring pooled resources and collaboration. It might be justified by the historic and geographical circumstances of development, as in Canada, but it was no solution to our governmental problems in the United Kingdom. Rather, it was a distraction from them.

My visit to Canada had its lighter moments. As we were travelling by coach through Stanley Park, Vancouver, our pretty young guide pointed out a flock of Canada geese 'we are trying to preserve for posterity'. 'Yes, yes. They must be preserved at all costs,' said a turbaned gentleman from the Indian continent seated beside me. 'They make wonderful curry.'

Separate devolution bills for Scotland and Wales were heralded in the Queen's Speech in November 1977 and published soon after. I spoke in the second reading debate on the Government of Wales Bill and wound up the debate on the guillotine motion, which was carried by a majority of 27. The Scotland Bill was similarly carried through into its committee stage without let or hindrance. They

were interesting debates with Enoch Powell well to the fore defending the unity of the United Kingdom. Labour critics of the devolution
proposals kept a low profile and were rumoured to be holding their
fire for the referendum campaigns promised by the prime minister.

Speculation about the date of the next election was endless.
Would it be in the spring of 1978 or October of that year? Spring
or October 1979? Before or after the referendums? In April 1978,
Cledwyn thought the government would lose because people were
tired of it and wanted a change. By the end of the month and our
committee stage on the Wales Bill, I agreed with him. Wales was as
antipathetic to devolution as ever. A poll by the local radio station,
Swansea Sound, showed more than 50 per cent against and only 30
per cent in favour. In early May, after the bill had secured its third
reading, Cledwyn announced that he would not be standing again
for Anglesey, which he had represented for twenty-seven years.
Although we belonged to opposing parties, he had been a true
friend and mentor to me and a wonderful source of anecdotes and
gossip. Little did we know then that his retirement from the
Commons would not be the end of his political career – far from it.
He became Labour's leader in the House of Lords.

Julian Critchley (Con., Aldershot) talked of Margaret and the
shadow cabinet as 'Snow White and the Seven Dwarfs'. I was
certainly worried about our election prospects and our lack of
impact on the electorate. Nick Edwards had been quite ill and had
spent a fortnight resting in the Bahamas before leading for the
opposition on the Wales Bill. Stress had taken its toll on other
colleagues' lives, including mine. The government was campaigning
harder than we were and I told Margaret as much in July.

I had an oral question to the prime minister on 11 July, the day
after my birthday. I asked him to explain why every Conservative
government since the war had left office with more people in
employment than when it came in while every Labour government
had left office with fewer in work than when it started. I bumped
into Jim in the library corridor afterwards.

'I never know what you're going to ask me when you stand up,' he
said.

'Always a fair question,' I answered. He seemed to agree.

When the House rose for the summer recess, many of us expected
an October election. The Lib–Lab pact had faltered and the Scottish
National Party had refused the government its support. I was attend-
ing an Inter-Parliamentary Union conference in Bonn in early
September and was distinctly worried that the election might be

called any day. The prime minister quashed such speculation in a personal broadcast on 7 September: he was clearly determined to carry on regardless, although his party was losing its core support in the country because of unemployment and cuts in public expenditure.

Early in 1979, in anticipation of the referendum, I wrote a number of newspaper articles on the Government of Wales Act and recorded a variety of interviews (later described as powerful by journalist W. John Morgan). However, the campaign began with a well-attended public meeting at Aberystwyth, addressed by Neil Kinnock, Lord Gibson Watt and myself as opponents of the act. Elystan Morgan, the local Labour MP, and others put the case for a 'Yes' vote. At the very end of the meeting when a substantial number of people had left, someone called for a vote to be taken which our side lost. The dubious circumstances surrounding the vote made it of no consequence, but it was the only vote the 'Yes' campaigners won.

The unpopularity of the government against a dire economic background, the lack of clarity in the government's motives in putting forward the devolution proposals, coupled with the split in the Labour Party on the issue, combined to ensure its defeat in the referendum on 1 March, St David's Day. Even in the nationalist bastion of Gwynedd, the voting was two to one against. In Wales as a whole, it was four to one against. As John Morris, the secretary of state for Wales said, 'You have to recognize an elephant on your doorstep.' This was indeed an elephantine defeat for the government.

It was soon to be followed by a vote of confidence on Wednesday, 28 March. Before the day, the government was scratching at every door for support. On Tuesday of the preceding week, I asked the PM on the floor of the House if it was true that the government had offered Plaid Cymru MPs a compensation scheme for slate quarrymen suffering from silicosis in return for their votes. And was this not a despicable bit of bartering? (I was particularly irked by the fact that I had been pressing the quarrymen's case since the start of the decade.)

I did not know at the time that the PM had been resisting pressures to barter with the smaller parties and had to be galvanized to agree the deal by the chief whip, Michael Cox, and the Lord President, Michael Foot. The PM was caught on the raw. Neither did I know that Nick Edwards was making a similar bid for Plaid Cymru support for our side. He told me I should not have put the PM on the spot. The facts were soon out in the open and all, especially the PM, were castigated by the press. There was some argument on our side as to whether we should allow the quarrymen's bill a free passage but I committed us to supporting it in principle when I questioned Michael Foot. I believe I had Margaret's support. In the event, the government lost the confidence motion by 1 vote. At 2 p.m. the following day the PM announced that there would be a general election on 3 May. He had reached the end of his remarkably long tether.

Might the Callaghan government have fared differently if it had not made their devolution legislation such a flagship of their policy? Without it and the support it generated from the Liberals and the nationalists, the government could not have survived as long as it did. Callaghan certainly believed in devolution and after the referendum famously said that it would not go away. He was proved right some twenty years later. He made the promise of a referendum personally at the second reading of the original Scotland and Wales Bill. It was the fulfilment of that promise that brought about his downfall. It focused public disaffection with the government in Scotland and Wales and gave a foretaste of the election result to come. But it was the government's failure to manage the economy and the country's finances that put paid to its reputation. The fall in the value of sterling in 1976, the need for stand-by credit from the International Monetary Fund and the advent of the IMF team to 'examine the books', was followed by very real and damaging cuts in public expenditure. Continual failure to control the trade unions and hold their wage demands in check culminated in the Winter of Discontent in 1978–9 when production fell to the level of Heath's three-day week in 1974. Jim Callaghan returned from Bermuda to face a mounting crisis only to ask 'What crisis?' These events, coupled with high unemployment, deeply discredited the government in the eyes of the electorate. I always admired Jim Callaghan as a man and politician. In more propitious circumstances, he might have been a great prime minister but time and chance were against him.

The 1979 Election

Even Margaret Thatcher, sturdy as she was, described the years before the election as gruelling. What made them so was the perpetual uncertainty. We were led up the hill to engage in battle time and time again only to be marched down after battle had been postponed. For Margaret as our leader it was a period of consolidation, not only within the Conservative Party in Parliament but in the country. Men thought that being a woman, she was very vulnerable and we all behaved like Knights of the Round Table. She had our absolute loyalty. We wanted her and willed her to succeed.

In some of her early speeches, she tended to hector the House and use the unparliamentary 'you' in arguing her case which would normally have resulted in a reminder from the Speaker that she was talking to Right Honourable and Honourable Members not himself. But George Thomas liked her and she got away with it. Her forensic skills stood her in good stead. She was to hone them and improve her performance no end over the years ahead. She always looked smart at the despatch box and added a barely audible 'Hm' of satisfaction at the end of her sentence when she had scored a point.

My parliamentary day usually began with a coffee at the Conservative table in the tea room where Ray Mawby (Totnes) would enlighten us on the intricacies of the orders of the day. As a former assistant postmaster general in the Macmillan government, he received first issues of Post Office stamps free and of right for years afterwards. He accumulated a valuable collection. My colleague and namesake, Michael Roberts, had a great affection for Mawby and once passed me some doggerel he had scribbled.

> My name is Raymond L. Mawby
> Collecting stamps is my hobby
> Which is not surprising, you see
> Since I was once APMG.

Another regular at our table, Sir Raymond Gower, inspired Michael to versify as Raymond spoke in the Welsh Grand Committee:

> The brain of Britain is in flower
> Alias, Sir Raymond Gower;
> He walks about while we have tea
> Just like an aborigine.

It was a perfect description. These hilarious morning sessions set us up to cope with the trials of the long day, which seldom ended before a ten o'clock vote, and often much later.

Afternoon gatherings in the tea room were very serious affairs. Margaret would come in after Prime Minister's Questions to hear reactions. Airey Neave, who had been her leadership campaign manager and was now shadowing the secretary of state for Northern Ireland, would not be far from her side. The murder of this quiet hero of Colditz by the Irish National Liberation Army in the precincts of the Palace of Westminster on Friday, 30 March 1979 was a terrible shock to us all. The bomb in his car exploded as he drove from the underground car park in Palace Yard. I had been with Airey at the BBC the night before his murder. His death caused a gnawing fear in our hearts that we too would be highly vulnerable to attack during the coming election campaign.

My diary tells the campaign story as I lived through it.

Monday, 9 April 1979

A good adoption meeting at the Town hall, Llandudno; the ground floor was full but not the gallery. Airey Neave's death and the threat of more violence have meant strict security; the police have been round every night since I have been home, checking the car and the premises.

Jim Callaghan opened his campaign in Glasgow tonight and called this the 'devolution election'. I am surprised, in view of the referendum results, that he should pursue this line even in Scotland. I wonder whether he will do the same in Wales?

Margaret does not open her campaign until next week. She may be right. She said on television tonight that it was going to be a long campaign and that people would get tired of it. Certainly, the television coverage tonight was dense with Ted Heath saying that we had a lower standard of living in the UK than Communist East Germany.

If we lose, Margaret's slowness off the mark compared with Jim's celerity will be blamed. I delivered a long address. The only part of our Welsh policy I am worried about is our line that Welsh should be optional in schools and subject to parental choice. How do we justify treating Welsh differently from other subjects?

My strategy is to tackle the outlying areas of the constituency and work my way into the urban centres of Llandudno and Bangor.

Tuesday, 10 April 1979

Tonight, hardly a soul at Betws-y-Coed and Dolgarrog but I was not surprised. Neither place has ever given me an audience to speak of although Betws is strongly Tory and Dolgarrog 90 per cent Labour.

The prime minister in Manchester was saying that a Conservative government would create more unemployment.

The Liberal, Richard Wainwright, on television was calling for proportional representation. He sounded very unconvincing about the Liberal hope of forty to fifty seats.

Canvassing, I found that our idea of selling council houses to sitting tenants was going down well, especially with the young.

Wednesday, 11 April 1979

I canvassed Bryn Pydew, Glanwydden, Craigside, Penrhynside and Craig y Don today. It was rainy and cold. This evening, I had meetings at Bryn Pydew and the Conservative Club, Llandudno. CID men told us they had searched the car ten times in our absence. They are clearly expecting a follow-up to Airey Neave's killing.

Bangor Conservative Club gave us £1,000 towards the Election Fighting Fund and Llandudno Club gave us £350. There has been some trouble between the Association and the Llandudno Club, which may account for the disparity.

Thursday, 12 April 1979

I think the government is showing the first signs of cracking up. Shirley Williams was on television last night suggesting we might increase school meal charges. It sounded phoney. They are trying to turn the attack on to us but failing and there are still almost three weeks to go. They are on the run.

We now have a weekend of no campaigning when people can assess the situation. Margaret Thatcher had a good launch for our manifesto in which the most credible item is our pledge to reduce taxation. We are not so strong, in view of the past and our confrontation with the miners, on our pledges to deal with secondary picketing and the trade unions' closed shop.

Saturday, 14 April 1979

Our literature still has not arrived from Central Office, which is worrying.

The polls still give us a lead but it has fallen, as it must before polling day.

Callaghan is campaigning well and on the attack. Today he was criticizing our policy of selling off successful nationalized industries and teasing us for condemning nationalization as unprofitable. He had a standing ovation from a public as opposed to a party audience.

Chris Butler sounded depressed at Wales Area Office. We have not been getting much of a showing in the *Western Mail*.

Easter Monday, 16 April 1979

Margaret Thatcher at Swansea and Cardiff spoke about the decline of moral values.

Glasgow Herald shows Labour gaining in Scotland from us and SNP.

Margaret is always shown in a hurry by television cameras while Jim looks relaxed. Margaret is constantly attacking. Jim is like a magician pulling card after card from thin air. No single issue has emerged yet. People seem to have made up their minds but appearances are deceptive.

Tuesday, 17 April 1979

A warm day and bigger audiences at Penmachno and Dolwyddelan this evening; heartened by door-to-door canvassing in Bangor and Penmaenmawr earlier in the day.

Enid is despondent and believes Margaret is inferior to Callaghan on the box. I agree. Margaret is too strident, too aggressive. She is a demolition expert but lacks imagination and the warmth that springs from it.

Our literature is inadequate, indeed poor. Yet I think we shall win if we can stay the course.

Wednesday, 18 April 1979

We are holding our own but there are a worrying number of Liberal posters in the windows in Llandudno. We had a similar flurry of posters in February 1974 and then they seemed to fade away.

Best line of the day on Labour: 'They've had their chance, now give us ours.'

Friday, 20 April 1979

Too tired last night to write a word; it has been an exhausting week.

Both Margaret and Jim showed signs of it in their interviews with ITN.

M. Th.'s voice was hoarse – a weakness she is prone to – and Jim, I could have sworn said 'We had a bad budget prepared . . .'

Reasonable socialists in my audience have now twice tackled my thesis of more jobs – lower taxes. 'It's a gamble I am not prepared to take' (student at Penmaenmawr). 'Some will succeed – the able and energetic – but the rest will go to the wall' (lady in Trefriw).

Our worst faux pas to date as far as I am concerned is over the pensioners. We have promised them little. Labour have a better appreciation of their electoral importance.

We have not made enough of the Labour Party's drift to the Left.

Saturday, 21 April 1979

I feel very refreshed after a day drenching Llandudno with my loud-speaker comments. We have this aspect of campaigning down to a fine art.

Tonight, I spoke at Penrhyn Bay and Ysgol John Bright on pensions and education. I hope the *North Wales Weekly News* does not lose my copy for next week's edition as they did last week. I suspect there is a saboteur somewhere.

Liberal posters everywhere. We hope it will stimulate our people to put up theirs.

St George's Day and Shakespeare's Birthday,
Monday, 23 April 1979

'To be or not to be' for Callaghan and 'Once more unto the breach, dear friends' for us. The election is hotting up with Jim attacking Maggie over prices but getting as good as he gave.

To Cardiff by car yesterday to record a television programme. Returned by air – 4 p.m. take-off – and was on my feet at Llan-fairfechan by 6.15 p.m. thanks to Zachry Brierley and his Rolls at Hawarden airport.

Wednesday, 25 April 1979

Spent all morning with our candidate, Jim Paice, at Caernarfon. Not much hope for anyone there except Plaid's Dafydd Wigley. He should double his majority. Visited Anglesey this afternoon. Keith Best could win it if he had a go at the rural areas. Labour are divided locally and Holyhead, a Labour stronghold, is not playing an active role because its favoured candidate (Will Edwards) was not selected to fight the seat. The Liberal is a windbag and Plaid's candidate is standing there for the third time.

At home in Conwy, I am worried by the apparent strength of the Liberals. Labour are very weak.

Monday, 30 April 1979

The Labour Party have almost disappeared from the local scene. The Liberals could well come second. They will take votes mainly from Labour but they might take some from me too.

HTV reported tonight that Nick Edwards was attacking Plaid in Pembrokeshire for encouraging their faithful to vote Labour and oust him.

Tuesday, 1 May 1979

This has been a television/radio election but attendances at recent public meetings have been good. An enjoyable gathering at University College, Bangor, today and a good crowd at Llanfairfechan this evening. A poll in the *Daily Mail* gives Labour a narrow lead. Uncertainty prevails.

Friday, 4 May 1979

I was too hard pressed to write a note on the eve of poll or yester-day. On the eve, I really thought my support would falter; the Liberals were triumphant on television and their postering locally was excellent. My meetings at Conwy and Llandudno were only moderately well attended.

On polling day, my president, Fred Sunter, and I toured the polling booths and committee rooms from 7.30 a.m. When we arrived at Conwy at 5 p.m. we were told that exactly the same number had voted by that time as had voted in October 1974 but that this time I had 37 per cent of the votes cast compared with 32 per cent five years ago. This was the first cheerful indication I had of the impending result.

Enid sent me to bed at 8 p.m. and I slept until midnight. Then we went down to the count at Aberconwy School. It was soon obvious from the voting paper bundles that I was in the lead and the final result was the best I have ever achieved.

After the declaration, we had a quick celebration at the Ravenhurst Hotel with the Carringtons and other supporters. Then I retired to bed about 4 a.m. to be woken by a BBC driver at 7.30 a.m. and taken to their Bangor studios to do interviews in both languages almost non-stop all day.

It has been a great victory for us in the country. We have also done very well in Wales to gain Anglesey, Brecon and Radnor, and Montgomeryshire. This brings our total number of seats in Wales to 11.

Nick Edwards will probably get the job of secretary of state. My only concern is whether to accept an under-secretaryship if offered. The thought of replying to all those adjournment debates in the early hours is very off-putting.

Sunday, 6 May 1979

Michael Jopling, the new chief whip, telephoned me this morning. He said, 'Margaret would very much like you to be a parliamentary secretary at the Welsh Office.' He told me that Michael Roberts would also have a similar post. This cheered me up and I accepted, as one must in these circumstances.

I telephoned Michael and Nick Edwards who suggested we meet in London on Tuesday morning to get down to business, division of responsibilities, a Welsh insert in the Queen's Speech etc.

It was indeed a famous victory. We had a clear majority of 43 over all other parties and a national swing of 5.6 per cent from Labour to Conservative. Reading Margaret's own account of it later, I was touched by the fact that there was some concern about her voice which, typically, she mentions only to deny it any significance. She had scented victory about the same time as I did. I was horrified to read of her conflict with the party chairman, Peter Thorneycroft, and of his proposal to bring back Ted Heath at one point to rescue the campaign. It was after all Margaret's chance – Ted had lost three elections – and it was her victory too.

I must explain my seeming reluctance to take office. I had long come to the conclusion that I did not have the egotistic drive to take me to the highest peaks of politics. I was not forceful or single-minded enough. My colleague Michael Roberts once kindly and euphemistically described me as 'a scholar and a gentleman'; I certainly preferred to belong to that genre of mankind rather than the nakedly ambitious, self-seekers and go-getters who infest political life. But humility contains its own strength. Besides, I loved Wales and its people and my party needed me. I could hardly refuse to serve.

Sea of Troubles

The areas of responsibility allocated to me were little different from the list I had drawn up for myself before the meeting with the secretary of state, Nicholas Edwards, my fellow parliamentary under secretary of state, Michael Roberts, and the permanent secretary, Sir Hywel Evans. They were health, local government, housing, water, the Welsh language, the arts and tourism. Michael, a former headmaster, was a natural choice for education. He also took responsibility for the roads programme – the biggest part of transport – and planning. The secretary of state took personal responsibility for industry and agriculture and he had overall responsibility for all our spheres as well. We decided to meet every morning at nine.

On Monday, 14 May I was the first to arrive for dinner at No. 10 and to hear the Queen's Speech, read by the Cabinet secretary, Sir John Hunt, in advance of the opening session of the new Parliament next day. I was a few minutes early and Ian Gow (Con., Eastbourne), the PM's parliamentary secretary whipped me into his office to chat with Richard Ryder (Con., Norfolk Mid). Then I was directed upstairs to be greeted by Margaret, resplendent in a pale blue evening gown. When she asked me how I was, I said: 'Surviving!'

She was taken aback by my rather flat response. She was still wildly elated by the election results. Curiously, when I went with colleagues to Buckingham Palace to meet the Queen nine days later, Her Majesty's last quiet, unforgettable words to us before she left for dinner were: 'I hope you all survive.' I did not know then that I would outlive Margaret herself in government and survive in office for more than fifteen years.

Being the only Welsh speaker in the government, I was sharply aware of my unique position and had already thought of answers to the most pressing problems related to the language. The Welsh Language Society (Cymdeithas yr Iaith Gymraeg), largely composed

127

of young people but backed behind the scenes by Plaid Cymru academics and politicians, was busy defacing road signs because the Welsh place name came second to the English. It degraded the language in their eyes. My simple and very practical answer was to give priority to the Welsh-language place name in those counties like Gwynedd where Welsh speakers formed the majority of the population and to give the English version precedence in places like Gwent where English predominated. The policy was introduced without fuss soon after we came into office and the campaign of defacing road signs petered out.

But this was only one aspect of the language problem. It extended to education, broadcasting, housing and other facets of Welsh life. The country's rural and religious life, the bulwarks of the language, had been in continual decline throughout my early years. The war, which increased people's mobility and disrupted families, had hastened the decline of churches, chapels and their Sunday schools and Welsh popular culture had suffered. If the people had abandoned God, they had not abandoned the state. 'The State is the march of God through the world,' Hegel had said, and under Labour it had certainly marched through Wales.

The inevitable reaction to linguistic and cultural decline culminated in the nationalist leader, Saunders Lewis's disturbing broadcast in 1962 *The Fate of the Language (Tynged yr Iaith)*. He urged that it should be made impossible to conduct the business of local or central government unless Welsh was treated on a par with English. Although he said that this was a policy for a movement to pursue rather than individuals, many zealots, backed by the Welsh Language Society, were inspired to fight for their rights through the courts. The principle of the equal validity of both languages was enshrined in the Welsh Language Act of 1967 but the act stated that, in the event of a semantic dispute, the English text should prevail. This concession of superiority to English soured the atmosphere. Spirited protests flared up at the least provocation.

We Conservatives had pledged ourselves to support the language in our Welsh election manifesto. If only we could divert the energy devoted to destructive protest into more constructive efforts to support the language, the sensible core of the population – Welsh and non-Welsh speakers alike – would support us.

There were already a number of voluntary and non-political organizations working in this field: the National Eisteddfod, the Welsh League of Youth (Urdd Gobaith Cymru), the Nursery School Movement (Mudiad Ysgolion Meithrin), the Welsh Books Council and others. Support for them would be consistent with our Conservative beliefs. The state helps those who help themselves.

I propounded my views to Nick Edwards who agreed the policy and we both spoke to it at the Welsh party conference at Llandrindod Wells in June. Later that year Nick secured half a million pounds of new money from the chief secretary to the Treasury, John Biffen, to implement the policy in the following year. I interviewed represen-tatives of the voluntary bodies, always saying at some point: 'Supposing the government were able to help financially, what would your priorities be?' I could not tell them of the new money we had in our back pocket because it had not yet been announced. They were all bubbling with creative ideas, except the Welsh Language Society who said: 'This government will never have money to help the language. Never ever.' I had no alternative but to let them stew in their own prejudice.

In April 1980, the secretary of state made a ground-breaking, heartening speech on Welsh-language policy before Gwynedd County Council at Maenan (where Edward the First had resettled the monks who occupied the site of the castle he was to build at Conwy in 1285). Things were looking up for the language; there were grounds for hoping that the tide of decline might be turned with the support of a surprisingly sympathetic state. The predominantly nationalistic audience for the speech was certainly surprised by its tone and content.

I had also thought hard about broadcasting, which had long since replaced the pulpit as the nation's forum; sons of the manse, like myself, had taken to it like ducks to water. There were Welsh-language programmes on BBC and HTV – the Welsh commercial broadcaster – but, although the competition was healthy and stimulating to programme makers, a political demand had developed for the concentration of these programmes on one national channel. Successive commissions and committees – Annan, Crawford, Siberry – had endorsed this proposal for a Welsh national service and the Labour government had accepted the principle. The problem was how to finance such a service. The Labour government had no answer.

The fourth channel was becoming available and ITV were keenly bidding for it. One of their arguments in favour of the allocation of the channel to them was that it would enable them to produce more programmes for minority audiences, including Welsh speakers. It struck me that if the ITV companies, who at that time were still raking in good profits, could afford to produce extra Welsh programmes, they should be able to sustain a basic national service for Wales. I discussed the idea with Nick Edwards who told me to see Willie Whitelaw, the shadow home secretary.

'Will it work?' asked Willie.

'There is no reason why it should not.'

On 23 May 1977, I staked our claim to the proposal on the floor of the House:

> I suggest that the proper solution is for both BBC and HTV Welsh programmes to be transmitted on the Fourth Channel under the control of the IBA . . . The IBA would bear the capital and operating costs of transmission while the BBC and HTV would bear their own production costs as they do now. (*Hansard*, Column 1083)

I also proposed that the BBC should 'continue transmitting selected programmes on its main Welsh channel and thus maintain the Welsh language presence on that channel in accordance with the Annan recommendation . . .' The last proposal was a safety measure, in case the fourth channel failed. There was no certainty that it would be a success. I had after all witnessed the bankruptcy of the Wales, West and North Company (Teledu Cymru) in the early 1960s.

In October 1977, Lord Harlech, chairman of HTV, argued in his company's annual report for the allocation of the fourth channel to ITV for mixed-language broadcasting in Wales. A summary of our views appeared in the Conservative policy bible, *Campaign Guide Supplement 1978*:

> The Government's attitude to the establishment of the Fourth Channel in Wales is favourable in principle but it claims that the resources are not available in the current financial climate. In contrast, Mr Roberts's proposals would allow a rapid establishment of the Fourth Channel at little or no extra cost to the public.

The Welsh manifesto of 1979 contained a commitment to implement this policy.

This was to have been the crowning glory of our new Welsh-language policy and a shattering blow to our nationalist opponents. Alas, we had reckoned without Willie Whitelaw's infinite capacity to vacillate – in the face of determined opposition from civil servants (notably Mrs Littler) – and our own inability in the Welsh Office to dictate broadcasting policy to the Home Office.

Welsh Office ministers were not consulted about the proposal to abandon our policy but there had been some discussion at Cabinet level by the time Willie asked to see me on Tuesday, 11 September 1979. I had an awful feeling before the meeting that the battle had already been lost and that I was the last man left on the field.

> However, I began by telling Willie [I noted four days later] that we were flying in the face of successive reports – Annan, Crawford and Siberry – and our own manifesto commitment. He appreciated this and said 'but you would lose out if you only had one channel for Welsh-language programmes'. It emerged that it was planned to produce about ten hours on BBC2 and twelve hours on ITV2 and to have consultative machinery to prevent programme clashes.

On the whole it was a reasonable deal but I warned Willie that there would be a public outcry over the volte-face. Willie's clinching argument turned on the future safety of the language and I had to admit that it would be safer on the two established channels than on one channel, unknown and untested as yet.

Willie announced his change of policy three days later at Cambridge and there were immediate howls of protest from Labour and Plaid Cymru. The Welsh Language Society announced a campaign of protest. We had handed them a just cause on a plate. We had broken a manifesto promise. The language was again a political football and we had started the game with an own goal. I did not consider resigning because the wrongdoing was not mine.

In January 1980 Willie told a deputation of MPs and others, led by Geraint Morgan, the Conservative MP for Denbigh, that he alone was responsible for the change of policy. By this time, many people, including Plaid MPs, were refusing to pay their licence fees.

At the end of May, Gwynfor Evans, the ex-MP and now president of Plaid Cymru, threatened to fast – Gandhi fashion – until the government changed its mind over the fourth channel. I made light of it at first: the man suffered from a martyr complex. On 31 May, I experienced half a dozen excited and frightened young demonstrators shouting abuse and throwing fourth channel pamphlets at me in the rain when I visited the Urdd Eisteddfod at Abergele. But there was an altogether nastier, more sinister campaign going on at the same time – the burning of holiday homes. There had been some thirty cases of arson and no arrests. The arsonists managed to avoid the homes where the police had set cameras to trap them. My diary takes up the story.

Thursday, 19 June 1980

Gwynfor Evans's threatened fast is having its effect on Whitehall. Willie Whitelaw called me this evening as I was about to leave the House and we went to his room. Of Gwynfor, he said, 'I am rather fond of the old man . . . we must fudge the issue. Nick saw me after cabinet this morning . . . your permanent secretary is worried. We must look for a way out.' I pointed out that the present Broad-casting Bill did not rule out the concentration of Welsh programmes on the fourth channel – I had said so during the second reading debate in reply to an intervention by Dafydd Elis-Thomas. Willie said he would get his officials to look at the point urgently because the bill comes up for report and third reading on Tuesday. Lord Goronwy Roberts greeted Michael and myself in the members' canteen with the gladiators' 'Ave Caesar, morituri te salutant' (Hail Caesar, we who are about to die salute you). There was no doubt that he was referring to Gwynfor. Many think he is serious about his threat. It will inspire a less noble breed to violence.

The Speaker has offered to go and talk to him. The archbishop has supported Gwynfor's stand.

My colleague, Michael, having in the past been in favour of the change from the manifesto policy, is now fearful of the consequences. Nick hammered him on the point and admitted that I was the only one who had expressed strong reservations about abandoning our commitment.

Sunday, 29 June 1980

Gwynfor's threatened fast continues to cause concern. In last Wednesday's debate, Willie said he would ask the BBC and IBA to report after the first year of operating the government's plan and 'if they prove the government wrong, we shall be prepared to make changes'. The offer was spurned by the gladiator of Llangadog.

These are the options as I see it. Either we return to the manifesto or keep that as an option for the future, which is the course we are currently committed to, or we stick to our guns and the two-channel solution – a course we are also committed to. Both lay us wide open to political pressure over a long period.

The deteriorating economic and industrial situation will exacerbate feeling and Gwynfor's fast will become symbolic of our heartlessness and obduracy as a government. His life will be equated – we may be sure – with the life of Wales, the nation and its people.

To find myself going back on a political promise is a novel experience for me and an uncomfortable one.

Sunday, 20 July 1980

Something of a rough house at Swansea yesterday with two or three thousand milling about outside the Patti Pavilion where the PM spoke at 11.45 a.m. She wore a blue dress with large red spots, 'just in case someone throws a tomato,' she said as she paced the anteroom, slowly, calmly and in complete silence, before going on stage. She had a very good line in her speech about the values she had worn all her life coming into their own again, like an old dress from the wardrobe coming back into fashion.

The party conference was well attended but it was the demonstration that made the news. The fourth channel protestors were there in force but they were greatly outnumbered by the Rent-a-Mob crowd drawn in by the left from heaven knows where.

I saw Barbara Castle at the Dragon Hotel. Later, I heard her on radio addressing the demonstrators. 'Welsh Conservatives!' she cried, 'the two are contradictory!'

Wednesday, 16 July 1980

At the Welsh Grand Committee, Nick outlined a proposal for a Welsh Language Television Committee. This will be incorporated in the Broadcasting Bill. It is nothing new to Nick and myself since we argued for it with the Home Office months ago – in vain. The new committee was presented as a lifeline for Gwynfor who is still talking about his death fast.

Sunday, 27 July 1980

Nick has been under severe stress the last week or so, ever since someone placed a firebomb in his son's bedroom at home in Gwent. Sir Anthony Meyer has put down an early day motion requesting the government to reconsider their fourth channel decision in Wales. Worried about the political consequences in the aftermath of Gwynfor's death fast, Nick and I saw Willie on Wednesday morning (23 July). Change of course would mean delaying the legislation, said Willie. It would also mean scraping £10 million from somewhere to cover extra costs and Nick preparing a paper for 'H' Committee. Willie promised not to oppose but it was clearly a difficult proposition.

I could feel both men shying away from it. Later we attended a Welsh Conservative MPs meeting. Young Best sided with Geraint Morgan who is very critical of the government. Sir Anthony was non-committal. At an IBA dinner that evening, Edmund Dell, former secretary of state for trade in the Labour government and now heading the subsidiary which is to run the fourth channel in the UK, said that he appreciated the political jam we were in but there was a financial penalty that would have to be paid if we changed course.

Sir Brian Young, director-general of the IBA, reinforced Dell's argument against change. Not only would the Welsh fourth channel be a write-off as far as advertising was concerned but there would be a massive switch of aerials by non-Welsh-speaking viewers in the populous north-east and south Wales to the English fourth channel in Granadaland and the West Country.

Sir Brian said that the IBA already subsidized Welsh programmes to the tune of £2 million and intended a further subsidy of £3 million from 1982 (by abatement of the rental paid by the contractor) but there would have to be a further contribution from the total budget of the channel if we reverted to our manifesto commitment. These are telling arguments.

We met Welsh Conservative MPs again on Thursday evening (24 July) and all agreed to toe the line except Geraint Morgan who blamed us for having made the manifesto commitment in the first place. Nick tore into him because he had not objected when the manifesto was in draft. Morgan's chip on the shoulder is as big as the hunchback of Notre Dame's.

Yesterday, protestors greeted me outside my surgery in Bangor. The presence of small children worried me; they could have been trampled under foot.

Dafydd Wigley, Plaid MP for Caernarfon is threatening chaos and attributing the fourth channel debacle to the devolution referendum defeat.

Saturday, 2 August 1980

My neighbour, Tomi Glyn Ucha, came to see me at home this morning. He feels strongly about the fourth channel issue although he is essentially a genial, fun-loving soul. He is one of the Plaid members who has refused to pay his television licence fee and is prepared to go to prison if necessary. I told him that we were living in a state of flux and that there might be a change of policy. He should keep out of prison.

Thursday, 7 August 1980

The eve of the summer recess and I sit here on the second floor of Gwydyr House waiting for some Parliamentary Answers I must sign. I got to bed at 6.50 a.m. and was up again at 8 a.m. for a fairly busy day. The sunset beams are warm on my shoulders. It has been a dreadful week at the House. We lost control of the summer adjournment and Consolidated Fund Bill debates and lost Tuesday's business. We recovered our ground on Wednesday with an all-night sitting.

Nick went to the National Eisteddfod and braved the fourth channel protestors. They threw themselves in front of his car, putting themselves in great danger. I am glad the recess is near. None of us could take much more of this.

Saturday, 30 August 1980

The economic outlook remains grim with fresh redundancies declared every day. Gwynfor's fast looms horribly but his water and salt diet – I read – has changed to water and glucose. I am saying little on the issue because I cannot trust Willie to stand firm on anything but I gave an interview to the *Daily Telegraph* which was fairly reported. I defended the government's position.

Thursday, 11 September 1980

Nick returned from America at lunchtime yesterday to join Willie Whitelaw in seeing the archbishop, Lord Cledwyn and Sir Goronwy Daniel, ex-permanent secretary at the Welsh Office. Nick gave me a copy of a paper he had written on holiday which concluded that the government had to change its mind on the fourth channel for purely political reasons – impending lack of support in the Lords and among Welsh Conservatives in the Commons and pressure from outside.

On Sunday, I went to see Dafydd Jones-Williams, the former local government ombudsman, to ask him, on behalf of the home secretary, if he would chair the proposed Welsh Language Television Committee. He was critical of the government's handling of the issue but agreed to consider our request. If he accepted, he said it would only be from a sense of duty. I advised Willie not to reveal his name at the meeting with Cledwyn yesterday but it came out. Everyone, including the Liberals, is now in on the act of trying to get the government to change its mind.

Gwynfor's publicity has taken off like a balloon. ITN's Glyn Mathias interviewed me on Monday and told me over lunch: 'This is my last chance to deal fairly with the issue. From now on it will be the Gwynfor story . . . will he, won't he, fast to death etc.'

The only part of my interview transmitted was a statement that we wanted people to live for the language, not die for it. They have licked us hollow in the publicity battle because they have the more newsworthy story. We can only react to it now.

What interests me most at this point is the psychoanalytical aspect. Gwynfor claims to be dying for the language. He is really dying with it as surely as a grieving widow. It's a kind of suttee. His followers have identified themselves with him but cannot follow him to death. Extreme disorder and violence will be the substitute.

Saunders Lewis, the nationalist hero, has told people to abandon television altogether. Return your sets to the makers – that is his message.

All this emotion has been translated into political terms. The government and television have been cast as the great killers. Television studios have been attacked; slogans have been daubed on magistrates' courts; some have gone to prison for refusing to pay their television licences.

If the government is to change course yet again, then the matter must go back to cabinet. The chancellor is known to be against the fourth channel anyway and Willie must fear that the entire argument will be reopened. Willie gummed up the works last session with the failure of his Official Information Bill. He is trying to foist the decision on Nick but the responsibility for abandoning the manifesto commitment is his and his alone. He is in a very hot seat indeed.

Saturday, 13 September 1980

Gwynfor has announced that if the government concentrate all Welsh programmes on the fourth channel he will give up his fast, subject to the 'small print' and other conditions being met – twenty-five hours per week, adequate financing etc. Nick telephoned me and confirmed his anxiety to accept. Willie too favours acceptance and wants an announcement as early as next Wednesday (17 September). I advised extreme caution. Nick's agitated state of mind worries me. I fear he and Willie will be trapped in another cock-up.

Sunday, 20 September 1980

I have just returned from a few days' break in Germany. In my absence the government – that is Willie and Nick – have completed their oval turn on the fourth channel issue and declared that the television licence fee must be raised by a £1 to finance the project.

'Silly Willie' proclaimed the *Sun* newspaper, but Gwynfor can now feast rather than fast.

Tuesday, 23 September 1980

I saw Nick in London yesterday before he left again for the US today. He was more relaxed. Apparently, they had tried to get me back from Germany and paged me at Frankfurt airport but missed me by five minutes – thank God! They had to go ahead with Wednesday's announcement because they wanted time to prepare amendments to insert in the Broadcasting Bill in the Lords where the government would have been defeated had it stuck to its proposals. Lord Belstead, the Home Office minister in the Lords, had assured them of that.

So it was the prospect of defeat in the Lords that proved to be the final turn of the screw necessary to get the government to revert to its Welsh manifesto commitment to establish the core of a national service for the Welsh-speaking minority. As far as I was concerned, and Nick Edwards too, conscience played some part in it. We did not like breaking promises and fought against it as hard as we dared.

It is not easy now to appreciate the uncertainty that surrounded the whole fourth channel venture in the UK. Its success was not assured. As far as Wales was concerned, the Broadcasting Bill wisely provided that in the event of failure the Welsh programmes would revert to the two-channel system for their presentation to the public. In the event, the Welsh service – S4C (Sianel Pedwar Cymru) – succeeded beyond all expectations. Typically, Willie Whitelaw admitted later that he had been wrong to oppose it. The Home Office too consulted the Welsh Office on Welsh broadcasting matters from then on.

There was more than a tinge of sadness in the whole business for me because the Conservative government gained minimal credit for the establishment of the Welsh service. The hero of the hour and for many years to come was the gladiator-cum-martyr, Gwynfor, with his will and determination. The beneficiaries were his nationalist followers and the lesson of his example was not lost upon them. Our Welsh-language policy would have to be rebuilt against a background of suspicion and hostility among those it was intended to serve.

Pussyfooting

Every department had its complement of ministers, headed by a secretary of state. Below him were ministers of state and below them, parliamentary under secretaries of state, shortened to PUSS and referred to by that acronym within government. We were the government's foot soldiers. We deputized for our secretaries of state, attended cabinet committees when he was not available, sat on the front bench in standing committees dealing with bills, took oral questions, answered debates and authorized answers to written questions.

Some wag said very unfairly that Pusses were like mushrooms – kept in the dark and showered with manure from time to time. The truth is that we received most of the papers circulating within Whitehall whether they concerned our departmental responsibilities or not and were consequently well aware of what was going on across the board. We had offices at the Commons as well as our department's headquarters – in our case, Gwydyr House – and lunched and dined there most days when the House was sitting.

Gwydyr House, which fronted on Whitehall just beyond the Ministry of Defence, derived its name from the sixteenth-century home of the Wynn family at Llanrwst on the borders of my constituency. It was an old building and the lift – one of the slowest in London – was pushed up from below rather than drawn up from above. The secretary of state occupied the first floor, I the second and my colleague Michael the third. My room was very spacious compared with the anteroom occupied by my private secretary, Richard Mason, and his typist, but there was nothing we could do to adjust the spatial balance. Michael and I shared a car and driver who would take us and our precious papers to our meetings in other departments and occasional engagements elsewhere in London.

The Cabinet Office, where many ministerial committee meetings were held, was just across the road from us and simply involved a dash with one's briefing folder across the Whitehall traffic. Behind the Cabinet Office building's modern façade and the security entrance was the old Cockpit Passage, with suits of armour, swords and pikes and, at the far end, two large portraits of fighting cocks, one of them titled *Old Tradgon*. The inner sanctum, where our meetings were held, was a gallery of portraits of our bewigged eighteenth-century predecessors. The deck of tables around which we sat enclosed the well-worn, smaller table used by William Pitt's Cabinet.

Our 'Old Tradgon' was the Lord Chancellor, Quintin Hailsham. He chaired the Legislation Committee, which gave the final authorization for the publication of bills when all departmental differences had been resolved. It decided in which House they were to be introduced – Lords or Commons – and how they were to be handled. Both chief whips attended, along with the leaders of both Houses, the chief secretary to the Treasury and other key ministers.

Quintin, who always signed his letters with a beautifully elaborate 'Q' or his full title of 'Hailsham of St Marylebone' in his immaculate, copperplate hand, always arrived for the committee with his folder in a canvas bag, slung schoolboy fashion around his neck. It was a hangover from the days when he used to cycle around Whitehall. He could be formidable in the chair. I once heard him thunder at a cowering minister whose bill proved faulty: 'Nothing discredits a government more than failure to get its legislation!' They were memorable words. I have never forgotten them.

Quintin could be endearingly amusing. On one occasion, before the start of the meeting, he sang in perfect pitch the entire 'Marsellaise' as rendered by the Free French in the Congo. It was a bravura performance at 10.25 a.m.

Willie Whitelaw, deputy prime minister as well as home secretary, was a mischievous chairman of committees. If he disliked the views being expressed by a minister, usually at excessive length, he would roll his eyes to heaven and pull faces, which had the rest of us in stitches. Then, suddenly, he would lash out at the offending minister with pretence at anger that left the minister nonplussed. Such meetings seldom lasted more than an hour and were an effective way of conducting government business.

Cabinet Committee meetings chaired by the prime minister took place around the Cabinet table at No. 10. I had attended two such Economic Committee meetings by the end of October 1979. At the first, the PM totally demolished a paper on pit closures produced by the secretary of state for energy, David (now Lord) Howell, and rightly so, I thought. The PM gave me my chance to contribute to the discussion and I said that the closures should be presented more positively, as part of the coal industry's reconstruction. At the second meeting I attended, she snapped the chancellor's head off when he referred to a subcommittee with the acronym 'FANG'. 'Get rid of it,' she said. She went on and on about it until poor Geoffrey Howe (now Lord) must have felt quite ashamed of himself – like a small boy who had wetted his trousers in class.

While the government wrestled with the major problems of rising inflation, reducing the increase in public expenditure planned by its optimistic predecessor before growth faltered and coping with a thirteen-week steel strike, I laboured alongside John Stanley (now Rt. Hon. Sir) and Geoffrey Finsberg on our flagship Housing Bill. It gave sitting tenants the right to buy their council homes at favourable discounts.

John, essentially a shy man but an easily irritated perfectionist, knew his bill and his subject backwards and we made progress in Standing Committee with only one very late-night sitting before securing a guillotine. A feast of bacon sandwiches, provided by the whips in an adjoining room punctuated the late night. Gerald Kaufman, who was leading for Labour on the committee, was invited to join us and he did, unaccustomed as he may well have been to the non-kosher fare.

A mystery woman sat in the press section of our committee room throughout our lengthy proceedings. Later, this lady, Monica Ferman, published a detailed description of the participants in the *New Statesman* (21 November 1980). She said that I dealt with amendments with 'the panache of a steamroller', flattening everything in its path. The description caught on with lobby journalists who added their own embellishments as the years wore on. We had completed third reading and report before the May Bank Holiday (4 May). John dined the Conservative members of the committee at his home and we had a wonderful meal prepared by his wife, Susan. The pudding pastry was angelic and the fruit within was out of this world.

The news, which broke in mid-November 1979, that Sir Anthony Blunt, Keeper of the Queen's Pictures, had confessed to being the arch-traitor behind Philby, Burgess and Maclean interested me greatly after my experience of our betrayal in Vienna thirty years before. It was sad that all this treachery had gone on for so long and that the guilty man had been so dangerously close to the Queen.

There was a hushed silence in the House as the Attorney-General, Sir Michael Havers, described the scene at Blunt's house when the Security Service was interviewing him for the eleventh time. For the eleventh time he denied his involvement, 'and then he was offered the immunity [from prosecution]. He rose from his chair, looked out of the window, poured himself a drink . . .' At this point the House collapsed with laughter. Perhaps that was Michael's intention.

Talk at the Savile Club was of loyalty to one's friends and the E. M. Forster theme that this was at least as sacred as loyalty to one's country. (Graham Greene apparently took the same view of his friendship with Philby.) The 'climate of treason' that gripped the 1930s persisted for decades after. Distrust of the intelligence services is still with us.

The closure of Shotton steelworks in north-east Wales had been agreed before the strike. Shotton was the victim of overcapacity in the industry and the dilatoriness of the British Steel Corporation in dealing with it. More redundancies were necessary later in south Wales and elsewhere before the industry became internationally competitive. People felt a special sympathy for Shotton, partly because the plant might have survived had it not been nationalized and partly because Shotton people were special.

I saw this for myself when about forty of them came to London to make their plea to Sir Keith Joseph. I sat beside him and listened. When their spokesman, the chief executive of Clwyd County Council, went on too long, Keith stopped him and invited the others to speak. They all did, briefly and in an impressively measured way. Keith, who had a persistently bad throat and sipped tea with honey, whispered to me: 'These are very good people.' They could not have had a better hearing or a better listener than Keith who understood their position and their feelings. But there was no turning back, no U-turn to save them.

I attended the cabinet committee Keith chaired in November 1979 when trouble brewed at the Govan shipyards. The Scottish secretary, George Younger (the late Lord) put a strong case for a dicey deal to stave off trouble.

'We have a choice between two evils,' I said to Keith as we emerged.

'That is our business as politicians,' he replied, 'choosing between evils.'

One sensed the puritanism of the man.

Those of us who had been first elected in 1970 celebrated a decade in the Commons with a dinner at St Stephen's Club in June 1980 and the prime minister as our guest. Margaret was in a flirtatious mood and positively glowed when she spoke of the decade ahead. Chancellor Schmidt of Germany, who had recently visited the UK, had told her that her government's economic policies were right. Her fresh approach to the country's problems was gaining approval in Europe. She welcomed particularly the return to self-reliance as opposed to dependence on central government. But could we expect 60 million people to be self reliant, I wondered.

These policies were tough and uncompromising and not everyone in the Tory Party endorsed them. A few weeks earlier, an anonymous article had appeared in the *Observer* describing Margaret as 'didactic, tart and obstinate'. It was personally hurtful to her and the anonymity branded the author as cowardly. He was clearly a 'wet', and belonged to the soft heart of the party. Julian Critchley (Con., Aldershot) came under suspicion and soon owned up to being the author. Curiously, although many of us had our private doubts of one sort or another about the policies and suspected that the British people had become too soft under socialism to take such harsh medicine, this snide, personal attack on Margaret rallied us strongly to her side. Julian became an isolated figure, lunching early and alone at the long Conservative table in the members' dining room.

The PM asked to see me at No. 10 on the Monday of party conference week in 1980. (Nick was away in the US drumming up investment for Wales.) When she sat down on the edge of her settee and beckoned me to take a chair, I had no idea what subject she was going to raise. It was typical of her thorough knowledge of what was going on – or not going on – under her administration, that she had discovered that Anglesey's local authority was prevented under the government's Local Government Bill from using the half a million pounds of revenue they received from the Shell oil terminal at Amlwch. I guessed from her quiet tone and demeanour that she wanted the council to have use of the money. I was not mistaken and she left it to me to ensure that a way was opened for the council.

The obvious explanation for her interest was that Keith Best, the lad from Brighton who had scored a remarkable triumph by winning Anglesey in 1979, was still recovering from a dreadful road accident in August in which his woman agent had been killed. Warned by friends at the hospital that Keith intended to hold a press conference at his bedside although he was suspected of having a fractured skull, I had rushed to see him and dissuade him if possible.

He had been remarkably cool and composed. Margaret never mentioned him by name and neither did I. 'Women are devious,' I noted afterwards, 'and she is no exception.'

On his return, Nick took over the issue of the Anglesey oil terminal revenues and advised the PM that there was no way the new legislation could be circumvented. The PM reluctantly accepted his advice. Nevertheless, she thought a political mistake had been made. Soon afterwards, the Lords carried an amendment to the legislation that allowed such revenues to be spent by a local authority. Anglesey had won.

By the summer of 1980, I had decided to leave the Savile Club, convivial as it was, and take a flat in Little Smith Street within easy walking distance of the Houses of Parliament. It was not easy to give up Gordon Chittenden's morning cup of tea. (Gordon had joined the Royal Navy as a boy of fourteen – he fibbed about his age – and had seen action in the Battle of Jutland. He was seventy-eight years old and got up at five every morning. He shamed us all.)

I spent a summer evening with Professor G. P. 'Chip' Wells, the genial son of H. G. Wells, who also lived at the club. When I mentioned how my father always used a broad, steel-nib ink pen, he quoted an advertising couplet from the 1920s that identified it perfectly:

> They came as a boon and blessing to men –
> The Pickwick, the Owl and the Waverley pen.

All three – Pickwick, Owl and Waverley – were different kinds of pen made by the same company.

Wynford Vaughan Thomas had been in the club earlier with Kingsley Amis. I quizzed Wynford about Marie Debortes Delmar, the copious but secretive nineteenth-century French woman poet. He knew all there was to know; Kingsley had never heard of her. They had an endless litany of limericks one of which I remember:

> There was a young lady called Gloria
> Who was wronged by Sir Gerald du Maurier,
> Jack Hylton, Jack Payne, and Sir Gerald again
> Then the band of the Brixton Astoria.

Wynford showed me a copy of a ribald poem by Dylan Thomas, scribbled from memory for someone in a pub. The writing tailed

144

off drunkenly towards the end. Dylan did this kind of thing when he ran short of money.

Savile Club, Thursday, 25 September 1980

This may well be my last night here in Room 14 and, late though it is, I must make a note of my immediate environment.

To the left as one enters, there is a bachelor-size single bed and, overlooking the bed, a large oil painting of a man with an open manuscript on his knee. There have been times when I feared that this literary worthy – it turned out to be Algernon Blackwood – might fall on me as I slept but he has been as good as his trustworthy face and generous bow tie. He knows his place and has stuck to it. Also on the left wall is a drawing by R. Schwebe of the old Savile Club at 107 Piccadilly, dated 1927.

The window overlooking the garden is still open to expel the prandial odours that rise from the kitchen below. Of course, I shall miss this room although it has been little more than a place to keep one's clothes and sleep in.

Why am I moving out? Perhaps only to return and relish the pleasure of being here at some future date. To be tired of London is to be tired of life; to be tired of the Savile is impossible. But it is, after a while, rather like Aladdin trying to live in his cave of riches – too much of a good thing.

Walking the Plank

On Monday, 28 January 1981 I had lunch with the prime minister at No 10. There were eight of us in all. I was the first to arrive and tagged along with Margaret as she examined the flower arrangements. They had her approval. She had a well-watered whisky and I a gin and tonic. Then the others arrived and after some light talk, she asked one of her staff:

'Has the cook finished cooking?'

She added under her breath, 'I have to ask because things are not as they should be.'

Over lunch, she began drawing us out individually but got no further than Grey, Lord Gowrie, minister of state at the Department of Employment, who said more jobs could be created if money could be raised by nationalized industries and excluded for accounting purposes from the Public Sector Borrowing Requirement. His bow tie or his argument was a red rag to a bull. Margaret pawed the ground, charged, tossed him up and gored him until there was nothing left except the bow tie dangling from her horns.

I thought it was a waste of time on her part to concentrate on putting one of us on the right track when she could have spent the hour eliciting the views of others. But perhaps there was method in her madness. The government was at a crossroads and she was determined to show that there was no easy way out, no turning back.

Industrialists were holding on for grim death and if orders did not pick up soon, there would be massive lay-offs and redundancies. I had been warned of this at a lunch with Alcan, the aluminium company, a few days earlier. Either we would be inspired to stick to our guns by such glimmers of good news as Datsun's decision to invest in the UK or the bubble of confidence would burst.

The miners' strike in mid-February and the water workers' threat to strike added to our woes. A Radio 4 programme, presented by my erstwhile socialist friend, W. John Morgan, ended with a question to journalist, Adam Raphael, whether the lady was for turning. His reply was: 'Yes, I think the lady is for turning when she knows she's beat!' What a tip-off that was for the water workers!

The media's constant attempts to undermine Margaret and the government riled and angered me. I knew that if we lost her, we would have lost all. She remained steadfast in spite of all adversities.

Margaret came to Cardiff to address the Conservative Central Council on Saturday, 25 March. My colleague, Michael, and I went down to the Park Hotel at 10 a.m. to check her speech and were surprised, when ushered into her presence, to find her still in her dressing gown, buttoned up to her throat, and working on her speech. Ian Gow, her PPS was there and two writers. There was another younger man sitting on the floor, clearly exhausted after an all-night bash at the speech.

The PM was tearing the speech apart, line by line, word by word and shifting paragraphs about. The silence was awesome, punctuated only by her criticisms and suggestions from the writers. I contributed one amendment. The draft had: 'I do not care what people think about me. I do care what they think about my country.' She did not like it and neither did I, so I suggested it should read: 'I do not care what people say about me but I do care what they think about my country.' She preferred my version and gave me a distant, thoughtful look of appreciation.

When she had finished with the draft – an hour before she was due to deliver it – she said, 'I knew I should have stayed up last night . . . I have half a speech . . . I had better get down to some notes.' She also had to dress.

When she came to the City Hall at twelve o'clock, the welcoming cheers were overwhelming. From behind her on the platform, I could see when she deviated from the typewritten script to her copious handwritten notes. There was no difference in style or delivery and her peroration was perfect. It brought us all to our feet in a spontaneous upsurge of admiration for her incredible quality and unwavering strength. It was an immaculate performance.

By July 1981 and after the riots in Toxteth (Liverpool), Southall and elsewhere, even the PM looked weary on television. 'She has suddenly aged,' said my private secretary who had also seen her on the box. Was the strain telling on her as it was on so many colleagues? My own secretary of state, Nick Edwards, had been unwell off and on for some time. On Budget day morning, at the end of a long meeting, he had his head down on his chest and complained of pain in his stomach. Rumour had it that his liver had gone. The PM asked me about his health towards the end of the month and I told her he was suffering from exhaustion but that his indefatigable spirit would keep him going. Michael too suffered from an enlarged heart and took pills by the handful in Strangers' Bar. He had not been the same since the death of his lovely daughter, Caroline, the previous year. I struggled against the consolations of alcohol. Mercifully, I never quite succumbed.

The government reshuffle in September saw the departure of Christopher Soames, leader of the Lords, Sir Ian Gilmour, Lord Privy Seal, and Mark Carlisle, secretary of state for Education (both late Lords). Norman St John Stevas had already gone in January. But the Cabinet was still regarded as being riddled with 'wets' waiting for their chance to ditch the leader. It looked as if their time had come during the party conference at Blackpool.

Ted Heath spoke in the Wednesday economic debate and began by saying that the party faced a crisis greater than Munich, Suez or the leadership crisis of 1963–4. He called for national and inter-national measures to combat unemployment and recession. He had a mixed reception, with some booing from right-wingers who thought it bad form that he should speak at all.

Essentially, Ted's plea was for reflation, although why he should have made it again now when it had ruined his own government in the early 1970s was a mystery to most of us. However, Michael Heseltine made much the same point and got a standing ovation. Geoffrey Howe delivered the *coup de grâce* to Ted by quoting the 1970 manifesto declaration that the party in government had to stick to its policies, which we had manifestly failed to do between 1970 and 1974. 'The worst thing we could do is to lose our nerve now,' said Geoffrey tremulously.

Francis Pym embraced much of what Ted had said but pleaded for unity. I told him afterwards that his speech was a good paving stone for the PM's later in the week, uncompromising though that was. Her speech contained sentences worthy of the first Queen Elizabeth at her formidable best.

I will not change just to court popularity . . . Indeed, if a Con-servative Government starts to do what it knows to be wrong because it is afraid to do what it is sure is right, then that is the time for the Tories to cry 'Stop'. You'll never need to do that while I am Prime Minister.

This was the Blackpool 1981 version of her Brighton 'The lady's not for turning' speech the previous year.

Although the conference was reasonably smooth on the surface, things were going on behind the scenes. George Lockhead of the *Daily Telegraph* told me that there had been a gathering at River House where Ted was staying. Francis and Michael Jopling (chief whip) were reported to be present.

'Maggie's on the end of the plank and so is Geoffrey,' said George. 'If they fail, Francis will be the next leader.'

The weekend press was full of speculation.

Michael Jopling and Francis were in the tea room the following Monday, obviously taking soundings. When Ian Grist (Con., Cardiff North) said that the electorate were more disappointed with the government than anything else, Michael said:

'Yes. And when my children come home drunk, having smashed the car and so on, I say to them "I'm not angry, just disappointed with you".'

It was a homely but telling rejoinder.

When I asked Ian Mikardo (Lab., Poplar) in the smoking room whether he was taking bets on the result of Thursday's by-election at Croydon, he said he was currently running four betting books. Two of them related to the Conservative leadership. The first was when, for whatever reason, Margaret Thatcher would cease to be leader of the Conservative Party and the second was on who would replace her. The other two were on how many members the SDP and the Labour Party would each have after the next election.

Margaret was in the House later that evening but few looked her straight in the eye, I noticed.

In royal circles 1981 was a momentous year and February's announcement of Prince Charles's engagement to Lady Diana Spencer was a joyous occasion. She had been pictured in a flimsy, translucent dress with a child in her arms in a nursery garden and that photograph, along with her peek-a-boo eyes, had already endeared her to the nation. In Nick's absence in Japan, I sent the congratulatory telegram on behalf of the Welsh Office. As the prince had learnt Welsh, I wished to add something in Welsh but was dissuaded on the grounds that the Post Office would only mangle it.

On the eve of the wedding on 29 July, the whole country was in a state of high excitement. The prince was Hamlet (without the neuroses) while she was the super girl next door with an extraordinary, natural charisma. Identification with one or the other was running amok in people's consciousness; every nubile girl fancied herself as Princess Di and every mother regarded Charles as an ideal son. Whitehall was concerned about security and the concern ran deep.

On the day itself, my driver called for me at 10 a.m. Whitehall was already closed to traffic and so was the Embankment but the police let us through. When we came to another police barrier at Horseguards Avenue, I told the driver I would walk. Whitehall was almost deserted but there was a strong smell of horses after the early morning rehearsal, which gave the air a rural tang. Whenever history is in the making, I told myself, there is this scent of horses. We watched the ceremony on television at the Welsh Office. Everything seemed to go smoothly and along with the entire nation, we shared in this great family occasion.

After their honeymoon in Scotland, Charles brought Diana to north Wales at the end of October for the start of their first official visit as a married couple. I spent Tuesday, 27 October with them in Llandudno and later at Plas Newydd, the home of Henry and Shirley, the Marquis and Marchioness of Anglesey. There was much speculation in official circles about the length of time it would now take for the couple to move through the crowds of well-wishers and from one place to the next. There was even more speculation when we were told in advance of their arrival at the Conference Centre in Llandudno that there was to be no smoking in their vicinity. (Was she pregnant already?)

I found her easy to talk to and marvellous with other people. She had slept well on the royal train the previous night, she said, which pleased me because she was to spend three nights travelling the length and breadth of Wales by train. I had spent a restless night on that train myself, travelling with Prince Charles from Euston to the opening of the Britannia Bridge over the Menai Straits. My wife, Enid, said that if she could survive three days in Wales, she could survive anything. Diana captured all our hearts when she was presented with a silver tea set at Llandudno. She turned a cup upside down and looked for the hallmark. Everyone tittered. She gave her Mona Lisa smile.

I saw her again enlivening the State Opening of Parliament on 4 November. Her radiant beauty dimmed the sparkle in her tiara. She had had a good start.

Monday, 21 June 1982

A prince is born to Charles and Di at 9.03 p.m. I sent a telegram:

'Wales and the world welcome your prince for Wales. Congratulations. Llongyfarchiadau.'

The Labour Party under Michael Foot's leadership was as shambolic as Michael himself with his duffle coat and stick. The intellectual elite, the Gang of Four – Roy Jenkins, Shirley Williams, David Owen and Bill Rodgers – had broken away to form the Social Democratic Party, nicknamed the Semi Detached or the Socialist Displaced Persons Party. But they had not taken many moderate and right-wing Labour members with them and the internal battle for the soul of the Labour Party continued.

While I was concerned about Margaret's position and attempts to undermine her as early as February 1981, I found Leo Abse (Lab., Pontypool) totally obsessed with the difficulties on his own side. 'Either we succeed in changing things in the Labour Party in October or neither major party will prevail in the general election and we shall have a coalition . . . government must go on . . . and the price of the coalition will be proportional representation,' he said. I agreed that his was one of many possible scenarios.

Labour's divisiveness was a running sore and contributed to the huge decline in their majority at the Warrington by-election in July 1981 which the Liberals and SDP also contested. Michael Foot made a stirring speech at the TUC conference in September but it did not pacify Arthur Scargill and the left who were determined to have their own way even if it meant splitting the Labour Party.

Denis Healey narrowly won the deputy leadership election later in September and put paid to Tony Benn's chances for the time being. It also prevented a massive defection from the Labour right to the SDP, which could well have happened had Benn won. But, able and clever as Benn was, he never had the full confidence of the left. He was not one of them. Healey was not short of enemies either. Opposition to the government in the winter of 1981 was unfocused and disunited. It would remain so for many months to come.

James Callaghan, the former prime minister, reverted to being a backbencher with remarkable ease. He attended the Welsh Grand Committee and my colleague Michael and I often joined him at lunch in the members' cafeteria. The talk was mostly of their beloved Cardiff. I encouraged Jim to write his autobiography.

'Your shadow grows no less,' he told me once, meaning, I suppose, that I was putting on weight.

'Thank God for that, sir. I would be more worried if I was losing it.'

The Falklands crisis was a bolt from the blue. This is how I saw it develop at the time.

Friday, 2 April 1982

3 p.m. I have just returned from the Commons where Francis Pym made a statement that there was nothing further to add to what Humphrey Atkins (Lord Privy Seal) had stated at 11 a.m. There had been no invasion. Meanwhile, the BBC carried Argentinian reports that they had invaded with 2,000 troops, taken the airfield and Port Stanley.

There were few members in the House. I was only there because the payroll vote (members of the government) was whipped to defeat possible amendments to the Goods and Services Bill. Those interested scurried to photostat the Argentine navy's complement as given in *Jayne's Fighting Ships*.

I lunched with Tony Buck (Con., Colchester North) and Jim Lestor (Con., Broxtoe) in the members' dining room. John Nott (secretary of state for Defence) said in passing to another table that the invasion was not expected until 2 p.m. and that the Argentine navy was not as strong as it appeared.

There was a war cabinet this morning – Nick told me. This could be another Suez for us. So much is clear. If the Argentinians take the Islands, we shall have to take them back and that is a major undertaking. The implications for John Nott and Humphrey Atkins are also clear and Carrington too. If we muck this up, we are done for as a government.

The truth is that we cannot counter a non-nuclear threat with a nuclear one. Or can we? This is a terrible question. Most people would rule it out completely and yet . . . Why be a nuclear power at great expense if we are not prepared to use 'gunboat' diplomacy with nuclear weapons? We have used nuclear weapons before as a deterrent? Then there are the very powerful arguments against. What if the Argentinians called our bluff?

Monday 5 April 1982

It has been a terrible weekend for the party in government. Everything that I suspected on Friday has been confirmed. Humphrey Atkins had not been in touch with the governor of the Falklands at 10.30 a.m. as he told the House. (Why did Francis not correct it at 2.30 p.m.?) Now, Carrington, Atkins and Luce (Foreign Office) have resigned as they damn well should and the Foreign Office has been caught napping.

We have launched an armada to retake the Islands but there are doubts whether it is adequate.

Francis has been appointed foreign secretary and John Biffen leader of the House – both good appointments – but Francis may still have his come-uppance on Wednesday if he is pressed on whether he knew the falsehood in Humphrey's statement or not, last Friday afternoon.

I was not at the House on Saturday because I had a premonition of what might be revealed. Indeed I had reconciled myself to it on Friday. I told Ian Gow tonight that I almost offered him my services for the weekend. Such was my concern. I now wish I had.

Best remark of the evening: 'They've turned the smoking room into a job centre.' I can't remember who said it.

Wednesday, 7 April 1982

Letter to Ian Gow, prime minister's parliamentary private secretary.

My dear Ian,

1. For the next fortnight or so this is going to be a media war in the UK. My guess is that every facility will be given to the television people in the Argentine to film the shipment of troops etc. to the Falklands and the media will be inundated with this material. Someone must talk to the BBC and the IBA about balanced presentation. (Material is much easier to get from Buenos Aires than from the Task Force.)
2. Secondly there is a serious danger that the television media will adopt the same approach as they have to Northern Ireland while there is a political element in the UK that is critical of the Government. In other words they will set themselves in the judgement seat. Again, I suggest they must be talked to.
3. Although I am against political interference in the professional judgements of servicemen, bearing in mind what I have said in

paras 1 and 2, I must say to you that there must be winning moves or events, diplomatic or military, over the next fortnight to uphold the pro-Government, jingoistic mood. The alternative is defeatism from which we shall never recover either as a party or as a country.

Yours ever

PS. I began writing this last night after the PM's excellent briefing of junior ministers. What I am really saying is that we must be seen to be winning from now on in, i.e. a troopship must be sunk and so must their key destroyers before the Task Force ever arrive. Sorry to be so blunt but I mean every word.

Acknowledged by Ian on the 8 April. He said he had shown it to the PM.

Sunday, 18 April 1982

It has not been a good Easter break for me but any kind of break is better than none. It looks as if my letter to Ian Gow has been acted upon. (It was a timely warning about the effect of television media coverage on people's morale. Television showed endless footage of Argentine soldiers climbing aboard ships and little or nothing of our troops embarking and preparing for battle. It was very demoralizing.)

Tuesday, 20 April 1982

There was a combined Foreign Affairs and Defence party committee meeting tonight and Robert Rhodes James (Con., Cambridge) reported to us – ministers are not allowed to attend unless invited – that Michael Mates (Con., Hampshire East) had spoken well. Mates is an ex-military man and knows his stuff.

Mates took the view that, to secure air superiority, we had to bomb the Argentine mainland. It took about ninety minutes, he said, to turn a Harrier around on board an aircraft carrier while a Mirage fighter could be turned around much more quickly on a landing strip. But what would war on the mainland entail in all? No one knew the answer.

Jim Lestor too was dove-ish on the grounds that members had not 'thought it through'. We would have to negotiate at the end of hostilities virtually on the same basis as we had begun. There are rumours that the Cabinet is divided (Keith Renshaw, *Sunday Express*) and that Maggie should fire the dissidents. There is a Cabinet meeting this evening. My guess is that most will toe the line for fear of dismissal or being accused of abandoning their posts in the country's hour of need.

Thursday, 22 April 1982

It has been a curiously quiet week with the Falklands problem hovering in the background of everyone's mind. I had lunch by chance with Jim Callaghan earlier this week. He was all for quick and decisive action. Colleague Michael has been quite the reverse and highly dubious about any action to support 'the sheep-shaggers' as he calls them.

Monday, 26 April 1982

Good news from the Falklands in that we have taken the dependency of South Georgia. The PM did well in the House today and tonight on *Panorama*. Someone said that the reaction in the chamber was muted and so it was. We know that the fate of the government hangs on the fortunes of war and we do not relish it.

Yesterday, I read the lesson at St John's Methodist Church, Llandudno. The first verse was ominous:

'But the end of all things is at hand; be ye therefore sober and watch unto prayer' (1 Peter IV: 7).

Dined with Sir Derek Walker Smith (Con., Hertfordshire East) who explained what David Owen had been driving at when he questioned the PM. We could vest sovereignty of the Falklands in the United Nations and secure trusteeship of them. (A neat solution but a lengthy process. Any disposal of sovereignty would be anathema to the PM.)

Wednesday, 28 April 1982

I have returned to the flat early because I have a rare chance of a respite. We have announced today that there will be an air blockade over the Falklands as from midday Friday. I gather from Nick that Haig, the US secretary of state, has put some non-negotiable terms to both sides, which are being kept secret for the time being. If the Argentinian junta accept them, we shall have political difficulties at home. If they reject them, then the path to independent action on our part is cleared. But the position is probably more complex. I am only surmising from what Nick told Michael and myself in the strictest confidence this afternoon.

Thursday, 29 April 1982

I was elevated by tonight's Commons debate on the Falklands. I listened to it on the BBC's London Radio and heard rather more of it than if I had been at beck and call in the House. It was a very fair debate but, listening to it, I felt impelled to telephone the whip to say that not enough had been made of the troops' position and the urgent need to get them ashore from the very high seas battering them. Francis did cover the point briefly at the end of the debate.

Tuesday, 4 May 1982

The inevitable . . . one of our ships, *HMS Sheffield*, has been sunk. Mirage aircraft using Exocet missiles did it. It just goes to prove that we should have knocked them out on their mainland bases long before this. Maybe we will now.

I am sick almost to the point of resignation about close government control of our forces. I warned Thatcher against this. Strict political control over operational forces is suicidal.

Wednesday, 5 May 1982

It is 12.30 a.m. and the end of a long day. I attended the House this afternoon to hear the Falklands statements by Francis Pym and John Nott.

Our political control of the Task Force is not, mercifully, as tight as I had feared; they operate within a general code and considerable freedom is given to operational commanders. However, I still feel that we are pulling our punches. Our submarine could have sunk some of the ships accompanying the *General Belgrano* as well as the cruiser herself.

A small 'Stop the War' demonstration outside Downing Street – only seventy-four people, according to Keith Best who counted them.

The PM wore a dark suit for the Commons this afternoon.

My early fears about the conduct of the media have been fully justified. Jack Page (Con., Harrow) and others have complained about the BBC's excessive use of Argentine material. Colleague

Michael takes the view that it is virtually impossible to wage a modern war; the country has no stomach for it and the media ensure that it has not.

Saw Geoffrey Howe who confessed his astonishment that 'these dreadful weapons we pay so much for, actually work'.

Thursday, 6 May 1982

Two Harriers lost. The problem of establishing air superiority has always been worrying. I continue to doubt whether we can do it with Harriers operating from aircraft carriers against Mirages operating from mainland bases. The carriers are a target while the mainland bases are not. This must give the enemy an enormous advantage.

So far I have made no substantial comment on the Falklands crisis but here are some points to note.

The first is the almost accidental nature of the outbreak of hostilities. Had the Foreign Office's assessment been more accurate, we might have been able to take preventive action. I suspect that the Argentinians were led to believe by successive ministers that we were not averse to being rid of the responsibility for the islands. Some chance remarks may have led to foreign minister, Costa Mendez's advice to the junta that the islands were there for the taking.

Secondly, there is the great principle of sovereignty. If what is lawfully yours is taken by force, then you have the right to take it back (UN Article 51 and Resolution 502). There are three parts to the Resolution – cessation of hostilities, withdrawal and negotiation. We have been stressing withdrawal.

Thirdly, as colleague Michael has been pointing out, the opposition are fully safeguarded. If the government succeeds, they can reap the reward of having supported the action and if things go wrong they can castigate the government for their errors.

Finally, we are placing ourselves in the lap of the gods – the gods of war – and that is dangerous. While the PM presents herself very successfully as the wronged Boadicea, we must not forget how that lady ended her career – nobly, but not winning an election. Of course we must pursue peace initiatives but we must also beware of the enemy. Time could be on their side. Their withdrawal is a must; the alternative is invasion.

Monday, 10 May 1982

As I suspected over the weekend, we are already delaying military action – at great risk – for diplomatic reasons. There is talk of Maggie losing her premiership if things go wrong. If the inner Cabinet is composed as I believe it is, there could be a majority against the PM and direct action. Francis will play hard for any peace initiative, John Nott is not aggressive and Willie is vacillating if not timid on the key issue.

Tuesday, 11 May 1982

It looks as if we are on the verge of invading the Falklands. I do hope that we do not delay beyond the end of this week and the expiry of the UN secretary general's current peace initiative. Of course a landing is only the beginning but I have faith in our forces to make a reasonably quick job of recapturing the islands.

Thursday, 13 May 1982

We had our fifth debate on the Falklands and the split in the inner Cabinet became apparent; it is between those who favour a diplomatic and those for a military solution, between the Foreign Office and the Ministry of Defence. Heath told Pym not to heed criticism but to pursue negotiations; Powell spoke of the need to restore unity of purpose. They were far more critical of the government than anyone on the opposition benches.

I have just returned from the House. There is a curious aftertaste to the debate. John Nott did not answer Ted's point that there is little difference between the Argentinians and ourselves over the Peruvian proposals. Then there are the idiots on our side who shout 'sell-out' whenever negotiations are proposed. They lay us open to the charge of being warmongers.

Monday, 17 May 1982

The invasion is imminent and heaven knows how it will end. Abraham Lincoln provides solace:

I do the very best I can and I mean to keep on doing it until the end. If the end brings me out all right, what is said against me will not amount to anything and if the end brings me out wrong, ten angels

158

swearing I was right would make no difference. (Quoted by Stanley Baldwin in a speech on Peace and Security, 2 July 1936)

Tuesday, 25 May 1982

The invasion has happened. British troops landed at San Carlos last Friday.

A 'Vigil for Peace' has been set up in Bangor in my constituency. Of course, we are all for peace but not at any price. The terms do matter. I cannot say that war is obscene, deplorable and ignoble in all circumstances. It spells the failure of more civilized means of resolving disputes and is in that sense a relapse into barbarism.

London, Tuesday, 1 June 1982

It was a very brief Whitsun recess for me. I was called back to London to attend a meeting of the Civil Contingencies Unit under Willie's chairmanship. We faced the possibility of having to call on the services and their ambulances to counter the NHS auxiliaries' strike on Friday. The meeting was cancelled because England and Scotland said they could cope with the help of their voluntary services and the police. We stiffened our resolve to act similarly in Wales.

Today is my son Geraint's twenty-fourth birthday. We climbed up to Llyn Eigiau on Saturday and, trudging through the miles of heather, we made frequent reference to the likely conditions faced by our troops in the Falklands. Geraint, who served with the TA, should have been a professional soldier but I never pushed him in that direction. My heart is with the men of peace, including Pope John Paul who has had a tumultuous reception wherever he has gone in this country.

Alas, we do not have an international force to back mandatory UN resolutions; the League of Nations was similarly unsupported. Surely we must press for such a force now after our Falklands experience?

Much has happened since the troops landed just over ten days ago. I have kept in touch with events – the taking of Darwin and Goose Green, the death of Colonel H. Jones of No. 2 Parachute Regiment and 16 others on our side and some 250 Argentine soldiers. We are now poised to take Port Stanley and must do so.

To put it crudely, we must teach the Argentinians a lesson so that they leave us alone in future. It is a dreadful way to put things but it is basically right. Some people have to learn the hard way. The tragedy is that those who teach the hard lesson must suffer too.

Monday, 7 June 1982

I have worked non-stop since my last entry here. I thought of dining in the Savile but Reagan is staying at Claridges and the area is blocked off by bobbies. The Americans are playing fast and loose with us over the Falklands because they are interested only in protecting their own backsides in Latin America. De Gaulle never trusted them and he was right. The sooner we lick Europe into defensive shape, the better; but we do not have a common language and we do have a common mistrust. Perhaps the only way we shall achieve unity of purpose in Europe is through the Christian Church, which united us and inspired our common defence against Islam in the Middle Ages. We in Europe need a major rethink about ourselves.

Monday, 14 June 1982

The war is over. The PM made a statement after the ten o'clock division. The House was very excited and there was a row as to whether we should finish the day's business – an opposition prayer. It was not moved. The razzle-dazzle and ragbag of feelings offended me.

Wednesday, 16 June 1982

Throughout the last stages of the war, my eyes filled with tears whenever I listened to the news. True, we had some all-night sittings that drained me emotionally but the fact is that my antipathy to war has been building up throughout. What I heard towards the end – of its physical violence, the cries of men in battle – was unbearable and so were the measured attempts of commentators and reporters to ennoble the killing into anything other than the carnage that war actually is. The refinement of the process of attaining military victory only made things worse; the killing that results is more cold blooded, more calculated. Thank God, the worst is over, but we have lost 250 lives and the wounded are many. We hold 15,000 Argentinian prisoners.

Sunday, 11 July 1982

Canberra and the Royal Marines arrived home today. I cannot help feeling that the PM should have been there, thanking and welcoming each man on his return if that had been possible.

Tomorrow's commemorative service at Llandaff Cathedral for the Welsh Guards lost in the blazing inferno of the *Sir Galahad*, will be a different scene and hard to bear for many.

A Friend Falls

As 1982 drew to a close, I began a fresh volume in my diary. Glancing back through the previous volume, I saw very clearly how late nights and the relentless pressure of government business had vitiated my thoughts and actions and I concluded that I might have to pay the penalty in the reshuffle due in the New Year.

There was some speculation that Nick Edwards would have to retire because of ill health. I told him that he did not have to decide by Christmas – as he unwisely put it about. He thanked me for my offer to 'carry him' for a month or two. The press wondered who would succeed him but the speculation evaporated when he appeared to recover. The curious consequence was that Michael and I became more uncertain about our positions.

I viewed the prospect of dismissal with comparative calm. Rejection is the ultimate fate of all politicians in a democracy – I told myself. Besides, all of us in the government faced the possibility of rejection by the country in the next year or so because the election was looming and we lacked imaginative ideas with a strong appeal to the electorate. The PM had asked every department to submit positive action plans by 31 December. I had seen some drafts proposing further reform of local government and more privatization but they did not amount to a 'winning line' that would see us safely re-elected.

The reshuffle at the start of the New Year was minimal as it turned out. John Nott left Defence and Michael Heseltine took his place. Tom King took charge of the Department of the Environment. There was no change at the Welsh Office. We all resumed our speculation about the timing of the election. I favoured October rather than June because it would give more time for the economy to recover.

Amusing remarks such as the Scottish peer, James Douglas Hamilton's relieved my own total engrossment with the passage of

162

the Conwy Tunnel Bill: 'I was told that criminals, lunatics and Peers were debarred from the House of Commons. When I arrived, I found that all three groups were well represented,' said James.

The PM opened and closed the debate on the Franks Report on the Falklands War (26 January). The opposition called it a 'whitewash'. Although she spoke largely off the cuff in her wind-up, she did not falter and won the day decisively. No government, she said, had ever subjected itself to such detailed scrutiny and it accepted the committee's verdict. Her brave words rang in my ears long after.

There was a Welsh Day debate on the floor of the House on Thursday, 10 February 1983. Colleague Michael was to do the wind-up. He had done so brilliantly the previous year and earned the PM's enthusiastic compliments and an invitation for us both to join her for a celebratory drink in her room. This year's debate had a very different ending.

Thursday/Friday, 10/11 February 1983

It is 3.35 a.m. and I am at the flat. Surely I shall remember every detail of this night till the day I die but I must record them now.

About 8.30 p.m. Michael said he was going for a drink. Whether he did so or not, or simply went to his room to assemble his notes, I do not know. He returned to the front bench about 9 p.m. – certainly he heard the whole of Donald Coleman's (Lab., Neath) final speech for the opposition.

Earlier in the day, I had told my private secretary that Michael had had an unnecessarily hard week, replying to a Consolidated Fund Bill debate in the early hours of Tuesday morning, which I could have done, and replying to today's debate as well.

He got up at the despatch box shortly after 9.30 p.m. and had been speaking for less than a minute when he stopped. I thought he was searching his notes for the name of a member but he was collapsing before my eyes. I shot to my feet to support him on one side and Nick did the same on the other. Even as we tried to lower him to the bench, Nick's eyes met mine and the question flashed between us: who's going to finish this wind-up. It was never openly asked. Michael's dead weight was too much for us; we could not lift him to the bench. His body slid to the floor.

One of the messengers, Ken Butcher, appeared at my side, quickly throwing off his coat and kneeling beside Michael's prostrate body. He took off Michael's tie and tried to resuscitate him where he lay in front of the Mace. Nick had sped out of the chamber for help. I did not move from the despatch box but tried to shield my fallen friend from the press gallery where reporters were moving about to get a better view of what was happening on the floor below.

Dr Roger Thomas (Lab., Carmarthen) came down from the opposition benches and Dr Maurice Miller (Lab., East Kilbride) joined him moments later. Both pressed his chest and thumped his heart and tried to blow air into his lungs through his mouth and nose. At no time did he show signs of reviving. I saw him heave a couple of times and then the wind came out of him. His eyes and lower face were blue. A third doctor, who had been dining in the House, came on the scene. 'He's gone,' he told me.

The chief whip, Michael Jopling, strode down the centre of the chamber and gestured to the press gallery to leave us to our distress and they left sheepishly. The public gallery was quietly emptied too. My dear friend was taken away on what seemed a totally inadequate stretcher. I was about to pick up my corner of the stretcher when a messenger took it and I found myself alone at the front bench. I picked up Michael's spectacles, well-worn, navy tie, his pen and papers, the secretary of state's papers and my own and took them out to the waiting hands of civil servants. One of them, Margaret Evans, rushed me to a telephone to tell Eileen, Michael's wife, at their flat in Dolphin Square before she got the news from the media. I told Eileen he had collapsed and had been taken to Westminster Hospital.

When I arrived at Eileen's flat with Margaret and Mike Chown, Michael's private secretary, Jim Callaghan and Ian Grist were already there. Jim had some doubt whether I had the right hospital. He phoned the Westminster and spoke to our whip, John Cope, who confirmed that Michael was there in the intensive care unit and that they were battling hard for his life. When we got there, Eileen was hustled to a side room and then John told us there was no hope. Michael was dead.

Anne Edwards offered to spend the night with Eileen but she preferred to be alone. She telephoned their son, Hilary, and told him to take care of the dogs rather as I had instinctively picked up the debris around the despatch box. Jim Callaghan rang the Foreign Office to ask them to let Michael's brother know the sad news. He is our ambassador in Beirut. I got back to the House in the secretary of state's car and Cyril, his driver, pointed out that the chief whip's car was still in Speaker's Court. Something made me call on him, only to find him in full conference with his whips and going over the whole tragedy in detail. The ambulance had been slow in coming. I referred to the third doctor; no one else had been aware of him.

The last person to die in the chamber had been Dugdale, MP for West Bromwich, in 1963. Tributes had been paid the following day. Jopling phoned No. 10. Ian Gow was picked up by car and brought over. The PM had agreed to deliver a tribute at 9.35 a.m. Ian Gow and I drafted it with Ian Grist at our side. It was read out to the whips and approved. Relevant people were informed. The Speaker was said to be very distressed.

I brought Ian Grist home with me and he is now asleep in the next room. Poor dear, he was in a pitiful state before I cooked him some baked beans. It was all I had to offer. We washed them down with a glass of wine. I envied him his weeping.

Dear Michael is now with his beloved daughter, Caroline. He had a strange love of death and almost courted it after she had gone. He is probably laughing his head off as he looks down at me and tomorrow's headlines. He will remember John Donne: 'Any man's death diminishes me because I am involved in mankind. And therefore, never send to know for whom the bell tolls; it tolls for thee' (1641).

Friday, 11 February 1983

Michael would have been pleased with today's proceedings. The PM wore black and spoke the words we had written. Our front bench was full. Others spoke: Michael Foot nicely, and similarly D. Wigley (Plaid Cymru), Jeffrey Thomas (SDP), Donald Stewart (SNP) and Albert McQuarrie (Con., Banff and Buchan). The Speaker was close to tears. The House, having restored its spirits, moved on to other business. I recorded two tributes, one in English for ITV and one in Welsh for S4C. I also drafted a piece for *The Times*.

Saturday, 12 February 1983

Tears welled up in my eyes as I breakfasted alone in the flat this morning. I decided to stay here for the weekend as yesterday slipped away with Michael's obituaries and because there was a threat of snow at home and elsewhere over Sunday. Enid wanted to come down but I dissuaded her; she was very fond of Michael and would only have stirred up my emotions. There was also a red box on the way to me and some submissions addressed to PUSS (M) as Michael was known at the Welsh Office. I could not face them yesterday but today I felt strong enough and tackled all with vigour at Gwydyr House. I had finished by lunchtime.

Michael hated loneliness – Eileen told me that – and any arrangement to meet up was always sacrosanct in his eyes. If I failed him, he would berate me. But he recognized me as an introvert, happy in my loneliness. It was this contrast between us that brought us so close. When I dropped into Annie's Bar yesterday, May, the barmaid, said:

'He was a helluva nice man.'

He would have enjoyed that tribute and that of the waitress in the members' cafeteria:

'Why is it always the nice ones who go?'

Of course, some thought it was I who had died rather than my namesake. I thought this might happen and had telephoned Enid from the hospital. Ted Garrett (Lab., Wallsend) who told me yesterday of Thursday night's confused bulletins, said:

'I knew it wasn't you and I told Peggy "that bugger will live till he's ninety".'

Monday, 14 February 1983

I awoke with a heavy heart, donned my black tie and sallied to the Welsh Office.

Nick looked gaunt at the debate on the water strike. I removed a bit of dog's fluff from his suit. He left after the opening speeches. He chatted with the Speaker and George told me later that his eyes were full of tears. Not only has he to cope with his own illness but his wife Anne is also unwell. I must try to care for him. While I was on the front bench, a message came that the Speaker would like to see me in his chambers after the debate.

So I went along to find George alone. He poured a generous whisky for each of us. We spoke of Michael's death, I for once outdoing him in verbosity and giving him every detail which I knew he wanted to hear and which I – let's face it – wanted to give. He had clearly felt the whole tragedy keenly. He too was a Cardiff member. He recalled how Michael had mischievously appeared with a loud hailer outside his house in Cardiff during the 1979 election and he, George, who as Speaker was being returned unopposed, had gone out shouting for his right of reply.

The whisky flowed very freely; George was not returning to the chair. He was for Ian Grist as Michael's successor at the Welsh Office.

We also needed a minister of state in his view; he said he would talk to the PM about that. We also talked about his own successor and the story in tonight's *Evening Standard* about a private dinner he had had with Francis Pym. 'Who else did I tell about that?' George mused.

Michael's funeral will be at Llandaff Cathedral at noon on Wednesday. George urged that the PM should read the second lesson and that it should be the immortal passage from Corinthians. George's eyes melted at the thought of it and so did mine.

Later, I spoke to Ian Gow and to Michael's son, Hilary. They agreed. Both George and I are to travel down to Cardiff with the PM on Wednesday in her plane.

Tuesday, 15 February 1983

Enid and my youngest son Huw were trying to get my black overcoat and bowler down to Cardiff via the HTV courier from Bangor but there was great uncertainty about the success of their efforts. I dashed to buy a new coat at Aquascutum in Regent Street.

I then waited for the outcome of Mike Chown's meeting with Hilary and the dean of Llandaff. The last had decided that the prime minister's services were not required nor those of the secretary of state. There would be only one lesson, read by Canon Winton, a friend of the family.

This afternoon, I went to the House of Lords to witness the second reading of the Conwy Tunnel Bill. It was accompanied by a string of tributes to Michael from Janet Young, Cledwyn, Emlyn Hooson and Boyd-Carpenter. They were very sweet (in my father's spiritual sense), benign and more subtle than the Commons' tributes which were really designed to get the place going again after the shock of the night before.

I learnt in the course of the day that if you die within the royal palace of Westminster a Coroner Royal has to be appointed with a jury composed of members of the royal household. That is why death never happens on the premises. It always occurs outside. (The last case of an actual death was of a maid who got herself locked in a cupboard: her body was found some days later.)

I know that Michael died on the floor of the House of Commons but, technically, he died at Westminster Hospital.

Dined at the chief whip's table, with Willie Whitelaw and Victor Goodhew (Con., St Albans). They were very understanding and spoke of other things.

Friday, 18 February 1983

I awoke early – heaven knows why – full of admiration for the PM. She is another Elizabeth I. I spent Wednesday with her and the Speaker when we flew to Cardiff and the funeral. I have to say that they really are magnificent people; they do more than you ever expect of them, with the PM leading the way.

On the way there, the PM listened and I kept prompting George, who sat opposite her in the plane, to tell some of the stories he had told me a couple of nights before. Returning, she was jovially full of the day's events, sad as they had been.

'Let's have a drink,' she said when we were safely airborne. 'Michael I am sure would approve.'

So most of us had a much needed gin and tonic. She stuck to her well-watered whisky. Europe came up in conversation and the threat of a milk flood from Normandy.

'We drink so much of their wine; why should we drink their milk as well?' she asked. But it was not so much what she said that made her extraordinary, but what she was. Simply to be with her was, I found, tremendously exhilarating. She was a goddess among satyrs.

It was announced today that John Stradling Thomas (Con., Monmouth) who has been deputy chief whip, is to be minister of state at the Welsh Office. It is a sideways shove for John, engineered by the chief whip, and he does not like it at all. He has told me as much this evening. He would not be Nick's first choice for a close colleague either because I have seen them fight like dogs. Whatever the ins and outs of his transfer, I am glad it is now acknowledged that the Welsh Office needs a minister of state.

I suffered the inevitable trauma after Michael's death but there was no time to indulge in it or recover properly. Political life is a pressure-cooker and you are either in or out of that cauldron of events. The coming election occupied our minds.

Willie Whitelaw joined Janet Fookes (Con., Plymouth Drake) and myself at a table in the members' dining room on Monday, 29 February. He agreed with me that the SDP–Liberal Alliance was too much of a rogue elephant at the moment for us to risk an election in June. He said that the Conservative Party had always made a mistake when it rushed into an election as it did in February 1974.

'Margaret must not lose her integrity, her honesty, or we are lost' – one can never quite quote Willie but this was the gist of what he said.

He was coming up to his sixty-fifth birthday and babbled on about 'being of some use to the party or none'. I had heard him say this before, at the end of the Heath government. Willie is a large, dominating personality who makes dwarfs of those around him. 'Everyone needs his Willie,' as Margaret famously said. But I could never forget his atrocious mishandling of the Welsh fourth channel. I am sure he knew my feelings and reciprocated them in kind.

Monday, 6 March 1983

I have had a traumatic weekend. It came to a crunch on Friday when an idiot of a guard on the train from Euston put out my baggage, including my locked and labelled ministerial briefcase, as 'unattended luggage' at Milton Keynes, just under an hour out of London. I fumed at the man for his unmitigated folly. I had to get off the train at Crewe and wait for my luggage to come up on the next train. I was still in an agitated state when I eventually arrived home. To cap it all I had a dreadful cold. Even Enid thought I was done for. I went to bed for an hour.

At the annual general meeting of my Conservative Association that evening I knew I had to pull out all the stops. I had seen the Speaker, George Thomas, do it when he was under the weather at a London Welsh dinner at the Savoy and the memory of it and George's sayings inspired me.

'It is the values we hold that decide the contribution we make . . . We take miracles for granted . . . Some things are unchanging, faith, integrity. I cry "Order! Order!" And I'm the only one who listens . . . Women are very lucky, they have no wives . . .'

George was a master at blending humour and seriousness. I tried to emulate him and at least got away with it. There are occasions in politics when every one and everything are against you and you must draw on all your last reserves of energy and will. Heaven help you if you have none left.

Tuesday, 15 March 1983

Today was Budget day. Geoffrey did not pull an obvious rabbit out of the hat and the Budget is no election winner. We must let the Alliance people get bogged down in their differences and rely on the Tory Party to rally when the trumpets sound. So the election recedes from June and October looks more likely.

I delivered a highly significant speech on our mental handicap strategy at Glan Clwyd Hospital on Thursday. It was of great interest to health and social services professionals but not to the media. I am genuinely proud of the strategy, which is to transfer mentally handicapped people from mental hospitals into the community.

It all began when I came across a fourteen-year-old mentally handicapped child in one of our mental hospitals and was told that the boy would neither get better nor worse and would spend the rest of his life in hospital. His parents did not want to know him. It worried me. I spoke to Nick about it and he was equally concerned.

'How many other children are in the same position?' he asked.

The best estimate civil servants could give me was that there were about seventy-five such children in Wales. My suggestion that they should be brought out of hospital to live in the community with caring couples fell on fertile ground. A senior civil servant, R. A. Pengelly, having tested my resolve, set himself to work up a strategy, not confined to children but including mentally handicapped adults as well. It extended over a period of ten years and would eventually cost £34 million a year.

It was pioneering stuff, which might pave the way for the return of other kinds of patients, particularly the elderly, from hospital to their communities if there was proper care for them. England too might follow our example.

The strategy was still at an early stage but we were making progress.

After the speech, I inspected the new roads by-passing Bangor and Llanfair P.G. on Anglesey. What a vista of the future we have there! The new roads are superb.

Tuesday, 22 March 1983

Alec Jones (Lab., Rhondda), leader of the Welsh Labour opposition has died over the weekend – a repeat of the massive heart attack he had about seven years ago. His close friend, Ted Rowlands (Lab., Merthyr Tydfil, now Lord) is pretty shell-shocked. Alec was a professional, noble and true as befits a man who is prominent in a major party. Jim Callaghan made him a Privy Counsellor although he was never more than a parliamentary under secretary – a rare honour. He had a wonderful wife in Mildred, a woman who believed in his kind of socialism. The world never matched their aspirations but that never stopped them from aspiring. I shall go to Alec's funeral at Tonypandy on Friday. I keep consoling myself with Michael's greeting to him in the 'Great Taproom in the Sky':

Michael: 'What kept you so long then?'
Alec: 'My exit was not quite so spectacular as yours . . .'

Wednesday, 23 March 1983

Sir John Eden (Con., Bournemouth West, now Lord) spotted Lord Molson dining alone and invited him to join our table. Molson was first elected as the member for Doncaster in 1931. He had cut his teeth in Aberdare in 1929 and had been criticized then for not putting some Welsh in his election address. He had intended to fight Bassetlaw in 1931 but stood down in favour of Malcolm Macdonald, Ramsay's son, who was the National Government candidate. Philip Snowden thanked him for his patriotism. He won Doncaster because the sitting Labour member had abandoned his miner's cottage and gone to live on 'the bankers' ramp' – the wealthier end of town. Too many of his constituents had been calling on him at home in the miner's cottage over the weekends!

Sunday, 10 April 1983

I am back, slightly becalmed, after the Easter recess.

I was surprised by the general confidence in the government – at the Bangor Conservative club, for instance, who gave a thousand pounds towards our election expenses.

Wednesday, 20 April 1983

In terms of hours, I am sure I travel more than the foreign secretary. It was more than twenty-five hours last week and this is not untypical. I live on the triangle between Conwy, Westminster and Cardiff.

I went to London by train on Monday (four hours) and returned by car on Tuesday to RAF Valley (six) to welcome the Irish Republic's minister, Paddy O'Toole, who is interested in our support for the Welsh language. Both the Foreign Office and Northern Ireland Office are backing the visit, which is part of the Anglo–Irish inter-governmental arrangements. I stayed with Paddy at the Bodysgallen Hotel, near Llandudno and close to my home. I wanted nothing to go wrong.

On Wednesday, we spent five hours visiting places of interest to him in north-west Wales and similarly on Thursday in north-east Wales. On Friday, I flew down to Cardiff (three hours in all) and came home by car on Saturday (five).

All the travelling was pretty gruelling but I learnt an invaluable lesson from Paddy, that it had been a mistake to make Gaelic a compulsory subject in schools in the republic and that the policy had to be abandoned in 1974–5.

Thursday, 21 April 1983

All the talk is of a June election. Nick confessed to me this morning that he was a member of a small group considering the precise date. It could be the 27th. Dined tonight with Paul Dean (Con., Woodspring, now Lord), Sir Walter Clegg (Con., Wyre) and David Crouch (Con., Canterbury).

David was all for June but the rest of us were not. I warned Margaret weeks ago that to go early would be regarded as a 'cut and run' affair, contrary to her character. We are not ready yet with well-formed policies to take us through the next ten years. To win we must lay out a hopeful future for the country, based on right principles and aspirations.

Tuesday, 26 April 1983

The PM dined at Gwydyr House last night. It was her first visit. John Stradling Thomas was put out and so was I that we were asked only to the pre-dinner drinks. But I understand Nick's viewpoint. He is jealous of his position and will brook no rivals. He is currently restored in health and in superb form.

We are in the process of setting aims for the department. In our discussion with civil servants I was struck by the divergence between what they thought to be their role and the secretary of state's functions and responsibilities. They have no role independent of him.

Wednesday, 11 May 1983

Our dear Prime Minister has decided to call an election on 9 June in spite of my warnings about the charge of 'cut and run'. My God, she has heard that phrase a thousand times since! We have all worked like fiends at the Welsh Office the last few days. Nick has done a marvellous job of the Welsh manifesto and of our record of achievements over the last four years but it was left to me to devise the final sentence: 'We look to the future; our opponents look to the past.'

God knows how we shall fare in the campaign. I am off to Pembrokeshire tomorrow to speak for Nick at Tenby. He intends to spend little time in his constituency and to campaign the length and breadth of Wales. Anne is in hospital till Friday.

Saturday, 11 June 1983

The election came at us with astonishing speed. Labour and the Alliance began their campaign a week ahead of us and were at each other's throats in no time. We launched our manifesto on Wednesday, 18 May and the Welsh edition the following day – with Nick in the south and myself in the north.

With the Alliance and us attacking Labour, they were virtually demolished in that first week or so. Their employment policy was contradicted by their proposal to withdraw from the Common Market and their unilateral disarmament policy seemed to be a total surrender to Russia.

Healey stepped forward to take the lead from Foot and promptly dropped a clanger over the Falklands by accusing the PM of glorying in slaughter. Kinnock followed him into the pitfall. When commenting on Margaret Thatcher's guts, he glibly contrasted her with those who had spilled their guts in the Falklands. The comparison repelled people.

The Labour candidate in Conwy was a trade unionist from south Wales, named Ira Walters. Ira is a girl's name in the north. When that little bit of confusion had been cleared in people's minds, another was added to it. 'Who is this IRA Walters?' some innocent asked.

The Alliance gave me a run for my money locally and came second by halving the Labour vote. My own vote stood up well and my majority at 4,105 was much the same as in February 1974. We have done extremely well in Wales.

David Steel, the Liberal, outshone Roy Jenkins (SDP) on the media and took the lead towards the end of the campaign but they gained few seats. There are now four elements in the opposition – Liberal, SDP, moderate Labour and the extreme left. The future looks promising.

Devils Rampant

It was not until November 1983 that I began to feel that our policies were starting to work and turning the economy around. Inflation was on the way down and there were signs of recovery and growth. But the government had its critics. Francis Pym, now out of office, attacked the government's tight control of the money supply and tough stance on public spending. He was critical too of the prime minister's style of leadership. The problem as I saw it was that it was not enough to roll back the frontiers of socialism; the frontiers of capitalism had to be rolled forward too – into the public services and elsewhere. For this to happen, the private sector had to shed its defensive wariness after years of socialism and develop a new entrepreneurial confidence to advance into areas it had not ventured into before.

The miners' strike which ran from March 1984 to March 1985 was a sub-plot that threatened to take over the whole play of national revival and become the dominant theme. The battle scenes between the police – many of them mounted, others with shields and riot gear – and massed pickets at Orgreave Colliery in May 1984 were reminiscent not only of similar clashes in the 1973 strike that shook Ted Heath's government, but of medieval encounters. The difference was that the ugliness of violence was visually brought home to the public by television. People did not like what they saw. It reeked of rebellion against the legitimate authority of a recently elected government by the trade union barons who had held the viewers of Britain in thrall for too long.

The miners' struggle in defence of their declining industry and against the closure of uneconomic pits appears inevitable in retrospect, once Arthur Scargill had become president of the National Union of Mineworkers (1981) and Ian MacGregor had become chairman of the National Coal Board (1983). MacGregor soon produced his plan for a massive reduction in the workforce – 64,000 over three years – to bring the heavily subsidized industry into balance. But there was to be massive investment in new pits as well. These two men were the leading players in the sub-plot unfolding before us. As usual, there were many crowd scenes and ancillary characters. There were interactions too with players on the national scene, including Margaret Thatcher and Peter Walker, secretary of state for energy, and the leader of the opposition, Neil Kinnock.

Arthur Scargill had been a member of the Young Communists League and was an avowed Marxist with his roots in the Yorkshire NUM. He had become Yorkshire president in 1973. Not only had he played a part in the 1973 conflict, but he had also been prominent during the Winter of Discontent which had contributed to Jim Callaghan's downfall. He did not accept the result of the 1983 election and very shortly afterwards he was saying openly that he did not believe 'that we are landed for the next four years with this government'. He was clearly intent on overthrowing the government if he could. He believed in himself and his cause and had the will, ability and followers to back him. He was impulsive – it was a mistake to call the strike in spring – and ruthless, but it suited his 'no holds barred' approach.

Ian MacGregor had all the tough qualities of a Scot, brought up in Edinburgh and Glasgow and tempered in the hard school of American business. He had proved himself as chairman and chief executive of the British Steel Corporation between 1980 and 1983 when he drastically reduced its manpower and laid the foundations for an internationally competitive steel industry. His will was backed by the business logic of his plans to convert the coal industry as he had converted steel. He was supported by the prime minister and Peter Walker, one of the ablest ministers in her government, a man who could have run the government in the unlikely event of her being run over by a bus.

I heard Margaret speaking at the Welsh party conference at Porthcawl in June when the strike was in its fourth month. The Grand Pavilion there had been the scene of many NUM and Labour Party gatherings. (Will Paynter, the Communist president of the NUM in the 1950s, had confessed to me privately there that he wanted to see all the pits closed in south Wales and the Valleys become green again.) She made a strong appeal to the miners to return to work. She referred to Jim Griffiths, the Labour stalwart from Llanelli, and Harold Finch, the former member for Bedwellty, and their descriptions of miners' hardships in the 1920s and 1930s. She contrasted the grim past with the hopeful future conjured up by the government's new investment of £3.8 billion in the coal industry – '£2 million for every day we've been in office'. Though strong, it was an emotional appeal touched with gentleness. Alas, there were no picketing miners to hear her in the pavilion or outside, only women who claimed to be miners' wives. Someone threw an egg, which landed on Maggie's front. It barely showed on her 'egg and tomato' dress.

The government's problem was to keep the dispute at arm's length. The dispute was between the NUM and the NCB. Of course, the government had prepared for the miners' challenge after the brush in 1981 by ensuring that the power stations had adequate supplies so that the rest of industry and the public could not be held to ransom. And when the dispute escalated and other unions became involved – especially the dockers – the dispute became such that the government could not allow the NCB to lose without losing face itself as the ultimate guardian of the nation's interests.

The maintenance of law and order by locally controlled police forces and the rights of those who wished to work to do so without the threat of violence, particularly the Nottinghamshire miners and the lorry drivers who supplied the steelworks, also drew the government into the vortex of trouble.

On 21 November 1984 there was uproar in the House of Commons when Norman Fowler (now Lord), the secretary of state for social services, made a statement about withdrawing benefits from striking miners. About twenty-five Labour MPs herded round the Mace. They were led by Eric Heffer (Liverpool Walton) and David Nellist (Coventry South East). The Speaker suspended the sitting. When he returned ten minutes later, he appealed to members to resume their seats. They refused and he had to adjourn the House.

Later the same month, the whole country was deeply shocked when a concrete block, deliberately dropped from a bridge, killed a Merthyr taxi driver, David Wilkie, who was taking a miner to work. It was the worst of many criminal incidents, which showed what could happen when things got out of hand. Wisely, the government kept its distance from the action, while keeping a very watchful eye on the battlefield and reserving its views for the media and the House of Commons.

I had seen Neil Kinnock, now Michael Foot's successor as leader of the Labour Party, cornered by miners on the committee room corridor of the House of Commons in 1973. I loitered there because he looked pale, frightened and physically threatened. I thought he might have to be rescued one way or another. The miners were telling him that if the Labour government had not closed down so many pits, the then Tory government would not have dared carry on the policy. I was quite fond of my Welsh Labour colleague and, as a former television producer, I had once told him not to draw his finger across his lower lip when speaking because it was a sign of uncertainty on his part. He had taken my tip and never done it again. Neil had extricated himself from that particular corner but he could not avoid supporting the miners as Labour leader a decade later. His constituency of Islwyn was in the heart of the south Wales valleys. He was no match for Margaret at the despatch box. In a censure debate in the House of Commons in December 1984 she challenged him to state his position:

'Throughout the strike the Rt. Hon. Gentleman has had the choice between standing up to the NUM leadership and keeping silent. He has kept silent. When the leadership of the NUM called a strike without a ballot, in defiance of union rules, the Rt. Hon. Gentleman stayed silent. When pickets tried by violence to close down pits in Nottinghamshire and elsewhere, against the democratically expressed wishes of the local miners, the Rt. Hon. Gentleman stayed silent. When the NUM tried to impose mob rule at Orgreave, the Rt. Hon. Gentleman stayed silent. Only when the General Secretary of the TUC had the courage to tell the leadership of the NUM that its tactics were unacceptable did the Rt. Hon. Gentleman take on the role of Little Sir Echo . . . I challenge the Leader of the Opposition. Will he urge the NUM to accept that agreement [the NCB's offer] or will he not?'

Hon. Members: 'Answer!'

'He will not answer because he dare not answer.'

As Scargill and the NUM lost ground, so did Neil Kinnock as Labour leader. He was not only sponsored by a trade union; he was their captive. It was the unenviable position Nye Bevan had privately foreseen and feared as union influence and power over the Labour Party grew in the 1950s. Neil's experience of the strike helped change many of his ideas about this time. He changed his mind about devolution and Europe. He had been opposed to both. It was fertile ground for the seedling ideas of a new Labour Party.

As the strike faltered, the myth that the NUM could overturn governments at will faded into legend. It was Harold Macmillan who had said that there were three forces that no prudent person would wish to meet in combat: the Roman Catholic Church, the Brigade of Guards and the National Union of Mineworkers. The last had now lost their invincibility. Margaret took their place.

Under Margaret's determined leadership, the country was at last freeing itself from the domination of the trade union barons. Never again would they have the power they once wielded to force governments to accept their demands whatever the cost to the rest of the nation. She had won despite the 'wets' in her own party and the Church and despite Scargill's attempts to seek assistance from abroad.

When the strike was over, the lobby columnist Alan Watkins, not a government sympathizer, wrote a shrewd analysis in the *Observer* (10 March 1985):

> If Arthur Scargill had accepted the terms the Coal Board offered last July . . . he could plausibly have claimed a victory. It is a fair summary to say that Mrs Thatcher has won because of Mr Scargill and despite Mr Ian Macgregor. But won she has.

'Militancy no longer delivers the political or industrial goods,' he wrote, and he concluded that there was now a chance for socialist moderates.

Margaret's victory had freed the Labour Party too. In her view, if anyone had won, it was 'all of those people who kept the wheels of Britain turning and who, in spite of a strike, actually produced a record output in Britain last year'. Her reputation as a strong and determined leader rocketed at home and abroad. Her position was unassailable.

The outcome might have been very different had the IRA bombers succeeded in their attempt to blow her to kingdom come at the Grand Hotel in Brighton during the party conference in October 1984. I was at the Grand the night before the explosion, picking up my colleague, John Stradling Thomas, to bring him back to London with me and my red boxes. I stayed the night at the flat in Little Smith Street.

It was the secretary of state's driver who telephoned me early that fateful morning of Saturday, 13 October, and told me of the explosion during the night at the Grand. I hurried there immediately. As we drove down to Brighton, we heard of the casualties on the radio. Norman Tebbit and his wife had been badly injured but brought out of the rubble. John Wakeham was still trapped. John's wife was dead and so was Anthony Berry, who had always been a personal friend. Margaret was all right but had spent the night in a police station somewhere. We went straight to the Conference Centre to give what help we could.

Someone said it was important that the platform should be full for the prime minister's speech when the conference session opened at 9.30 and I hurriedly took my place. I was sitting next to Diana, George Younger's wife, who had got her dress from Marks and Spencer that morning. After the explosion, George had opened their bedroom door into a gaping void, she told me. There was an astonished hush of relief, an intimate quiet, when the prime minister entered. I watched anxiously from behind as she spoke her opening words, calmly, reassuringly. Yet, I trembled for her when she reached for the glass of water from its tight fitting socket in the tilted podium. But I need not have worried. She returned the glass straight to its narrow confines without so much as a twitch, a quiver, or a tremor, although she had been up most of the night. The Iron Lady had nerves of steel.

'Her major theme, the rule of law, ran like a glittering stream through her entire speech', I wrote later that day, 'and embraced the violence on the picket lines as well as the murderous IRA. She had a beautiful quotation from Theodore Roosevelt for Arthur Scargill. "No man is above the law and no man is below it; nor do we ask any man's permission when we require him to obey it. Obedience to the law is demanded as a right – not asked as a favour".'

'The PM came through it all, not only unscathed but also triumphant and her final words from the conference platform are still ringing in my ears: "Democracy shall prevail." It is only now that the full horror of last night's experience is denting the numbness in my mind.'

The following day, the PM attended a church service and broke down momentarily under a ray of sunlight. Norman Tebbit, I thought, would recover and have the strength to bear the tragedy of a dear wife possibly crippled for life. John Wakeham had been trapped for hours under a hot water pipe, which poured its contents on his thigh. It was some weeks before he called me aside one night in an empty 'Aye' lobby and said: 'Look, I can walk without my stick.' And so he did.

My lovely, blue and white sheep dog, Carlo, was dying at home that weekend of the Brighton bombing. He had been with us for fifteen years and we had raised him from a pup with our boys. He was very intelligent. I had sworn that I would never have him put down but when I saw him a week later unable to get to his feet and read the plea for release in his soft, kindly, old eyes, I had no option but to grant his wish. It was strange how my grief for him mingled with grief for friends killed or maimed at Brighton.

Pot-Pourri

It was Francis Pym who famously said in the course of the 1983 election campaign that 'landslides on the whole do not produce successful governments'. True or not, his timing was deplorable; it was a gaffe of the first order and could have debilitated our efforts. Margaret countered that she could handle a landslide majority. When she got it – 144 over all other parties and 188 over Labour – she decided she could manage it without Francis's services. There were other casualties. Nigel Lawson replaced David Howell at the Department of Energy and Janet Young made way for Willie Whitelaw as leader of the Lords. Our minsterial dinner at No. 10 on 22 June was a merry affair. The PM gave us special praise for our achievement in Wales where we now had more Conservative MPs than at any time since 1874.

I sat next to Nick Ridley (Con., Cirencester and Tewkesbury) whom I knew well ever since we had paid a parliamentary visit to Israel together. He was a fine watercolourist and whipped out his easel at every opportunity. He used a sponge as well as brushes and could capture a scene quickly. I have his picture of Mount Hermon and still cherish it along with my memory of him.

Nick said that with high inflation the rich got richer and the poor poorer. The socialist dilemma was how to enrich the poor in inflationary conditions, which their policies tended to create. It could not be done, he said.

Little did I know then that Cecil Parkinson, party chairman and newly appointed secretary of state for Trade and Industry was in deep trouble. The PM had known since polling day. It blew up into a national scandal when his pregnant secretary, Sarah Keyes, sent a letter to *The Times* which they published on the Friday of the Blackpool conference in October. A contemporary doggerel summed it all up:

Sarah Keyes was difficult to please
After she'd been laid
By the Minister for Trade.

The loss of Cecil was to be a severe blow to Margaret, who valued his abilities. He had master-minded the election campaign brilliantly. Beneath a handsome, sporting exterior – he ran for Cambridge in his student days – he was full of Lancastrian nous and common sense. His wife Ann was a strong character cast in Margaret's own mould. They were friends. Margaret would have kept him in her government had she been able to.

When Cecil fell, Nick Ridley entered the Cabinet as secretary of state for transport. He too was a monetarist and a truly aristocratic, independent spirit – a man after Margaret's own heart.

I was to savour Ridley's brilliance as an engineer and planner when Nick Edwards and I went to see him in his office at the Department of Transport in the now demolished three-tower block in Marsham Street. We were to press him hard to provide the second crossing over the River Severn because the first bridge – I had seen it built in the 1950s and opened by the queen in 1966 – was now approaching its full capacity and carrying more than 50,000 vehicles a day. There were endless traffic delays caused by high winds, resurfacing and maintenance.

A new bridge was urgently needed to promote the prosperity of south Wales and the new manufacturing industries that were coming in. Although part of the bridge would be in Wales, it was essentially an English project. Nick Edwards and I were fully armed with maps, plans and papers and were taken aback when we saw the lean Ridley lounging nonchalantly behind an empty desk with nothing on it except his packet of cigarettes. Nick Edwards launched into our presentation with his usual vigour. After he had been speaking for a couple of minutes, Ridley began to fidget impatiently with the cigarette packet and then raised his hand to stop Nick in mid-flow.

'No, no' he said, 'this is what we shall do.'

He then propounded his plan for the design, build and operation of the new bridge in conjunction with the operation of the existing bridge – all to be paid for by tolls over a lengthy span of years. It would require legislation, which was at that moment being drafted. It was a grandiose but simple scheme, breathtaking in its vision. There was not a single aspect of the vast project that he had not considered. Nick Edwards and I left in the certain knowledge that the project was in masterly hands.

On 20 July 1983, I watched Alan Clark (Con., Plymouth, Sutton) speaking for the first time at the despatch box as a humble parliamentary under secretary of state at the Department of Employment. Everyone knew that he was the son of the life peer, Lord Clark, who had distinguished himself on television with his superb series on the history of civilization, but Alan had all the airs and graces, appearance and pretensions of an heir to a hereditary title. There was nothing obviously *nouveau* about him except his love of classic cars and the leather headgear and goggles needed to drive open-top vehicles. He had the flavour of the flapper era about him. He listened more than he talked in the tea room. Privately, he could be mischievous and once told me that there was a wager among unnamed friends as to who would be the first to make love to a girl on the Woolsack in the House of Lords. He had clearly considered the challenge. No one suspected that he was anything as plebeian as a diarist.

There was nothing untoward about Alan's debut. He was the kind of man who might have treated the House with disdain and been ruthlessly cut down to size by a hail of off-putting interventions but he was wise enough to restrain himself on this occasion. His physical posture helped. He looked as humble as a member of Nabucco's slaves' chorus. Nevertheless, Hugo Young of the *Sunday Times* found him arrogant and said so.

On a later occasion, after a wine tasting, his disdain came through when he read verbatim the gobbledegook with which his civil servants had provided him to introduce an abstruse departmental order. His performance on that occasion earned him notoriety but he got away with it, possibly because his contempt was for the material he had been given rather than for the House. My guess is that he had a narrow escape from dismissal and remained in the government on sufferance. There were more 'incidents' to come.

My close colleague, John Stradling Thomas, was settling down with difficulty in his new post as minister of state for Wales after his years in the whips' office. He was still to be found in the late evening ensconced in the smoking room and indulging his talents as a raconteur. He had a charming secretary, desired by every policeman in the Palace – our driver, Eileen, told me.

John had perfected the whip's technique of putting down obstreperous members and was an outstanding practitioner of the art. I saw him use it with great effect on Keith Best, who had been quickly elevated to the position of PPS to our secretary of state. He had unfortunately been absent from his proper place in the House, directly behind his master, during our session of oral questions. The dialogue in the smoking room was as follows:

John: What will you have?

Keith: A Scotch, please.

John to barman: Make it a large one.

Keith: That's generous of you.

John: Where have you been the last few weeks? We've missed you.

Keith: I went to Chile . . . absolutely fascinating place.

John: But being a PPS, shouldn't you have been back for Welsh Questions?

Keith (laughing nervously at the sudden change in tone): Perhaps . . .

John: There's no perhaps about it. You should have been here supporting your secretary of state, not effing about in Valparaiso or wherever. Or do different rules apply to you?

Keith: I can see you're getting agitated . . .

John: But your place was here . . . you forgot all about that, didn't you? What do you think people here feel – including your secretary of state – when you behave like you have done? You had better toe the line . . . I'm telling you.

Keith (sheepishly): I know . . . would you like another drink?

John: No, thank you.

Keith (to me): Can you give me a cigarette? (He was normally a non-smoker)

And that was for starters. The dialogue continued in this hectoring vein until Keith, who was as resilient as they come, was ground down by every trick known to the professional whip to the point where he could not resurrect himself. Not long afterwards, Keith lost his job as a PPS for refusing to return from Geneva for a division in the House. The disciplinary regime was still tough and to miss an important vote was a cardinal sin.

It was a testing time for the new 1983 intake as a whole when any hidden errors in their past or character defects would surface and become common knowledge among members. Keith Raffan (Con., Delyn) was a quick-witted performer of great promise but he was suspected of contributing to the satirical revelations of *Private Eye*. This put him beyond the pale. It was a testing time for us all. The slightest whiff of scandalous behaviour became pungent gossip in the tea room and bars. Such gossip was always picked up by the whips and reported at their meetings. The government was on the lookout for new talent but there was no future for anyone who transgressed. The seriously ambitious were selective in their choice of company and kept silent.

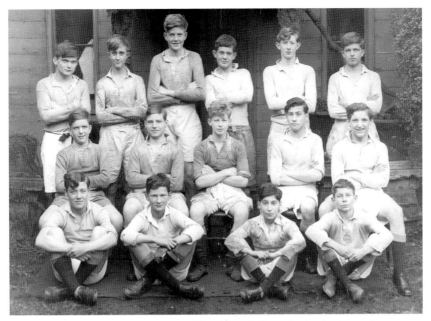

The Head Master's House, Harrow School, 1946. Our winning junior rugby team:
Evan Griffiths (captain, centre, second row), self (extreme right, same row),
Colin McEvedy (second from right, top row).

Sunday best at Harrow: topper and tails.   Playing Falstaff, summer 1947.

Quizmaster of T.W.W.'s *Gair am Air* (word for word) – one of a series of popular quiz programmes introduced by the company.

Filming in Moscow, 1965, with Gwyn Thomas and Colin Voisey.
The Ukraina Hotel is in the background.

Enid and I with our three sons, 1971. Left to right:
Huw, Geraint and Rhys.

Campaigning with Margaret Thatcher in the 1970s.

Poring over the Severn Estuary and a second crossing with secretary of state,
Nicholas Edwards, and colleague, Michael Roberts, 1983.

The prime minister visits the Welsh Office, Gwydyr House, Whitehall, 24 April 1983.
Left to right: Keith Best, John Stradling Thomas, Nick Edwards, the PM and myself.

Our home, Tan y Gwalia, in the Conwy Valley under snow.

Enid lends a hand in the library at Tan y Gwalia.

Greeting Prince Naruhito of Japan – now Crown Prince – at Colwyn Bay, 1985.

With President Jordi Pujol of Catalonia in Barcelona, 1991.

Opening of the Conwy Tunnel by HM the Queen, 25 October 1991.

Her Majesty at Conwy Castle, with 'Taffy' the goat of the Royal Welch Fusiliers
in the background.

The last of the oil well fires at Burgan 118, Kuwait, 1991.

Inspecting one of the fire extinguishers.

With Dr T. S. Lin of Chungwa Tatung, Taipei, 1994. Sir David Rowe Beddoe of the Welsh Development Agency is to his left.

Enoch Powell (Official Unionist Party, Down South) set the proper tone for them in his brief exchange with the House barber – a loquacious and excitable Zionist, as it so happened, fond of stressing his point with a flourish of his cut-throat razor:

'How would you like your hair cut, Mr Powell?'

'In silence. In silence.'

Having cared for a minister from the Republic of Ireland in Wales, I was invited to spend a few days there as their guest and to visit the Gaeltacht – those pockets of the republic where Gaelic was still in every day use.

I flew to Dublin on Tuesday, 26 July 1983 and spent the night at the residence of the Ambassador, Alan Goodison. The mansion was originally built as a retirement refuge by an Irish-American gangster called Crooker. When I woke up next morning and looked out of the window, I saw an officer with a sub-machine gun walking along the far edge of the lawn. It was a sharp reminder that a former ambassador had been assassinated on the drive to the house some years before. The spot where his car was blown up was pointed out to me as we drove to the office in the city where the minister, Paddy O'Toole, and my Garda escort were picking me up to fly from Shannon to the west of Ireland.

The media were on strike throughout the republic except for the local Gaelic radio station in Galway. While we were there, the minister, fluent in Gaelic, gave an interview, which was broadcast live. He explained my presence as a British minister visiting the Gaeltacht and mentioned, incidentally, that we would be spending the night at a local hotel. I could see the Garda nervously loosening their shoulder holsters when he named the Hotel Carraroe. Of course, the minister was encouraging visitors but no one, least of all the Garda, wanted the wrong kind. They did not relish a shoot-out with would-be IRA assassins wishing to add a British minister's scalp to their collection.

When we got to the hotel, I found some Gaelic literature and a language-learner's handbook. That night I learnt a word I hoped would stand me in good stead if there was an ominous knock on the door and my name was called. 'Niel!' (Not here!) The Garda told me next morning that they had kept watch all night. They were a formidable looking bunch, armed to the teeth. When we returned to Shannon, the airport thronged with armed Garda personnel.

'They're not all for you,' said Paddy slyly. 'The Taoiseach is due back from Brussels.'

The persistence of the IRA threat in the republic and high official awareness of it surprised me as a visitor.

There was a great deal happening in Wales. The old economy, excessively dependent on coal and steel, was being transformed and manufacturing companies, attracted by government grants and willing workers, were coming into the south and north-east. There were never enough local entrepreneurs like Alf Gooding to anticipate and match the needs of newcomers from North America, Japan and elsewhere but attitudes were changing and the spirit of enterprise freshened the air.

In May 1984, I accompanied Prince Charles to the opening of the huge Dinorwic Power Station in north Wales which Peter Emery (Con., Honiton) had approved in 1974 when he was minister for energy. I recalled that day and the moment when Peter had turned to me on the windy mountainside at Merchlyn, now the site of the upper reservoir, high above Llyn Padarn at Llanberis, and uttered the understatement of the decade: 'It sounds all right to me. What do you think?'

This magnificent project, estimated to cost £135 million, made sense to me too. It meant pumping thousands of gallons of water from the lower lake through the heart of the mountain to a high reservoir during the night when electricity consumption was low. The power would then be converted back into electricity by releasing the water through turbines in the daytime when consumption was at its peak. It was an investment on the edge of my constituency that would benefit the entire country. The foundations were also being laid at this time for new hospitals and vital east–west road links.

Over Christmas 1984 I wrestled with the problem of developing two subsidiary renal dialysis units, one in the south and the other in the north. Official advice was that one should be allocated to the private sector and the other to the NHS. I decided that both should go to the private sector in the interests of fair competition; they would be attached to NHS hospitals but independently run on a contractual basis. There would be no cost to the patient. The secretary of state backed my decision and we went ahead despite mutterings of likely opposition. In the event, there was none. Wales soon had one of the best dialysis networks in Europe.

Millions of pounds were paid in grants to improve homes and houses, many of them built pre-1918. Whenever I travelled by train from Paddington, I used to count the new roofs I could see at Newport. It was pleasing to see where the taxpayers' millions were going. The sale of council houses to sitting tenants was going with a swing. People recognized a bargain when they lived in one. Home ownership went up by leaps and bounds.

As ministers at the Welsh Office, we were not idle either on the conservation front and I presided over the newly established Cadw: Welsh Historic Monuments from its inception in 1984. We moved quickly to protect and promote our built heritage which ranged from prehistoric and Roman sites to Edward I's castles, Tintern Abbey and a host of other treasured edifices. There was hardly a building or a site of any archaeological or historical value in Wales that escaped the attention of Henry Anglesey and Professor Glanmor Williams (late Sir). We plotted their acquisition and restoration with loving zeal.

Came the day when the secretary of state was to open the magnificent, restored Roman baths at Caerleon. I had decided that the plaque marking the occasion should be in Latin but I was not satisfied with the draft translation. Eventually, I sought Enoch Powell's assistance as a former professor of classics but even then I suspected there was a grammatical mistake in the text. I did not have the guts to confront Enoch with his error. My college friend, Christopher Elrington, then general editor of the *Victoria County History*, confirmed the error, corrected it and gave the text a final, superb polish. I sent the amended text to Enoch who fully approved. The plaque is still there on the wall. I have never heard any criticism of the Latin from the many scholars from all parts of the world who have gazed on it.

The Welsh Language Society, who had been no more than a discomfiting nuisance with their blaring loudspeakers in ministers' ears at National Eisteddfodau, excelled themselves when they imprisoned me in my surgery for constituents at Bangor one Saturday morning in December 1984. I was on my own – apart from the redoubtable Sheila Jenkins who organized these surgeries for me. Suddenly, about thirty youngsters, of both sexes, led by an athletic young man, invaded the large room. They barricaded themselves in with chairs and sat down – an ugly picture of disciplined stubbornness. Some of them whispered among themselves in English. I did not move knowing that sooner or later one of them would have to go for a pee. I remonstrated with their leader that they were obstructing my constituents in the exercise of their right to see me as their MP but he was not very communicative. I made the same point to the *Guardian* freelance reporter who had slipped in with them and added that the only 'story' was that most of them did not speak Welsh and came from outside my constituency. Mrs Jenkins had called the police and an officer appeared outside the building. He did absolutely nothing and neither did I. My captors reminded me of the snapping dolls in the film, *Barbarella*. Mercifully, they were not ordered to torment me. After an hour or so, they left in as orderly a fashion as they had entered.

The police charged their leader with some trivial offence and I gave evidence before the magistrates who enjoyed the publicity as much as the accused. It was the Hitler Youth style of misdirected discipline that irked me more than anything and the time-wasting folly of it all.

Tom Hooson, our member for the tricky rural seat of Brecon and Radnor, had fought a losing battle with cancer and died in early May 1985. I had known him off and on since the 1950s when he was a young man of quality and charm with a playful, confident smile. He had made his fortune in advertising in the US and produced a definitive Conservative policy for Wales with his friend, Geoffrey Howe. The smile had gone from his life in his later years. His disease probably accounted for the change. His death would mean a by-election and I doubted whether we could hold the seat. I thought the Alliance would win.

Home and Abroad

West Germany was among the major investors in Wales and it occurred to me that, while we were actively courting potential American and Japanese investors, we were doing little to attract more investment from Germany. I spoke some German and had spent short holidays in the Rhineland in recent years. It was therefore agreed that I should lead an exploratory mission set up by Winvest, the inward investment arm of the Welsh Development Agency.

Our first target was increasingly prosperous Bavaria and I flew to Munich towards the end of May 1985. I stayed at the Hotel Deutscher Kaiser again, where I had stayed in the 1970s, although it appeared to have been out-starred by the Hotel Eden Wolff nearby. In the evening, I paid a quick visit to the huge *bierkeller* within walking distance of the hotel. The clientele were much younger this time – tourists mainly – and there were fewer *lederhosen* about but the 'helles bier' was as much in demand as ever and the band was as oomphatic as before.

The first company I called upon was Staedtler, the lead pencil and ball-point pen manufacturer in Nuremberg, who already had a subsidiary plant at Pontyclun in south Wales. I had of course familiarized myself with the Welsh plant before visiting the company's headquarters in the heart of the city. A Welsh dragon flag flew in my honour at the entrance to the plant. Dr Herman Egger, one of three trustees who ran the company, showed me round the factory. I was impressed by his close personal knowledge of every employee we met and the fact that they trained young apprentices on brand new machinery. 'We train them on the machines they are going to use – not the old stuff,' Dr Egger explained.

The company was cramped in its inner-city premises but they were planning a new factory on the outskirts and hoping to expand their factory in Wales at the same time to meet growing, worldwide

demand for their products. I encouraged Dr Egger and his colleagues to proceed with all speed. We would assist as best we could;
my ministerial visit was an earnest of our government's goodwill.
My visit to Staedtler was the beginning of a lengthy association
with Dr Egger, which proved very fruitful to the company and
beneficial to employment in Wales. I did not foresee it all at the time
but the promise was there.

Another German plant I had visited in Wales was Ina Bearings at
Llanelli. It was a subsidiary of Shaeffler of Herzogenaurach and
badly in need of fresh investment, the local German manager had
told me. The Shaeffler plant was enormous – employing 10,000, its
chief executive said as he gave me a rapid tour of the factory. They
were breaking into the American market with their roller bearings
and hoping to start production in China. As we climbed to the second
floor, I wondered how on earth I could bring this man's busy mind
back to Llanelli, which we had talked about only briefly. He had
brushed it aside as a minor concern. Then an idea came to me. I
paused on the stairs and turned to face him:

'You really have achieved a great deal here. You have good reason to
be personally proud of your achievement,' I said with all the
sincerity I could muster.

We continued up the stairs. Out of the corner of my eye, I could
see a smile of satisfaction playing on his face. I had been right in
thinking that no one had given him such fulsome praise for a long
time. As I left the premises and wished him well with his company's
expansion plans, he put his arm around my shoulder and said: 'And
I shall not forget our plant in Llanelli.' He was as good as his word
and the new investment, creating a hundred new jobs, was
announced a few weeks later.

My ministerial party lunched with the Bavarian Vereinsbank and
its chairman, Dr Peter Reinpell. We touched on the shortage of
skilled workers. Siemens were said to be short of 10,000 skilled staff
in spite of the acknowledged superiority of the German training
system. I had no compunction about attracting German companies
to Wales when they were so short of the skilled labour we could
provide. The problem of a divided Germany drifted into the conversation and someone quoted the French statesman's smart remark
that he loved Germany so much he was glad there were two.

We travelled down the Rhine to Darmstadt by car. Stephen
Steiner, who was attached to the consulate at Frankfurt, did the
driving. Stephen, with his blonde hair and Aryan features, looked
more German than the Germans and he accentuated the fact by

wearing a black leather raincoat and hat. He might have walked off the set of the television farce *Allo, Allo* having just played the role of a heel-clicking member of the Gestapo. He was deep into German politics and gave us a range of prognostications. Chancellor Helmut Kohl was a bore and 'to be a boring politician is a crime'. The Americans he described as 'overbearing, overeating and over here'. Of me, he said: 'You speak German without an English accent.' He was curiously amusing company as we sped along the autobahn.

Darmstadt was the centre of Wella, the ladies' hair products manufacturer. They too had a plant in Wales, run by an ardent patriot Eddie Rea. We were welcomed and shown around the premises, which included a museum, full of art deco furniture and fittings, and devoted to the development of ladies' hairdressing and toiletries in the twentieth century.

The brief visit to Germany had opened our eyes to fresh possibilities and given us new contacts which Stephen would pursue after our return to the UK. Next time, we would visit companies known to wish to expand to the UK but undecided about the location. We would tempt them to Wales. Meanwhile, we had encouraged some of those already established in Wales to enhance their operations.

On Saturday, 27 July I entertained Prince Naruhito of Japan to dinner at the Hotel Seventy Degrees at Colwyn Bay. The grandson of the old Emperor Hirohito was taking a break in Snowdonia from his studies at Merton College, Oxford, before returning home. I took immediately to the diminutive prince and his quiet, courteous humility and led him to the dining room set aside for us. Henry and Shirley Anglesey and my wife were there and a young local girl playing the harp.

Prince Hiro, as he was known, made a beeline for the harpist and listened attentively before her as she played and sang items from her repertoire of folk music. As the minutes passed, I began to think that the young man had suffered the celibacy of Oxford for too long and was desperate for female company when he turned to me and said: 'My mother plays the harp.'

Over dinner, we talked about Oxford and the thesis he had written on the upper Thames canal system. He had all the characteristics of a true scholar, which endeared him to me even more. He promised me a copy of his thesis. We spoke too about the influx of Japanese companies to Wales – the result of Nick Edwards's expeditions to Tokyo and elsewhere. The prince invited me to call on him if I should come to Japan. I could see no immediate prospect of that happening but I made a mental note of the invitation. I also promised to send him tapes and scores of Welsh harp music and singing to harp accompaniment to give to his mother, the crown princess. I had been deeply impressed by his cultured, scholarly approach to life and his naturalness. His thesis was duly published a few months later and a copy of the book arrived with the quaint, handwritten inscription on the frontispiece: 'To Mr Roberts. Naruhito.' Three years later, I visited Japan.

By May 1986 we were ready for another inward investment foray to West Germany. My party arrived at the consulate in Düsseldorf and, in the evening, Peter Bryant and his wife took us to the opera house. It was a mediocre performance of Mozart's *Escape from the Seraglio*: the soprano Constanze's hat fell off and the tenor, Belmonte, was booed at the end of the performance. But the patrons clearly enjoyed themselves in the lengthy intervals and talked as if there was no tomorrow. The opera house was clearly their social centre.

On our way to Hamburg, we called on the burgomaster of Soest – twinned with Bangor in my constituency. He was also the head-master of the local secondary school; the whole town looked well disciplined and peaceful. We drove on to Gutersloh and the Sprick cycle factory which already had a plant at Pontypool.

Julius Sprick was tall and fair; his wife Ute was a brunette who matched him perfectly. Her eyes were as receptive as his were piercing. Both looked very fit and loved hunting. The entrance hall to the factory had a wall of stags' heads and trophies. They were a striking couple. Herr Sprick said: 'If you have a joyous marriage, then you are creative with it. I have been fortunate in my marriage and therefore successful in my business.'

He maintained that a man with a personal problem could not devote himself properly to his work. He based his business life on empathy between his fellow workers and himself. I asked him who had instructed him in his approach to life. He replied that he owed it all to his mother. I guessed that Ute now provided all the mother-love and inspiration he needed. He said that all his problems dissolved in her company. I had high hopes that his operation in Wales would expand, but he had his problems and I was saddened to hear a few months later that he had gone bankrupt.

The Hotel Vier Jahreszeiten (Four Seasons) at Hamburg was reckoned seventh best in the world. When I greeted the head porter outside the main entrance, he returned the greeting with a detailed weather forecast. We gave a dinner for local businessmen. Our consul, Alec Goldsmith, fresh from Hong Kong, was glad to be introduced to them in such style. We toured the port in the harbour master's boat the next day, saw the concrete, wartime submarine pens, sniffed the spices in the warehouses and saw some of the great freeport's import-export activities with the East, so disliked but tolerated by the European Commission. Hamburg's trade extended down the Elbe to Czechoslovakia and into Eastern Europe and Russia via the Baltic. The port was prosperous. We netted one valuable development, by Klockner Pentatuck at New Tredegar. It made the week's efforts worthwhile.

As I feared, we lost Brecon and Radnor to the Alliance on 4 July 1985. Nick Edwards thought that the government had alienated too many interest groups – teachers, health workers and so on. In spite of a stirring speech at the Welsh party conference at Llandudno in June, Margaret had become 'that bloody woman' to many voters and our candidate, Chris Butler, had distanced himself from her in his campaign. There were some in the upper echelons of the party – notably the Centre Forward Group led by Francis Pym – who shared that antipathetic view. Personally, I did not waver in my support. Thanking her off the cuff at a lunchtime gathering at Llandudno after her speech that morning, I said: 'Great speeches come from great people. You have achieved greatness and it walks with you. You are imparting it to Britain and to Wales.'

While the secretary of state was away in India (10–26 September) I held the fort at the Welsh Office with my new colleague, Mark Robinson (Con., Newport West). John Stradling had gone under in the reshuffle. The first announcement was that he was resigning with a knighthood but next day the truth was out. He had been sacked. I was not surprised. I had seen him in his office the last day before the recess, smoking a cigar with a glass of sherry, and an alarming tableful of neatly stacked files waiting for his attention.

Towards the end of the month, I attended a string of bilateral meetings between the chief secretary to the Treasury, John MacGregor, and individual secretaries of state to finalize their departmental budgets for the following year and beyond. I had attended such meetings in previous years and knew the form. The meetings always took place at the Treasury in an airless room overlooking Parliament Square and the lower end of Whitehall.

If a window was opened, traffic noise drowned the voices of the shirt-sleeved occupants and traffic fumes sharpened the odours of sweat, biscuits and tea. On the right of the entrance was a picture titled *The Lamp* by Anthony Harrison and dated 1955. It suggested midnight oil and toil. My first day's attendances ran, off and on, from half past eight in the morning to eleven at night and embraced several ministries.

The chief secretary always had a standard opening to the effect that Cabinet had agreed in July on the total amount that could be spent. His job was to ensure that the sum of departmental bids for money came within that total. At present, they far exceeded it and had to be reduced. The secretary of state now facing him, eyeball to eyeball, would say that he understood the chief secretary's position perfectly but that in the case of his own department . . . and then he would launch into his argument for more expenditure than was due to him. The arguments advanced would be ingenious – the cleverest that the best brains in the department could devise – but the Treasury mandarins flanking the chief secretary were no fools. Demolishing notes would be passed to him to counter the arguments put forward.

When everyone was on the point of suffocation, the chief secretary would say: 'It's getting warm in here,' and take off his jacket. Twenty people would do the same, draping their jackets round their chairs. It was then that the smell of sweaty armpits wafted about the room. Someone would ask whether a window might be opened. The chief's private secretary (Richard Broadbent) would shake his head and I for one would suspect a Treasury ploy – to suffocate us into submission. Sometimes the going got tough, formal titles were dropped and Christian names came into play:

'I'm not playing games, John.'

'I know you're not.'

'But surely Treasury must fork out the money for measures announced in the Budget?'

'The chancellor promised future cuts in taxation but we are always having to review our promises.'

At this point, the secretary of state would push his chair back and adopt an attitude of resignation before some new line of attack occurred to him and he would return like a bull to the charge. They were not secretaries of state for nothing; faint hearts were not their distinguishing characteristic.

My function was to safeguard Welsh interests and to weigh into the argument if necessary. I knew that terriers were not welcome in this fight between bulldogs and usually kept my interventions to an absolute minimum. We got a percentage share (5.85 per cent that year, corresponding to the Welsh share of the population) of the budget spend won by our colleagues. It was important for us to know how they fared, who had been successful in their bids and who had not. Our own bilateral would come in due course and Nick would be back for that.

Enoch Powell came to address the Churchill Club at the St George's Hotel in my constituency in October.

'You look remarkably well,' I said in greeting him.

'You clearly know the three ages of man,' he said. 'Youth, middle age and "you look remarkably well".'

We were all quite chirpy at the eve-of-new-session dinner at No. 10 on 5 November 1985. The PM looked resplendent in a blue dress, edged with gold. Her husband, Denis, was caught inside the room when she ordered the chief whip to: 'Guard the door!' before Sir Robert Armstrong read the Queen's Speech to us. Denis was let out like a naughty school boy. The incident made us all relax and that atmosphere prevailed throughout. I sat down for dinner at Nick Edwards's table with David Hunt (Con., Wirral) and Lynda Chalker (Con., Wallasey). It was Nick who first spotted that the pictures had changed. 'She's raided the National Portrait Gallery,' he said. Romney's portrait of Pitt the Younger now hung over the mantel-piece. When Margaret came to our table, Nick remarked that she had reshuffled her pictures as well as her government. 'Well, we had three pictures of young boys here and I didn't think that was quite right.'

Ian Gow (Con., Eastbourne) bubbled with good humour, was able and loveable. After being the prime minister's PPS for four years – a job he did well – he became minister for housing and construction. My impression is that he was not really suited for ministerial work. My first close personal experience of him occurred on Thursday, 7 February 1985 when he was faced with a debate on water charges. He proposed to open and close the debate himself – provided I had no objection – but he wanted me near to him because he was not too certain of the Welsh dimension. Water charges were a hot issue in Wales because Welsh water was cheaper in Liverpool and Birmingham, which Wales supplied, than it was to Welsh consumers. Ian asked me to go over to the Department of Environment to brief him on the day of the debate.

I therefore attended his 10 a.m. meeting with his officials, believing that I would be free to attend a luncheon engagement. But, after the meeting with officials had ended, he pressed me to stay while he rehearsed his opening speech aloud – word by word, line by line, with a running evaluation of every point and nuance by himself. In the course of the morning, the whips' office telephoned to say that he might not be able to close as well as open the debate. No one could speak twice without leave of the House and it was doubtful whether the opposition would agree to his doing so. The conversation ended with Ian saying: 'You will try to get the opposition's agreement and ring me back . . . Good man!'

Shortly before one o'clock the whip rang back to say that Labour was adamantly opposed to Ian's speaking twice. There was a lengthy conversation about all conceivable possibilities and then the whip went off to try yet another tack with the opposition. At this point, I thought it advisable to cancel my lunch engagement. Sandwiches were brought in. At half past two, the whip called again. The opposition would not budge. My name was clearly mentioned because Ian said, 'He's right here with me.'

Only at that point – within an hour of the start of the debate – did he ask me if I would do the wind-up. I grabbed his most knowledgeable civil servant and took him to another room to knock up some key speech notes for me. All went well and we celebrated with Ian's favourite white lady cocktails in his office afterwards, but it had been an extraordinary, day-long performance. Ian's ebullience made it highly amusing but I never quite understood it.

I was not surprised to hear in November 1985 that he had resigned over the Anglo–Irish Agreement. He had been secretary of the party's Northern Ireland Committee when we were in opposition in the 1970s and he was a principled unionist. Ian joined me and Peter Thomas (Con., Hendon South) in my room overlooking Whitehall to view Prince Andrew and Sarah Ferguson's procession in the honeymoon carriage from Westminster Abbey on 23 July 1986. It was one of our last intimate meetings. His murder by the IRA on 30 July 1990, when he stepped into his car in the driveway at his home, was a gratuitous, senseless killing of a man unflinchingly opposed to such acts of terror and the evildoers behind them.

The Westland affair, which occasioned Michael Heseltine's resignation as secretary of state for Defence and Leon Brittan's as secretary of state for Trade and Industry was a veritable battle of the Titans. Michael made much of the issue of whether Westland's best prospects lay in Europe or with the Americans. Michael favoured Europe. Westland was synonymous with Britain in Michael's eyes but, significant as the helicopter company was to Britain's defence and economy, Michael's feelings on the issue were excessive. His dramatic resignation led one to think that it was the climax of a conflict that had been raging in his mind for some time. It certainly had its repercussions afterwards. Here are some edited entries from my diary:

Saturday, 11 January 1986

The House meets on Monday to the discordant music of Michael Heseltine's resignation over the Westland takeover. There are suspicions that this is the occasion rather than the cause of his departure from the government. My own view is that he has become overwrought. Six and a half years in office is a long time and in major offices too, first Environment and then Defence. Environment is a killer. I know how it blasted Patrick Jenkin's cranium.

Michael's appearance has changed over the last six months or so. His skin seems different, like Keith Joseph's when he went through a traumatic period as secretary of state for industry. I feel sure his judgement has faltered over this issue. Whether the European or the American bid succeeds, the PM wins because she has said 'leave the decision to the shareholders'. The government's future does not hang on the future of Westland. The key to that must be the performance of the economy as a whole.

Tuesday, 14 January 1986

Leon Brittan's denial yesterday on the floor of the House of the existence of a letter from British Aerospace to the PM caused such a furore that he had to make another statement last night. It made matters worse because he admitted that he knew the letter existed. He had therefore misled the House in his earlier reply.

Both he and the PM at Questions today sought refuge in the private and confidential nature of the letter, which they extended from its contents to its existence. The opposition failed to nail either Leon or the PM. Roy Jenkins got nearest to it.

Wednesday, 15 January 1986

Although he defended himself well in the wind-up. Leon did not cover himself with glory and I would not be surprised if he had to go simply because he is going to be a continuing liability. The lid has been taken off the process of government. MPs, let alone the public, have been astonished at 'the goings on'. The dissatisfaction in our own ranks is enormous. The popular line is that the answer for Leon is in the British Aerospace chief executive's name – Sir Raymond Lygo! He has featured prominently in the controversy.

Sunday, 19 January 1986

Much has happened since I last wrote but Leon appears to have saved himself, not so much by his exertions as the fact that his guilt is shared by the PM. If he is soundly thrashed by the Select Committee now examining the issues then, by implication, so will she.

Monday, 20 January 1986

Life for the party is one long banana skin; we seem to be more on it than off. Our minister, Mark Robinson (Con., Newport West) 'dried up' at Welsh Questions today. I had a session with him afterwards to make sure it does not happen again. Whatever the question, whether one understands it or not, one must always have something to say in reply.

Wednesday, 22 January 1986

Leon is still in trouble but it is now over the Solicitor-General's letter to Michael Heseltine, leaked to the press by DTI. Tam Dalyell today named the culprit as Colette Bowe, their press officer. The PM is to make a statement tomorrow – 'robust' we are told.

Thursday, 23 January 1986

Nick told me after Cabinet that the government had reached a critical point. The Lord Chancellor had urged cabinet to rally round the PM. Willie had urged complete frankness. Nick said he had never seen his colleagues so downcast.

The PM's statement and answers afterwards were surprisingly sound but there were some questions left unanswered including when she had been first informed. She maintained that it was only yesterday that the full facts had been presented to her – after the leak inquiry. Yet it was No. 10 who had authorized the leak.

The 1922 Committee were tonight baying for Leon's blood while asserting their loyalty to the PM. We have lost our credibility and it will be a long time before we regain it.

Monday, 27 January 1986

Leon resigned last Friday. The PM cleared the air a little today. She said she had not consented to the leak but, of course, there were a lot of unanswered questions. Both Michael Heseltine and Leon Brittan confirmed her account. John Biffen, winding up, said that the debate was an El Alamein not a Dunkirk.

Monday, 3 February 1986

The Westland row has now moved to the Defence Select Committee who want to interview a host of civil servants. Tonight it was announced that the head of the Civil Service, Sir Robert Armstrong, would appear.

Meanwhile, Michael Heseltine was seen lobbying members after the seven o'clock vote. And Sir Anthony Meyer (Con., Clwyd North) was calling on people to question whether Mrs Thatcher is the best person to lead us in the next election. (He was to challenge her leadership and stand against her as a stalking horse in 1989 – a prelude to Michael's own challenge a year later.)

I dined with Lord (David) Renton and Sir Paul Dean (Con., Woodspring). David tried to cheer us by saying: 'You should read *The Times* and *Guardian* at the time of Suez. The Tory Party was done for according to them but within three years we had one of our greatest election victories.'

The Westland episode and its immediate aftermath should have proved to diehard supporters like myself that the Iron Lady was vulnerable. But I do not recollect that it had that effect. The fact that she escaped unscathed only added an extra dimension to her invincibility.

Towards a Third Term

The Suez Crisis was very much on the minds of the older Conservative members in Mrs Thatcher's middle years as prime minister. Julian Amery (Con., Brighton Pavilion), who addressed the Churchill Club in my constituency in May 1986, recalled Winston's comment on it: 'I am not sure that I would have started on it but I am certain that having started, I would not have dared stop.' Julian was talking in the context of the current discontent with Margaret's conviction politics and urging us, in his own way, to stand fast.

Willie Whitelaw was as active and amusing as ever. When Quintin was at Willie's side, we were guaranteed a comedy. The offence of digging up badgers was up for discussion at a Cabinet Committee. Willie said:

'The Duke of Beaufort used to dig them up.'

'But no more,' said Quintin.

'No. They're digging him up now!'

Powerful as he was, Willie occasionally ran into trouble himself. On 20 July 1986 the *Sunday Times* ran a story about a conflict of views between the Queen and the PM over Rhodesian sanctions. Suspicion fell on Willie as the source. He denied it strongly but the purpose of the story was unmistakably to undermine the PM and Willie was not above suspicion by some on his own side.

After John Stradling Thomas's fall from grace, we had our own reshuffle of portfolios in the Welsh Office. Mark Robinson took over health and housing while I became responsible for education and transport – mainly consisting of our roads programme. Education was not as direct a responsibility as health because we had to work through the local authorities who owned the schools and colleges and managed them from day to day. I familiarized myself with the scene by school and college visits. The children and their teachers were wonderful and the buildings atrocious. The truth of Jim

Callaghan's remark over lunch one day was brought home to me: 'We are trying to provide first-class public services with a second-rate economy.'

There was a daunting shortage of money and no certainty that, if it was provided, it would be spent where it was most needed. Local authorities had a knack of diverting resources to their own grandiose ends. Their county halls were spanking new, rivalling the Taj Mahal in splendour, while their school buildings leaked and their further education colleges overflowed into rickety Portakabins. The more I saw, the more resentful I became at the implicit lack of respect for young people and their needs.

I chaired an advisory board on further education composed of chairmen of local education authorities. Some were fine people capable of rising above their local interest and of taking an all-Wales view. Our main function was to allocate resources in the most beneficial way possible and to encourage the development of worthwhile courses in engineering, electronics and information technology, while at the same time not inhibiting the choice young people made for themselves. All the girls, it seemed, wanted to be hairdressers; in retrospect, they were probably right.

Friday, 13 June 1986 was a beautifully sunny day and, together with Kenneth Baker, newly appointed secretary of state for education, and Michael Ancram, the Scottish education minister, I attended a tea party at Lancaster House for hundreds of exchange teachers from the US, the Commonwealth and the European Community. The Queen Mother was there, chatting tirelessly with one group after another for at least two hours. Her endurance amazed me. At 5.15 p.m. she descended the steps with us and said with a sweet smile:

'I shall go home now.'

I looked around for her car. It was not in sight; neither was her equerry. There was no one to look after the old lady. On impulse, I said:

'Shall I accompany you, ma'am?'

'What a splendid idea,' she replied.

I did not know where her home was until Kenneth thankfully joined me and pointed out that Clarence House was only fifty yards away. I have always been glad that we walked her home in the sunshine of that late afternoon.

The national committee that looked after schools in Wales – the WJEC (Welsh Joint Education Committee) – comprised all the education authorities and representatives of other interested parties. It was a large body, predominantly Labour, with its own chief officer.

It also provided the examining board for Welsh schools. Towards the end of 1985, it was under mounting pressure, from within and without, to form a special committee to safeguard the interests of schools where pupils were taught through the medium of Welsh. Such schools were becoming popular not only with Welsh-speaking parents but with English-speaking parents too because the teaching was good.

I had a difficult meeting with the leaders of the WJEC in late November. They were divided on the issue of a special committee and it looked as if they would not set up such a committee at all. A few days later I buttonholed the toughest opponent, Philip Squire, and in return for a promise of fresh funds for his local polytechnic he agreed to 'oblige the minister'. But the WJEC was still desperately slow in giving a positive response. Meanwhile, the Welsh Language Society was becoming increasingly vocal in its demands. Some members had already wrecked a health exhibition at the National Eisteddfod at Rhyl in 1985 by putting their boots into computers and other equipment. To civilized people, their vandalism was horrendous.

On 19 April 1986, I addressed Parents for Welsh Medium Education in Welsh at Pontypridd and outlined the substantial progress made since 1979. The increase in the money provided to support the language was a fair measure of such advancement. The speech was well received but the question session afterwards was marred by diatribes by young Welsh Language Society members accusing the government of failing to support the WJEC's special committee. On my way out of the building, my private secretary, Simon Morris, whispered to me that the exit of my official car was blocked by protesters but that our press officer's car was waiting – with its engine running – just beyond their barricade. I headed for the official car and then turned quickly at the last moment to the press officer's vehicle. Realizing that they had been duped, some of the protesters ran after us and one threw himself on the bonnet. When the car swerved at the end of the drive, he slid off onto the grass verge. The entire scene was captured on camera and shown on television news that evening. Sadly, the young man on the bonnet, Steffan Webb, had injured himself in his fall.

A similar scuffle, this time involving the police, took place when I visited Gwynedd County Council in Caernarfon in July. I have a distinct recollection of the protesters' leader, Angharad Tomos, with her face and long, wild hair pressed for an instant against the car windscreen before she was peeled off by a burly gentleman in blue.

I saw the chairman of the WJEC, Councillor Fred Kingdom, and the language and culture chairman, Councillor Emyr Currie Jones, in Cardiff on 4 August. I pressed them to set up the Welsh Medium Education Committee and we agreed how it might be financed but I was left to issue a press notice on my own because they had to have the approval of their main body. The WJEC formally announced the setting up of the committee in December – more than a year since we had first discussed the proposal. Not long afterwards, their offices were burgled and the Welsh Language Society accepted responsibility. Heaven only knows what they had hoped to find.

A highly respected man who had devoted his life to young people in Wales spoke to me later about Welsh Language Society members: 'Protest is their life. If they are not protesting, they are not doing anything of any significance to their generation. You have become their focus. When you've gone, God knows what they'll do.' It was one way of looking at it. I was always cool and more concerned about their safety than my own.

Enid and I were in London for the first weekend in May 1986. The Russian nuclear reactor, one of four at Chernobyl in the Ukraine, had exploded a good week earlier (24 April) and was now on fire. It rained heavily and I told my wife that I was glad we were not at home in Snowdonia because the mountains attracted nuclear fall-out. There had been a scare some years earlier when high levels of strontium 90 were found in the hills. Although I did not know it at the time, I was right to be concerned about the fallout from Chernobyl. Radioactive matter was being borne on the wind as far north as Lapland and across the North Sea to Scotland, Cumbria and Wales.

On Tuesday, 6 May Lord (Walter) Marshall, chairman of the Central Electricity Generating Board, lunched with us at the Welsh Office. He had visited Chernobyl in the past and had seen the reactor – a military-type installation without the safety features of nuclear power stations in the UK. What worried Marshall was that the Russians were trying to put out the fire with sand and lead, dropped from helicopters. He feared that radioactivity would continue and that there might be another fearful explosion in a month to six weeks.

Nick Edwards was back at the office after a spell in hospital but he had not yet fully recovered and I was still taking his place at odd meetings. Reports began to emerge that radioactive matter had been found in lichen in Scandinavia and that herds of reindeer had been contaminated and slaughtered to prevent pollution entering the food chain. One day, I was summoned to deputize for Nick at an urgent meeting with Michael Jopling, the agriculture minister. There was no brief, which worried me a little since agriculture was not one of my normal responsibilities.

I found Michael's room crowded with ministry vets. We were informed that sheep in the uplands had been found to have high levels of radio caesium. Lambs were coming on to the market in large numbers and steps had to be taken urgently to stop the caesium from entering the food chain. 'What do you suggest?' asked Michael. One senior vet said that the only way to be absolutely sure was to take a kilo of meat from the neck of every lamb killed, test it in a laboratory and then if it was free of contamination, the rest of the carcass could be safely eaten. I shook my head at Michael. The whole process would take far too long. The sheep industry would be totally devastated. I asked whether it might not be possible to isolate the farms where the caesium levels were high, much as we did when there were outbreaks of foot and mouth disease. This was the thinking that eventually prevailed and by early August I was meeting local representatives of the farming unions, hard hit by the movement restrictions imposed on their flocks. It could have been far worse for them had that vet's view won the day.

I got some relief from the pressures of office fishing for salmon at the Beaver Pool in the River Conwy near Betws-y-Coed. The fishing rights were owned by Jack Flynn, an ex-Mancunian bookmaker turned hotelier, and an old friend of Bill Swan, the retired owner of an organ and piano shop at the Arndale Centre, Manchester. It was Bill who inducted me into the salmon fishing business. He was a vociferous Tory and once draped himself in a Union Jack when he spoke at a party conference. He had not touched a drop of liquor until his thirties and remembered the days when he had gone around singing a travesty of the gospel song:

> Dare to be a Daniel,
> Dare to stand alone
> Dare to pass a public house
> Dare it on your own.

He had made up for his abstinence in later years and carried a whisky cabinet with him on our fishing expeditions. He was prone to fall asleep after listening to the news in his car – always parked as near to the river bank as possible – with his line still in the water and wound around his thumb in case he had a bite. His tackle box contained everything from illegal salmon paste he swore he never used to a spinner bought in Florida named Marilyn Monroe because of the way it wiggled seductively through the water. I never caught anything in Bill's presence although he landed a couple of fine salmon himself.

I made my first unforgettable catch on Friday, 4 September 1986. I recorded this momentous event in my diary at 6.30 a.m. the following day.

Saturday, 5 September 1986

That fishing had become an obsession was clear to me by Thursday evening when, after arriving home from the river, the vision of the dark, whirling waters and their kingly contents persisted in my mind. Seeing some corks bought years ago for bottling wine, I thought they would be excellent for floating a line gently downstream and avoiding the rocks below. I put in light staples to secure them to the line a yard or so from the bait.

When I arrived at Jack Flynn's fishing hut beside the pool, there was no one about and so I was able to make my preparations calmly and to cast my line, cork, small lead weight and triple hook loaded with worms into the lightly foamed current. Of worm bait, Jack had said: 'They're like a T-bone steak to a salmon.'

Freddie Ormett, a retired drummer whose presence on the river Jack just about tolerated – 'his pipe frightens the fish' – arrived about noon. Both of us took a fairly pessimistic view of our catch prospects. The previous day's spate had subsided and the water was becoming clearer by the hour. True, a large fish had been leaping regularly the previous evening at the spot where I was now fishing but he had probably long gone upstream to the spawning grounds with his mate. All I was hoping for was a hungry sea trout. Suddenly, my cork bobbed down below the surface and up again.

'You've got a fish there,' said Freddie. 'Snatch it.' And so I did.

No one was more surprised than I to feel the line truly tight and a fish coming in quietly as I reeled it towards me. I kept my rod well up. It was only when the fish came within sight of land that he began to fight back.

'You've got a salmon there,' said Freddie. 'Don't hold the line too tight.'

But I kept on reeling him in.

'Tire him out first,' said Freddie.

By this time, the fish was fairly close and I caught sight of him turning in the water. He was big but there was no telling how big and then he began his real fight to get away. My line was too tightly wound and I was afraid it would break under the strain of his powerful tugs but as it held my confidence grew. His great tail rose above the water in the distance.

'He's tiring,' said Freddie, but it did not feel like it.

There was another strong pull away from me and the tense spool groaned on the rod. But the line did not snap. The fish was coming in closer, to the right of the jetty where Freddie was poised with his landing net.

'Try and get him to the other side . . . it's easier there,' said Freddie.

The fish must have heard him and obligingly fought his way round the head of the jetty but, when Freddie tried to net him, he shied away to the depths once more. His tail came up again and I now saw his broad side, twisting and writhing against the thin line whose frailty I was so conscious of under his dying weight as I dragged him back to be scooped out of the pool. We did not have a priest to hand and Freddie stunned him with a stone.

'It's a cock,' he said. I did not ask how he knew. I simply stood in amazement over this enormous, yet so graceful creature, my first salmon, and tried to guess his weight.

'It's more than a fourteen pounder,' said Freddie, 'bigger than the one Jack caught. Must be about seventeen pounds.'

'Get him to the bank,' I said, as the great mouth opened and closed. I still believed he could leap right back into the water and I was probably right. Freddie extracted the hook from his mouth and we carried him up to the hut and put a sea line around his tail because he kept slithering from our grasp. We could not find a weighing device and Freddie went off home to get one.

'Phone Enid,' I shouted, 'and ask her to phone Jack Flynn.'

Freddie's sister-in-law, Mrs Sharrocks-Carter arrived with an oil painting she had made of the Beaver Pool which I had promised to view that day. I bought it on the spot. She took photographs of the salmon and me. When Jack and Enid arrived, he told me:

'Enid left a message for me to call her urgently . . . I thought Bill Swan had snuffed it.'

Towards evening, I went down to the riverbank for a last look at the pool. The light was beginning to fail. Suddenly, there was a great splash on the far side and a little later I saw my salmon's mate leap again. She was looking for him. A sadness began gnawing somewhere inside me.

I told Jack what I had seen. He was sceptical.

'No. His mate is probably down in Conwy by now – claiming her widow's pension.'

Politicians are always thinking of the next election, especially in the last couple of years before it takes place. In the early months of 1986, it seemed to me that we had run too far ahead of the electorate and should pause to explain and enable people to catch up with our thinking.

The economic situation, though better in many ways, was still disappointing. The euphoria that should have come from a successful steel and a reformed coal industry was not materializing. The cost had been great and we were still breathless from our exertions. Unemployment continued to be a burden though the unemployed themselves were not as dismal as Labour politicians made out. I visited a job club at Shotton and found the members highly motivated in their search for work. Nevertheless, the sore and hurt of the steel plant closure still rankled. I had hoped the country would be in far better spirits by now.

At the Welsh Office, we were pursuing some positive policies to enliven the economy. New investment from abroad was trickling in. There was a Valleys Initiative to be unveiled in a month or so and a Rural Enterprise Initiative. The problem was to secure enough money to make them significant.

Personally, I was grappling with the reform of careers education where I found diverse groups of officials working in different areas quite independently of one another. I discovered one such group, over a hundred strong, not directly responsible to anyone. They had never met a minister until I called them together. Cohesion was desperately required.

The March 1986 Budget was sound and promising. I felt that we were in a better position to win the next election than our opponents. Both opposition parties were committed to devolution for Scotland and Wales, primarily because they feared the nationalists. I had long considered the devolution issue and concluded that Wales would be well served so long as it had a powerful secretary of state with a voice in the Cabinet. Nick had the voice all right, strong enough to fill a cathedral. The Labour benches were comparatively weak. But we were still trailing the opposition in May and it was only at our highly successful party conference at Bournemouth in October that I sensed that our juggernaut was beginning to roll. Themes that I had touched upon in constituency speeches the previous month were fully amplified: popular capitalism through privatization, better presentation of our achievements and the fundamental weaknesses of our opponents. Unforeseen events might yet derail us but my heart was set on another victory at the polls. The 'events' came sooner than I expected.

The Jeffrey Archer scandal broke early in November. 'It did not rock the party,' I noted, 'but the Shepherd's Market episode – if indeed it is true – surprised many of us. I was personally much amused by a *Daily Telegraph* cartoon of two street girls with one saying to the other: "No, but I've read the book and seen the TV series." Lord Chesterfield's maxim was much quoted: "the price is exorbitant, the pleasure transient and the position ridiculous".'

Jeffrey had entered the House through a by-election at Louth in 1969 and I had been impressed by his impersonation of Iain Macleod. He had not stood in 1974 because of his failed investment in a venture called Aquablast but he had made a fortune with his books. One of my colleagues had seen him walk out of a film-rights auction in New York 'a million pounds richer'.

Labour was presenting its new rosy image with great success and would promise the earth to be returned.

In the afternoon of Thursday, 11 December, Nick Edwards told my fellow minister, Mark Robinson, and myself that he would not be standing again for Pembrokeshire. I had thought for some time that he did not intend carrying on as secretary of state because over recent months he had been garnering initiatives and starting developments, such as Cardiff Bay, which would occupy the Welsh Office for months and possibly years to come. Nick was like a pedigree horse and when he got the bit between his teeth there was no holding him. He had become as close as an elder brother to me, always watchful, always critical; yet there had never been a cross word between us.

But he had not enjoyed good health while he was at the Welsh Office. (He has given an account of his illness in his book *Westminster, Wales and Water.*) The miracle was that he survived as long as he did in spite of weight loss, extensive travel and a devastating burden of work that would have flattened a less spirited man. I had become increasingly concerned as his health visibly deteriorated. Occasionally, when I feared he might collapse, I sat beside him on the front bench clutching a copy of a statement he was making. He put every last ounce of energy into his performances and I could only marvel at his power and endurance. But his lifestyle was killing him and he wanted out. He had discussed the matter with the PM and an announcement would be made next day. My first concern was that we would miss his strong, forceful leadership in the coming election.

Back in February, Sir George Young (Con., Ealing, Acton), under secretary of state at Environment, had pointed out to me that we two were the last of the 1979 batch of parliamentary under secretaries. The others had either been promoted or ousted. I had begun to feel that I was only being kept on because of my Welshness and at as low a ministerial level as possible, in spite of frequent calls by colleagues that I should be promoted, especially after Sir John Stradling Thomas's departure.

Nick's impending resignation prompted me to write to the PM and the chief whip asking that I should be made a minister of state so that we should not be leaderless in the coming campaign. It was a fair not a selfish point but the PM brushed it aside and when the old year ended, I was in the doldrums wondering if I should bother to stand again. The mood passed during the recess and I wrote in my diary:

> I shall return to Parliament without much relish for the fray ahead but I shall rely on my professionalism. We must succeed. I do believe that it is necessary for our future development as a country. Labour are ill prepared for office and the Alliance are very wishy-washy, all things to all men.
>
> Sadly, I feel that the days of the Tory revival in Wales are numbered unless we have good leadership and we do not have it at present. Nick has his eyes set on the Lords.

In the early months of 1987 the timing of the election became tricky. There was a deep undercurrent running against both us and the Labour Party and the Alliance was attracting a substantial protest vote.

Willie Whitelaw addressed the Churchill Club in my constituency and told me a lot. Nick had let us down by not standing again. He wanted some other office but there was nothing for him. He could not be secretary of state for Wales sitting in the Lords – a story floated by Peterborough in the *Telegraph*; there would be an almighty row. I suggested Michael Howard; he was Llanelli bred. 'No, You must be humble . . . you cannot come down to Wales and tell people what to do.'

I wrote to Willie afterwards and told him he had cheered me up. Sir Anthony Meyer and other Welsh members were strong in their support for me.

The PM came to north-east Wales on Friday, 13 March 1987 and I accompanied her throughout her visit to Flint and elsewhere. She must have captivated me totally because I wrote next day:

> I am now beginning to understand the core of goodness in her that gives her an inexhaustible supply of energy. Her sustained vitality, her interest in all things and her great humanity flow from that inner core.
>
> She is more of a saint than a statesman. Wrong headedness on the part of others only highlights her own rectitude; she counters it with her own view and a determination that it shall prevail against a sea of evil.
>
> She finds her own goodness reflected in the common sense of ordinary people she meets – nurses, patients, young people and workers.
>
> If the electorate rejects her, it will be for the same reason as saints are always rejected. The forces ranged against her will vitiate her image, her motives, her policies.

I do not appear to have mentioned to her my personal ambition at all. Her performance was beyond any such triviality.

A couple of weeks previously, Julian Critchley had told me that there were two nameless members who had wagered as to which of them would be the first to lay Mrs T when she first entered the House in 1959. Neither had won the bet. 'But she screwed you all!' I said, mindful of the fact that Julian was still waiting for his knighthood. I could now add myself to her collection.

We had a good Budget the following week – 2p off income tax and higher allowances with the borrowing requirement kept down to £4 billion. Interest and mortgage rates fell. We launched a fierce attack on the Alliance who were running second to us in too many seats (268). They ran second to Labour in 48 only.

There was still one unhappy event to come: multiple share applications for the British Telecommunications issue.

'What has your friend in Anglesey been up to?' asked Eric Cockeram (Con., Ludlow) when he joined my table at dinner. It turned out that he too – like Keith Best – had put in more than one application. I asked him why he had not put one in his wife's name.

'Never thought of it,' he said.

Both he and Keith had to withdraw as candidates.

The local government election results in May were favourable to us and the PM closeted herself at Chequers to finalize her decision on the election call. On Sunday, 10 May we looked set to win on 11 June on a stable government ticket. The Labour Party would argue that it was time for a change and the Alliance would plead that they should hold the balance of power, whichever major party won. Personally, I looked forward to three weeks away from Westminster and Whitehall but I did not relish the prospects thereafter.

If I am asked to be secretary of state, I shall accept knowing that there will be a couple of years of very hard work ahead. I am getting no younger – I shall be fifty-seven in July – but I still have good health. If I am not asked to serve in the top job, I am not keen to continue in my present role. If I refuse to serve, that will be the end of my political career and the beginning of a serious decline in our Conservative fortunes in Wales. It will be countered in due course by a resurgence of nationalism in one form or another.

Sunday, 14 June 1987

The election has come and gone. Mrs Thatcher and the Tories have been returned with a majority of more than a hundred; a unique and historic event and the first time since Lord Liverpool for a PM to be elected for a third term. The victory is even more remarkable considering that we did not run a very good campaign and that Labour rose to new heights of presentation, packaging Neil Kinnock as a president and selling him on the media with great expertise.

At the end of the day, people vote according to their interest. Thatcher and the Tories are trusted while Labour are not. The militants and the trade union bosses were in the wings all the time and people were conscious of it. The Alliance were soft and never broke through. Labour did well in Scotland and Wales where they took five of our seats because of the Alliance collapse. My majority fell because Labour performed better than last time. I did not cavort about the country but campaigned vigorously at home and on the media.

When it became known that I was the only surviving Welsh Office minister, there was strong speculation that I would be made secretary of state. I certainly did not fancy the possibility of a young outsider coming in to cut his Cabinet teeth on Wales. Surprise! Surprise! The PM appointed Peter Walker whom I regarded as an old friend and respected as a minister of great experience. He was the only Cabinet minister who had visited my constituency during the campaign. I thought he would be good for Wales and never felt a twinge of personal disappointment. In truth, I found myself anxious to stay in office if Peter wanted me. At fifty-five, he could be the next prime minister.

We spoke and I told him the line I was taking with the press who were hounding me every hour – 'an inspired choice . . . tower of strength . . . a very strong voice for Wales in the Cabinet'. He asked me to be his number two and I agreed. (Nick had recommended me.) Whether the PM would give me a minister of state's position depended on the number of such posts she had to give, said Peter. I did not attach great importance to it but Enid did. It would be a sign that the PM appreciated my eight years of service and loyalty to her. Peter asked me to meet him in London on Monday at 6 p.m.

5 p.m., Monday, 15 June 1987

The PM telephoned me at 3.50 p.m. to ask me to be minister of state for Wales. The dialogue was brief:

PM: How are you?

Me: Fit as a fiddle. (She seemed taken aback by my abruptness.)

PM: I want you to be minister of state . . . a mark of respect . . . you are the only Welsh speaker in the government . . . I am sure you will do it well.

Me: I am honoured Prime Minister. My wife will be delighted. I have arranged to see Peter at six tonight.

For some reason, I added to my note of the conversation Mitterand's comment on her: 'She has the eyes of Caligula and the lips of Marilyn Monroe.' Perhaps I intended it as an antidote to my hero worship of her.

Walker's Way

Peter Walker was the cleverest man I have ever worked with. He had the intelligence to grasp quickly what needed to be done and the experience to know just how to do it. He also had an extraordinary ability and industry to drive his ideas to fruition with a smile and seeming effortlessness. He was a political 'striker' par excellence and a joy to watch achieving his goals. He was also a homely man, with a lovely wife, Tessa, and five adorable children. He had made his fortune before entering politics and had the independent spirit of a man of substance. (Curiously, he and Jim Slater had taken over a company that had belonged to my friend, John Lotery's father.) Peter had been a political 'whiz kid' and on the Conservative front bench since 1964. He had managed Ted Heath's election as leader and had subsequently served as secretary of state for the Environment and later for Trade and Industry in Ted Heath's government (1970–4).

He had remained on the front bench in the intervening years and Margaret had appointed him minister for agriculture, fisheries and food (1979–83) and later secretary of state for energy (1983–7). His politics were known to differ from hers – he was an interventionist of Harold Macmillan's 'Middle Way' school – but his formidable talents were highly valued. He and Margaret had reached some kind of tolerant, pragmatic accommodation over the years. When Margaret asked him to become secretary of state for Wales, he accepted on condition that he could 'do it my way'. (He tells the story in his autobiography, *Staying Power* (1991)). I genuinely welcomed his appointment because I thought he would be a tonic for Wales and he was.

I met Peter as arranged at his home in Cowley Street and over a goblet of champagne, we discussed personalities at the Welsh Office. Ian Grist (Con., Cardiff Central) who had been a colleague in the Commons since he was first elected MP for Cardiff North in 1974, had now been appointed a PUSS and came up to London the following day. Peter gave us a splendid lunch at La Capanini's in Romilly Street. It was to be the last of our post-election celebrations before we got down to serious work.

It was only a matter of weeks before Peter took up the formidable challenge of restoring the south Wales valleys and he tackled it with a will and determination all his own. It was the biggest challenge in Wales, faced only spasmodically over the years by his predecessors who tended to shrug their shoulders when they came up against the grim enormity of the task. The valleys were Labour heartlands, ruled by Labour local authorities and returning Labour MPs with vast majorities. They were shrouded in their own black clouds of pessimism. No one was more embarrassed than Labour by Peter's cheerful commitment and they tried their best to disparage his efforts. But the psychological effect of his persistent optimism was considerable and the valleys people took to him as their new Messiah.

His Valleys Initiative began with a concentration of all the resources available from various budgets – health, education, roads and so on – and developed momentum as he secured more resources. They were devoted to land reclamation and factory building by the Welsh Development Agency and environmental improvements by all and sundry, from Barratts, the housebuilders, to the brewers, Whitbread and Bass. It was a good story and Peter made sure it was told. The telling was part of the business of focusing public attention on what was being done and encouraging people to do more. The opposition called it 'hype' but there were many places that had a facelift and looked brighter and better as a result. Even Margaret was impressed when she visited the Rhondda in Peter's company.

It all involved some very hard work on his part. On one occasion, when he had set off at 5 a.m. from Cowley Street to address a businessmen's breakfast in Cardiff and returned to answer Welsh Questions at Westminster in the early afternoon, he asked me if I would take over his engagements for the rest of the day. His youngest, Marianna, was unwell and he wished to be with his family; his car and driver would be at my disposal. I readily agreed without knowing quite what I was in for.

Within the hour, I was on my way to Cardiff to present awards on television to young entrepreneurs. It was a substantial programme, requiring rehearsal before a live transmission. It was past midnight before I was back in London. It was not an untypical day for Peter Walker. He liked challenging schedules as I found again when I took over one of his foreign engagements. It involved flying to Lisbon one morning and ending the day at a late dinner with members of the Portuguese cabinet. Next morning, I flew to Madrid for a whirlwind round of engagements and returned to London that night, shattered by my exertions and dazed with fatigue.

But I am rushing ahead – as one always did when Peter was around. We had the usual eve of session dinner at No. 10 and, having arrived early, I had a chance to thank the PM for my appointment as minister of state. She seemed more concerned about the absence of drinks and, when they arrived, she kept on urging us to keep our glasses charged for the loyal toast at the start of proceedings. When Sir Robert Armstrong came to read the Gracious Speech, she said: 'And Bobbie, here's a soapbox for you!' Someone pushed the little box towards him and he stood on it as she did herself when she addressed us.

I sat between Tom King and Lord (Bertie) Denham, captain of the Gentlemen at Arms or government chief whip in the Lords. Tom described how he was chaired and carried shoulder high after his election victory in Bridgewater. Bertie told me the story of how Bill Molloy (later Lord), originally from Swansea, had been unable to take up a scholarship at the Royal College of Dramatic Art and had passed it on to one Richard Jenkins of Taibach, alias Richard Burton.

Michael Heseltine – still in the wilderness after the Westland affair – joined my table at the House for dinner twice in the first week in July. He was vehemently opposed to the community charge – already rechristened the poll tax – and was girding himself to play a leading role when the Local Government Bill came before the House.

Richard Ryder (Con., Norfolk Mid, now Lord) and a whip was with us on the second occasion when we spoke of the PM's worries about the conduct of the election campaign, shortly to be published in *The Selling of the Prime Minister*. Richard knew the author, Rodney Tyler. I jokingly asked whether Tyler was also writing a book about the poll tax and Wat Tyler, the leader of the Peasants' Revolt of 1381. The long shadows of coming events were already beginning to form.

The summer recess was busier than usual and included two inward-investment missions – one to the US (29 August–8 September) and the other to Germany (27 September–1 October). I had an embarrassingly heavy cold when I arrived at the Hotel Plaza in New York. The humidity and a soaking in a shower of pencil long rain when we walked to lunch with the British Tourist Authority did not improve it.

There was no 'down-time' either but I managed to take my new private secretary, Ceri Thomas, on a humid Saturday afternoon to Dylan Thomas's haunt, the White Horse, in Greenwich Village. The down-at-heel pub seemed totally different from the establishment I had previously visited in the 1960s but there were historic posters advertising a performance of *Under Milk Wood*. Dylan's reputation seemed to have died a death.

We visited a score of companies in New York State and then headed north. There were two major companies in Michigan with subsidiary plants in Wales – Dow Chemicals and Dow Corning in Midland – and there were two more in Minnesota – 3Ms, best known for their videotapes, and the Advance Machine Company at St Paul's. I was impressed by 3Ms' stated aim that a high proportion of their sales should consist of products developed in the last five years and by the elaborate steps they took to encourage employees to work up their ideas to enhance the company's performance. Time and resources were made available to all.

The Advance Machine Company was owned and run by a larger-than-life character, Bill Pond, who collected Second World War planes as a hobby. The company made mechanical sweeping and brushing machines. Pond had converted one of his machines into a people-carrying buggy and we toured the acres of factory space with him at the wheel. All these companies were in an expansionist mood and wanted to increase their sales in Europe from a sub-sidiary base in the UK. My visit helped concentrate their minds on the advantages of expanding their production facilities in Wales.

I spent a weekend at St Paul's and attended a hymn-singing festival which had attracted more than a thousand people of Welsh extraction from all over the US – including a much loved, former teacher of mine, 'Miss Davies Welsh' as we called her at Beaumaris. On Sunday, there was a well-attended chapel service, including a Welsh sermon. It was a warm day and the women cooled themselves with wheat-coloured fans. Many of 3Ms' employees – migrants from Gorseinon, Wales – were in the congregation.

Some months previously, I had browsed in a fascinating volume titled *History of the Welsh in Minnesota*, published in the 1880s. I remembered seeing, among the plans of chapels, a drawing of a vast scaffold for a mass hanging of more than a hundred Indians after the Sioux rebellion of 1863. Their crime had been to take all the women and children from the Welsh settlement into the wilds.

The Indians had returned them when the rebellion collapsed, hoping for forgiveness. But the women's tales were harrowing. The president, Abraham Lincoln, intervened and some of the Indians were spared but the majority were hanged. Hardly any traces remain of the original Welsh settlements.

My visit to Stuttgart, Germany, was full of intriguing possibilities. I paid a courtesy call on the Land government of Baden-Württemberg and was greeted by their economics minister, Dr Leibing. He told me how their premier-president, Lothar Spath, was fast developing relationships with the neighbouring Rhone-Alpes region of France, the province of Lombardy in northern Italy and Catalonia in Spain. They called themselves the 'Four Motors', as the foremost enterprising regions in Europe, and were striving towards ever greater prosperity. It struck me immediately that this was the kind of grouping that Wales should try to belong to: it would connect us directly to the heart of Europe and associate us with powerful, go-ahead regions, rather better off than ourselves. We could learn from them and they from us. We would sidestep the bureaucracy in Brussels. Wales was smaller in population but we would have the backing of the UK government. Car engines made in Wales by Ford at Bridgend were already being transported to Stuttgart. If car parts could travel, so could people. I broached the possibility of Wales joining the Four Motors at my first meeting with Leibing and we both agreed to consult with our superiors.

My key adviser was the British consul-general in Frankfurt, Julian Hartland-Swann. He was most anxious that I should meet the oberbürgermeister of Stuttgart, Manfred Rommel, son of 'the Desert Fox' as the German field marshal was known to our troops in North Africa during the war. There were good reasons why I should meet this executive lord mayor. Stuttgart was twinned with Cardiff but, even more importantly, relationships between the city and the UK were at a low ebb because we had closed down our consulate there. (The British ambassador had been snubbed when he tried to visit the city officially.)

Rommel, who had been cared for in England by Montgomery after his father's suicide at Hitler's command, invited me to dinner. He spoke English fluently and told me all about Stuttgart, its people and its problems. The Swabians were an industrious lot, he said, so much so that one had asked that his ashes should be put in an egg-timer to give him something to do in the afterlife. They had their own word for poor quality work – *pfusch* – and so he went on. As oberbürgermeister, he was the head not only of local government but of the health service as well; his powers extended far into the business and economic life of the community. I told him of my ambitions for Wales and the possible association with the Four Motors. Hartland-Swann chipped in with the potential benefits for the city, which had not been lost on Rommel. We parted on very cordial terms, convinced that Anglo–Stuttgart relations were on a better footing than before.

As a matter of interest, Stuttgart was the birthplace of the philosopher, Hegel. The poet and dramatist, Schiller, lived there. It was also the birthplace of Gottfried Benz and the headquarters of Mercedes-Benz. Robert Bosch, founder of the firm that bears his name, was also of Stuttgart. Bosch were later to establish a major plant at Miskin in south Wales It was a city worth cultivating for cultural as well as business reasons.

On my return, I reported all to Peter Walker, who gave his enthusiastic support. Lynda Chalker at the Foreign Office was also pleased with our progress. Not long after, Dr Leibing and I drafted an agreement for Wales's association with Baden-Württemberg. Peter went to Stuttgart and Lothar Spath visited the UK. Peter introduced him to the PM. She apparently spoke non-stop and barely allowed Spath to get a word in edgeways. Perhaps it was just as well that she did not know too much about what we regionalists were up to. Meanwhile, I was determined to tackle Lombardy and Catalonia when I had the chance.

During the recess, my desk at home was piled high with papers relating to the coming Education Bill. We had set off with the sound notion that we should safeguard English, maths and science as core subjects in the curriculum and ensure that they were not displaced by 'softer' subjects, as appeared to be happening in many schools. But what was to be the fate of other subjects – history, geography, domestic science and physical education and so on – when the core subjects had been enshrined in statute? What was going to be the status of Welsh, particularly in Welsh-medium schools? The Department of Education and Science, then sited at the Elephant and Castle, and our educationists at the Welsh Office had latched on to the concept of foundation subjects and this appeared in the first draft of the bill.

Peter was away and I attended two Cabinet Committee meetings at No. 10 on Wednesday, 28 October 1987. In the morning, we discussed the future of television broadcasting, especially the fourth channel, including S4C. I was relieved to hear the PM say, with some fervour, that she did not propose to reopen the Welsh issue. Willie Whitelaw said amen to that. The future of S4C seemed secure whatever regime was established for the fourth channel in the rest of the UK. I did not have to fight my corner.

At the afternoon meeting, the subject was education and the PM tore into the education secretary, Kenneth Baker's paper on the National Curriculum where he proposed foundation as well as core subjects. She was opposed to anything apart from the core.

'We started off with a good idea and you've ruined it,' she said.

'With respect, Prime Minister . . .'

'Forget the respect . . . let's get it right.'

In retrospect, I think she was correct in her view. Baker was trying to get a quart into a pint pot, but I did not intervene and put my head over the parapet. I had already agreed Kenneth's paper and I was not going to let him down. Had she pursued a softer, more persuasive approach, the outcome might have been different. (Kenneth later objected to the record of the meeting.)

My own paper was only lightly touched upon towards the end of this sharp exchange and I made much of points that I knew would appeal to her. Welsh would not be a compulsory subject in all schools in Wales although there would be a presumption in favour of it. (I had not forgotten what I had been told about the Irish experience with compulsory Gaelic.) It would of course be a core subject in Welsh-medium schools. We would have our own Curriculum Council. The paper was accepted – pro tem!

I circulated a draft document on Welsh aspects of the National Curriculum within government with a deadline for comment set at 'close of play' (6 p.m.) on Thursday, 19 November. A copy was sent to No. 10. I was concerned as to what the reaction from the PM might be – it was just the sort of esoteric stuff she might read – but as the days passed and there was no comment I began to relax. On the Thursday, I was in Cardiff and when I caught the 5.25 p.m. train back to London I must have had a smirk on my face. It was soon wiped off when I arrived in Paddington. Eileen, my driver told me: 'The prime minister wants to see you as soon as you get back to the House.' I gulped a large black coffee and went along to her room. Her PPS, Archie Hamilton (now Lord), offered me a whisky. I accepted but did not touch the contents. I knew I had to win through the tirade to come or perish in the storm.

She began by venting her dissatisfaction with the bill as a whole. All she had wanted were the core subjects but those people at the

Department of Education, her secretary of state and I had betrayed her. We had succumbed to our officials. She knew how devious and manipulative they could be: she had been education secretary herself once. We had introduced foundation subjects, including Welsh, and the entire bill was a mess and so was my consultative document, which she had boldly underlined in red here and there. It lay open on a low coffee table along with a copy of the bill. She was strutting and moving about like a boxer looking for an opening.

'But we are taking a power to exempt schools from teaching foundation subjects . . .' I said.

'You will have to consult before exercising it. Don't you realize that you will be laying yourselves open to judicial review? You'll never get away with it. You will have all kinds of applications for exemption . . . from history, geography and certainly Welsh . . . you will be flooded with applications . . . And you will consult? On each and every one of them? You will be at it till doomsday . . .'

There was no holding her now: she was in full spate.

'I don't think it will be as bad as you make out, Prime Minister.'

'You wait!' and she was off again, like a thoroughbred from a starting gate.

At one point she got down on her knees on the carpet beside the coffee table to hammer home to me what the bill actually said. I leaned down beside her.

'That's an early draft. It's been changed,' I countered.

'Get me the latest,' she ordered. Someone ran to Kenneth Baker's room to get the latest version from his desk. Thank goodness, my memory of the change was right but there was no let-up in her barrage of criticism.

'You can do what you like in your Welsh-speaking schools but look here . . . you define them as schools where "the majority of subjects are taught through the medium of Welsh". Don't you see that your nationalists will exploit that definition, use a bit of Welsh in teaching all sorts of subjects and claim to be Welsh-speaking schools even though their pupils are monoglot English?'

'Not a chance, Prime Minister. Welsh-medium schools are clearly identified. You can't change a school overnight as you are suggesting . . .'

I was on safer ground now but if she wanted 'more than half' instead of 'the majority' of subjects, I was prepared to concede. It was the only concession I made and the only one noted in the following day's brief report from her office of our contentious meeting. But other things had been said which were hurtful and lingered in my mind for days. Wales and Scotland were holding England back.

'You have nothing! You contribute nothing!' she said with great emphasis.

I was tempted to say that we had a lot of Japanese companies – more than England – but I refrained. I knew that she would make a mountainous denunciation of our inadequacy from such a reply.

'The only Conservatives in Wales are the English who moved in.'

I did not let her get away with that – I had hundreds of Welsh-born Conservatives in my constituency and told her so.

We had been at each other hammer and tongs for an hour and forty minutes and I had not been worsted as far as I was aware. I knew that it would be fatal to give in to her. My blood would be on the carpet and my brains on the curtains. The ten o'clock division was coming up and Archie Hamilton moved in with some presentation whisky bottles for her to sign. She did so automatically while still talking to me – a little less strident now. 'I thought I could do things with a few like-minded people on my side but I find I am on my own.' It was to be her recurring theme from then on.

I ventured to sip the small whisky Archie had poured me before our humdinger of a row began and left the room as she moved on to other things. As the door closed behind me, I heard her laugh out loud. I wondered whether she was laughing at my performance or her own. She had probably enjoyed the fray.

Later, Archie asked me if I had been 'rattled' and I replied that I had not. He told me that I was not alone in being subjected to post-prandial inquisitions of that kind. News of the altercation sped around Whitehall. Kenneth Baker told me: 'I hear you've had a taste of what I've been having for weeks. Why did you send your document to her? I keep everything away from her.' Professor Brian Griffiths (now Lord), her adviser at No. 10, told me that he was not res-ponsible for the line she took and was sending her a note. Peter Walker also sent a letter I had drafted with officials.

I saw Margaret looking hard at me in the division lobby a couple of nights later. I spoke to her, to prove that I bore no scars or ill will. But I was beginning to have my doubts about her infallibility. She had allowed the bill and the thinking behind it to proceed too far before intervening. This was where she had gone wrong. If she could be wrong on this, how could she be right on everything else?

The Education Act of 1988 was a landmark piece of legislation comparable with the Butler Education Act of 1944. The Welsh language was given a statutory place for the first time in the schools' curriculum. Some were disappointed that it was not being made a compulsory subject in all schools, but I knew that we faced a difficult enough task in ensuring that language teaching was available to those who wanted it. I had visited a small primary school at Cwmffrwdoer in Gwent where the teacher, Mrs Thomas, had told me that she was only one step ahead of her pupils on the learning curve. Her dedication, and the fact that the language was returning to an area where the last remnants of it was on the gravestones of the children's great-grandparents in the local cemetery, moved me deeply.

The year 1988 was particularly appropriate for the introduction of the act in Wales because it was the 400th anniversary of the translation of the Bible into Welsh. The commissioning of the translation had been an act of state by Queen Elizabeth and Archbishop Whitgift. The translator, William Morgan, later given the bishopric of St Asaph, had spent some weeks polishing his work at Westminster Abbey before it was published, shortly after the defeat of the Armada.

The Bible's frontispiece stated it had been printed by the Queen's printer. It bore the Tudor coat of arms, enclosed by the garter and circled by 'Honi soit qui mal y pense' – like Cranmer's Bible of 1539 and modern Welsh Office documents. No greater proof was needed in my view that the government of the day was fully behind the translation. There was a special service at the abbey to celebrate the anniversary.

This favourable aura boosted our determination to promote the language and Peter encouraged me to establish a committee to find the way ahead. Its first meeting was held in Cardiff on 25 January. On my way down from north Wales in the train, I saw that the notice in the lavatory prohibiting its use at a station was printed in four languages – English, French, German and Japanese. Underneath some wag had scribbled:

'What about the Welsh lingo then?'

Below that, there was a crude Welsh translation, obviously done in anger:

'Y mae'n anghyfreithiol cachu mewn steshon' (It's illegal to shit in a station.)

And below that again was another contribution:

'Welsh shit doesn't understand English!'

The graffiti illustrated with uncanny accuracy the variety of feelings prevailing at the time and the need to defuse the antagonism surrounding the language. Petty-minded and insensitive officialdom was the root cause of much of the trouble.

At my meeting with the committee, one of the members, Winston Roddick QC, argued that a legal obligation should be placed on all public bodies to respect the language and treat it on a par with English. As our meetings progressed, so the pressure for legislative action grew. The committee members were unanimously in favour. As chairman, I was snookered. Peter too realized that we had no chance of securing legislation if the PM's attitude over the Welsh provisions of the Education Bill was anything to go by. Wisely, he advised me to quit the chair while the committee was re-established as a board with an independent chairman, John Elfed Jones. We consulted within the government but not with No. 10. It was July before we had the official launch of the new board but the Welsh Language Society had got wind of it and campaigned with redoubled vigour for a Language Act. They scented victory and wanted to be in the vanguard of success.

But this was not the only sphere where Peter and I were sailing close to the wind and a cosh from Margaret's handbag. Our agreement with Baden-Wurttemberg had been ripe for signing since the end of 1987. Peter had his understanding with the PM that he could do things his way and he had got more money out of the Treasury for his Valleys Initiative on the strength of it, but how far would this freedom extend? To signing an agreement with a semi-independent, German Land government? To a Welsh Language Act, under pressure from nationalists? (Dafydd Wigley, the Plaid Cymru MP had introduced such a bill the previous year; it had failed to make progress for lack of time.) Neither of us had much appetite for a battle with the PM over these issues when there was so much else that needed to be done. Peter was a superb tactician. I had noticed that, while he solved most problems quickly and with ease, he took all the time available with difficult issues. As for the PM, she was in a strange mood: the poll tax debate was not going her way. George Thomas had warned me that she would have to look to her laurels if she wished for a fourth term. She had said in a BBC interview at the Llandudno conference in June that there would be no Welsh-language legislation. 'If people love the Welsh language, why do you need compulsion?'

The archdruid, at the proclamation of the National Eisteddfod at Llanrwst, accused her of having spat on the language. He got some mild applause. Peter suffered the usual baptism of bawling from society members when he visited the National Eisteddfod at Newport in August. They daubed the Welsh Office with slogans. A suspension of hostilities all round in the summer recess was very welcome.

Around the World

Investment in Wales by companies from different countries was reaching new heights. During Peter Walker's three years as secretary of state, Wales secured 22 per cent of all the inward investment coming into the United Kingdom. Our share of the population was just over 5 per cent. The largest number of projects came from North America but the most novel were the Japanese. We had the biggest concentration of Japanese companies in Europe. They liked to visit the Welsh Office and be visited in return. It was planned that I should go to Japan in the autumn of 1988.

During the summer, I went to see a dozen of the Japanese companies already established in Wales and invited the heads of the remainder to brief me over dinner at the Holiday Inn in Cardiff. I was deeply impressed by their factory operations – the high-tech products, advancing automation and robotics, excellent hands-on management and a high proportion of production going to export. The European Single Market, targeted for 1992, was already a reality for most of them. I liked their priorities too: the customer came first.

Our first stop was a monsoon-drenched Bombay in the middle of the night where we stretched our legs for twenty minutes in a large, humid corridor of small airport shops. Substantial groups of human beings – twenty, thirty or forty people – sat unsmiling on the floor here and there in this laundry-smelling atmosphere. I tried to focus on individual faces as I passed but none registered in my mind. Everyone dissolved in the mass. I could well believe that all of India was like that, a place where individualism, political philosophies and even religious creeds dissolved and were absorbed into the vastness of the whole. I was glad to get back on the plane.

We were royally greeted in Hong Kong by the governor's adjutant in full uniform, with white epaulettes, and driven to the residence. Sir David (now Lord) Wilson and his wife were there and I was shown to a beautiful suite, recently occupied by Princess Anne. It was so large I never did find the drawer with the residence note-paper to record events during my three-day stay. The slim, towered edifice of the China Bank – a foretaste of things to come in 1997 – now dominated this fine residence building which dated from a less crowded era. We dined the first night at the Jumbo Restaurant, afloat in the harbour, with academics from local colleges. I was struck immediately by the profusion of human life. The people, being small in size, differed from us in their sense of appropriate body space. If you stood in a queue, someone would pop into the gap between you and the person in front without touching either.

There was concern about what would happen when Hong Kong returned to Chinese rule in nine years' time but domestic property prices remained high and the economy was vibrant. Some were said to be seeking Canadian or Australian citizenship in case Communist rule proved unbearable but the prevailing view was that the Communists were unlikely to put Hong Kong's prosperity at risk. They had much to gain from its continuation. Some were reported to be secretly educating their children at Hong Kong institutions just as some Eastern European Communists were sending their sons to English public schools. I was invited to broadcast on local radio one morning and I said that if I were young again, I might well come to live in HK. I hoped it was a reassuring message.

We flew to Osaka on Saturday, 1 October and a princely welcome at the Hotel Nikko. I sent an appreciative note to the manager who promptly presented me with a clock. The Japanese could hardly ever be outdone in generosity in those days. We spent a restful Sunday at Kyoto, viewing the Nijo Castle and treading its Nightingale Gallery; then it was the Myoshinji Temple with its powerful painting of a dragon on the ceiling before lunch on the banks of the Nagara River where they fished with tame cormorants on leads. A special delight, off the well-beaten tourist track, was a visit to the Eurian nunnery garden. I swore that I could still smell the camphor rising from a very old wooden bridge. One of the nuns, a gnarled old lady, told us of a card game (karuta) that had been devised there many, many years ago. You matched word cards to make up a haiku – the Japanese form of poetry.

Then our race around companies began in earnest at Osaka, Kobe and Nagoya. I soon noticed that many of their subsidiaries in Wales, being new, were technically more advanced and better equipped. They were not short of plans for future development and their men in Wales, freed from the hierarchical restrictions of the older generation of businessmen at home, were pressing hard for investment and raring to go.

We had been invited to dine at home – a rare invitation in Japan – with the Bando brothers, two restaurateurs who lived in a house on the outskirts of Osaka. The house was more than a century old and had withstood countless earthquakes and tremors. It was therefore highly valued. The wife of the elder brother greeted us just inside the doorway on her knees in her kimono. We took off our shoes and were supplied with slippers. We were five – four males and a female. We sat around in the lounge talking to the brothers and having drinks Western-style when someone said that Mrs Bando, who was hovering at the door, thought we should eat. We moved to another room and sat on cushions with our feet under a long table, beautifully laid for a multitude of courses. I sat to the right of our host at the end of the table and facing an arched hatch where our chef's head briefly appeared. Our host told me that he had trained the chef at our hotel. I was about to have the best, most exotic food I have ever had in my life.

We began with some appetizing delicacies and Mrs Bando filling our cups with warm sake that seeped down to one's toes. We graduated through a light consommé to the distinctive 'soup of the house', the foundation of further courses, and then we escalated through a series of tasty dishes to a magnificent crown of Pacific prawns which I thought must be the glorious climax of the meal. Not a bit of it. A mouth-watering mountain of sushi – soft sea urchins, choice lobster pieces and heaven only knows what – followed the giant prawns that had tempted me to surfeit on them. And all the while Mrs Bando ensured that our sake cups were full. Gradually we descended from the eximious heights of the sushi to exquisitely thin slices of Kobe beef, produced – I was told – by lifelong massage of the animal's body so that all the fat is absorbed into the meat. We ended with a pudding of pure delight but I had lost count of the courses and was full to the brim. The all-important rice was specially grown by the family and our host never travelled abroad without a supply, which he could cook, if necessary, in a hotel bedroom, his brother said.

After the meal, Mrs Bando relaxed and became a different woman. She joined us with her son and daughter – both educated in England – for an exchange of presents and laughter in the lounge. Mrs Bando said that the meal expressed her gratitude for the kindness shown to her children. Our host was opening an eating house in California and then he would consider London and perhaps Wales.

During my stay in the Kansai, I quickly detected the spirit of rivalry with the capital. They told me that in Osaka one said 'Maido orchini' to express thanks, rather than the standard 'Domo arrigato', but they warned: 'Don't say it in Tokyo or they'll laugh at you.'

When I arrived in Tokyo on the bullet train, in time for dinner with the ambassador and his wife, Sir John and Lady Whitehead, I found that some of the businessmen guests were from the Kansai. Of course I played on their provincial roots and got a hearty laugh when I ended a short after-dinner speech with the Kansai thank you. Respect for a people's language is a sure key to their hearts.

A strange thing had happened shortly after we arrived at the embassy. I was upstairs changing for dinner when I heard a loud-speaker blaring in Japanese outside. I could have sworn that occasion-ally the voice was saying 'Wyn go home' and adding some gross English and American obscenities. I thought for a moment that the Welsh Language Society had found out where I was and engaged friends in Tokyo to harass me. I listened more intently. What was being said in the course of the diatribe was 'Queen go home'. John Whitehead explained that in Japan, if you thought someone had wronged you, it was quite usual to hire a verbal protagonist to blast at the wrongdoer in this fashion. A travel company in Hong Kong had left some Japanese tourists in the lurch in northern Australia and the outburst outside the embassy was the result. Because Hong Kong was British, the Queen was wrapped up in the blame.

The high point of my visit was to be an address to the Keidanren, the biggest organization of Japanese businessmen. It had been organized by the Invest in Britain Bureau under the auspices of the Department for Trade and Industry and it had been agreed that I should speak for Britain but with a special reference to Wales. The meeting hall was crowded on the day because the old emperor, Hirohito, was slowly dying and the news bulletins that week antici-pated an announcement at any moment. In that event, we would have to cancel everything – at great cost.

As we waited to go on stage, John Whitehead teased us that he had just had some bad news from the Imperial Palace. The IIB man turned pale and looked as if he was at death's door himself. But the bad news did not come that afternoon and I had the pleasure of addressing the largest gathering of Japanese businessmen ever addressed by a British minister. Alf Gooding, the Welsh businessman, who had come to Tokyo at his own expense, also had his say.

Afterwards, I was whisked in the ambassador's Rolls to the walled Togo Palace to pay my respects to the scholar prince, Prince Naruhito, whom I had entertained at Colwyn Bay three years before. He was genuinely glad to see me because he had been very isolated during the emperor's illness. We chatted over green tea and imperial cake. He had the rare ability to make one feel close to him while he kept his distance and personal integrity. I gave him a book about the Montgomery Canal and more harp music for his mother. The palace interior was very reminiscent of the buildings I had seen at Kyoto, fine, light and undecorated. A message came to the embassy that evening that the Crown Princess Akihito (now Empress) had enjoyed the music. I did not know then that one day I would meet her in person in Cardiff.

There were more company visits. Sony showed me their latest digital television sets and cameras, very novel at that time, and the superior quality picture they produced. These digital developments and the technology behind them were going to revolutionize television broadcasting worldwide and Sony were at the cutting edge. The prospects for their fast-growing plant at Bridgend were very promising if public demand matched the new technology and its products. Sony believed it would over time.

I had been to the Hoya plant at Wrexham where they manufacture spectacle lenses and I was due to meet the head of the corporation, Tetsuo Suzuki. Mr Annesley Wright, who ran the Wrexham plant had taken one look at me and said:

'You would not go to see Ford in a Japanese car, would you?'

I agreed.

'Well, you cannot go to see Hoya without wearing Hoya lenses.'

He had made me a pair of superb, coated lenses on the spot to be framed by my own optician. Hoya had a number of retail outlets in Tokyo and the name was prominently advertised. I met Mr Suzuki over dinner. He was getting on in years and suffering from a cold but it did not stop him quizzing me hard about Wrexham and the potential of the lenses market in the UK. Sitting beside me was a man he had brought back from holiday in Hawaii. He did not know why he had been recalled until Mr Suzuki told him that he was to come over to the UK to assist with the company's expansion at Wrexham. The Japanese had taken to rugby football with enthusiasm and I saw Sanyo play against Toshiba in the Tokyo sports centre on the Saturday before I left.

Mrs Bando had shown me that the role of women in Japan was not as inferior as it might seem at first sight. They had always controlled the family finances and had played historic role in the early development of Japanese writing. Like every other foreigner, I was intrigued by the kimono. I was told that a little girl of seven might be bought a kimono, which could be so altered as she grew up that she might still be wearing it at twenty-one. To the discerning, the *obi* at the midriff reveals the wearer's status, married or single, spinster or widow – and more. During a visit to the Meiji Shrine on our very last day in the city, I glimpsed a bevy of about twenty beautifully dressed young women on their way to a tea ceremony in the adjacent gardens. The Cha-no-yu ceremony is derived from Zen Buddhism and I came across a Portuguese priest's description of it, written in the late sixteenth or early seventeenth century. 'The aim of this art of the Cha is to produce courtesy, politeness, modesty, exterior moderation, calmness, peace of body and soul without pride or arrogance, fleeing from all ostentation, pomp, external grandeur and magnificence.' That is a tall order but one that the best of Japanese womanhood still try to meet. It inculcates a self-discipline that is uniquely appealing when achieved.

It is only when you cross the Pacific that you realize its vastness; it is twice the size of the Atlantic. It was raining and cool when we left Tokyo and boiling hot when we reached Hawaii. We had a couple of days to spare before our next engagements in California. We needed a little time to recover after our hectic week in Japan.

The new Otani Hotel on Kaimana Beach at the extremity of Waikiki looked out on the clear, blue expanse of the Pacific vanishing in the haze to join an equally blue sky on the horizon. A dip in the warm sea and a restful hour or two on the sand restored our spirits and our energy. It was too hot to walk any great distance and I toured Honolulu by taxi. The driver called himself 'Honeyboy'. He told me that locals like him were very concerned that the Japanese were buying so much property on the island that house prices had risen beyond their reach. It was a problem I was all too familiar with at home. There was much to see, including the haunting remains of Pearl Harbour.

On the plane to San Francisco, I sat next to a computer boffin who was a regular commuter on this 2,000-mile journey. He entered an in-flight competition to estimate our precise time of arrival but the winners were two seven-year-old girls. The twins were most disappointed to find that their prize was a bottle of champagne. We stayed at the Holiday Inn at Fisherman's Wharf and found time to tour the city on a Gray Line coach with Melvin Stroud as our priceless driver-commentator. As we made the sharp descent by hairpin bends from Twin Peaks, he said: 'If some of you are worried, then you should do what your driver does . . . close your eyes.' His humour was closely related to the places we passed through. At one point he referred to a local comedienne and her ribald remark: 'Aids! I bet you hope you don't catch that again!'

Over lunch with the British consul at his residence in Pacific Heights, I met his Indian counterpart who told me that Gandhi had derived some of his ideas about passive resistance from the American Thoreau's essay on civil disobedience. But many prominent Americans, from Thoreau himself to Emerson, Robert Oppenheimer and Martin Luther King, were heavily indebted to Indian thinkers and their writings.

We flew across the US to New York. From my hotel window near Kennedy Airport I could see the Big Apple glowing beneath the night sky. It was a tempting sight but we had Concorde to catch in the morning. We reached London in three hours and ten minutes, an hour less than it took me to travel from Conwy to London by train. And so, I had completed my first journey around the world and found it full of wonders. I would not have missed the trip for anything. A journey round the world is a 'must' for anyone who can make it.

Open Road

Having seen Peter Walker launch himself heart and soul into his Valleys Initiative in south Wales, I was keen to harness his energy and expertise to a similar initiative in north Wales. On 21 November 1988 – the eve of the new parliamentary session – I noted:

> I suggested to Peter Walker today that he asks me to head an inquiry into prospects for the north after the completion of the A55 Chester to Bangor road in the early 1990s and he agreed. I have been concerned for some time about the reluctance of the north Wales local authorities to accept proposals for development which would bring economic benefits to the area.

When Peter adopted a suggestion, he made it his own. He put his own stamp of thoroughness on the actions that stemmed from it. No stone was left unturned and if you were the stone digger, your fingers would be bruised by the time you had finished. Over the next few months I visited all the local authorities in north Wales and urged them to prepare for the developments that would assuredly follow the new expressway that would shorten the journey time from Chester to Bangor to an hour.

We had already found that the extension of the M4 in south Wales was an all-important key to greater prosperity: much-needed new factories had come in its wake to Newport, Cardiff and Bridgend where such developments were welcomed. The attitude towards factory development was similar in the industrial north-east but the situation was different in north-west Wales. People welcomed the removal of traffic congestion in black spots like Conwy but they were wary of change and fearful of its effect on their way of life. They cherished their comparative isolation.

I had a prime example on my doorstep in Conwy where the river would soon be crossed by a submersed tunnel. A gigantic basin had been dug beside the estuary for the construction of the tunnel sections (close to the point where the Mulberry Harbour was built in great secrecy for the Normandy landing in 1944). When the sections were completed, the basin would be flooded and the huge sections floated out and submerged in sequence in a massive trench dredged out of the riverbed.

Already our thoughts at the Welsh Office were turning to the possibility of converting the casting basin into an attractive marina with appropriate housing nearby. I was amazed to find strong local opposition to the project on the grounds that the houses would be taken by 'yuppies from Manchester', and this kind of argument found supporting voices in the local council and the press. Few were prepared to recognize the potential benefits of the marina development to local shopkeepers and traders. As the minister responsible for the roads programme, I was determined that the basin would not be filled in (at great cost) and the opportunity for development lost.

There were other difficulties that mercifully did not become public knowledge at the time. There was mounting pressure in south Wales to provide what became known as the 'missing link' in the M4 – the Baglan to Lonlas section across the River Neath. It was a vital conduit to bring new industry to the Swansea area and south-west Wales. I was told by civil servants that there were insufficient funds to meet this urgent need in the south and, at the same time, tunnel through the formidable mountain at Penmaenmawr to complete the A55. I resisted the proposal to abandon the Penmaenbach tunnel with all the strength I could muster because I knew that, once abandoned, it would not be easy to bring back the scheme into the roads' programme. Furthermore, the delay would make nonsense of much of the work already done and simply shift congestion westwards. Our long-established political commitment to make the A55 dual carriageway all the way from Chester to Bangor would also be called into question. It would be political suicide for me in my own constituency. As it turned out, we managed to find the resources necessary to pursue both schemes to completion.

Peter Walker came to the north in June 1989 to open the Penmaenbach tunnel on the A55 and he took the opportunity to meet Gwynedd County Council to discuss how it proposed to exploit the advent of the new road. A week later I opened another section to the east, the Northop by-pass. Yet another section was opened in October the same year, which took traffic out of the seaside towns of Penmaenmawr and Llanfairfechan, Gladstone's favourite sea-bathing resort. These townships, which had been choked by heavy traffic for years, now had a new lease of life and a chance to develop their tourist potential.

We finalized our *Road to Opportunity* document in November and launched it on 6 December. Its main purpose was to open the eyes of all authorities – local and national – with a stake in north Wales to the potential benefits accruing from the new road. The industrial north-east certainly seized all the chances open to it to attract new industry and the tourism businesses along the coast took full advantage of their closer proximity to the populous conurbations of Greater Manchester, Merseyside and the Midlands. The document also stressed that the survival of the Welsh way of life, its language and culture, depended on the Welsh people themselves and the use they made of their greater prosperity.

Things did not always run smoothly. During the first week in February 1988 Edwina Currie (Con., Derbyshire South) sat beside me at table in the members' dining room. She had been forced to resign in December the previous year from her post as parliamentary under secretary of state at the Department of Health after saying that 'most egg production' in the UK was infected with salmonella. The statement had caused an almighty furore and knocked the egg industry for six. She was now her buoyant self again and kept on pressing me about the Japanese in Wales. She wanted to know all about them. I should have been alerted immediately by her questioning because Toyota were searching for a site for a major development and it was almost a foregone conclusion that they would choose north-east Wales.

Within a month, it was announced that Toyota's main plant would be established in her constituency in Derbyshire and the engine plant alone would come to north-east Wales. Many of us were mystified by the decision. The prime minister hinted privately to Peter Walker that there were political reasons why Toyota should go to the Midlands. I recalled my conversation with Edwina. She had clearly been tipped off. I had no idea then that she had been so friendly with the chief secretary, John Major, as she has subsequently revealed.

The Conservative Party's failure to hold on to the Vale of Glamorgan constituency after Sir Raymond Gower's death in February 1988 was an early signal that the party was not in good heart and that Labour's fortunes were reviving. Sir Raymond, although an outstanding constituency member, had seen his majority fall from 10,000 in 1983 to 6,000 in 1987. Even so, I had high hopes of our candidate, newscaster Rod Richards, whose face was well known to the public. Yet, when I went to campaign for him on Wednesday, 26 April I came away with the impression that we were not putting enough effort into the fight. We were not helped by an open attack by Nick Edwards, now Lord Crickhowell, on Peter Walker's record as secretary of state. Labour converted our 6,000 majority into a similar majority for their candidate.

Peter Walker was very helpful to me in dealing with Welsh-language issues. It was not the strategy for the preservation and promotion of the language that caused problems but the tactics. The activists were determined that any progress made should be as a result of their clamour, their protests, their struggle and not the result of government policy. They often wrote nicely to us to find out the government's intentions and if we so much as hinted at our objectives, they would then campaign vociferously for the same ends. This cat-and-mouse game reached a point where we refused to answer their letters unless they gave us a guarantee of good behaviour. We never received it.

I had already persuaded the Welsh local education authorities, much against their will, to set up a special committee to examine the problems relating to the teaching of Welsh in schools. Even before the committee had produced acceptable recommendations, I was faced with a huge demand for funds and my resignation if I could not meet it forthwith. Undeterred and flanked by the leaders of the educational establishment, I launched our proposals for Welsh in the National Curriculum in July 1989. There was no way that the activists could claim these proposals as their own. But, as well as watching them, I had to keep a wary eye on the prime minister. She had sent an apology for her absence from the Welsh Conservative conference the previous month and had gone out of her way to mention that schools could apply for an exemption from teaching the language. Of course, I too referred to this option at the launch, but I expressed the hope that most schools and most children in Wales would take the opportunity to learn their native tongue. I knew I was sailing between Scylla and Charybdis; I had no choice but to negotiate the passage.

I thought that the policy stood a fair chance of gaining popular approval. Already, 80 per cent of schools were teaching Welsh and 64 per cent of children were learning it. In the event, opting out was never a major issue. We readily granted exemptions to schools in 'Little England Beyond Wales' (Pembrokeshire) where there was no tradition of learning the language and to schools on the English border with a high proportion of pupils from homes in England. There was no large-scale, adverse reaction at the time. It was only when certain education authorities, notably Dyfed, pursued the policy with excessive zeal that an adverse reaction developed and that came from Welsh-speaking parents!

In the autumn of 1989, the Welsh Language Board we had established with John Elfed Jones as chairman produced its proposals for a new bill. John was a trusted confidante familiar with the workings of the Welsh Office. He had been my first choice for the chairmanship of Welsh Water when it was a nationalized industry in the early 1980s and I had helped him through to a successful privatization. He was an uncompromising advocate on Welsh-language matters. We met Peter Walker on Wednesday, 18 October. My note of the meeting reads:

> Peter explained (to John Elfed) the enormous difficulties involved in getting the bill accepted by colleagues and their departments – difficulties which are very real indeed – and the doubtful benefits of the bill as envisaged. (It relates mainly to the status of the language and other imprecise but controversial matters.) John did not seem to get the message that it was simply not 'on'!

Peter and I both knew in our hearts that we could never get such a proposal past our foremost colleague, the prime minister, and we had the sense not to try. The following day, I wrote:

> The nub of the Welsh-language issue is that those who cry for 'Deddf yr Iaith' ('Welsh Language Act' – the activists' slogan) believe that its preservation can be ensured by law. If so, they have more faith in the law than I have. Beyond that again is a wish to force the English to recognize the official status of the language. For some people, the demand for legislation is a virility symbol. Others are beginning to see that legislation of itself will achieve little in practice.

After we had kicked the proposed bill into touch, it was only a matter of time before the activists found out and began to hound us. As luck would have it, someone leaked its contents in December 1989 and all hell was let loose on its imperfections. John Elfed talked of resignation. We had a good excuse for sitting back and doing nothing, which was all we could do while Margaret was PM. It was then that I began to think that if we were to have fresh legislation, we would have to get away from the old battleground of equal validity with English and be more constructive in our approach. Our purpose should be to create the right ambience in adult life for all those youngsters who were now learning the language at school.

Peter Walker was a delight to work with and he proved himself a good friend to me. When he wished me a happy Christmas, he added 'and if the New Year isn't good for you, it will not be good for me either'. He knew that I was very loyal to him – as I had been to his predecessor – and he set great store by loyalty as I did myself.

In May 1989 the prime minister celebrated her tenth year in office. I too received plaudits for having served a decade at the Welsh Office. But the truth was that we were all suffering from a strange political malaise at that time. Even the prime minister was more testy than usual. My own philosophy of service had taken a battering. For me, prosperity had a social purpose, but the government's emphasis appeared to be on the material benefit to be reaped by individuals. The controversy over Margaret's denial that there was any such thing as society did enormous damage and portrayed us as a bunch of greedy, self-seeking egotists.

I spent a great deal of my time travelling on the Conwy, Westminster and Cardiff triangle and over the years this endless journeying by train and car had begun to take its toll. My wife too was affected by the loneliness of our home in the Conwy Valley and her sense of security was not enhanced by the fact that my name appeared on an IRA hit list found in a house in Clapham. In July 1989 I received a parcel bomb of sorts at home; it was an amateurish device – the experts said – posted from Aberystwyth. But all this paled into insignificance beside the fact that I had crossed swords with the prime minister.

Peter was not enjoying the best of times himself. Rumour had it that if we lost the Vale of Glamorgan by election, he would leave office, but we had lost and he remained. Nevertheless, it was reported to me by Peter himself (16 May) that the PM had ordered the whips to canvas support for Chris Patten as secretary of state for Wales. 'She [the PM] needs me more than I need her,' he told me. In early June, Julian Critchley updated me with the gossip that John Wakeham had told the PM that unless she wanted her arch-rival, Michael Heseltine, to succeed her, she should sack Walker. Walker would do all the work so that Heseltine would get the prize. Julian wanted not so much a reshuffle of the government as a completely new pack of cards. Bearing in mind what was to happen shortly – Sir Geoffrey Howe's demotion as foreign secretary followed by Nigel Lawson's resignation as chancellor – the government was not a happy ship to be sailing in. The rocks of future disasters were almost visible under our bows in the summer of 1989.

Dissension within the government's ranks on European issues, especially the ERM (exchange-rate mechanism), was the most direct link with the challenge to the prime minister's leadership by my neighbouring MP, Sir Anthony Meyer (Con., Clwyd North West) at the start of the new session in November 1989. Sir Anthony was an ardent Europhile and had contact with all the malcontents in the parliamentary party, they knew that he was standing simply as a stalking horse to assess the extent of opposition to the prime minister. He gained 33 votes but there were 25 abstentions, which meant that about a fifth of the party did not support the prime minister. She polled 314.

There were those within the government or who were former members of it who bitterly complained about Margaret's autocratic style and its outcome in actual policies. I vividly remember one Cabinet committee meeting under her chairmanship, which dealt with possible exemptions from the poll tax. I was astonished to find that most of those around the table were wholly opposed to the tax including the chancellor, then Nigel Lawson. The possible exemptions included those in holy orders dedicated to poverty and vagrants with no fixed address. Margaret was determined that no one should be spared from payment. It was clear as daylight that the tax was uncollectable compared with rates levied on property. It was her persistence in the face of a united opposition that best described her style. Francis Pym could be vitriolic in his criticism of it and even Quintin Hailsham had the odd gripe.

Even so, I still felt bound to Margaret by a political umbilical cord and I never wavered in my support for her. In November when the air in the Commons reeked of trouble and the whips were not rallying in her support, I wrote a letter of encouragement to her saying that 'Your political instincts are still true and we shall need their guidance more than ever over the next few years.' I knew that she would be preoccupied with events in Europe over the coming months and it worried me that she would not be able to apply herself fully to home affairs. The economy too had taken a turn for the worse and interest rates were rising: Nigel Lawson's legacy was a poor one for John Major, the new chancellor. I received a warm response to my letter.

The first hard blow of 1990 was literally that for us in Wales. A combination of high tide and high wind smashed the coastal defences at Towyn, near Rhyl, and the sea poured in, flooding the railtrack along the coast and hundreds of caravans and houses in the low-lying areas. I flew up to Hawarden from Northolt on Tuesday, February 13 in a ferocious gale. As we approached the runway to land, the plane zigzagged, drunkenly, before dropping at near-stalling speed (90 knots) on to the tarmac.

An eerie scene greeted me at Towyn. From a bridge over the railway, I could see acres of holiday caravans half-submerged in seawater. A television crew tried to interview me but the wind was so strong that it blew the interviewer and myself apart. The survivors had been taken to Bodelwyddan Castle where I found them quietly resigned and clutching their pets for comfort. They were glad to be alive. I talked to as many as I could.

Peter Walker had always said that he would only be at the Welsh Office 'for a couple of years', but the news that he was resigning and would not be standing at the next election came as a surprise over the first weekend in March. Speculation was rife in the media that I might succeed Peter but I would be sixty in July and, although I was a Margaret supporter, I was never 'one of us'. The Education Bill still rankled. Nevertheless, I dropped her a note saying that I was ready to carry on if she so wished. My guess was that she would look for a promising, younger man and I feared that if she chose the wrong person, it would add to the credibility of Labour's burgeoning devolution campaign. The chief whip, Tim Renton, phoned me to say that David Hunt (Con., Wirral West), who had shown his mettle as local government minister defending the poll tax, had been appointed secretary of state.

Shortly afterwards, I was asked to see the chief whip, Tim Renton (now Lord). He told me that the PM wanted me to stay in office and that she intended to give me something that would please my wife in the June Honours List. That could only mean a knighthood. I told Tim that to be knighted in office was almost unheard of – one had to go back to Sir Winston Churchill's era for a precedent – but Tim reaffirmed the PM's intention and I accepted it in good faith. When I met David Hunt at the office, he too pressed me to stay. Knowing that my services were at least appreciated, I had no sensible alternative but to see David get to grips with his new responsibilities. I had known him since he first came into the Commons as Selwyn Lloyd's successor in 1983. My wife had canvassed in the Wirral constituency on his behalf. With two years to go to the election, this was not the time to quit.

The scenario confronting us in March 1990 was of deepening unpopularity as inflation rose. I anticipated that inflation would fall later in the year and that a return to growth in 1991/2 might give us a chance of winning an election in the spring of 1992. But I also noted that 'there is an underlying hatred of the PM and what is increasingly perceived as her uncaring attitude. This is socialist claptrap but the danger is that the electors will opt for Labour simply to be rid of her.' The result of the by-election in Mid Staffordshire, which saw a Conservative majority of more than 14,000 converted into a Labour majority of 9,000, confirmed my personal analysis of the situation and the unpopularity of the government. 'We must get our act together,' I wrote, 'or we shall lose the next election. A new leader will be called for.'

Monday, 26 March 1990

I have a distinct feeling that the party has lost heart with the loss of Mid Staffordshire, the Budget and the poll tax. We are boxed in and my guess is that even a new leader would find it very difficult to get us out of the mire.

4.45 p.m., Saturday, 31 March 1990

A gigantic demonstration against the poll tax massed in Trafalgar Square from about 2.30 p.m. onwards. It was organized by the Socialist Workers' Party, judging by the banners. Some of the girls were wearing sweaters with 'Bollocks to the Poll Tax' printed on the front. A tall clown carried a placard with the legend '600 years opposition'. I saw all this as I walked up Whitehall and across the square to St Martin's Lane. The square was pretty full then; it was packed when I returned at about four o'clock.

As I worked my way along the frontage of St Martin's in the Fields, I noticed a smart young couple, immaculately dressed in spanking-new, black leather outfits, bristling with chrome buttons. I thought to myself that the outfits alone would have more than paid their poll tax. My instinct told me that they were hell bent on mischief.

I veered towards Charing Cross Station and down towards the Embankment where there was a long Socialist Workers' Party procession which tailed back across Westminster Bridge. They were a jumbled, easily led crowd, some whistling for courage and excitement but generally good humoured. Some were very young and carrying placards bigger than themselves. I had no difficulty crossing the procession at one point.

When I got to the flat in Little Smith Street, I switched on the television set. There had been some scuffles with the police and an injured officer commented: 'There was a lot of black leather about.' The smart young couple I had seen flashed back in my mind. Tony Benn was shown addressing the crowd and playing Wat Tyler in Trafalgar Square.

10 p.m.

I have now seen more pictures of the violence in Whitehall and Trafalgar Square. It is reckoned that about 50,000 took part in the demonstration and that about a hundred police and demonstrators were injured. I pity the organizers because all was peaceful until the unruly elements took over and exploited the occasion for their own concerted violence and mayhem.

The effect could be highly damaging for the Labour Party but the PM and the government will not escape censure. We shall be accused of being confrontational. The PM spoke at Cheltenham of having 'stomach for the fight'. With whom? It will be asked. With those who cannot afford to pay the poll tax?

A Funny Old World

Discontent ran like an underground river in Margaret Thatcher's government throughout 1990. It bubbled to the surface from time to time. She seemed to be marooned in her own world with a rarified, radical vision others were unable or unwilling to comprehend. Was it their egotism that blinded them to the meaning of Thatcherism or was the vision so amorphous that it was indefinable? Occasionally she would meet someone who appeared to understand her approach.

Enid and I were invited to lunch at Chequers on Sunday, 22 April. It was a misty morning for the hour's drive down from Westminster but Sir John Stradling Thomas – also invited – kept Enid amused with his chatter. Someone had asked him if they could be on first-name terms. Sir John had replied that as far as he was concerned 'Sir' would be all right. He defined an alcoholic as 'a man who drinks as much as you do but you dislike'. Policemen armed with shotguns and sub-machine guns loomed on the driveway to the PM's weekend retreat.

Of the twenty sitting down for lunch after an aperitif in the great hall, I knew all except the Reverend Charles and Mrs Robertson. He was the parish minister of Canongate (the kirk of Holyroodhouse, Edinburgh) whom Margaret had 'found' during a visit to Scotland. He was now a member of the Broadcasting Standards Council and clearly a man after Margaret's own heart. He sat opposite her at lunch and she devoted most of her attention to him. She must have realized by then that her government and party had lost a great deal of ground in Scotland where the poll tax had been introduced a year ahead of England and Wales. Scottish nationalism was in the ascendant again and her abandonment of devolution for Scotland meant that the Conservatives were out of the race between Labour and the Scottish Nationalists to win a Parliament for Scotland.

She expressed surprise to me that Labour had launched themselves yet again into a pro-devolution campaign in Wales considering that they had lost the last referendum by four votes to one. I said that Labour feared the nationalists who were actively challenging them at local level. The truth was that the referendum defeat of 1979 was largely due to the unpopularity of the Callaghan government. I did not add that the next referendum might be a protest vote against us! It was not the kind of truth you delivered to your host over a relaxing Sunday lunch at Chequers.

My colleague, Ian Grist, and I gave a farewell dinner to Peter Walker in the Elgar Room at the Savile Club on Wednesday, 2 May. Colin Shepherd (Con., Hereford), Peter's PPS, was the only other guest and we were able to talk freely. Peter's political intelligence – a comet-like phenomenon – came into play when we discussed the party's prospects. He thought we might have a chance at the next election if John Major's judgements as chancellor turned out to be right and he then led the party. It was a correct prognostication in the event but, at the time, we were more mystified by Peter's lack of enthusiasm for Michael Heseltine as the next leader.

When I next met Margaret at a Cabinet Committee on Tuesday, 12 June it was to sort out a difference over planning legislation between Chris Patten, secretary of state for the Environment and Nick Ridley, secretary of state for Trade and Industry. The PM listened to both sides of the argument and sought everyone's view including mine. We were evenly divided. She had only just returned from Russia and had not had time to study the latest exchange of correspondence. It ended with Chris being sent away to think about it all. It was the PM at her sweetly reasonable and feminine best.

Her mood was different in mid-July. For the first time, she talked about the possibility of defeat at the next election. Her remarks were en passant but the certainty of victory was noticeably absent. Perhaps the will to win is fading, I noted afterwards. The new scene in Europe and her known antipathy to it may have been conducive to her defeatist spell. It did not last long. When I attended a reception at No. 10 on 26 July, she greeted me with: 'We're going to win sixteen seats in Wales next time!' It would have exceeded our best result ever. She did not appear to have been affected by Nick Ridley's enforced resignation over some ill-judged remarks about Germany at a lunch with Dominic Lawson, although Ridley was one of her strongest supporters. Ian Gow's murder by the IRA happened shortly afterwards. Both events must have been highly damaging to Margaret's personal morale.

It was a strangely happy time for me personally. The announcement of my knighthood in the June Honours List resulted in a great flurry of congratulatory letters from all and sundry who had ever known me. Other recipients of a knighthood will agree that it is far and away the most popular accolade a person can ever have. The fact that it was bestowed while I was still in office and that the last recipient in a similar position was Sir Anthony Eden in 1954 made it a truly signal honour in my eyes. My dubbing at the palace did not take place until Tuesday, 27 November 1990, when I lined up for the ceremonial bow, kneel and tap of the sword on the shoulder just ahead of Sir Jimmy Savile. 'Fifty quid if you curtsy,' he whispered mischievously behind me as I stepped forward.

The Japanese ambassador, Mr Kazuo Chiba, also gave a dinner at the embassy in my honour. I only noticed that I was the chief guest at the last moment – no one had told me. In my impromptu speech of thanks, I proudly referred to the fact that there were now thirty-three Japanese companies established in Wales, representing an investment of £400 million and employing more than 10,000 people. It was no mean achievement on our part and theirs.

I had the first standing ovation of my life at the Welsh party conference at Llandudno when I abandoned my scripted peroration and let the words fly free – the only sure-fire way to get an audience to its feet. I flew straight from the conference to Dresden with David Hunt who had quickly established himself as a capable and industrious secretary of state. He was a strong pro-European and heartily approved of my policy of developing relationships with the Four Motor regions.

In September, I paid one of my most enjoyable visits to North America. It began with a stay in New York at the home of John and Sarah Rhodes and their two sons, Jack and William, at 770 Park Avenue/73rd Street. My private secretary, Martin Hum, and I arrived on Saturday afternoon, 15 September, and Sarah took us for a walk with her two small boys in Central Park. At one spot young people were dancing on roller skates to beat music but all eyes were glued to a particular young lady on single-track rollers who gave a riveting display of her athletic dancing skills. She was a star performer, who knew it and loved it.

Sunday was a little cooler and we toured around Manhattan Island by boat before brunch at the Inter Continental on Lexington/48th Street. In the evening we dined over in Brooklyn and John took us as far into Harlem as he dared (126th Street). We went up Madison Avenue and came back down Park Avenue and saw the stark contrast between wealth and poverty in the Big Apple. Barely a mile separated ugly apartment blocks without air conditioning and fronted by vandalized cars from the luxurious residential blocks like our own with a complement of twenty-one door and security men, mostly of Irish descent. Tom Wolfe's *The Bonfire of the Vanities* was compulsory reading and presented a very accurate picture of New York at that time.

On Tuesday, 18 September, after visiting some potential inward investors, we moved on to Toronto. We were taken straight from Pearson Airport to the acting consul's home in Garfield Avenue, Lawrence Park, to welcome about eighty people who had come to taste a tun of Felinfoel ale, specially shipped from Wales for the occasion. Among the guests was Olwen Stephen, originally from Llanon, Cardiganshire, who had stayed at our home in Anglesey as a young teacher at the beginning of the war. She had married a Polish soldier and emigrated. It was a joy to see her again. All the ale was consumed.

I addressed the British Canadian Trade Federation on Thursday and had a very good reception to the proposal that we should organize a trade mission of Welsh companies to Toronto and Chicago. Colwyn Rich, chairman of Champlain Industries and a brother of Geoff Rich, editor of the *South Wales Echo*, was very supportive of the idea and a natural local ambassador for Wales.

There was much talk about the election upset, which had seen the Liberals out and the Socialists in. The new premier, Bob Rae, a former Rhodes scholar, was personally well thought of, but regarded as having a hard job forming a cabinet since only 13 of his 74 members had any previous parliamentary experience. The most widely accepted explanation of the election result was that the electorate was fed up with the two major parties – the Liberals and the Tories – who had dominated the political scene for too long and lost touch with ordinary people and their aspirations. The Liberal minister, Monty Kwinter, whom I had met at Dresden in July, was still at his desk pending the appointment of a successor, but powerless to initiate the link I desired between Ontario and Wales. I saw Don Rickard too at the Max Bell Foundation. He knew Bob Rae personally and thought he would continue the policy of extending Ontario's relationships in Europe. He offered to raise the possible Welsh connection with Rae at the appropriate time and I knew he would be as good as his word.

Chicago – The Big Onion – was a city after my own heart. I was immediately impressed by its fine array of skyscrapers of different styles and periods. There were attractive smaller architectural items too, including Frank Lloyd Wright's home and another house he had built for a cardinal.

Chicago business people were highly critical of their brethren in New York. 'Those guys in New York are just finding out what their paper's worth.' The mid west economy had an independent strength of its own like the west coast, they argued, and pooh-poohed the threatening recession. 'Our industries are going full swing; there's no sign of recession here.' The Canadians, they said, had been over-pricing themselves for years and now, after the latest free trade agreement between the US and Canada, US businesses were swallow-ing up the Canadian market.

Sam Zell, head of Great American Management, personified Chicago with his unique style. He rode to his company offices on a motor cycle and prided himself on the fact that he had no office of his own. He used other people's. As for the nature of his business:

'There are a lot of good companies with poor balance sheets. We buy them up. We raised a million dollars to begin doing it – me and fifty others. Took us six months.'

When I asked about his evident, personal success, he said:

'I've never had a job, so I don't know what I can't do.'

His staccato sentences seemed characteristic of 'the city of broad shoulders'. Even the coffee stall notices were brusquely direct: 'Eat it and beat it. We don't want no stool warmers here!'

By Saturday, 22 September, I had reached San Francisco. Over the weekend, the British consul, Anthony Ford, an Aberystwyth graduate, and his wife Lynda took us up to Napa Valley for lunch at Inglenook. I learnt all there was to know about commercial wine making and tasting. Anthony also gave a dinner at Pacific Avenue so that I could meet businessmen with an interest in Wales. Some guests came up from Los Angeles.

In the course of my stay, I met three cab drivers on separate journeys and made a point of talking to each of them about the developing crisis in the Gulf. The first, a family man in his thirties, saw his livelihood threatened by rising gas (petrol) prices and was fearful of the consequences of deeper US involvement. The second, a young black man, was all for a quick military solution because 'that guy [Saddam Hussein] will still be there if we don't get him'. The third was a non-practising Muslim. He feared there might be a conflict of loyalties in groups like his own and internal antagonisms within the US. It was a fair cross section of opinion.

The situation in the Gulf had been very threatening for some weeks. Saddam Hussein had proved he was no fool. He had made peace with Iran and invaded Kuwait. Now, with the United Nations forces, led by the US gathering in Saudi Arabia, conflict seemed inevitable. The question was how long it would last and who would suffer most, Iraq or the west.

When I returned to the UK, it was to a sense of growing concern among colleagues about the outcome of the next election. Many had come into the Commons with the Conservative tides of 1983 and 1987 and were nervous about the future. We were facing a new Labour Party which had abandoned its traditional dogma and appeared to be without principle. The collapse of Communism, which should have helped the Conservative cause, was really helping our political rivals to shed their Marxist beliefs and present themselves in a new light. Britain was faced with grave uncertainties abroad, not only in the Gulf but in Eastern Europe and within the European Union. Personally, I still had faith that Margaret would instinctively defend British interests but she would need all her intuitive antennae to sort out where those interests lay. I trusted her to succeed.

Wales had changed drastically over the last few years. It was now a manufacturing country, no longer dependent on coal and steel but very sensitive to consumer spending patterns. Farming incomes had plummeted under the impact of high interest rates and were only maintained by a thick rug of subsidy. My conclusion was that to win the election, we would require a miraculous economic recovery. It was nowhere in sight.

News of Sir Geoffrey Howe's resignation on Thursday, 1 November, came to me at the Holiday Inn in Swansea via Robert Adley (Con., Christchurch) who was also staying the night there. Neither of us was surprised. Geoffrey had been at odds with the PM ever since she deprived him of the Foreign Office and made him leader of the House and, with reluctance, deputy prime minister. It was known that they differed on European policy. There was an immediate Cabinet reshuffle and the media had an anti-Thatcher field day. Meanwhile the prospect of a war in the Gulf was hotting up and it looked as if Saddam Hussein would be attacked before Christmas if he did not withdraw from Kuwait. We began the new session of Parliament with the party in a petulant, disgruntled mood. There were too many egos punctured beyond repair and there was talk of a leadership election. I thought the prime minister would win but it would be a pyrrhic victory if too many in her party were seen to be against her. I recorded events in my diary.

Sunday, 18 November 1990

The end of a momentous week and the start of another. Geoffrey Howe delivered his scathing attack on the PM in the Commons on Tuesday and Michael Heseltine entered the lists to tilt against the PM on Wednesday. Voting will take place on Tuesday next. Many of today's newspapers have declared themselves for Heseltine because the polls show him as favourite to win the next election. This may sway a lot of the younger members in marginal seats anxious to save their skins. Much as I like Michael personally, I do not really trust him as a leader and prime minister. He is too impulsive. We have grave problems at home and abroad and only Margaret has the resolution to pull us through.

The current disunity in the party over the leadership issue may extend beyond Tuesday to a second and possibly a third ballot. The only gainers will be the opposition.

Wednesday, 21 November 1990

There was mounting consternation as we waited for the declaration of the result yesterday in Room 10 on the committee room floor. As the minutes ticked by I sensed that something had gone wrong. There must have been a hundred press people milling outside the doors and then John Lee (Con., Pendle) shouted 'The press have got it!' He shouted out the figures. John Taylor (our whip) came in looking like a scalded cat. Those making the announcement had gone to the wrong room! Margaret was 4 short of the outright majority required. She had polled 204 and Michael 152.

This morning, I called Derek Conway (Con., Shrewsbury and Atcham), my PPS, who told me that the PM's support was flaking away – he and others were joining the Heseltine camp. This is a curious development. I would have expected people to rally to her rather than to him – she had more votes after all. But that is not to be. They will inflict a crushing defeat on her if she stands for the second ballot on Tuesday.

[News of the previous night's mysterious meeting at the deputy chief whip's flat – Tristan Garel-Jones, now Lord – was not yet common knowledge. Was it there that the decision to scupper Margaret began to mature? Those present deny it.]

Mistakenly from their viewpoint, the opposition have thrown Margaret a lifeline with tomorrow's confidence debate. She will have a chance to show her mettle and so will Heseltine. But she will need a miracle to save her now.

I drifted around the House tonight and had a drink with Hal Miller (Con., Bromsgrove). He said:

'What do you do with a wounded bird? You kill it.'

The rebellion against Margaret was clearly too big to bear in Hal's view.

'Our lot aren't interested in the eighties – they're into the nineties,' he said.

I had been down to the House earlier in the day to hear the PM's statement on the Paris treaty she had signed the day before. The change in atmosphere when she entered the Chamber was electrifying. She irradiated the place with her presence and positively glowed at the despatch box. Our side gave her vociferous support and they will do so again tomorrow but they will kill her on Tuesday if she has not resigned by then.

The chief whip and the leader of the House have been to see her to tell her of the haemorrhage of her support but she will have none of it, I am told. Half the cabinet are said to have joined Heseltine already but she is determined to fight to the bitter end. The latest bulletin is that John Wakeham has replaced George Younger as her campaign manager with Michael Fallon, Francis Maude and Michael Portillo as his lieutenants. Had she assembled this team at the beginning, the story might have had a different ending. But the tumbrel has begun to roll for her, I fear, and stopping it now will take more than their combined, coercive efforts. The loyalty which produced last night's 204 votes for Margaret has crumbled before a tide of self-interest, self-preservation and survival at the next election.

PS. There was trouble in my private office yesterday when a housemaid called Fran cooked onions in the basement and the smell wafted up to our third floor. Sue Cobbold, who is allergic to onions, hit the roof. Sue runs our lives in that office.

Thursday, 22 November 1990

The PM was right yesterday to remind Paddy Ashdown when he referred to her 'twilight', that there were twenty-four hours in a day. This has been a long day for me after a troubled night riddled with nightmares. In one horrible dream, I was on my knees in stockinged feet in the House of Lords trying to deliver a message which was missing from my papers! I caught the 9 a.m. train from Paddington, full of foreboding about the day ahead. Shortly before arriving in Newport, we had news by phone that the PM had resigned. I spent the day at the Panasonic factory in Cardiff and giving an endless stream of interviews to the media. My nightmares had somehow drained the shock from my system.

Tonight, I wrote to Michael Heseltine offering my support. Douglas Hurd and John Major are also standing but my guess is that they will split the anti-Heseltine vote. Michael will win through, possibly in the third round. David Hunt phoned me from the Far East to say that he too is likely to support Michael. Ian Grist has already done so in the first round.

Monday, 26 November 1990

John Major and Douglas Hurd have moved very quickly and their support has grown over the weekend. John Major who has been away with dental trouble, was in the tea room with Norman Lamont and others. I told him I was glad to see him back. David Hunt is the only Cabinet minister to have joined Heseltine's camp, which now includes Howe and Lawson. David spoke to me twice over the weekend to tell me of the timing of his letter to Michael and its contents, which he is going to make public. I suggested to him that one of us should support Major to hedge our bets as a ministerial team at the Welsh Office and that I was minded to switch my support to him. But David wanted us to present a united front and I have gone along with it although I now have a feeling in my bones that Major will win. It now looks as if Michael Heseltine, who has been blamed for Margaret's fall, may not secure the 187 votes he requires tomorrow for a clean victory. If he fails, he will be overwhelmed on Thursday when second preferences will count. Personally, I am weary of the whole business. Its one redeeming feature is that the PM has been able to retire with dignity of a kind.

Friday, 30 November 1990

A momentous week is an understatement.

Tuesday saw my dubbing at the palace in the morning and the proclamation of a new prime minister in the evening. Michael failed to get the requisite 187 for a clear victory but John Major got within two of it with 185. Douglas got 56. Heseltine and Hurd immediately withdrew, leaving John Major in possession of the field.

Wednesday saw much toing and froing and the main Cabinet changes – much more extensive than expected. David Hunt's skin was saved – God he was worried! I was in his room when he telephoned his family with the good news. But there will be further repercussions at our office because Nicholas Bennett (Con., Pembroke-shire), an abrasive little fellow, was a strong Major supporter and will be pressing for a job. David suggested I might be the fall guy on grounds of age.

Thursday: shortly before 9 a.m. David and I followed up the previous day's discussion. I said I was quite willing to go if required. David asked me what my plans were and if I had thought of the Lords. I told him I planned to contest Conwy again but would not expect to serve in the post-election government.

Ian came to see me late morning to say David had spoken to him and he was out. No. 10 wanted his job as a PUSS rather than mine as a minister of state. I saw David after PM's Questions (3.30 p.m.). Ian had been wrong to 'have a word' with me; everything was still to play for, he said.

Sunday, 2 December 1990

I spoke to Ian on my way to Paddington on Friday morning and reported David's view but by the time I arrived in Cardiff he had had a message that the PM wanted to see him on Monday. He expected to be sacked.

I kept wondering what my late friend Michael Roberts would have said. He would have been critical of Ian for leading with his chin and openly supporting Michael Heseltine from the start. He would also have criticized me for not following my instinct and switching to John Major when I realized he was winning. I did not do so because I preferred to be loyal to David Hunt even when I knew he was wrong. We should never have allowed Bennett to be the only Major supporter in the Welsh camp. Loyalty to friends is very important – possibly too important – in my personal philosophy.

I have a dreadful feeling that the assassins who brought Margaret down will fail John Major one by one. Alan Clark, who was present at Tristan's late-night meeting after the first ballot, is in trouble over the supply of arms to Iraq. The air is thick with rumours. John Major is said to be 'estranged' from his wife Norma.

Monday, 3 December 1990

Ian did his bit superbly at Welsh Questions this afternoon considering he had been fired this morning. There is a sour, guilt-ridden atmos-phere in the party and a feeling that things will never be the same again.

Our run-up to the election will not be smooth. I see deep troubles ahead.

Wednesday, 5 December 1990

John Major spoke yesterday about an open, compassionate society as his aim and that may be right and good but is it what we were elected to achieve? He is indebted to the right-wing 'No Turning Back' group for his election as leader and I do not think they care a fig for such a society. The politics of this country are polarized – much as French politics are – by the extreme left and extreme right, with those of us in the middle trying to preserve the moderate approach. Success at the next election depends on who is best able to define acceptable policies. Labour have had more time to think things through but have they the ability to present their views in a credible fashion?

There is a daft, 'head in air' attitude among some of my younger colleagues. They know the future is theirs, now that Margaret is out of the way, but they do not seem to realize that politics is a serious business and that other people matter.

Ian Grist had more plaudits today at the Welsh Grand Committee than he will have in his obituaries.

As Margaret said on her departure from Downing Street: 'It's a funny old world!' Was it the world of the over-tired woman, succumbing to pressure and 'seeing the world as the world's not', that finally got her down? She was at her best as a critic, working her way with others towards a solution. She was at her worst when she struck out regardless of others and on her own. Too many in the Conservative Party in Parliament had lost faith in her ability to lead them to further triumphs. She had become a liability rather than an asset in their eyes. Their belief was never to be put to the test of a general election; hence the lingering sense of betrayal, not by a concerted plot but by a general failure to support her.

One thing is certain; we shall not see her like again. As the first woman prime minister, her statue deserves its place on the empty plinth in the members' lobby.

Major in Charge

As soon as he became prime minister, John Major announced that he wished to create a nation more at ease with itself. It was a brave ambition in the face of his 'unpromising inheritance', as he later described it, but his words signalled a return to a more traditional form of Conservatism, which I for one felt more comfortable with. He knew from his own experience of life, and certainly from his years as minister for Social Security and later the disabled (1985–7), that there were those who could never take full advantage of the society of opportunity and needed a helping hand. How his softer approach would go down with the new, hard breed of Conservative MPs was anybody's guess.

I had known John from the time he entered Parliament in 1979, when he still had a slight limp from a car accident in Nigeria. He was always in the tea room after Questions, talking and listening, and it was no surprise when he became a whip and later under secretary of state for Social Security. His rise within the government since joining the Cabinet as chief secretary to the Treasury in 1987 had been truly meteoric but not unexpected and he had lost none of his friendliness. He was businesslike rather than profound.

When he became prime minister, he was shrewd in his choice of Cabinet colleagues. Michael Heseltine took charge of the Department of the Environment and had the unenviable but essential task of sorting out the poll tax. There was not much time to lick the country and the party into shape for the next election but, if anyone could do it, John Major was the man. I had a personal stake in winning that election since I had decided to stand again and had given a substantial sum to my association to rescue them from financial difficulties. Meanwhile there was a war to be waged and won.

When I surveyed the world scene at the end of 1990, I was more concerned with China and Russia than with the Gulf. The spirit of change which had seized the world and taken off so bravely on the

252

wings of hope and freedom had faltered and was threatening to come crashing down about our ears. What had happened in China the previous year should have been a warning to us. The old rulers realized that freedom is an intoxicating brew and that, without discipline, it degenerates into licence and divisiveness. The unity of the entire country was threatened and so were the benefits brought to the masses by internal peace and a better food supply. So the rulers took the hard line, which led to the repression in Tiananmen Square and elsewhere.

The USSR appeared to be on the verge of a similar course. Perestroika, launched in 1985, was still failing to reform the old economic order and the break-up of the union, now to be proposed in a referendum of the Soviet peoples, must surely cause political instability. It was hard to believe that the disintegration of the USSR could happen peacefully and without a bloody turmoil, which could only be suppressed by force. In retrospect, it was only President Gorbachev's strength of will and genuine patriotism that ensured the worst scenario did not happen.

The situation in the Gulf was enigmatic and the outbreak of hostilities imminent. My diary entry on Sunday, 23 December 1990 ran as follows:

> I find it strange that many in the west believe that Iraq can be defeated by a powerful strike over a period of six weeks or so. Saddam Hussein will stick at nothing and will use all the weapons and forces at his command. It is known that he has chemical weapons and that he is not far from acquiring a nuclear device. His people are accustomed to war – they fought Iran for eight years – and they can endure hardship. He threatens to involve Israel, which may divide the Arab states ranged against him. I foresee a long-drawn-out struggle, costly to both sides.

When the attack on Iraq began in mid-January 1991 with an aerial bombardment equivalent in destructive power to the atomic bomb dropped on Nagasaki, opinion varied on its eventual effectiveness. I spoke to Jim Callaghan at Donald Coleman's funeral at Neath at the end of the month and he recalled the controversy about 'Bomber Harris' and the bombing campaign towards the end of the war in Europe. We agreed that a blitzkrieg could never end a war, although it had its place in softening up the enemy.

John Major was calm and right for the occasion. As the Gulf War developed, his standing in the polls rose to Churchillian heights. But there were mutterings within the party about his greyness and there were those who wanted to see Margaret Thatcher back. But the war came to an end sooner than I expected, although I should have known better after Bob Boscawen (Con., Somerton and Frome) had told me that the Iraqis did not have the command structure to wage war successfully. Their resistance crumbled under the Allies' ground assault and, by the end of February, they had been driven out of Kuwait and the main objective of the United Nations had been achieved. Margaret Thatcher spoke in the Commons for the first time since her dethronement.

My worst fears of a prolonged war were not realized at the time – thanks to the success of the Desert Storm forces commanded by General Norman Schwarzkopf. Yet, twelve years later, the United Nations were in much the same position as before, with Saddam Hussein still allegedly armed with weapons of mass destruction and still posing a threat. He did not use his diabolical weapons in 1991, as he had against Iran and the Kurds, because he had been warned of the horrendous retaliation that would follow. Then, when his forces were retiring from Kuwait and caught in a turkey shoot on the road to Baghdad, the US decided that enough was enough. In the words of secretary of state Colin Powell: 'The American Army doesn't do massacres.' So Saddam Hussein was saved for another day and another President Bush to unearth him from his hole in Tikrit on 13 December 2003.

It was only when I arrived in Kuwait to see the last of the oil-well fires being extinguished in November, nine months after the formal Iraqi surrender on 3 March 1991, that I saw something of Saddam Hussein's capacity for evil. His troops had not only deliberately set the oilfields on fire but they had mined them too so that the fires would be more difficult to put out. At one stage there were more than 700 fires billowing black, acrid smoke that blotted out the sun and rained soot on the entire desert landscape. There were stagnant lakes and ponds of oil everywhere, some burning, others menacingly static. It was not easy to breathe in this polluted atmosphere. 'If Hell had a national park, this would be it,' a fellow visitor said. I could not better that description.

The Americans had estimated that it would take two years to extinguish the fires but the Kuwaitis had pulled out all the stops. They had mobilized 10,000 people, comprising mine-disposal experts and fire-fighting teams from twenty-seven different countries and using a variety of techniques. The Hungarians used a turbo jet engine mounted on a huge truck to blow out the fire at its base. The job had been accomplished in six months and twenty-one days and the last well fire at Burgan 118 was blown out and capped on Wednesday, 6 November. I was there representing the British government because I happened to be in the region. It was an important occasion for the Kuwaitis. The lakes and ponds were still burning over a vast area and the hellish scene surrounding us was a monument to Saddam Hussein's monstrous capacity to wreak havoc.

There were other mementoes of the dictator's barbarity in Kuwait City. Before they left, Iraqi troops had taken hundreds of men, women and children indiscriminately from public places, mosques and homes. Nothing had been heard of them since. The homes where they had lived were now draped with yellow banners protesting at the outrage and commemorating these lost human beings. Saddam Hussein owes the world an explanation for their disappearance. The world is still waiting.

The Kuwaitis I spoke to blamed themselves for their weakness and inability to resist the Iraqi invasion. Too many rich and prominent citizens were absentees from their country and spent too much of their time abroad. The country had become too dependent on foreign labour, especially Palestinians, and when the invasion came, the will and capacity to resist was not there. They had been taught a hard lesson.

There were now moves afoot to rebuild Kuwait and an exhibition on this theme had been arranged in neighbouring Bahrain where I had led a group of interested suppliers from Wales. While they got down to business with their contacts, I visited the minister of commerce, Habib Kassim, whose guest I was, and the minister for health to explore their requirements and open up new possibilities for our business people. The Bahrainis were building a new hospital and specialists in my business group were quickly involved. I also had a lengthy discussion with the crown prince. He put Saddam Hussein among the devil-worshippers of the Arab world, totally alien to Islam and traditional Muslim beliefs. He believed that some good would emerge from the Gulf War in that people now saw the stark choice between good and evil rulers. He had faith that they would make the right choice if they were free to do so. Our talk was reassuring.

Over the weekend, I visited the magnificent Koranic Library which includes among its treasures the Koran taken from the body of the Mahdi by Captain Maxwell after the battle of Omdurman. On Sunday afternoon, at the Horseracing Club, I was astonished to find a well-watered race course of green turf flourishing in the desert and beautiful, sleek thoroughbreds galloping as if they were at Ascot.

On my return to the hotel, the manager told me that they were going to open the royal suite for me. I protested that I was quite content where I was and had no wish to move. He then unlocked a door next to my room. Inside, there was a truly palatial dining room complete with a spacious bar and kitchen. But what intrigued me most were the royal sleeping quarters beyond, with an enormous canopied bed and half a dozen luxurious pillows. Secretly and alone, I lay on the coverlet for a moment or two to imagine sybaritic delights that would have put the Old Man of the Mountain to shame. Then I noticed that there was a large television screen at the foot of the bed in this houri heaven. *Me miserum*! My imagination died on the spot. I switched off all the lights, which took all of twenty minutes, and retired to my own room next door.

There were rumours of an election being called immediately after the Gulf War but there was too much unfinished business, including the replacement of the poll tax and the restoration of the economy, to create a real window of opportunity. The loss of the Ribble Valley by-election on 7 March, where the poll tax was a central issue, put paid to all such rumours for the time being.

We busied ourselves at the Welsh Office with the Severn Bridges Bill, paving the way for the implementation of the plan that Nick Ridley had outlined to Nick Edwards and myself. The Welsh National Opera Company was in financial trouble – not for the first time – and David Hunt rode to the rescue with a generous grant. We also prepared to make higher education colleges independent of the local authorities – a move rightly welcomed by the colleges because it was the foundation of their future success.

Knowing Wales intimately, I knew its problems. I devised a Rural Initiative to stimulate activity in the countryside and encourage farming communities to diversify. David was grateful. He too had familiarized himself with Wales and asked me to take a special interest in the redevelopment of the port of Holyhead which had fallen on bad times with the decline in passenger traffic to and from Dublin. I agreed, although I knew some of the port's problems were intractable.

Just as the Gulf War ended, I composed my thoughts on the Welsh Language Board's legislative proposals and found them more to my liking than I had thought earlier. We could live with the package. But to gain approval within the government and in Parliament, the proposals would have to be put into a flexible framework, which could be modified over time. I recommended that we should legislate if colleagues in government agreed.

David and I met the chairman of the board, John Elfed, and one of his members, Winston Roddick QC, on Thursday, 23 May. Once again, I found that they had no idea of what was involved in getting approval for a legislative proposal within the government. (I had just seen Michael Heseltine lose a proposal for a cabinet-style local authority structure because of lack of support in a Cabinet committee.) Nevertheless, I thought that we could make an acceptable case for a Welsh Language Bill and might win if we had the law officers on our side. The present situation was auspicious. The Lord Chancellor, Lord Mackay of Clashfern, the Attorney-General, Sir Patrick Mayhew QC (now Lord), and the Solicitor-General, Sir Nicholas Lyell QC (now Lord), would not be antipathetic to our request as Quintin Hailsham might have been. Neither would John Major react as adversely as Margaret might have done. In July, I told the board that I accepted the need for some form of legislation and that I hoped it would give people not just what they wanted but what they had not dreamed of – a line used by A. C. Bradley in a lecture on Shakespeare in 1904!

It was February 1992 before we had obtained full government approval. Somewhere along the line, the prime minister asked David Hunt whether I personally was convinced of the need for legislation and David had given a strongly affirmative reply. Now, all that was required was a slot in the legislative programme but it was clear that none would be available until after the election.

The Welsh Language Society had been active but in a desultory fashion. They did not touch upon the government's agenda. In November 1991, a young woman, Branwen Nicholas, threatened to fast if I did not go to see her in prison after she had been jailed for vandalizing a government office in Colwyn Bay. I refused point blank: it was a form of blackmail. It was embarrassing because she was the daughter of the archdruid, James Nicholas, who had once helped me compose a sonnet. The media broadened the issue and asked why I was not prepared to meet these young people.

To diffuse this broader issue, I arranged to meet officers of the society in Aberystwyth in January but their suggestions for solving the holiday-home problem were impractical and would have deprived ordinary private home owners in parts of Wales of the open-market value of their properties. This was not acceptable. However, I was impressed by the quality of some of the young people I met, especially Alun Llwyd, a slight figure with impenetrable eyes and dressed in fashionable black with a Long Island belt. If only they could be persuaded to work constructively for the future of the language, there would be hope for us all.

Life was not without its grimmer side. I visited Sir John Stradling Thomas at Westminster Hospital in February 1991. He had lost a great deal of weight and the use of his legs, he told me. He also had some obstruction in his chest. But he was as belligerent as ever and I thought he would survive, although the gloomy conditions at the hospital, then destined for closure, were hardly conducive. The news about his condition that filtered through subsequently was dire and his death at Easter was no surprise. 'Nihil sed bonum de mortuis,' said Nicky Fairbairn (Sir Nicholas, Con., Perth and Kinross) when he saw me struggling with an obituary. 'Stradders was no saint,' said Jack Weatherill (now Lord) in his commemorative address at St Margaret's, the parish church of Westminster. Most of us would have agreed with that sentiment but I had to deliver a similar address shortly afterwards in John's constituency of Monmouth. I took infinite care over the contents.

The British Consulate in Milan is one of my favourite locations. The residential quarters look out over the ancient church of St Ambroglio and we had gathered there in anticipation of my signing a letter of intent to conclude an agreement between Wales and Lombardy next day, Wednesday, 20 March 1991. The president of Lombardy, Guiseppi Giovenzana, was there along with the prefect, the chief of police et al. – all invited by our indefatigable consul, Julian Hartland-Swann. The reception was a pleasing prelude to the following day's proceedings. The signing established a further link between Wales and the Four Motor regions of Europe and gave a valuable entrée for Welsh businesses into the rich north Italian market. One of the early results was that the Welsh Development Agency secured an office at the Lombardy Chamber of Commerce, which had no fewer than a thousand businesses on its books. After the signing and lunch with Giovenzana, I paid my first but not last visit to Milan Cathedral – the Duomo – and was overwhelmed by its intricate grandeur, the product of centuries of design and labour. Julian was a superb host and relished the novel inter-regional link we were developing.

Early in October, I headed for Barcelona to sign a similar agreement with Jordi Pujol, president of Catalonia, whom I had met at Dresden. The agreement was to be in English, Welsh and

Catalan – certainly the first ever. Pujol was well known in Europe for his devotion to the regional cause and to his native Catalonia. He was anxious to see the European regions make more progress but he knew that Europe did not divide itself easily into regions; they were rivalled by the great cities that had an independent spirit of their own, running back to the communes of the Middle Ages. Still, he was hopeful that the regions would win representation at European level, which in time they did.

Pujol was a talkative, likeable man with an astute brain. He realized the importance of leadership. He also realized that, unlike Catalonia, which is one of the most prosperous regions in Spain, Wales was very dependent on the rest of the United Kingdom. In our relations with Catalonia, we had harnessed the strength of the United Kingdom to our legitimate ambitions. This kind of benevolent cooperation was not characteristic of Spanish–Catalan relationships in the past – far from it – but it was to develop in the near future with the staging of the Olympic Games in Barcelona. The games required a huge investment by central government in Madrid to prepare the city for that amazingly successful event. Others outside Europe were thinking along the same lines as we were. A great character, Governor Hiramatsu of Oita province in Japan, visited Cardiff in the autumn of 1991. His message was: 'Think globally, act locally.' His aim was to inspire his province to produce the best, whatever the product, and so win a place in the global market. David Hunt, like Peter Walker before him, thought that Wales should have a provincial link with Japan in view of their investment in Wales. I am sure it was right to develop such a link with Oita on the same lines as our contact with the European regions and later Ontario. My greatest fear was that these relationships would become too diffuse and that we would be unable to do justice to them all.

I received a letter from the prime minister in early May 1991 saying that he was minded to make me a Privy Counsellor; this would be announced on 15 June. This honour means more in political circles than outside and is an acknowledgement of the individual's eminence and worth to the state. It entitles you to the status of 'Right Honourable'. Privy Counsellors have a special code of honour among themselves and can talk to each other on 'Privy Counsellor terms' which raises the conversation above party interest and ensures absolute secrecy. On Wednesday, 24 July I presented myself to the clerk to the Privy Council, Geoffrey de Deney (now Sir), at the Cabinet Office building in Whitehall at 11.30 a.m. We were soon joined by the lord bishop of London, David Michael Hope, who was also to be made a Privy Counsellor that day.

Mr de Deney first explained the nature of the ceremony to take place at Buckingham Palace later that morning and then took us to the office next door where footstools and kneeling cushions were laid out to match the real scene ahead. Mr de Deney's instructions were immaculate, from the first neck-bow on entering the Queen's presence to a similar bow on departure. There were two oaths but we did not have to repeat either, I was assured; Queen Victoria had abandoned the practice during her grieving after the death of Prince Albert.

After the rehearsal, we stepped out into Whitehall and my driver, John Satchell, drove me to the palace. The Lord President of the Council, John MacGregor, the home secretary, Kenneth Baker, and Ian Lang, the Scottish secretary, arrived hard on our heels. As we ambled upstairs, we were joined by the Queen's private secretaries, Sir Robert Fellowes and Sir Kenneth Scott. We spoke about Her Majesty's coming visit to Conwy in October to open the tunnel under the river.

The ceremony was to take place in the White Room, not the Blue Room normally used, and we waited for the tinkle of a bell within – the Queen's summons to us to her presence. The doors were opened and the Queen greeted each of us in turn. My name was called by the Lord President and then the lord bishop's. We both knelt. The clerk to the Council read the oath of allegiance – a substantial, unequivocal oath – and then each of us, with a Bible in his right hand, said 'I do' in unison. Shifting the Bible to my left hand, I moved forward, knelt and kissed the Queen's hand. It was a small, cool hand and I found the experience very moving. James Shirley's famous lines that once terrified Cromwell, raced through my mind:

> The glories of our blood and state
> Are shadows, not substantial things;
> There is no armour against Fate;
> Death lays its icy hand on kings:
>   Sceptre and crown
>   Must tumble down
> And in the dust be equal made
> With the poor, crooked scythe and spade.

When I got to my feet, the Privy Counsellor's oath, pledging absolute loyalty to the sovereign, was read out to us and again the lord bishop and I said 'I do'. I shook hands with the Lord President and his line-up of fellow Counsellors which we now joined. The meeting continued. The Lord President read out a list of Orders in Council made in Her Majesty's name. After each one, she said: 'Approved.' When the formal proceedings were over, Her Majesty said to Mr de Deney: 'You managed to get a lot in.' Then she questioned the home secretary closely about the situation on the Broadwater Farm estate which was causing a great deal of concern. It was one o'clock; the Queen left the room and we all parted, the lord bishop and I clutching our Bibles which on closer inspection turned out to be the New Testament with Our Lord's words printed in red and the Book of Psalms added at the end. Glued inside the front cover, there was a personal presentation slip commemorating the occasion and signed by the Lord President. It had been a memorable morning.

The Queen duly came up to Conwy on 25 October and I met her at Llandudno Junction Station. She told me she understood that I was to travel with her to the tunnel entrance in her car – I had heard talk of it – but I declined her gracious offer. We were coming up to an election and I did not wish to take advantage of her to enhance my personal political prospects. Perhaps I was being excessively finicky, especially as I was giving an address before her at the opening ceremony and accompanying her throughout the day. After her speech, a little girl approached us with a pair of scissors on a velvet cushion. I picked up the scissors and gave them to Her Majesty to cut the ribbon at the tunnel entrance. When she handed them back to me and I similarly to the little girl with the cushion, the Queen was about to present the child with the traditional gold coin given to a person who presents her with a sharp instrument, when one of her officials said: 'To the minister!' She performed a quick half turn and gave the coin box to me. I have always felt that her first instinct was right.

She clearly enjoyed her visit to Conwy Castle and paused to admire the noble Taffy, the Royal Welch Fusiliers' goat. He was in a frisky mood and his head had to be very firmly held by his handler. The Queen questioned him about Taffy's behaviour and he, standing stiffly to attention, explained through gritted teeth:

'Time of year, Ma'am! Time of year!'

Taffy could probably smell the she-goats on the Great Orme not so far away. Later, we travelled to Holyhead. My car was directly behind the Queen's and I saw people's faces light up with joy as she came into view.

'I've seen her!' they cried.

The sight of their Queen still quickens people's hearts.

The election was certainly looming from January 1992. I reckoned that we had until March before it was called. My guess was that John Major would play it as long as he dared because he was growing in stature while Neil Kinnock was declining. Neil's verbosity was becoming a national joke. He did not have the quality of a prime minister in waiting. 'We are not going to have an economic recovery under way to help us win but hopefully, we shall have a useful Budget, with a tax cut to boost demand,' I wrote. By Sunday, 19 January I was 'more convinced than ever that we are heading for an election on 9 April. The chancellor will announce the date of the Budget this week and if that is 3 March, we shall be on course.'

My greatest consolation was that past general elections showed an average swing of no more than 2 to 3 per cent at most and if this continued we should still be returned with a majority of 30 to 40. Of course, statistical runs could never be relied upon but Labour needed an 8 per cent swing to win. For us to lose an overall majority of nearly a hundred was unthinkable. The 'Budget for Recovery' – a week later than I anticipated in January – did not disappoint, especially the 20 per cent rate of tax for the low paid. The following day, the PM went to see the Queen and called the election for 9 April. On Thursday, 12 March, Margaret Thatcher made a stunning appearance in the House in a shimmering, light-blue evening dress, billowing with pleats. It was her final farewell to the Commons.

I looked forward to three weeks of fresh air and running door to door in the constituency but I was concerned about our lack of a clear vision of the future and the divisions within the party on Europe. There were rumours that a former Conservative prospective candidate would stand against me as an independent.

The election campaign lacked 'oomph and fizz', as Margaret said at one point, and got bogged down mid-way in a propagandists' war over 'Jennifer's ear' – an NHS case featured in a Labour Party political broadcast. John Major stomped the country on his soapbox but the campaign was dominated by the media and the pollsters rather than by personalities and issues. The two main parties ran neck and neck until a MORI poll reported in *The Times* on 1 April that Labour were 7 points ahead.

That night Labour held a rally of 10,000 supporters in Sheffield with all the razzmatazz of an approaching victory and Kinnock leading the 'Ra . . . Ra . . . Ra' cries of triumph and celebration. It was all seen by the electorate on television. If it was meant to convey that the campaign was all over bar the voting and that the outcome was now a foregone conclusion, it misfired badly. I remember the personal bitterness I felt at the sheer presumption and effrontery of it all. There is nothing more calculated to antagonize British electors than to presume that they have cast their votes when there is a week to go before they do. Electors relish every moment of a campaign when they have the upper hand and candidates have to grovel for their votes and woe betide the party which takes them for granted. Labour never recovered from the effects of that premature celebration at Sheffield. It put the seal on Labour's folly as a party and branded their leader, Neil Kinnock, as a buffoon. They lost their credibility and the country's trust. The average Labour lead in the polls was 1.6 per cent at the start of the campaign and 2.3 per cent at the end.

The Tories ran well over the last lap and pressed home their key messages that Labour could not be trusted. They were the tax and spend party. The negative campaigning worked. John Major and his party won a record high vote of 14 million but there were not enough Conservative votes in the right constituencies to give us more than an overall majority of 21. Still, a majority of 64 over Labour and a fourth term in government was an astonishing triumph. I held my seat at Conwy with a reduced majority. I had had an independent Conservative to contend with as well as my usual opponents. Party Politics won the Grand National on 4 April and I had backed it to win.

Black and White Wednesday

The 1992 election was a surprise win for the Conservatives, which some thought we might have been better off without. A spell of government under Neil Kinnock and a Labour Party unsure of itself would have given the Tories a much needed respite and time to freshen up their thinking for a strong comeback later. But this was speculation on a scenario that never was and flourished only when the party's difficulties in power reached such proportions that the prime minister was totally exasperated and many of us maddened by the lemming-like behaviour of our colleagues.

One of the immediate consequences of the election was a government reshuffle and I was surprised to hear publicly that Kenneth Baker, the home secretary, had twice been offered the post of secretary of state for Wales and had turned it down. Kenneth confirmed it to me at the eve-of-session dinner at No. 10. We both scoured our minds for an appropriate quotation but the best I could come up with was W. H. Auden's gem:

> Put the car away; when life fails
> What's the good of going to Wales?

Kenneth left the government to pursue other interests but his departure also left David Hunt, the current secretary for Wales, in an unenviable, precarious position. Rumour had it that John Major had not forgiven him for his outspoken support for Michael Heseltine in the battle for the leadership in 1990. Outwardly unfazed, David continued as secretary of state for Wales until May 1993 when he was moved to the Department of Employment, already doomed to be amalgamated with Education. (I foresaw the need for this closer inter-departmental relationship in Wales and took steps to bring school, college and training at the workplace closer together well in advance of the formal departmental amalgamation in England.)

We had lost our brash hotspur of a junior minister, Nicholas Bennett (Con., Pembroke) at the election along with my former, much loved colleague Ian Grist, at Cardiff Central. Ian had been dogged by ill health ever since he had fallen through an open trapdoor into a cellar at a Conservative Club in Cardiff where he was holding a surgery for constituents. Gwilym Jones (Con., Cardiff North) a quiet, reserved, family man bravely stepped into the ministerial breach.

The prime minister visited north Wales on Friday, 4 September. He greeted me warmly at the Kinmel Manor Hotel near St Asaph, where I joined his party and he made a splendid speech at a party luncheon. I told him afterwards in the car that the speech reminded me of Lord Salisbury's declaration at Caernarfon in 1888: 'We are part of the community of Europe and we must do our duty as such.' He was intrigued by the quotation and said he was minded to use it the following week. I faxed the details to No. 10. At Llandudno's Arcadia Theatre, which dated back to 1894, Caitlin's Pierrot Troupe performed a brief, nostalgic history of the theatre in song. John was touched and thanked the troupe with great charm: 'My father did this kind of thing between the wars – in this theatre for all I know – and I remember him singing these songs.'

He joked about my longevity at the Welsh Office and said I had been there since the time of William the Conqueror. His instant and easy rapport with people was quite remarkable. I had planned that we should go to Llanberis – his next destination – along the A55 expressway so that he could travel through the Conwy tunnel and see our achievements for himself. But there was a security scare and we were advised to take the alternative, up-country route through Llanrwst, Capel Curig and Pen-y-Pass. I pointed out the Pen-y-Gwryd Hotel where the Everest climbers stayed while they trained for the Himalayas. The ex-prime minister, Jim Callaghan, too liked the wild isolation of the place and stayed there from time to time. 'It's a different world up here,' said John 'and people's lives are different.'

Although he enjoyed the mountain landscape, he became uncomfortable in the heavily armoured, claustrophobic car as we swung and rolled around the sharp bends between massive rocks on our descent from the foot of Snowdon into Llanberis Pass. He told the driver to slow down and asked me how far we were from Llanberis. I was worried that he might feel unwell when we emerged from the car but, if he was, he showed no sign of it. We alighted at the new factory he was to open in the constituency of his parliamentary

265

pair, Dafydd Wigley, the Plaid Cymru MP. Afterwards, I accompanied him to RAF Valley and he clasped me warmly with both hands before he boarded his plane. I felt our old familiarity and friendship return and I privately vowed to help him as best I could. 'He is his own man and will grow with the years if he does not tire of his exacting office,' I noted, 'but I wish he would not lower his voice at the end of sentences; it is very unprofessional and unexpected in a man of the theatre.'

Ministers sometimes find themselves in incongruous situations, even when fulfilling official engagements. On Wednesday, 16 September 1992, I was due to celebrate 225 years of brewing at the Crown Buckley Brewery at Llanelli. It promised to be a merry break, away from the office. The press too had sensed the merriment potential of the occasion and turned up in force. I was appointed chief brewer for the day and, dressed in a white coat, I stepped up on to a raised platform and turned on the taps to fill a gigantic vat with all the ingredients of thousands of pints of beer.

Shortly after eleven o'clock, as I peered over the edge of the vat at the frothing, brown liquid swirling below, I noticed my quiet-spoken press officer, Elfed Bowen, signalling to me from the other side of the vat. Gradually, I got his message – the interest rate had been raised by 2 per cent. Of course, I was aware of the prevailing concern about exchange rates but hopeful that our membership of the ERM plus the fact that the lira and the franc were also under pressure would somehow save the pound. The 2 per cent rise, unwelcome as it was, was clearly a drastic, defensive move, intended to quell turbulence in the money markets.

When Elfed appeared again and signalled that the interest rate had been upped a further 3 per cent, I thought that the powerful aroma rising from the vat had overcome his normal sense of propriety and that his three-finger gesture and mouthing of words across the froth was really a testimony to the strength of my special brew. I descended from the platform to check Elfed's message that the interest rate had indeed been raised by a total of 5 points that day. Mercifully, the press, who had been imbibing all morning, were in no condition to ask awkward questions and I left the brewery as soon as I decently could to absorb the full implications of the day's alarms.

The sight of a shattered chancellor, Norman Lamont, on the television news told a grim story in brief. Nothing apparently could stem the fall in the value of the pound beyond its baseline in the ERM. The 3 per cent increase was cancelled as a hopeless gesture soon after its imposition and the ERM, which we had joined during

John Major's chancellorship, was reluctantly abandoned. Then the inquest began in earnest. Parliament was recalled ten days later.

While the period of high interest rates, which membership of the ERM demanded of us, helped to reduce inflation, the relief experienced by business and industry after leaving the system was enormous. Black Wednesday became White Wednesday in no time. But why had the government allowed this costly crisis to develop? Did they not see it coming? No amount of explanation could eradicate the impression of poor handling by the government. They had lost control of events.

Those events remained an indelible blot on the government's reputation for managing the economy and it never recovered its lead in the opinion polls from that critical day on. As Norman Lamont scathingly said later, the government was in office but not in power. We now know that John Major wrestled with the question of whether he should resign or not. Someone had to fall on his sword for this debacle and in the end it was the chancellor, Norman Lamont, who was cast for the role. It emerged that Norman had been unhappy with the Maastricht agreement too, although he had played a prominent part in negotiating it.

Taking a bill through Parliament is a tricky business. A bill to safeguard and promote the Welsh language had been promised in the Queen's Speech and we got down to its preparation straight away. I was fortunate to have a young civil servant with a fine mind, John Howells, in charge and he in turn worked with a supremely able parliamentary draftsman, Christopher Jenkins (now Sir). It was not usual for ministers to meet directly with draftsmen – a rare breed who keep themselves to themselves – but I did meet Christopher Jenkins and sensed immediately that the drafting was in a perfectionist's hands.

My first job was to ensure that the bill was ready to compete with others for a place in the legislative programme for the Parliamentary session beginning in the autumn. If it was not ready, we would miss the bus. Opportunities to legislate are not abundant and Parliament can only cope with a limited number of bills in any session. Getting a bill through Parliament is like walking through a minefield with no mine detector other than your own mental antennae. Your bill can be blown sky high at any moment.

The world outside Westminster now understands the legislative process much better than it used to, thanks in part to the expert, full-time lobbyists employed by major organizations whose vital interests are affected. To cultivate public sympathy for legislation in advance can obviously assist its passage through Parliament and I realized that I had much work to do in this field with my bill when, in July, I saw a young girl at Bala wearing a T-shirt bearing the satirical, alliterative legend: 'Deddf yr Iaith: Dim Dannedd' (Language Act: No Teeth). Little did she know that the act was not yet drafted!

I thought that the bill would be ready for approval within the government by early October and for publication soon after. News of the imminence of publication appeared in the press and activists – anticipating publication – actually demonstrated against the bill in Cardiff on Saturday, 31 October. It was a damp squib because the bill was not yet published. The draftsmen working on the bill had been switched to another, more urgent measure with a higher priority.

It was not until Wednesday, 11 November that I saw the first print of the bill. It was a far-reaching document which affected the past as well as the future: it repealed the Tudor Acts of 1536 and 1543 which united Wales with England. I wondered how this proposal would be received by my colleagues and prepared for battle. The simple truth was that the union no longer depended on these anti-quated laws which aroused such bitter resentment and antagonism among patriots of all political hues.

The final authority for presentation and publication of bills was the Cabinet's Legislative Committee – 'L' Committee for short. I was a regular attendee and had seen many bills come to grief there over the years because the presenting minister was faced with a question he could not answer or an issue arose that could not be resolved. The date fixed for me to present my bill was Tuesday, 15 December 1992. I knew that the key to success was to clear up any potential difficulties in advance. The Treasury's view was particularly important so I tackled the chief secretary, Michael Portillo, informally, at the House.

'Are you lobbying me, Wyn?' he asked with a smile.

'Not exactly. There's no problem for you with the Bill . . . all expenditure will be contained within the department's budgets.'

'I shall read it very carefully – now that you've mentioned it!'

Ugh! It was a mock-serious exchange but I knew that if I could not get the bill approved by colleagues in 'L' Committee, no one else was likely to be able to for many years to come. I anticipated that it would be the most difficult and crucial battle of all. There were centuries of inbuilt prejudice to be overcome. Only the argument that the Welsh language was part of the British heritage and required the government's support would carry the day. I lobbied the chairman of 'L' Committee, the Lord President, Tony Newton, before the appointed day to ensure that there were no un-anticipated problems.

In the event, my presentation went smoothly. There were no un-answerable questions from ministerial colleagues and no insuper-able difficulties. They trusted my judgement. It was decided that the bill should be introduced in the House of Lords, which pleased me because it was there that I anticipated any real fundamental criticisms would emerge. I launched the bill publicly in Cardiff on Friday, 18 December, knowing that it would be denigrated by those who could never be satisfied by anything done by a Conservative government. My concern was for those who genuinely cherished the language and wished sensible steps to be taken to enable it to survive and prosper.

The 1991 census had shown that the decline in the number of Welsh speakers had slowed down over the preceding decade when we had been in office and the number of young speakers (aged three to fifteen) had increased from 18 to 24 per cent. The policy and actions of the government, in education, broadcasting and in support-ing voluntary bodies concerned with promoting the language, had helped these trends and were in tune with the deep aspirations of many. The new Welsh Language Bill would provide a further boost to these efforts and provide a framework for the use of the language in adult life. It would also give the language a new and enhanced status.

On Wednesday, 9 December 1992, I accompanied Prince Charles on a visit to Holyhead to boost the morale and reputation of the town. The prince was his usual self, chatting interestedly with everyone he met. About noon, my press officer whispered to me that news of his separation from Princess Diana had leaked and that there was to be a statement in the Commons by the prime minister. I spoke to the prince's equerry. The prince carried on with his engagements, appar-ently unaffected by the impending announcement, and earned my admiration for his calmness and fortitude in the eye of a sad national scandal. He took off in his helicopter shortly afterwards.

My memory took me back to happier days when, as a newly married couple, they had come to north Wales for their first official engagements together. The princess was a demure young bride then, only a breath away from the children's nurse who had captivated the nation's heart. Much had happened since then. I also recalled a lunchtime conversation I had had in June with Nicky Fairbairn who thought that Diana, deprived of love in her childhood, could never have enough attention and affection to satisfy her in later life. He thought she belonged to the Marilyn Monroe category of woman-kind – along with Jayne Mansfield and Princess Grace of Monaco – beautiful but doomed to a tragic end. Nicky went on to say that Diana's devotion to Aids sufferers and identification with landmine victims reflected her own subconscious death wish. It was an in-triguing analysis at the time, which proved to be closer to the truth than we realized. I saw the princess later when she opened a new artificial limb centre at Wrexham. She was on her own and I could not but notice the change in her. Her self-confidence had grown enormously; she was now a star in her own right. When she left the building to face an extended semi-circle of spectators – fifty or sixty yards long – she did not make for the shortest exit route but shook hands with everyone from one end of the crowd of well-wishers to the other. She enjoyed their surging adulation; it was entirely hers and hers alone.

The Welsh Language Bill had its second reading in the House of Lords on Tuesday, 19 January 1993. As a Privy Counsellor, I could sit on the red-carpeted steps below the throne and listen to the thirteenth Earl Ferrers, deputy leader of the House and minister of state at the Home Office, deliver the opening speech. The bill could not have had a better presenter. Robin Ferrers was a past master of the distinctive style – cultivated, witty and refined – characteristic of the best performers in their Lordships' Chamber.

A week later, I briefed their Lordships privately on the details of the bill before they examined it in committee and was relieved to find that there were no insuperable objections. There was an argument about the fact that, although Welsh was now to become an 'official' language in Wales, there was no statement to that effect in the bill, mainly because no one knew its full, practical and legal impli-cations. Did everything done in English have to be done in Welsh as well and vice versa? The Liberal, Lord Hooson, a lifelong personal friend – I had once drafted his election address – called a division on the issue but it was defeated by 39 votes.

There were other bones of contention – later to be chewed over more vigorously in the Commons. Why were the bill's requirements confined to public sector bodies and not intended to cover the private sector as well? The answer was that I did not wish to burden private companies with linguistic demands and give them an excuse to leave Wales or not to establish there on language cost grounds. Besides, private firms, left to themselves, might well lead the way – I hoped – and use the language in novel ways to attract customers.

I knew that the bill's passage through the Commons would not be as easy as the House of Lords because the opposition was hell bent on mischief. Although the government had a majority in the Commons, the Labour Party dominated the Welsh Grand Committee of Welsh members where Welsh bills had in the past been dealt with. Ron Davies (Lab., Caerphilly) who led the opposition, pressed for a second reading and a committee stage in the Welsh Grand Committee. But I set my face firmly against his proposal because it would mean that we would lose control of the bill and Labour, Liberal and Plaid Cymru members could play havoc with its contents. I did not fancy being at their mercy. The government supported me in my resolve.

On Wednesday, 21 April, the Lord President and leader of the House, Tony Newton, secretary of state, David Hunt, Murdo Maclean ('the usual channels') and I decided that we should have second reading of the bill on the floor of the House. This would be followed by a motion to set up a standing committee with an inbuilt government majority. Discussions about the precise composition of the committee seemed to go on interminably. At one stage, the whips thought that the bill might be used to give concessions to Plaid Cymru in return for their support for the Maastricht Bill, which had run into heavy weather. Thankfully, they did not make progress with their dastardly ideas and we had a second reading debate of my bill without a division on Wednesday, 26 May. The following morning, I heard that a government reshuffle was well underway and before the end of the day my colleague, David Hunt, had left us for the Department of Employment. Political life is fraught with uncertainty.

The motion to set up a special committee of twenty-eight MPs to deal with the bill was taken on the floor of the House on Monday, 7 June. Our new secretary of state, John Redwood, opened the debate and I closed it in a minor tumult. In my excitement, I failed to sit down before ten o'clock in time for a division to be called. It meant that the debate could have gone on much longer had the opposition had the stomach for it. Luckily for me, they did not.

Tuesday, 22 June 1993

The first session of the Committee on the Welsh Language Bill and we managed to deal with the first batch of amendments relating to the status of the language. I am sure the government is right to resist populist calls for vague declarations of principle – with no definitions attached – that would only lead to court proceedings to seek meaning and interpretation. I am determined to have a piece of legislation which will stand the test of time and can be built upon by future generations.

Michael Heseltine's heart attack in Venice is a severe blow. The prime minister is hounded by the media and the opposition on account of Michael Mates's presentation of a gold watch to Azil Nadir. We have reached our nadir all right!

I must get my bill if it's the last thing I do.

(Jenkins, our parliamentary counsel, is a noble, clear headed fellow, firm of mind and purpose.)

Thursday, 24 June 1993

Another morning on the bill. It is going well but slowly. The Labour Party is bored and Plaid Cymru is making a meal of what should be a snack. We must hurry on next week or we may lose the bill, I fear.

11.50 p.m., Tuesday, 29 June 1993

A long day on the bill. Dafydd Wigley threatened to vote against third reading if there were no concessions given to him. Roger Evans (Con., Monmouth) muttered his dissatisfaction with the proposal to repeal the old Tudor union laws. Talk of Scylla and Charybdis!

Ted Rowlands (Lab., Merthyr Tydfil, now Lord) is the man who has really grasped and understood the bill best. The proposed new board will explore all the enthusiasts' aspirations for the language and deal with all the complaints too. It will promote and facilitate its use. That should be the end of the language issue politically and legally but, of course, it will only shift the battle on to new ground – probably the financial resources available for its implementation. We shall spend £1 million and create a lot of vested interests but they will only ask for more.

Michael Neubert (Con., Romford) who was at the Ministry of Defence told me Alan Clark was an impossible man to work with at the MOD because he always broke the rules. 'Alan believed that government should be by Old Etonians for Old Etonians.'

Thursday, 1 July 1993

Completed committee stage of the bill of which I am very proud. It is a positive piece of legislation of great potential benefit to the language.

The Welsh Language Society is disappointed that it does not impose statutory bilingualism which I abhor and so does Labour. The people would not tolerate such an imposition. Furthermore, it would kill the language rather than save it. Plaid Cymru is playing to the gallery of critics who would find fault with God if they had Him in the dock.

Thursday, 15 July 1993

Five hours in the Chamber dealing with report and third reading.

Plaid Cymru voted against third reading and Labour abstained. The media tell me that some twit has been calling for my resignation! I know that there is no such thing as gratitude in politics but this is ridiculous. We produce a sound bill, which will mean the investment of a great deal of money in Welsh-speaking Wales. And Welsh MPs turn it down! So much for their professed love of the language and their concern for the best interests of their people.

When the bill received Royal Assent, we appointed Lord Elis-Thomas as chairman of the new language board. He was not universally popular but his credentials were impeccable. He was a former Plaid Cymru MP and had cherished left-wing views at one stage but I had always found him more understanding and amenable than his colleagues on language issues. Like me, he did not treat the language as a political football. At the National Eisteddfod in August, he robustly defended the new act while others gathered names to petition for a new bill, which they must have known was a non-starter. One of the people approached to sign was Michael Fabricant (Con., Lichfield) who had been engaged by a television company to comment on the Eisteddfod. When he refused to sign, he was told to go home. 'No wonder the Eisteddfod field is so empty,' said Michael.

The departure of David Hunt as secretary of state and the advent of John Redwood was a sub-plot in the Welsh Office drama as far as I was concerned. I was now sixty-three years old, too old for a new job in the government and unlikely to stand for Parliament again. I had soldiered on, largely because of the Welsh Language Bill which I wanted to see on the statute book – it is still there more than a decade later – and partly because the government was under attack from all sides and I did not want to rock the boat. Loyalty mattered to me and if ever there was a time when loyalty was at a premium, this was it. At the beginning of the summer recess of 1993, I wrote to the PM to cheer him with a reaffirmation of my personal faith in him. I noted in my diary:

> We have been through hell this last year or so and he has borne the brunt of it. Although I painted a reasonably optimistic scenario, there is another, far more depressing prospect – continued infighting within the party and a press determined to oust us from office. People like Nick Budgeon (Con., Wolverhampton South West) and Bill Cash (Con., Stone) have found a new importance for themselves as dissenters and will disagree for the sake of it. The Cabinet is a cabal of plotters.
>
> I propose in my letter to the PM to counter this with a reassertion of basic Conservative principles and strong leadership based on these principles. It is as good a strategy as can be devised and should see us through if our will does not falter.

It was 'Back to Basics' in essence, the policy that famously back-fired and failed to rescue John Major's government.

David Hunt had done many good things during his tenure of office and had been very generous in his support for my endeavours. He had fully endorsed my efforts to link Wales with the leading regions of Europe. He personally launched a series of overseas visits by Welsh companies to help them find export markets for their products. I led a number of these visits and was always surprised by the rich haul of orders that we brought back, thanks to the efforts of our businessmen and women.

David had also embarked on further reform of local government in Wales and was deeply enamoured by the idea of unitary authorities, to replace the two tiers of county and district/borough councils. I had been involved in the local government reorganization carried out by the Heath government in the early 1970s and knew only too well of local sensitivities and the difficulties of setting up a new system. Michael Heseltine, who was pursuing the same unitary approach, soon sensed what he was up against in England and abandoned the idea of a uniform system statutorily imposed. David stuck to his guns in Wales and prepared to legislate to restore the old county identities as far as possible. I should have been more vigorous in my criticism of the new system with its twenty-two councils – too small to deal effectively with large-scale responsibilities like transport and planning that went far beyond their boundaries. Cooperation, enforced by statute, was the proper answer but it was not included in the bill. It is true that we were reducing the total number of local authorities and that was super-ficially attractive, but the whole system reeked of weakness and I viewed it all with foreboding. I had further opportunity to give vent to my doubts about local government reorganization when John Redwood took over and pronounced that the reforms should go ahead. He thought there would be savings; all I could see were add-itional costs. Every little authority would have its own director of education and we would have twenty-two of them instead of the five we had had before.

John Redwood was a fellow of All Souls, Oxford, the hallmark of intellectual ability. Another fellow of All Souls had once described his colleagues to me as 'clever as hell but short of common sense' and the verdict had stuck in my mind. I decided to watch over John as carefully as I could and infuse some common sense into his decision making, given the chance. Alas, the chance occurred infrequently. I quite liked John as a person but the cartoonists did not. They spotted his resemblance to the humanoid Dr Spock in the *Star Trek* series on television and their caricatures of him spread into the written word. When he stood beside me on a party conference platform in Wales and tried to mime the words of the Welsh national anthem – a performance caught in close-up by a wily television cameraman – his fate was sealed. The clip was shown ad nauseam whenever his name was in the news.

David Hunt had secured a special adviser post to be attached to my office and I had found an ideal Welsh-speaking, Conservative history master at Rugby, Hywel Williams, to fill the vacancy. When John Redwood succeeded David as secretary of state, Hywel's appoint-ment had virtually been made and he was on the verge of joining us. John said: 'I suppose I had better see him but of course he will be working for you.' I arranged the meeting and the two of them struck up an immediate rapport. Hywel worked closely with Redwood from that moment on. They were both men of the right. (Later Hywel was to write *Guilty Men*, one of the most devastating critiques of the Major government.) The main thrust of John's ideas was to eliminate the dependency culture that undoubtedly thrived in Wales irrespective of the party in power. It was the product of decades of supportive, regional policies and redistribution of resources pursued by successive governments.

Labour justified these policies on grounds of regional need and their political interest. Under the Conservatives, the motivation was different although the resulting disparate expenditure was the

275

The Rt. Hon. Lord Roberts of Conwy

same. We regarded the money poured into Wales as an investment, which would eventually revive the economy and create an entrepreneurial society less dependent on Treasury largesse. Such a society might in time produce more Conservative voters. The transformation was happening to some extent during the Thatcher years but it was a slow process – too slow to produce a quick political return.

John Redwood, among others, believed that the government's generosity delayed rather than assisted the transformation and, true to his principles, he set out to reduce government expenditure, especially in areas where he considered it wasteful. There was nothing wrong with that – except the way he went about achieving his objective. He targeted the Countryside Council for Wales – a quango (quasi autonomous non-governmental organization) we Conservatives had set up. The Labour Party was already attacking other quangos, like the Welsh Development Agency, which they had themselves established. Rhodri Morgan (Lab., Cardiff West) had a mole at the WDA who unearthed all manner of defects in the operations of that body, including the scandalous recruitment of escort-agency girls as hostesses at official functions. It cost the chairman, Gwyn Jones, his job. Mid Wales Development, another Labour quango, also had its problems, which were laid bare by the National Audit Office and the Public Accounts Committee. Again, the top men were toppled.

John Redwood went on to reorganize our roads strategy, cancel advanced plans for various by-passes and improvements and give a new priority to the development of the Heads of the Valleys road, linking the upper ends of the south Wales valleys to each other and the Midlands. When he announced that he had thus saved a £100 million for the Treasury, he gave a hostage to fortune, which the Labour Party would use mercilessly at the next election.

By that time John Redwood had burnt his boats by standing against John Major in the leadership election of 1995. Challenged to 'put up or shut up', he had resigned as secretary of state for Wales and stood against the prime minister. The folly of his campaign was stamped on the first photograph of himself and his strange-looking associates – a blazered Anthony Marlow (Con., Northampton North) and glowing Teresa Gorman (Con., Billericay) et al. He lost. He lost again when he stood for the leadership of the party after John Major's resignation in the wake of the shattering Conservative defeat at the 1997 election. John Redwood was followed as secretary of state for Wales by William Hague but, even with his considerable abilities and lovely Welsh wife, Ffion, there was little he could do to repair the damage and stem the tide of New Labour. The Conservatives lost every seat in Wales in 1997. It was a *coup de grâce* from which the party has not yet fully recovered. But I am running ahead of my story.

East and West

One of the joys of life as a minister at the Welsh Office was that I was seldom engaged on one subject or in one place long enough to be bored. Life was well spiced with variety. After my stressful stint on the Welsh Language Bill, I led an export/investment mission to Singapore and Kuala Lumpur in mid-August 1993.

Thursday, 19 August 1993, Omni Marco Polo Hotel, Singapore

I never thought I would be back here quite so soon and in exactly the same room as I had in January. The smiling, young waitresses in cheongsams serving in the lounge downstairs, were as welcoming as the purple and white orchids on the table in my room – a delight to the eye and a joy to the heart.

I have had a busy day, breakfasting with our export missioners, visiting Singapore Broadcasting Corporation, lunching with business-men and talking to tourism chiefs. The latter's chairman, Leong Chi Wayo, thought that Wales was best known for its prison and I had to point out to him that Dartmoor was in Devon, not Wales.

Dined at the Fountain Food Court in Neil Road in the old Chinese quarter on a lethal mix of delicacies – chilli crab, pork ribs and sea slugs. Not surprisingly, I woke up in the early hours with fearful, gargoyle images rampaging in my mind.

Friday, 20 August 1993

Our mission ends tomorrow. Some of our people have done very well and established firm contacts. The Economic Development Board here is to send its own mission to the UK next month. I broadcast on Singapore Radio this morning and acquitted myself reasonably well.

A reception at the high commissioner's at Ladyvale this evening: I went, dressed in insect repellent, to meet members of the local St David's Society. The acting commissioner, Peter Ford, a ginger-haired Arabist, laid on an excellent buffet and I persuaded Eleri Roberts, a Pembrokeshire girl, to sing a lovely Welsh folk song 'Ar Lan y Môr' (On the Sea Shore) to the accompaniment of the cicadas. She gave a perfect rendering.

Since my last visit, I have read C. E. Wurtzburg's extensive biography of Sir Stamford Raffles who played a key role in establishing Singapore for the East India Company early in the nineteenth century. Suffering from recurrent bouts of malaria, he pursued very enlightened policies, which respected the native peoples and their culture. He established the Singapore Institution in 1819 – the precursor of the University of Malaysia – with the support of the Marquis of Hastings, then governor-general of India. Raffles died aged forty-five after a life of great achievement.

Saturday, 21 August 1993, 26th Floor, the Hilton,
Kuala Lumpur

It is just past midnight and I am looking down on some Indonesians and Philippinos sweeping the newly laid, fourteenth concrete floor of a large, floodlit building under construction below. This is a city in a hurry to grow, a Muslim city without too many of the trammels of Islam.

The Philippinos are everywhere. There was a group welcoming guests to the hotel when I returned from a gargantuan dinner at the Bankers' Club with Gareth Howells, director of the British Council here. I am off to Malacca with him and Mrs Howells tomorrow.

The workmen are still polishing their concrete.

6.30 a.m., Sunday, 22 August 1993

It has rained heavily overnight but the concrete floor at the construction site looks all right. This city is a concrete jungle compared with the lush, deep greenery of Singapore. There is some green grass left where the racecourse was but it is about to be built upon. Such a shame that it is not being kept as a park.

The day has begun to improve since Dino, a forty-year-old Malay-Muslim, brought me breakfast. He prays five times a day, has one wife and five children. He goes to the mosque when he feels like it. One wife is enough, he says.

6.30 p.m.

Malacca was a historical revelation. The church of St Peter was originally built by the Portuguese early in the sixteenth century. It was later renamed St Paul's by the Dutch. But there were Chinese and Muslim traders and settlers there at least a century before the Europeans.

There were a lot of Muslim mothers and children in the vicinity of the church and adjacent ruins. The women wore gay-coloured, long dresses and the *tudong* headdress, which covers the face. Mothers, I noticed, urged even their youngest children to cover their faces despite the breathtaking heat.

I was glad when we reached the cool interior of the family home of Tan Siak Choo and her husband, Walter. Her grandfather, pictured in Victorian dress complete with a wing collar and cravat, had established a shipping service between the Malaccan Straits and south China. As befitted a man whose motto was 'The Spirit of Righteousness', he had shunned the opium trade. His grand house backed on to the river and could be entered or exited by boat through a trapdoor in the floor.

On the return journey, we passed a prison-like compound packed with people. They were illegal immigrants, better treated now than they had been, I was told.

Monday, 23 August 1993

Quite a hectic day, beginning with a briefing at the High Commission at 8 a.m. We then went on to meet the very impressive, direct and dominating lady, Rafidah Aziz, minister for Trade and Industry. She is reputed to be the only member of the Cabinet who dares to argue with the prime minister, Dr Mahathir.

There is a touch of Margaret Thatcher about her. As she answered questions from our missioners, she lectured her civil servants *sotto voce* on minor points and told me to drink my tea. She is very media conscious. There was a battery of cameras in attendance as we walked into the conference room.

The country is set for continuing rapid growth but there is some doubt about the value of Western-style progress in the Muslim community, which is becoming increasingly fundamentalist. The young women are reverting to the *tudong*, which is not part of the traditional Malaysian wear. That consists of the sarong and the *kabaya* (top). Mrs Les Winters – first name Tunku – told me this at a High Commission reception this evening where I met members of the St David's Society of Kuala Lumpur.

Tuesday, 24 August 1993

Almost the entire day devoted to education and nurturing the links between the University of Glamorgan and the Help Institute. I was invited to make an impromptu speech to young law students and I spoke to them about their role as guardians of justice.

I lunched as a guest of former students at Aberystwyth. There were about forty in all. Afterwards, I made some impromptu remarks on the theme that peaceful economic development depends on political stability founded on a just system of government. Our educators have been in the vanguard in meeting Malaysian requirements but they are meeting tough competition from the American universities.

The British Council under Gareth Howells's leadership is coping well with a huge demand for English lessons, English being the lingua franca of commerce and business in the Far East.

Malaysia is eager to play a leading role in trade in the Association of South East Asian Nations (ASEAN). A link between Welsh and Malaysian companies could be helpful to both in securing entry to their respective markets in Europe and South East Asia with its 360 million population.

Our missioners tell me they have secured more than £1 million worth of firm orders so the visit has been financially worth their while.

I return to London tomorrow, concerned by the growth of Islamic fundamentalism and the troubles it might lead to.

I had another foreign visit arranged for September and spent the next few days recharging my batteries at home in the Conwy Valley. My political judgement at the time was that the government had lost its way but, with a fresh approach to law and order expected in the next Parliamentary session and a revival in the country's economic fortunes, we might regain our popularity. John Redwood had yet to make a favourable impression in Wales. I noted:

He is probably too detached by nature, too remote and too much in the shadow of his extrovert predecessors. If only we could galvanize Wales into concerted action on any front of real benefit! It is the age-old problem with this little country of ours – so small but with such a big appetite, wanting so much and yet prepared to do so little.

Thursday, 2 September, was one of the sunniest days of the year. In the evening I climbed the hill lane beside our home and strolled towards Tu Hwnt i'r Ffrwd (Beyond the Stream), the little farm house where Dafydd Owen and his aged mother used to live with no gas, electricity or running water. She lived to be ninety-four. Two pairs of buzzards soared and circled on warm air currents overhead and called joyously to one another.

Thursday, 9 September

I cut the first turf at Talacre in north-east Wales to signify the start of works at the landing site for the oil and gas Hamilton Oil has discovered in Liverpool Bay. It is a £2 billion project linked to the restored and adapted power station at Connah's Quay. I have been closely involved with the project for months since it is of crucial importance to the future prosperity of the area.

Fred Hamilton himself had flown over from his home in Denver, Colorado, for the occasion. He was the first to get oil out of the North Sea and could now add the Irish Sea to his achievements. He was a tall, slender man with rugged features, a fine mind and wide interests. He told me an alarming tale of how young black gangs were invading Denver from time to time to shoot a white person. This indiscriminate individual killing was the probationer's ticket to membership of his gang.

Monday, 13 September 1993, Stouffer Madison Hotel, Seattle

Still a little shaky after a long yesterday. The nine-hour flight added eight hours to my Sunday. We set off from Heathrow at 1.15 p.m. and arrived here at 3.15 p.m. Seattle time. I retired after dinner with Stephen Turner, the British consul, and slept fitfully, but the sunshine on Puget Sound and a hearty breakfast have restored me. The mat on the elevator floor with its 'Have a good Monday' also helped.

New York has its pretzels, Chicago its hot dogs and here in Seattle it's caffeine. To the newcomer, it may appear more of a frenzy than a fancy – with shouts of 'full double skinny, iced latte or dopio to go to a double espresso'. Seattle is certainly a smiling, welcoming city with or without coffee.

Tuesday, 14 September 1993

Visit to Boeing at Everett this morning to see how they assemble the six million parts of a 747; it is a real feat of organization, technology and timing. That aircraft has now been in operation for twenty-five years and has carried the equivalent of a quarter of the world's population. Its successors, the 767 and 777, were also on the stocks. Aircraft purchase deals are made in the air, I learnt, to avoid ground taxes.

Lunch at Smuggler's Cove and much talk of Bill Gates of Microsoft whose new home I saw under construction.

I also visited Mrs Mary Rosenberger (née Rowlands) who celebrated her hundredth birthday in July. She emigrated to Washington State from Wales when she was eight years old. This must have been wild country in her younger days. She spoke to me in Llanberis Welsh. I spent a pleasant evening with the Puget Sound Welsh Association at Bellevue and listened to Jennifer Nightingale reciting a passionate account of the demolition of a Welsh church and its cemetery in the neighbourhood.

The ferry boats are hooting in the sound as I write, reminding one of the area's past. The whistle of police-car sirens downtown and the sparkling lights of skyscrapers bring one back to the present and the precarious nature of life and its riches.

Wednesday, 15 September 1993

This morning I met William B. Stafford, executive director of the Trade Development Alliance of Greater Seattle. We talked about regional links and sparked off the idea of 'world regions'. It is a fresh and appealing concept. Just as the 1980s was the time to develop European regions, the 1990s should see the idea of world regions come into its own. These regions would have common trading and developmental interests and would assist each other for their mutual benefit. With our international links, we are well prepared for this in Wales. Bill Stafford is already engaged in bringing about this kind of synergy and the APEC summit (Association of Pacific Economic Communities), shortly to be held in Seattle, is helping him along. He hopes President Clinton will attend. He is also planning a major business mission to south-east Asia.

Thursday, 16 September 1993, Vancouver

Life for me is now a return journey – a privileged one – to the Canadian geese, the black and red squirrels of Stanley Park I last saw in the 1970s. Perhaps it was my respect for the totem poles at Prospect Point that brought me back. We came over the border by coach from Washington State.

I was interviewed for radio this morning by J. J. Richards. He has an unctuous voice and style to match. I put over my idea of world regions in a tentative form. I must try to develop it further.

Met Oksana Excell this afternoon. She is president of the British Columbia Trade Development Corporation, which employs over a hundred people compared with Bill Stafford's three! I could not avoid comparing the American and Canadian operations although this is probably unfair. The American was much more focused on 'the production of intended effects' (as Bertrand Russell defined real power). I picked up the Russell phrase from a magazine article about twenty-nine-year-old Terry Hui, the boss of Concord Pacific who is building a new city on the old Expo site at False Creek. (The Canadians are sore because they had to pay to clear the site.) Now, Mr Hui has stepped in with his $3 billion investment in 'Forty high rises and an equivalent number of low rises.' The money is from Hong Kong and the development is an insurance against things going sour there after China takes over in 1997.

Oksana told me that some Hong Kong families were establishing themselves in Australia at the same time as they sought a home in Canada and that it was not unusual to find families with this triple base spanning the vastness of the Pacific. So, the end of this decade may see the Hong Kong Chinese dominating the Pacific Rim from Guangdong to Queensland and British Columbia.

Tonight, a reception for missioners and guests, including Charles Lambert and his wife Sally who oversee this hotel as well as the Royal York in Toronto. The Welsh were here in force. Our missioners are doing good business. I greatly admire Owen S. Roberts of Tywyn Pottery who never misses an opportunity to sell his daffodil-decorated tea sets, Irish patterned jugs and Scottish tartan rugs.

Friday, 17 September 1993

Lunched at the University of British Columbia before going to the Science World Dome – not unlike our own Techniquest Centre in Cardiff Bay, which I helped Rudi Plaut to establish.

My chambermaid, Melodia (pronounced Meloja), is from the Philippines. She is saddened by the poverty of her country. The Filipinos are the *shardanah*, the wandering people of the Pacific; they show what can happen when a country's politicians fail.

Welsh cakes and folk dancing at a Welsh Society reception at Cambrian Hall this evening. The consul, Brian Austin, and his daughter Stephanie came with us. (Brian was at the embassy in Sweden when I called there on my quick tour of Scandinavia.)

Saturday, 18 September 1993

Went fishing today with John Quinn, an ex-CIA officer, in his superbly equipped cruiser, *Southern Cross*. He has a rare claim to notoriety in that his wife Nancy once fell overboard when he opened the throttle without warning and he did not notice her absence until he tied up the vessel and someone asked where she was.

Colin Green from the Welsh Office was on the expedition. He is an ex-naval lieutenant and was blown up during his service.

'Where?' I asked.

'Twelve feet up,' he said.

My day's fishing was very enjoyable although we caught nothing except a tiny rock cod in a quiet inlet. I threw it back, almost straight into the mouth of a waiting seal. There were too many seals about for my liking. That, plus Quinn's impatience with the throttle, accounted for our failure to catch, despite the availability of a sonar device to locate the elusive salmon. Of course, there were two lads on shore who had had all the luck and brandished a couple of large salmon provocatively as we passed. But we had a bellyful of fresh air and grand scenery with treetops towering above the mist and the spectacle of a forest fire being doused by helicopters filling their buckets from the inlet sea.

Wednesday, 22 September, Toronto 1993

I have been here at the consul's home as a guest of Peter and Elizabeth Davies since Monday. As a representative of an associate member of the Four Motors, I am given the same VIP treatment by the Ontario government as ministers of the full member regions. This was an unexpected bonus.

Ontario has been through a rough time in the recession. The economy is now growing again but unemployment remains high. Bob Rae's federal government is unpopular with the trade unions that helped secure his election victory in September 1990 when I was last here. Met Francis Lankin, minister for economic development and trade, and I was delighted to hear that they are determined to put some life into the Wales–Ontario agreement I signed with Ed Philip last autumn. I shall hear more at dinner with his deputy tomorrow night.

Yesterday, we flew to Sudbury to see the Inco nickel and copper complex. The pristine grandeur of Northern Ontario was mind-bending in its vastness and geological complexity – the result of meteorite bombing or volcanic eruption 1.8 billion years ago.

At the Science North Centre, there was a flying squirrel with wings like a stealth bomber and a propelling tail. It landed on Colin Green and made straight for his warm trouser pocket and deposited its calling card there too – much to his annoyance.

Today, we viewed Toronto from the summit of the CN Tower and, afterwards, visited the art gallery that has some fine pictures by Canadian artists like Lauren Harris who have tried to give distinctive form to their visions of this incredible country. The indigenous Inuit art, especially the sculptures, capture the effect of an unkind nature on the human face and mind. The tightly drawn lips, the lost sunken eyes and the weirdly powerful shapes all suggest the extreme cold that brings a shiver of dread to those who have experienced it.

Thursday, 23 September 1993

At dinner last night at Mclean House, Sunnybrook, Len Christino offered jointly to finance a trade conference for Canadian and Welsh businessmen in Wales early next year. This is the fillip they had in mind to give meaning to the Wales–Ontario agreement. I gladly accepted the proposal. With Terry Mathews (now Sir) of Newbridge Electronics and Dr Bill Morgan with a foot in both Canada and Wales, we cannot go far wrong.

Don Rickard, whom I saw at the consulate reception on Tuesday and who dined with us afterwards, phoned to say that he would meet me in London before Christmas to arrange the conference in Wales. Rickard, an Oxford-educated lawyer, played a prominent part in developing the Four Motors, as I found at Dresden. I told him of my world regions idea and he encouraged me to develop it.

Postscript: Our Boeing 747 could not land at Heathrow because of fog and, after two attempts, headed for Manchester. I got off there with one of our missioners, Mrs Drake, who was pregnant and felt queasy on the flight. She too lived in north Wales. The plane landed in Heathrow after the fog had lifted. Another missioner from north Wales recovered our luggage. Mrs Drake was none the worse for her flight.

Going, Going . . .

A s the 1992–3 Parliamentary session drew to a close after the party conferences in the autumn, there was a great deal I could look back upon with a fair measure of pride. Shortly after my return from North America, I had met Lord Elis-Thomas and agreed the membership of the new Welsh Language Board. I had every confidence in him and his chief executive, John Walter Jones, that they would get on with the job of implementing the act. Early October saw the opening of the 930-metre-long tunnel on the A55 at Pen-y-Clip, Penmaenmawr – the tunnel that almost never was had I listened to my top advisers. This astonishing piece of engineering, buttressed at its western portal by a concrete wall thirty-four metres high and bolted to the mountainside, was the last magnificent addition to the now completed Chester–Bangor expressway. A major extension to the Sony factory at Bridgend was opened by Her Majesty the Queen in the same week. Even with such achievements to our credit, the government did not stand high in the Welsh people's esteem. John Redwood had not endeared himself to the nation.

I returned to London on Monday, 18 October. The party conference at Blackpool was thought to have gone well. John Major had launched his 'Back to Basics' theme but he had been overshadowed in the media day after day by his predecessor, Margaret Thatcher. The *Daily Mirror* (5 October) purloined extracts from her autobiography criticizing the prime minister. Then serialization of her book began in the *Sunday Times* (10 October). We were all tarred with the past and feathered with her pique – if not fury – at her dismissal. But the government's malaise was more deep seated.

The entire government seemed to be discredited in the eyes of the people by innuendo – and crescendo whenever the media could manage it. Rumour and scandal had run riot after David Mellor's toe-sucking affair with a soft-porn actress, Antonia de Sancha. It had culminated in his resignation as minister for national heritage the previous year. The prime minister himself had been forced to take legal action against the *New Statesman* for regurgitating a scandal-sheet story that he had had an affair with the attractive No. 10 caterer, Claire Latimer. Now, jovial Steve Norris was being hounded as a sexual maestro with five mistresses who had given the Ministry of Transport a new meaning. 'Back to Basics' had returned with a vengeance. There were more casualties to come.

The rust of immorality and corruption corroded us all. We all became suspect and unsure of ourselves, especially when we found the rust had penetrated the quangos, supposedly being constantly watched by beady-eyed civil servants. Wales emerged scarred from a debate on the Public Accounts Committee proceedings on 25 October 1993 and I noted:

> The scope for dishonesty is vast! The ultimate consequences for Wales are serious. Both the Welsh Development Agency and the Development Board for Rural Wales will be discredited and maybe the whole quango system. There will be a case for making them directly accountable to a Welsh elected body – it will be argued – or for abolishing them altogether.

It took the irrepressible story-telling of Geoffrey Dickens (Con., Littleborough and Saddleworth) or 'Dickens of the House of Commons' as he called himself when he answered the telephone, to raise our spirits from this political trough.

Every day in one's life is special but Thursday, 4th November 1993 was uniquely so for me. I was at my desk in Gwydyr House, Whitehall, ploughing through papers when my private secretary, Huw Jones, told me that there was to be a meeting of the Privy Council at Sandringham later that day.

At 5.15 p.m. my driver, John Satchell, and I set off for Kensington Palace where a Wessex helicopter of the Queen's Flight and a red carpet was waiting. Peter Lilley, secretary of state for Social Security, was already inside and we were soon joined by John Wakeham, deputizing for the Lord President, Tony Newton, who was still on his feet in the Commons. Lynda, Baroness Chalker, minister for overseas development, and the clerk to the Privy Council, Nigel Nichols, also came aboard. We took off at 6 p.m. London from the air that night looked like a Christmas card, with Harrods's illuminations especially prominent.

After what seemed a lengthy flight, we landed in a floodlit clearing in the woods at Sandringham. The helicopter engine died away and an RAF man opened the door. We trooped out into a waiting Land Rover, drove along a track with rabbits scurrying for cover, and were soon at Wood Farm. The Queen's equerry, Sir Kenneth Scott, greeted us there and led us into a whitewashed waiting room.

The farmhouse was small and cosy but the gents' outside toilet had room for two. I went there with John Wakeham as soon as we arrived. When we got back to the farmhouse ante-room, Philip, Duke of Edinburgh, had appeared from somewhere. 'How will you know when you're summoned?' asked Philip and someone mentioned the bell. Sure enough, there was a tinkle beyond the latched door and we entered in order of seniority as PCs – Lynda, Peter and I. John Wakeham had preceded us.

The Queen stood with her back towards a blazing fire, flanked by two easy chairs, in the farmhouse parlour. She greeted us as we stood formally in line away from her as usual at Privy Council meetings. There was no one else in the room except the Queen, the clerk and ourselves. John uttered the words requesting Her Majesty's consent to prorogue Parliament and she replied:

'Approved.'

Almost in the same breath she said:

'To think that you should come all this way just to hear me say that!'

Yet, we all knew that, formal as it was, her consent as monarch – freely given and in our representative presence – to the prorogation of Parliament, was constitutionally important. No one was holding a gun to her head; neither was she acting alone.

As Prince Philip came in, the Queen suggested we might like a drink. Philip personally dispensed the gin and tonics and informality prevailed. She had been to visit the troops in Germany earlier in the day and had clearly enjoyed crossing the Wieser with the sappers and seeing a Harrier put through its paces. She looked younger, more relaxed and cheerful than I had seen her for some time. Philip was his usual buoyant self and full of zest. He saw us off at the door of the Land Rover.

We returned to the helicopter in the clearing and in an hour we were back in London. Our cars were waiting for us at the landing pad in Kensington and we sped off into our individual nights – the four of us who, with the monarch, had brought Parliament temporarily to an end in a remote farmhouse in England.

I had known since the 1992 election that I would not be standing again for Parliament. Neither did I intend to stay in office until the last possible moment – that would not be right in my book – and so I would have to resign (or be fired) at some point. My cherished plan was that I should carry on until some of the Welsh newcomers – Jonathan and Roger Evans and Rod Richards – had had a chance to prove their mettle and provide the prime minister with a choice of successor. The question at the back of my mind was when would be the best time to go. I did not wish to create a fuss.

On Tuesday, 9 November, I watched a television account of Margaret Thatcher's downfall where she described her individual meetings with members of her Cabinet as 'betrayal with a smile'. What she seemed to forget was that it was she who had appointed every one of them and that some of them were sycophants, not loyalists. The truth was that she had lost her will to win. I wrote:

> I cannot but feel that all the emotion surrounding her resignation and the public exhibition of it amounts to a betrayal of the party and that we shall suffer from it for a decade if something is not done to counter act it. It does not look as if anything significant can be done in the near future. We badly need success under John Major and it is, sadly, not in prospect.

Thursday, 18 November 1993

The Queen's Speech today at the opening of the new session. I had heard it at No. 10 last night, read by Sir Robin Butler (now Lord) and someone said to me 'You've heard a few of these!' Indeed I have. Included in the speech is a measure to reform local government in Wales, which I do not relish. It is going to cost a great deal of money – a £100–150 million for starters – and it will be contentious.

The secretary of state, John Redwood, is in a spot, not because of anything done in Wales but because of colleagues. His speech on single parents at St Mellons (on an estate where 66 per cent of the parents are single) had less to do with his Welsh responsibilities than with Peter Lilley's at Social Security. Then last week he made a speech highlighting the increase in the administrative costs of the NHS which poached on Virginia Bottomley's territory as secretary of state for health. There has been a flurry in the media and a leader in the *Evening Standard* saying he was right and his colleagues laggardly in reform.

David Lightbown, our whip, told me over dinner last night that John is in danger of drawing wrath upon his own head if he goes too far in highlighting defects in Wales which are even more painfully obvious in the rest of the UK. The government is trying to establish a united front and John is disrupting it.

Monday, 22 November 1993

I got as far as composing a letter of resignation to the chief whip, Richard Ryder. I shall have it in my bottom drawer over the next few weeks. The inspiration is my age, my wife's feelings and my antipathy to what lies ahead. I have no stomach for the Local Government Reorganisation Bill and today's debate confirmed my doubts about its value. Alex Carlile (Lib., Montgomeryshire, now Lord) sabotaged John Redwood's wind-up speech totally by raising points of order and calling a vote on 'I spy strangers'. Alex was inspired by a desire to hog tomorrow's headlines. As he is the only Liberal MP in Wales, he is a party of one and I can understand his behaviour.

Monday, 29 November 1993

Ted Heath joined my table at dinner and we chatted about the Far East. Chris Patten has gone wrong in Hong Kong and antagonized the Chinese in Beijing. I agree with Ted that our posturing is really monstrous. How can we assert the need for democracy in Hong Kong when we have denied it to them for so long? Our quarrelsome attitude towards China must affect our ability to trade. Ted knew the China trade figures, which show Japan in the lead followed by the US and with Britain trailing badly.

'We are still good traders,' I said.

Ted gave me a very dubious look.

Politics are not what they were, said Ted. There used to be a time between elections when both sides got down to the business of running the country. Now the electioneering never ceases.

Wednesday, 1 December 1993

I have caught a bug, which has cracked my voice and is causing a depression of Johnsonian dimensions. I asked Gwilym to wind up today's Welsh Grand Committee debate on the implications of the Budget for Wales. No one distinguished himself except Ted Rowlands (Lab., Merthyr, now Lord) – always a man to listen to. Ted said that most people including himself hated the dependency culture in Wales but there was no alternative; it was the existence of the welfare state that made life now so different from the 1920s and 1930s – and more tolerable. Privately, I had to agree with him.

We are now entering rough waters and they will be very testing. The Tory Party has lost a great opportunity in Wales over the years we have been in office. We should have been more proselytizing in our approach and made converts to strengthen the party's membership and organization. We have not done so.

I really must steel myself to hand in my resignation letter next week. I have no realizable ambition as far as Wales is concerned and I must get out.

Monday, 6 December 1993

My dreadful bug continues to debilitate me but I managed a reception at the Travellers' Club given by Peter Davies, our consul in Toronto, and his wife, Elizabeth. The Ontarians are still thinking of an event in Cardiff in March. It could be a gathering of the Four Motors. Could we get Prince Charles to open it?

Dinner afterwards with Hywel Williams whom John Redwood thanked me for finding, some time ago now. He spoke learnedly of Ximénez and the Spanish Reformation that never was and I of the Iron Age treasure found at Snettisham, Norfolk, on show at the National Museum in Cardiff. (I opened the exhibition on Friday.)

Enid was most understanding over the weekend about my intended resignation. I think she sees it as an escape hatch for herself too. She has put up with a great deal.

Midnight, Tuesday, 7 December 1993

Here I am with my resignation letter in my top drawer and I keep on bumping into the prime minister in the division lobby. At one point we were so close I overheard him tell Graham Bright, his PPS, of some woman that she was 'about my age, you know'. We exchanged greetings trustingly, on Christian-name terms. Presumption of trust must be a huge liability in his position. Graham looked sheepish but intensely aware of the ears around us.

Thursday, 9 December 1993

I put my letter to the chief whip, Richard Ryder, on the board at the Commons yesterday lunchtime – with some reluctance – and he asked me to meet him at No. 12 Downing Street at 12.15 p.m. today. I did not really know what I was letting myself in for – hence the hesitation on my part.

After some small chat about his wife, Caroline, Richard said that he had been sad to read my letter. I explained that I would be most unlikely to stand at the next election and that I would like some time on the back benches beforehand. In the new year, we would be deeply involved with the Local Government Bill and I could not properly abandon it until it had completed its progress through Parliament. This was why I had couched my letter in the terms I did; the timing of my retirement was for the government to decide.

He sounded me on my possible replacements and I ran over the three possibles. None of them could walk into my position as minister of state, Richard said, without serving for twelve to eighteen months as an under secretary. This would mean I could not vacate my post until 1995 at the earliest. We ended the conversation with Richard saying he would have to report to the prime minister who would probably see me before Christmas. I must therefore think hard over the weekend whether I want to carry on or not. If I do not have the stomach for it, my guess is that I must go now. Proving that I have the will to carry on – now that I have shown my hand – will not be easy.

8 p.m., Monday, 13 December 1993

My thoughts have not advanced a great deal over the weekend but my bug seems to have cleared and I am in better spirits. I gather from the press that the PM and his entourage are nervous about the immediate future and that I can well believe. There is stormy weather ahead.

Much depends on my encounter with the PM. If it is on a bon-homie basis of 'what's this about you wanting to resign etc.', I shall know he wants me to stay and I shall do so. Of course, his approach could be different in which case I shall go.

In that event, my regret will be that I leave a clever young man in charge of Wales, John Redwood, who does not know the people he governs. Redwood is very critical of Michael Griffith, chairman of the Countryside Council for Wales, not only for his running of the council but on account of some honest, critical advice given by the council to Prince Charles for a speech he made on Friday. I shall not see Michael hanged! He has served the government well.

Midnight

I spoke with the chief whip in between divisions and said 'the time is out of joint' for further discussion of my retirement. He asked me whether that meant that I would soldier on and I said it did. He said that I had been right to raise the subject. This means that I do not think the PM will wish to discuss it with me – a great relief – and that we can return to it at a later date. Of course, this is only my reading of the runes.

An HTV programme about my life, filmed earlier in the year, was transmitted this evening. The initial reaction has been favourable. In anticipation of a reception for Welsh MPs tomorrow evening, John Redwood told me jokingly in the lobby: 'I shall say I do not mind having a high-profile minister of state because it excuses me for having a low profile as secretary of state!'

The net result of the last few days is that I shall probably have a different future to the one I had anticipated. I must consider it carefully. I am overjoyed that my friends value me to the extent they do and that is a good starting point. This minor crisis was of my own making – possibly the effect of the bug and the late nights – but the fundamental problem remains. I must leave the government at some point, preferably of my own choosing.

There were so many scandal stories in the press at the start of 1994 that I had almost lost count after the first few weeks. They appeared in the broadsheets as well as the tabloids. Able Tim Yeo (Con., Suffolk South) and his offspring on the wrong side of the blanket led the field, followed by David Ashby (Con., Leicestershire North West), who admitted to a strange bedfellow, to the horror of his tempestuous Italian wife, Silvana. The Conservative member for Rutland, Alan Duncan's purchase of a house from Westminster Council at Gayfrere Street caused a rumpus. The death of the wife of Lords' minister Malcolm Caithness from a self-inflicted gunshot had a darker hue. One of Steve Norris's mistresses opined publicly that this was not the best time to 'move in'. Steve and Tim reappeared in the lobbies, looking chastened by sleepless nights – the real penalty of scandal.

The *Sunday Times* threw a bucket of acid in John Major's face in its leader columns. The newspaper was determined that the Conservative Party should do badly in the local government elections in May and the European elections in June and that these defeats should be followed by a leadership crisis in the autumn.

Good news such as the January fall in unemployment was ignored in favour of rumours – some originating in *Scallywag* – that there was a gay clique in the Cabinet and a bunch of right-wingers (the 'bastards') totally opposed to Major. All the prime minister's initiatives – from the Citizen's Charter to Back to Basics – seemed to have a hollow ring. The press was intent on scavenging for scandal and nothing would distract them from their pursuit. They were obsessed with dirt.

Late on Monday, 7 February, I heard the shocking news that Stephen Milligan (Con., Eastleigh), aged forty-five, had been found strangled at his home in Chiswick. I knew him by repute as a high-powered journalist and by sight as a somewhat strained looking individual. Later, I learnt that he died of self-asphyxiation. We were not spared the details.

Within a week of the Milligan tragedy, Hartley Booth, Margaret Thatcher's successor at Finchley and a former No. 10 adviser on law and order issues, resigned as PPS to Douglas Hogg, then minister of state at the Foreign Office, because of an unconsumated affair with a twenty-two-year-old research assistant, reported to be a *Guardian* contributor and occasional nude model. Our 'funny old world' was becoming funnier – in a mad sense – by the day. People were only too ready to believe that we were all the same. Even Dennis Skinner, Labour's 'Beast of Bolsover', was not immune to the paparazzi who caught him with his face wrapped in a scarf when he visited a female American researcher in Chelsea. The next to fall was none other than the chief of the Defence staff, Sir Peter Harding, aged sixty. On Sunday, 13 March, the *News of the World* revealed that he was on familiar terms with Bienvenida, until recently married to Sir Anthony Buck MP (Con., Colchester North), chairman of the Conservative back-bench defence committee. She was a stunning brunette when she married but she was pictured in the Sunday newspaper as a thirty-two-year-old blonde. All these scandals were uncovered in the first three months of 1994 and there were more to come right up to the 1997 election. I fell victim myself to a preposterous story in *Scallywag* linking me with a paedophile ring run by a mysterious Mr X. I was telephoned by the BBC in Cardiff and asked if I was going to sue. Everyone at Westminster knew that the magazine was not worth suing and I had the wit, mercifully, to reply that I would sue the BBC if they lent any credibility to the story.

These scandals were enormously damaging. The local election results in May were dreadful and the result at the Eastleigh by-election early in June equally devastating. There were four other by-elections the same day – four in safe Labour seats – and the average swing to Labour was 18.5 per cent. The prime minister wandered through the division lobby the following Monday evening looking distinctly forlorn; he spoke to those who wished to speak to him and they were few.

The European election results later that month were also cata-strophic. We lost 15 of our 32 seats – 13 to Labour and 2 to the Liberal Democrats. Despite a low poll (36 per cent) which usually favoured the Tories, there was a marked swing to Labour of 11 per cent. In Wales, the Conservative share of the vote was halved. Our supporters had lost faith in a tainted government and had deserted the party on a massive scale. Scandal (mainly sexual peccadilloes) and later sleaze – venal and selfish money-grabbing – accounted for much of that loss of faith. They sapped the confidence of the party in itself and its will to win.

I was glad that the earlier work I had done to promote Welsh relationships with the Four Motor regions came to fruition at this time. On Monday, 21 February, I went to Milan to sign a joint agreement between Wales and Lombardy with the new president, Dr Fiorella Ghilardottia, and stayed overnight with our ever active consul, Philip Whetton and his wife, Roswithe, in their wonderful apartments overlooking St Ambrosius's church. When I returned to London, it was to find the PM wearing out his nerve ends in the lobby. Only the momentum of events kept him going.

After answering Welsh Questions in the House on Monday, 14 March, I flew to Barcelona with an export mission of twelve. President Jordi Pujol was in fine form, girding himself for the next election in 1996 but fearful that they could no longer sustain their welfare state in Catalonia. Cheap imports from the Far East were also causing problems in traditional Catalan markets. I saw Gaudí's cathedral again in a new light. Those who commissioned him had immense faith in the enduring quality of his unique work. (Gaudí was killed in a tram accident in 1926.)

I returned on Wednesday to get a motion through the House setting up a standing committee of twenty-eight to deal with the Local Government (Wales) Bill. I was haunted by the late Henry Brooke's dictum that he who would govern Wales must win the support of the local authorities. We have not been able to carry them with us in this gratuitous upheaval. *Me miserum*, that I should ever have acquiesced! (I learned later that Peter Walker also thought the bill was a mistake.) The county councils supported us in our fight against devolution in 1979. I doubted whether the new authorities would do the same next time round.

Wednesday, 17 March 1994

I am concerned that Wales is again being reduced to a backwater in the multi-ethnic, multicultural sea that is modern Britain. It is partly because it has produced no political return – a fact stressed by John Major when David Hunt and I were called in to see him before the 1992 election – and partly because of the pressure, endorsed by John Redwood, to reduce government expenditure. Impoverished Wales is the last place where one should look for such reductions.

I have always deliberately been kept out of the leadership in Wales. I could – even at this late stage – make a bid for it and try, along with the Scottish secretary, Ian Lang, to appeal to the prime minister to see sense in a 'new deal' for the regions. This would mean a radical change of policy and I do not think the government is capable of it.

Wednesday, 30 March 1994

Dropped a line to the PM who has been going through hell recently – yet again. Whitehall rumour has it that he has been seeing Cabinet ministers individually – all very reminiscent of Margaret Thatcher's downfall. John Redwood is said to be very agitated over the qualified majority voting issue.

Thursday, 14 April 1994

The PM has replied to my letter – expressing his appreciation of his friends. I shall try to help him with the press.

We are into the committee stage of the Local Government Bill and I am taking the lead. Only the ineptitude of the Labour Party enables me to hide my true feelings about the bill. Jonathan Evans (Con., Brecon and Radnor) is about to drive a coach and horses through it. I shall try to stop him but I do not think I shall succeed.

Thursday, 21 April 1994

Defeated in committee on Tuesday as expected over Breconshire and again today over Radnorshire and Montgomeryshire. Jonathan Evans's career prospects are back to zero. I blame it all on David Hunt who promised a return to the shire counties in Powys before the 1992 Election. Jonathan took him at his word.

Reception at No. 10 last night. Lew Grade told me he knew Vere Harmsworth (*Daily Mail*) and would try to get him on side.

Everyone is speculating about the timing of a 'night of the long knives'.

Some speculation that Michael Portillo might give the country 'the smack of firm government' it needs.

Monday, 25 April 1994

Howard Davies, director of the CBI was sharp in his satirical comments at the Freight Association dinner at the Hilton. He described the Channel Tunnel as a 'feat of financial engineering' and the author of the rail privatization measure as a 'chartered accountant trainspotter on ecstasy'.

Thursday, 12 May 1994

Death of John Smith, leader of the Labour Party, announced just as we were about to begin our morning session in committee. We dealt with a couple of amendments and then adjourned.

Lunched with Lord Hanson, Eve Pollard (*Daily Express*), Lord (Brian) Griffiths and others. Much talk of John Smith's successor. Magnificently buxom Eve favoured Tony Blair. I thought Prescott would be the popular choice. They also spoke of the weakness of John Major's kitchen cabinet. I spoke of the dangers of a totally biased press. James Hanson was the perfect host.

Sunday, 15 May 1994

John Smith's untimely death had extensive ramifications at Westminster. There was an agreement between the parties to suspend campaigning in the European election until after his funeral and a campaign rally we had planned at Cardiff yesterday became an unusually quiet affair. A Central Office chap told me he had seen a press summary of my speech but had not bothered to bring copies to Cardiff!

I travelled back on the train to Reading with John Redwood and we were soon discussing the impending reshuffle. He thought Douglas Hurd would go and that Malcolm Rifkind would succeed him at the Foreign Office; Ian Lang would become party chairman and be replaced by David Maclean (Con., Penrith) as Scottish secretary. He, John, would stay in Wales. I suggested he might be needed at the Treasury or Trade and Industry.

Chief whip, Richard Ryder had clearly cast a fly over him about my possible successor. John had told him that I might stay as long as I wished as far as he was concerned. Rod Richards, whom I had helped into politics, is much favoured as an under secretary. It was left that I should consider my own wishes.

We got off the train at Reading where my eldest son Rhys was waiting for me. I introduced him to John who headed home to Wokingham while Rhys drove me to his computer heaven of a home at Chineham where he has a neat, little, portable Toshiba I greatly fancy. We were up at 7 a.m. today playing with the PC. He is now to order one for me – mouse, printer and the rest.

Midnight, Tuesday, 24 May 1994

We ended the committee stage of the Local Government Bill today. I quoted Shirley's poem:

> The glories of our blood and state
> Are shadows not substantial things.

as part of my tribute to John Smith. Rhodri Morgan looked perplexed or perhaps he was just being appreciative. The bill is better than I thought and may eventually do some good. But I am getting old and must retire at the next reshuffle, likely to be in July.

Our lively whip on the committee, Michael Brown (Con., Brigg and Cleethorpes) was caught up in a gay scandal and resigned a week ago. A great shame.

Enid is to see a specialist tomorrow about her throat condition. She is very stressed.

Monday, 6 June 1994

It has been a trying time politically and personally with the European campaign refusing to take off except on domestic issues and Enid's ill health. The specialist told her that her vocal chords were inflamed and advised rest for six weeks.

We got onto the theme of betrayal the other evening – in private and public life – and it is true that betrayal has become a feature of our amoral society. Loyalty and trust are things of the past.

The uppermost thought in my mind is of the coming reshuffle and my retirement from the government. All the daily tasks – the endless file-reading, signing of footling letters, meetings and journeying on the triangle between Conwy, Cardiff and London – have become burdensome. The lack of effective leadership and the perpetual dissension among colleagues are fast holing the government below the waterline. I foresaw it all last December and hated the prospect. That was why I offered my resignation.

Summer Clouds

The Labour Party's broadcast on the eve of the European election in June 1994 accused the government of lying and betrayal time and again. It was as if they had picked up the theme of Margaret Thatcher's betrayal and extended it to the country as a whole. Those who had betrayed Margaret had subsequently betrayed each other – disloyalty to the prime minister was rampant – and Margaret might well have said:

> All things betray thee
> Who betrayest me.

There was a Welsh dimension to all this. The scandalous goings-on at the Welsh Development Agency and the Development Board for Rural Wales, which I attributed to sleepwalking civil servants who had failed to inform ministers, fully justified a corrective, puritanical reaction on John Redwood's part. Their misuse of funds was a clear sign that they had too much and that cutbacks were called for. This accorded well with the Treasury's tighter monetary-control policies. But John Redwood's positive welcome to Treasury pressures to reduce public expenditure played into the hands of those who argued for a Welsh Assembly as a better defender of Welsh interests than an English secretary of state. I foresaw a situation developing where we would lose every Conservative seat in Wales and create a popular demand for a greater degree of independence – 'an Assembly of sorts to counter act the Rightist autocracy'.

On Thursday, 16 June, our very last day on the Local Government Bill, the *Western Mail* carried a profile of me and strongly implied that I was about to retire. Someone had clearly been leaking and wanted me out of the way. I suspected Rod Richards, my potential successor, rightly or wrongly. There were some embarrassing plaudits for me from the opposition during third reading, which I had to

302

parry, not very convincingly, by saying I had made no statement. A few days later, Dafydd Wigley and Mike Steele (HTV's lobby correspondent) urged me to stay on in the government. But I could see no grounds for optimism anywhere. Even old party warriors like Lord Harmer Nicholls thought that the divisions within the party were now so deep that they could not be bridged and only extreme folly on the part of the Labour Party could keep them out of office after the next election.

John Major showed his amazing resilience before the end of the month when he returned from a EU meeting in Corfu where he blocked Dehaene's appointment as Delors's successor at the head of the European Commission. Order papers were jubilantly waved again by our side at Prime Minister's Questions on Tuesday, 28 June, when Margaret Beckett, deputy leader of the Labour Party, was foolish enough to tackle him about family values. She had herself recently been lambasted in the *Daily Mail* for her own alleged marital misconduct. Everyone knew the story but John Major never mentioned it. These were minor triumphs in a sea of defeats.

Prince Charles's confession of infidelity in a television interview with Jonathan Dimbleby on 29 June had quite an effect on me, as it did on many other viewers. People argued about whether it would do him any good. I did not think so. He did not look a fit man in spite of all his exercise. He breathed in quickly twice as he answered questions. His eyes too were those of a defeated man, tired and in need of a long rest. He was spiritually and mentally exhausted. An introvert at heart, he showed the strains of being a public figure. There was no resilience there. He may have excited public sympathy but that would not be enough to sustain him. Public figures have to have an extraordinary ability to keep their personal egos unpunctured. John Major had it and a few others. No one can bare his soul without being seared and scorched by the media without mercy.

Charles had chosen the road to Canossa and worn sackcloth and ashes before his future subjects. It was a hell of a gamble. It would not pay off. Princess Diana was waiting in the wings with all the fury of a woman scorned. She had more of hell in her to wreak havoc on his life. He gave the impression of a man making a comeback. Why? Did he have a rival other than a wife he could not handle? Wrecking his plane landing on Islay did not improve his image.

Will Charles the Confessor ever survive to be king? I considered the question in my diary:

The Rt. Hon. Lord Roberts of Conwy

He has made a tremendous effort to regain his standing as heir to the throne with his twenty-fifth anniversary celebration of the Investiture. But I cannot help feeling that he is doomed. The public failure of his marriage, his abject confession of infidelity and the impression he gives of a man struggling against a sea of troubles, mark him out as a victim before whom only greater disillusionment lies.

'Uneasy lies the head that might have worn the Crown.'

I do not recollect ever having read the diary of events and feelings preceding a ministerial resignation – a unique happening when it is pre-meditated. These are my diary entries.

Wednesday, 6 July 1994

On Monday evening, Ed Blair, president of Hamilton Oil, and his wife Nancy gave a farewell party at the Four Seasons. Sir Peter Morrison, Colin Moynihan (now Lord) and I gave short speeches. I delivered a paean on Ed's pioneering work in the Argyll Field in the North Sea in 1975 and his successful battle to win oil and gas from the Irish Sea more than a decade later. He is one of the 'greats' in terms of industrial achievement.

I drew up a list on the train of the pros and cons of staying in office. They are overwhelmingly against but it is extremely difficult to bring oneself to the point of resignation. Age does wither one's ambitions but there is no future to excite me in politics. If I had only my own interests to consider, I would tender my resignation now, but my loyalty to friends and my anxiety to do right by them, even at the risk of being a pawn in their hands, is curiously supreme. So after my letter to Richard Ryder of December last year, I am inclined to leave myself to the angels for the time being.

Sunday, 10 July 1994

This was to have been a quiet birthday but the misfortune of my PPS, David Tredinnick, who fell into a trap laid for him by the *Sunday Times*, has put paid to my peace. David rang yesterday to forewarn me that the story was about to break but I was not at home and then the newspapers rang and I pieced the story together. He and Graham Riddick (Con., Colne Valley) had been set up by the Insight team to put down a question by a bogus 'businessman' for a fee of a thousand pounds. Alas, poor David! He fell for it. I cannot understand it; he did not need the money. The chief whip phoned me this morning to tell me David was to be suspended from his PPS post and his case referred to the Committee of Privileges.

My eldest son, Rhys, is here inducting me into the deeper mysteries of my Toshiba lap top and advising me on my response to the media.

Monday, 11 July 1994

Saw Derek Conway (Con., Shrewsbury) on the train and he, like David Lightbown last week, pressed me on whether I intended to fight the next election. I prevaricated with Derek because he had been my PPS at one stage but had unexpectedly resigned over Europe. I also suspected him of conspiring in Margaret's downfall.

'That's two bad choices you made – me and Tredinnick,' he said laughing.

'You were the whips' choices; I only accepted you,' I replied truthfully.

Derek said the reshuffle details had been worked out a month ago and might be announced this week, possibly Thursday.

I spoke to Enid a few minutes ago and she is relaxed about my imminent doom – as she sees it. Of course, I could save myself but I do not have the will to do so.

Tuesday, 12 July 1994

I stared into the abyss for a while this evening after I had read all my papers and then wandered down to the terrace where I met David Lightbown, his mountainous figure sandwiched between a cooling fan and a refrigerator to repel the warm air. We chatted about the coming reshuffle.

'You don't have to worry. You are all right . . . at least you were when I was last involved.'

It was remarkable how that remark – well-founded or not – cheered me up! The change from being an office-holder for fifteen years to being a backbencher is horrendous.

Thursday, 14 July 1994

Chief whip Richard Ryder asked to see me and we met in his office shortly before 7 p.m. He began by seeking my views on the Welsh Conservative members. Although he did not tell me in so many words, the prime minister is clearly prepared to accept my resignation – 'quite understands' etc. We then spoke of my longevity in the same office, unequalled in this century. I said it was time for me for me to go.

He was taken aback when I handed him a letter, dated today, which summed up my present feelings in favour of retirement but offering to assist if needs be. (I had updated the letter last week and kept it by me.) One thing was certain. I would not be standing at the next election.

Tuesday, 18 July 1994

This is the eve of the long-awaited reshuffle and I am walking about with my resignation letter in my pocket. I have concluded that I am bound to go this time. I have after all asked to be retired. The PM has not asked to see me – as yet.

Spent Sunday night at Doldowlod in Powys in the wonderful company of Diana and David Gibson-Watt, Sheila and John Lisburne (Irish peer) and Katie Macmillan, widow of the late Maurice. Katie told the curious tale of a French count who knew Goering personally as a flyer in the First World War and had used his influence with him to rescue a local man from the Gestapo during the German occupation of France. After the War he was accused of collaborating with the Germans and imprisoned for two years.

Diana told me David had backed Reggie Maudling against Ted Heath for the leadership of the party and had told Ted so. This must have killed any prospects David ever had of becoming secretary of state for Wales after the 1970 election. Bad enough to back a loser; worse to tell the winner that you did so.

I feel sweetly relieved already of the awful, dreary burdens of office but I suspect I shall miss them in the months to come. I took a last look at Room A in the Cabinet Office where I have attended so many meetings. On the walls around Pitt's Cabinet table are portraits of Henry Pelham and his secretary, John Roberts, and Robert Walpole and secretary Henry Legge. My dog, Jacko, died on Monday after a short illness – RIP.

Wednesday, 20 July 1994

The reshuffle was to have been on Monday but that day came and went and Tuesday too. Today was very hot and this morning I completed a round of interviews on our proposals to build a new, southerly by-pass of Newport.

A message came from No. 10 that the PM wished to see me in the course of the day. I was ready with my letter of resignation, polished and typed on Welsh Office notepaper, and a press notice.

Then another message came at about 2.30 p.m. from one of the private secretaries at No. 10 saying that the PM knew my position and suggesting we might leave it until we had a drink at the reception on Thursday. I smelt confusion and said no. I wanted to see the PM (to deliver my letter to him) so it was fixed for 3.30 p.m.

I was shown into the lovely upstairs drawing room with Turner and Lavery paintings and served a cup of tea. Then I was led down to the Cabinet room. The prime minister sat alone without officials and he seated me close to himself; he struck me as very vulnerable, spiritually and physically.

There was no opening statement from either of us, just a re-establishment of our intimacy, measured thanks for my services and my presentation of the letter. I also showed him the press notice. He patted my hand and thanked me. We spoke freely about the two Welsh members lined up for jobs (Roger Evans and Rod Richards).

He expressed his appreciation of the odd private letter I had sent him, encouraged me to contact him again if there was anything on my mind and, as we parted, he said:

'You have what you and I know as "bottom" . . . so many of our colleagues do not have it. They are a different breed. If I had a hundred like you, I would have a much easier life.'

As I walked back up Whitehall, I thought about his last remark. He too felt betrayed but he was still fighting. I had always abided by the principles of loyalty and service in the belief that some day someone would appreciate my stance but such principles had long been out of fashion. Naked, egotistic ambition was the order of the day.

When I got back to the office, there was a freshly opened bottle of champagne overflowing in my out-tray. It was an appropriate end to more than fifteen years of service in government.

The immediate aftermath of my resignation was more traumatic than I had anticipated. My wife too regarded herself as free now that I was no longer a minister and went off to stay with a friend. I spent some time at the House searching for a new office and found a niche in No. 1 Parliament Street. The entire block was a hive of bustling young Labour Party researchers, all serving the few faces I knew – Robin Cook and Peter Mandelson among them. Theirs was a very different world with its eyes firmly fixed on the future and power. My thoughts revolved around the theme of betrayal. There had been so much of it in my lifetime. There were the Windsors and the Fascist appeasers in the 1930s; the Communist spies, Blunt, Philby, Burgess and Maclean in the Cold War. Now, there was a more subtle form of treachery, a betrayal of people's trust and cherished personal and family values. The powers of darkness were working overtime.

A shoal of appreciative letters from Wales for what I had achieved in government gave me a much needed boost. My return at the weekend to the enduring tranquillity and beauty of the Conwy Valley completed my personal rehabilitation. I had left the government honourably and had no regrets. Subsequent events proved that I had timed my exit well.

The Sleazy Life

Returning to a backbencher's life in the Commons after nearly sixteen years, I was struck by the proliferation of the commercial lobbyists. Whereas in the 1970s lobbyists operated as modest individuals on behalf of the road haulage industry, Kentucky Fried Chicken or whatever, they now had burgeoning companies like Ian Greer Associates whose tentacles extended everywhere and who had a string of MPs on their books. Unbecoming conduct – soon to be described as 'sleaze' – was being openly tolerated and there was no one to say that it was wrong – except the press when it became gross enough to shock the public.

We had only just returned to the House in October 1994 to end the Parliamentary session when the *Guardian* broke the news of a fresh ministerial scandal. Neil Hamilton (Con., Tatton) and a minister at the Department of Trade and Industry, was alleged to have spent a whale of a weekend with his wife, Christine, at the Ritz in Paris, which was owned by Mohamed Al Fayed of Harrods. The prime minister had to face questions about it the same day (Thursday, 20 October) and joined us in the tea room afterwards.

Neil, I knew, had been educated at Ammanford Grammar School and the University of Wales, Aberystwyth, before going on to Cambridge, but he had never in my presence prided himself on his early Welsh upbringing. He appeared to have developed into a brash right-winger in partnership with his wife, Christine, who had once worked for Sir Gerald Nabarro MP. We all knew about Al Fayed and his fight for British citizenship, ever since his battle with Tiny Rowland of Lonrho over Harrods. Both had kept every MP well posted on their slanging match by sending us a blow-by-blow account on the richest notepaper we had ever seen. Involvement in this scrimmage between a pair of Cyclops proved irresistible to Neil Hamilton, even though, as a Minister at DTI, he was in grave danger of being compromised. After the *Guardian*'s detailed revelations about his sybaritic weekend at Al Fayed's expense, he did not immediately resign but issued a writ against the newspaper.

The prime minister acted quickly. On Tuesday, 25 October, he announced the setting up of a new inquiry under Lord Nolan to look at the whole issue of members' interests (but not trade union sponsorship of Labour members). Tony Blair's expenditure of £88,000 on his campaign for the leadership of the Labour Party was hardly noticed and no one asked where the money had come from. Hamilton resigned to pursue his writ and Al Fayed's allegations were referred to the Director of Public Prosecutions.

I attended Lord (Peter) Thorneycroft's memorial service the following day and heard Lord (Peter) Carrington contrast Thorneycroft's sterling qualities with 'the venal and selfish' reputation of the current batch of MPs. Never were truer words uttered.

Next day, tall, handsome and able Jonathan Aitken, ex-chief secretary to the Treasury and minister for defence procurement, was back in the dock over another stay at the Ritz in Paris and a bill he claimed his wife had paid. Others said it had been paid by a Saudi Arabian businessman. The issue was being relentlessly pursued by Peter Preston, editor of the *Guardian*, who soon proved that he would stop at nothing to get at the truth.

On Monday, 31 October, I dined in the Commons cafeteria with John Ward (now Sir), the prime minister's PPS. He told me John Major's personal standing had risen by 10 points in the polls over recent weeks and might rise still further if he survived the current outbreak of sleaze. Ward was doubtful whether Aitken would survive. On the way home across College Green, I met Winston Churchill and said:

'Jonathan's not out of the wood yet.'

'Just dined with him . . . some questions unanswered.'

The new session opened with another bombshell for the Tories and a bonanza for the opposition – the leaking of John Maples's paper on the state of the government party of which he was now vice-chairman after losing his seat at Lewisham West in 1992. His reference to Tories attacking Blair as 'yobbos' was particularly galling. I regarded myself as one of them. Gordon Brown's speech on the economy (23 November) consisted largely of material culled from Maples's castigation of the party.

Euro-scepticism in the party was fast developing into septicaemia. The government only managed to defeat a Labour amendment to the European Finance Bill, which increased our contribution to Brussels, by declaring it to be tantamount to a vote of confidence.

Even so, eight members abstained and had the whip withdrawn. This meant in effect that we now had a minority government. One of the more virulent rebels, Tony Marlow, said: 'They (the government) need us more than we need them!'

There was talk of challenging Major's leadership and Kenneth Clarke's name was bandied about but the deadline for nominations (30 November) passed. John Major joined our table for dinner in the members' dining room on Wednesday, 7 December. We spoke of Tony Blair's reluctance to commit himself to a referendum on Europe. I said that he would not commit himself to a referendum on devolution for Scotland and Wales either – a point Major used next day. He appeared to be in good form but Lady Olga Maitland (Con., Sutton and Cheam) told me afterwards she thought he was terribly tense.

The Dudley West by-election showed massive abstention among Conservative voters and a hefty swing to Labour, producing a 20,694 majority. The press called on the government to listen to the people but nobody was clear as to what the people were saying. Labour too was confused on Europe and torn between Old and New Labour over Clause 4, but Tony Blair and his allies represented their best hope and he was proving himself a fair match for the PM in their twice-weekly jousts at the despatch box.

The new year 1995 seemed to start well for the government but there were some reckless, hell-bent characters about. Teresa Gorman (Con., Billericay), one of the eight unwhipped, was rumoured to have a roomful of researchers paid for by Sir James Goldsmith of the Referendum Party. At the Welsh Office, Rod Richards was beginning to emerge in his most lurid, Rottweiler colours. He described Welsh Labour councillors as 'short, fat, slimy and fundamentally corrupt'. Some threatened to sue him; others, not surprisingly, refused to meet him.

Despair ravaged the Tory ranks like the plague. I dined with Michael Jopling (now Lord) and Ted Heath on Tuesday, 7 March. Michael described the party as being in 'free-fall'. No one knew how to arrest it. A week later I walked back from the House with Francis Pym (now Lord) and I told him that, according to the latest polls, our expected vote had been halved to 15 per cent in Wales.

'We used to get nearly 30 per cent in Wales. Now, we'll be lucky to get that in England.'

Francis agreed and took the view that John Major was too young to be prime minister. He did not carry authority. Only Douglas Hurd and Michael Heseltine had the necessary experience for the highest office. The rest of the Cabinet were run by the media, he said. There was a lot of truth in that. We soon turned to our old battleground of devolution:

'I did not expect to be fighting that battle again,' I said.

'I did,' said Francis. 'I knew we could win once but not again after Margaret turned her back on Scotland.'

I had persuaded the Welsh Select Committee and its chairman, Gareth Wardell (Lab., Gower), that we should look into the progress made with the regional links I had developed in Europe. I had met Jordi Pujol, the president of Catalonia, in London on Friday, 3 March. He was a great advocate of Europe of the Regions and I wanted members of the committee to savour his thinking. The Welsh Development Agency celebrated the fifth anniversary of the Wales–Baden-Württemberg agreement in April and this was another reason for the committee to activate its interest. Besides, devolution for Wales was firmly back on the Labour Party agenda and my colleagues could learn a great deal from the experience of the European regions.

In mid-May, the committee visited Stuttgart and met Ober-bürgermeister Rommel whom I knew well, and members of the Land government. The committee's secretary recorded the key points about the developing relationship with Wales (to be reproduced later in the official report, *Wales in Europe*) but Rommel told me something that I took a personal note of. He said democracy would never have survived in Germany after the war had it not been for the benevolent dictatorship of the Allied powers. Russia, he suggested, now needed a similar dictatorship to allow democracy to flourish. It was a novel proposition but Manfred Rommel was nothing if not an original thinker. (He was later honoured with a CBE.)

We went on to Milan and Barcelona where Pujol received us in style and answered the committee members' questions. We visited the chamber of the Generalitat, which was suspiciously empty. I asked the doorman how often it met and he told me: 'Not often these days. The president is very busy.'

We were approaching the end of our visit when a message came from the Welsh Office asking me to go to Taiwan with the chairman of the Welsh Development Agency, David Rowe-Beddoe (now Sir), to tackle a major company, Chungwa/Tatung, who were consider-ing a major investment in Wales. The prospect of 3,000 jobs in cathode ray tube manufacture was very enticing and I readily agreed to go at the secretary of state's personal request. (I knew that he could not go himself for diplomatic reasons.)

It was an arduous seventeen-hour journey to Taipei via Singapore, but David Rowe-Beddoe was good company and we finalized our case for investment in Wales during the flight. Our strongest point was that the Tatung factory would be located in Cardiff adjacent to the company that made the fine glass they required for their tubes. After a night's rest at the Ritz, we set out to meet the chairman of Tatung, seventy-five-year-old Dr T. S. Lin, and his two sons. I had been told that he was Taiwan's authority on the political philosopher, Adam Smith.

The Tatung complex comprised factory units and offices with a college building at its centre. It was at the college that we met the very civil and scholarly Dr Lin. I began by saying that I understood that the company wished to expand and establish in Europe.

'Why Europe?' asked Dr Lin. 'We could establish anywhere in the world.'

I spoke of the strength of the European market and the success of other companies from the Far East such as Sony which had operated from Wales since the early 1970s. Then I went on to talk about the Cardiff site we had in mind for Chungwa and the proximity of their main glass supplier.

'Our supplier tells us that they will provide for us at the same price wherever we decide to establish ourselves,' said Dr Lin.

This undermined our main argument but Wales had other advantages and attractions, which we advanced as strongly as we could. Dr Lin said that many of their customers were based in Scotland and that it was important to the company to be close to them. This was tricky ground for me. As a representative of the UK government, I was obliged to sing the praises of Scotland as well as Wales – once the possibility of an investment there had been mentioned.

As our exchange came to an end, Dr Lin presented me with three substantial volumes, in soft yellow covers: *The Analects of Confucius*; *The Theory of Moral Sentiments* by Adam Smith and *A System of Moral Philosophy* by Francis Hutcheson. 'All three agreed on the fundamentals,' said Dr Lin. Hutcheson, like Adam Smith, had been a professor at Glasgow University in the eighteenth century and the canny Scots had honoured Dr Lin too for his scholarship. The books were a fair indication of where the old man's heart really lay and of the company's eventual destination in the UK – Mossend, Lanarkshire.

Dr Lin left us to deliver a lecture and I asked one of his sons if I could see his father perform. He took me to a huge hall upstairs where 1,000 students were listening to the Mandarin speech of Dr Lin while two young women translated into other dialects at either end of the long platform where he stood. It was a remarkable sight. I was relieved to see that the students were half asleep, as students always are when they listen to lectures. But the educational appetite and industry of the Taiwanese is boundless and one of the wonders of the modern world.

As we drove to the airport, I was intrigued to see a child being trained by a 'lollipop lady' to guide his schoolmates safely across a busy road. It was an early lesson in social responsibility.

A dozen of us lunched with the PM at No. 10 on Monday, 12 June. Lunch was served in the alcove dominated by a bust of Isaac Newton. After the main course – a lamb hotpot – the PM asked me to set the ball rolling. I talked about the insecurity of the middle classes. Others took up the theme and then raised concerns of their own. Sir Peter Fry (Con., Wellingborough) and Sir Dudley Smith (Con., Warwick and Leamington) were critical of the Nolan Report on members' outside interests and urged the PM not to introduce the proposed measures until after the next election. It was quite clear that, faced with the choice of continuing to pursue their outside interests or remaining MPs, they would choose the former. I had little sympathy with them.

The PM was most interesting on his own leadership and said that he could have given firm leadership of the dogmatic sort but he remembered what had happened to Michael Foot who had done just that. He believed it was possible to develop a consensus and went on to say: 'Unless we achieve some sort of consensus, the Conservative Party will throw away the next election which will be a great pity since our economic prospects are better than they have been for many, many years.' There was a curious air of detachment about that statement, which prompted Sir Teddy Taylor (Con., Southend East) to urge the need for a crusade in the party and the country. I chipped in that it was high time we hammered out a consensus to be the substance of such a crusade. Afterwards, John Biffen (Con., Shropshire North) told me that an upturn in the economy and rising living standards might just see us through the next election. It was a pleasant occasion but the PM left me with the impression that, although he is a master of detail, he is no great strategist.

Within days, his leadership was under attack from the 'Fresh Start' group of Tories, led by Sir Peter Tapsell (Con., Lindsey East).

He had a rough meeting with them, which his critics made much of in the media and the press. There was talk of a leadership challenge. On Tuesday, 20 June, the PM dined with the 1970 intake of Conservative MPs and I had a chance to urge the PM – as I had already done by letter – to appear before the 1922 Committee flanked by his entire Cabinet, to settle the issue of the party's future. Unknown to me at the time, Winston Churchill, who sat between the PM and myself at dinner, was also giving him similar advice. The PM told us to await an announcement he would make shortly.

It came at a press conference in the garden at No. 10 two days later when the PM said he would resign his leadership of the party and face any challenger who would throw his hat in the ring. It was the 'put up or shut up' challenge and within days John Redwood, the secretary of state for Wales, had taken up the first option. I saw Tam Dalyell (Lab., Linlithgow) in members' lobby and he muttered to me: 'Serve them damn well right; they should have put you in that job!' John Redwood had a good press conference but whatever he said was eclipsed by the picture of him looking more Vulcanesque than ever, backed by a dominant Tony Marlow in a Wellington College blazer and a grim Teresa Gorman determined to dwarf Bill (Biggles) Walker behind her. It was a motley crew. The press had no difficulty in making mincemeat of them and the rest of the Tory Party who had made this Mad Hatter's tea party possible. Michael Portillo was reported to have said that Major was 'doomed' but he would not stand against him. Michael Heseltine also denied on radio that he would stand but the *Evening Standard* ran a front page story that he would (28 June).

The *Sunday Times*, the *Daily Telegraph* and *The Times* wanted the PM ousted, but when the vote came he did better than expected and gained 218 votes compared with Redwood's 89. Ian Lang and Archie Hamilton had campaigned well on his behalf. The champagne flowed in the smoking room and I joined in the celebration of our pyrrhic victory.

There was a minor reshuffle and Tristan Garel-Jones (Con., Watford) fancied he might be asked to go to Wales. I rehearsed him in the Welsh national anthem in the tea room – probably the first time it has ever been sung there by a couple of Tories. Jovial William Hague was appointed secretary of state for Wales. At thirty-four, he was younger than my youngest son. I pledged my support for him on the backbenches. It was not long before electoral defeat stared us in the face once more. 'We are heading for disaster on a massive scale,' I wrote in my diary on 5 July 1995.

Time for Change

In the long run up to the May 1997 election, no popular phrase crystallized the electorate's feelings better than this expression of conviction that the Conservatives had been in office too long and that it was time for a change of government. John Major was decent enough and had lost some of his early greyness. He had brought the country safely through the Gulf War and the Kosovo crisis and had had the rare courage to tackle the Northern Ireland problem with a real will to secure peace. The country was gaining in prosperity. But the prime minister was not master of his own house and it was this failure to control and lead his party firmly and with a clear sense of direction that featured in the media time and again. Tony Blair had his problems establishing New Labour's predominance over Old Labour but so strong was the common will in the Labour movement to wrest power from the Tories, that these difficulties were mostly suppressed and seldom made headlines. He had the halo of charisma about him.

Snippets from my diary not only give a flavour of the time but also indicate the factors and divisions contributing to the Conservative Party's decline and the government's eventual fall.

Wednesday, 29 November 1995

The Queen's Speech and now the Budget. The first was described as a 'mouse of a speech' and the second as a milestone in the government's demise. Somehow we have been persuaded of the truth of these dicta. Why? We hang more on the words of the opposition than we do on our own. We are, curiously, more convinced by them than we are by ourselves. We are mesmerized by them – that's the truth.

316

Tuesday, 12 December 1995

My old friend and whip, Sir David Lightbown (Con., Staffordshire South East) died today after a heart attack at the Oxford–Cambridge rugby match at Twickenham. I grieved for him as did Sir James Hill (Southampton Test) for the three of us often ate together. Otherwise, the party, like the media, only remarked that our majority was now down to 5. David was a strong man, ex-army, and the House was his barrack square. He was reputed to crush critics of government policy but he always claimed that he 'kissed them better'.

Tuesday, 19 December 1995

Our first defeat of this Parliament – on a motion to take note of a European Community document to do with fisheries. The defeat brought about by some defections on our side – Bill Cash (Con., Stafford), John Wilkinson (Con., Ruislip) and others – showed the government's vulnerability on European issues. It sent the Labour Party home for the recess with their tails up.

Saturday, 30 December 1995

News of Emma Nicholson's (Devon and West Torridge) defection to the Liberal Democrats. I believe she wanted to abstain on the fisheries vote and the whips had been rough with her. She is a rather odd fish herself: nice, rich and panting for fame.

The PM was on radio this morning, cheerful as ever in adversity. He reeled off the government's achievements to date and they are impressive. He harped on the risk the electorate will take if they opt for Labour but, alas, I believe they will and that the Tory party faces annihilation – Canadian style! The country has a deep desire for change. John Major is in the same boat as Harold Wilson. He is so close to events that he cannot see the future, let alone dictate its shape. He has to carry his followers with him but they are like a handful of eels. Pleas for party unity beg the question of unity around what; the answer should be principles and vision but there is little talk of either these days. Still, the PM claims to be steering a course from which he will not be deflected and that is the promotion of economic progress. He believes that the 'feel-good factor' will return 'as night follows day'. I think he is wrong.

Tuesday, 16 January 1996

Here we are at the start of a new year. The media pounced on Margaret Thatcher's Keith Joseph Memorial Lecture as being anti-Major and pro-right-wing Conservatism. Peter Lilley replied that the bulk of it was anti-Blair and anti-socialist. Alistair Burt (Con., Bury North) attacked Thatcher in a letter to *The Times* and Blair asked the PM if he had been reprimanded for so doing. 'What happens within my government is for me not you,' snapped Major.

Tuesday, 23 January 1996

John Major had an exceptionally good Question Time against Blair over Harriet Harman's decision to send her child to a grant-maintained school which had occasioned the resignation of the shadow education spokesman, Gerry Steinberg (Lab., City of Durham). Like Lloyd George, Major hit where it hurts.

Tuesday, 30 January 1996

Ted Heath on form in the smoking room. He pooh-poohed the Bank of England. 'You can't have a proper governor called Eddie George,' he said. He thought the handling of the Barings Bank crisis had been abysmally naive. The Bank of England should never have allowed the situation to develop unchecked as it did.

Thursday, 1 February 1996

I have just heard a fascinating analysis by David Trimble, leader of the Ulster Unionists, of the current situation in Northern Ireland. On relations with the UK government, he said that his party voted for or against the government according to the issue confronting them. They had not yet been faced with a confidence vote and he did not foresee such a vote in the near future. But he is clearly in close touch with Labour. Of Major, he said that they were all now walking up a garden path and that he believed Major had not yet decided whom to dump when they came to the end of it.

There is clearly not much trust about.

Thursday, 15 February 1996

The Scott Report on the supply of arms to Iraq has come like a fall

318

of snow – all six inches of it. Ian Lang, now president of the Board of Trade, made a good job of defending the indefensible, but Robin Cook's demolition job on the government's case was a superb demonstration of his forensic skills. He was helped by the fact that Scott did not list his conclusions, which allowed Cook to pick and choose the most damning quotations.

Monday, 4 March 1996

Ron Davies, the shadow Welsh secretary, has queried whether Charles is fit to be king. Others have declared their doubts and republicanism has reared its head. Charles has brought it upon himself, I fear. I was asked over the weekend by one of the whips to keep the issue alive in the media but I refused because I sensed that it could backfire, as indeed it did when George Walden (Con., Buckingham) criticized Blair for restraining debate and sided with Ron Davies. There are Conservative Roundheads too.

The government's majority is now down to 2 after Peter Thurnham's (Con., Bolton East) rejection of the whip for the petty reason that he had not been interviewed for Michael Jopling's Westmorland seat which Michael is to vacate.

Monday, 25 March 1996

The ministers for health and agriculture revealed the possible link between BSE (bovine spongiform encephalopathy) in cattle and Creutzfeldt–Jakob disease in humans on Wednesday last to a jittery public. Over the weekend, European countries and McDonald's have banned British beef and the BBC has been asking incessantly whether the national herd should not be slaughtered in its entirety and burnt.

Today's announcements have done nothing to restore confidence and the government seems to have surrendered power to the scientists. Scientists, like civil servants, are there to advise; decisions are for ministers. They should have announced plans to eradicate BSE and they will probably do so but I have heard nothing to that effect as yet.

Tuesday, 26 March 1996

Stephen Dorrell (secretary of state for health) lost his rag over BSE on a radio talk-in this morning and said it was not the cows who were mad but the people!

Wednesday, 17 April 1996

We lost David Lightbown's Staffordshire South seat with a swing of 22 per cent to Labour. Our majority of 7,192 was transformed into a Labour majority of nearly 14,000. The party's depression has plunged us into defeatism. We are totally lacking in vision and by-passed by the electorate as worn out and irrelevant. The will to win is totally lacking. The outlook for the local government elections next month is dismal.

The PM relishes his isolation; he is the boy on the burning deck, or the soapbox in his case. His extraordinariness blossoms in these circumstances and he knows it and loves it. He is happy to go down fighting but the party is not interested in noble, 'loner' heroes. It needs a bandwagon of success and a charismatic, extrovert Henry V on top of it shouting 'Once more unto the breach, dear friends, once more.' That might rouse our rabble. Tony Blair has some of that quality and drive.

Saturday, 20 April 1996

Today, Sir James Goldsmith, founder of the Referendum Party, held a meeting at Westminster Hall and called the government 'appeasers' on Europe. Goldsmith is prepared to invest £20 million in election candidates who pledge themselves to a referendum. Apparently, he has more pledges from Labour than Conservative candidates. They are less ingenuous than we are. This could well lead to a loss of Conservative seats at the next election.

Monday, 29 April 1996

I was successful in the ballot for PM's Questions for last Tuesday, St George's Day, and I had planned to ask the PM if he would outline his vision of the future for the British people and contrast it with the 'baseless fabric' offered by the Labour Party. But John Ward, the prime minister's PPS, pressed me to abandon my preferred supplementary in favour of a question on child benefit, then – embarrassingly for Blair – under attack from Labour. Perhaps I should have stuck to my guns but there was no point if the PM did not have a substantive reply to give me and the public.

Last week, I voted for Iain Duncan Smith (Con., Chingford) to have leave to bring in a bill to curb the power of the European Court of Justice. We lost the division by 6 votes. I found myself closeted in the lobby with the anti-Europeans who are a mixed bunch not entirely to my liking.

Tuesday, 7 May 1996

By an extraordinary stroke of luck, I was again successful in the ballot for Prime Minister's Questions and again I wanted to press the PM to put forward a positive Conservative programme to contrast with the 'vacuous, soundbite policies of the party opposite'. I telephoned John Ward from Crewe station to give him advance warning but he urged me to pursue the child benefit issue which had riled the opposition since I raised it on 23 April. Three shadow cabinet ministers, including Gordon Brown, had been on radio defending their position. So, I devised (and delivered) a useful supplementary to the PM.

> Will my Right Honourable Friend confirm that the Government will not take away the £560 per year child benefit that so many families rely on to get their children through 'A' levels. And does he not agree that Labour's plan to scrap the benefit for 16 year olds would devastate families and reduce the numbers going into further education?

It was a winner for us. Tony Blair sought safer ground.

As spring turned to summer, some of us began to think that if the government could survive until the recess then it might – with luck and dexterity – carry on until the end of its five-year term in the spring of 1997. People were better off than they had been for many years. But Labour craftily lulled them in their sense of well-being and security. Their prosperity was not an issue. The eventual fall of the government was taken for granted by the media because the opposition was consistently ahead in the opinion polls and the government's recovery to the point where it might win appeared to be out of the question. The will to win was not showing in the party. To win, John Major's solitary strength had to be transmitted nationwide in an electrifying fashion but most of us doubted whether he could do it. We wondered when he would break under the strain of office rather than when he would inspire the electorate with vision and fervour. Tony Blair too was in danger of over-reaching himself. His aim was clearly to win Middle England as well as the Celtic fringes on the assumption that he could do both, that traditional Labour voters in the heartlands would be with him anyway and that the real challenge was to win the middle classes of Middle England. But he could easily fall between two stools and lose credibility all round.

On Monday, 22 July, David Heathcot-Amery, the postmaster general, resigned over the issue of a single European currency. That night Steve Norris (Con., Epping Forest) told me that speculation was rife about further resignations in advance of a reshuffle. When I referred to the lack of a will to win, Steve said: 'Will to win? There's a positive will to lose in the Tory Party!' And so we slipped gratefully into the summer recess.

It was a summer of dissent for Labour. Diane Abbott (Lab., Hackney North) a member of the National Executive, criticized the leadership for their shady efforts to ensure the re-election of Harriet Harman to the shadow cabinet. Clare Short, Labour's overseas development spokesperson, called Blair's aides 'forces of darkness' and expressed the wish that 'Tony should be more of his principled self'. There was more in a critical vein from Paul Flynn (Lab., Newport) and Austin Mitchell (Lab., Great Grimsby). Paul objected to the ditching of traditional policies and Austin complained that Blair pretended to listen to the party and then did his own thing in their name. It was a promising scene of dissension for the Tories to play havoc with but few did with any effect.

When the party chairman, Brian Mawhinney, came to Llandudno in my constituency in early September, he told us that the party's current strategy was based on Harold Macmillan's 1959 winning slogan: 'You've never had it so good' with the addition 'Don't let Labour ruin it'. There had already been a poster campaign on the theme of 'New Labour, New Danger' showing Tony Blair with bloodshot eyes. The eyes had been described as 'demonic' by Peter Mandelson, Blair's master of spin, and there had been public controversy about the appropriateness of the portrayal. Brian argued that the controversy alone was worth millions in advertising terms. Clearly, ours was to be a negative campaign. The trouble with negative campaigns is that they do not inspire the rank and file of any party.

The party conference at Bournemouth went well with the PM nailing his colours firmly to his soapbox. We were closing the gap between us and Labour in the polls and for the first time in months I thought we had a chance of winning a fifth term provided there were no more sleazy skeletons to tumble out of the cupboard and be publicly gnawed by the media. I visited my constituency branches as usual at this time of year, conscious that, whatever happened in the election, these visits would be my last. With their support, I had won seven elections and by the spring of 1997 would have re-presented Conwy in the Commons for twenty-seven years.

The new session opened in October with an ominously short Queen's Speech. In the debate that followed, Tony Blair took a high dive into his election campaign and sought what is euphemistically called the moral high ground. It was soon shown to be political opportunism by another name. Gordon Brown was no match for Ken Clarke at the despatch box on finance and the economy and the political weathervane seemed set fair for the government. The election of officers to the 1922 Committee had gone smoothly in that the right-wingers were kept at bay. In early November, the government had a majority of 1 against an opposition motion criticizing its handling of the BSE crisis, but one was enough. The date of the election was projected by our 'experts' as 10 April 1997.

It was early December before the Conservative division on Europe surfaced with a vengeance. It was not only visible but risible too. Those of us who supported the government usually sat behind the front bench while the anti-Europeans segregated themselves and sat below the gangway. Their conduct reached new depths of absurdity during a European debate on Thursday, 12 December when they jeered pro-European speakers on their own side, much to the joy of the opposition and to the delight of the press gallery.

A few days later, the opposition won a division on an amendment to the Harassment Bill by 7 votes. The division had taken place earlier than expected and some of our people were absent from the House. It was an innocuous victory in that the amendment simply provided counselling for stalkers' victims, but a troop of Labour MPs – the majority of them women – descended on the smoking room and were soon singing 'The Red Flag'. They had the bit between their teeth and the unity which was so blatantly lacking on our side.

We drifted unhappily into the new year (1997). At dinner in the Commons, John Redwood joined our table. He took my point that I would find it hard to say what we would do over the next five years if we won the election: privatization was a worked-out seam, although there was talk of privatizing the London Underground. John did not have anything much to offer either.

On 15 January, I attended a presentation at Central Office by a top party official, Danny Finkelstein. He attached great importance to the voting trend revealed in local government elections which showed that, if the current trend continued, the Conservatives would be level-pegging with Labour in December of this year – too late for the inexorable spring election that confronted us. He went on to say that private polls showed that Blair was regarded as 'smarmy' and 'two-faced'. We had to stand for 'stability and against a step into the unknown'. This was obviously the basis of the negative campaign being pursued by the party. I was not enamoured of it.

We had another vote before the end of January where the government had a majority of 1. It concentrated minds wonderfully on the imminence of the election. News leaked that the Cabinet had met at Chequers to finalize the manifesto (on 27 January) and everyone seemed to be taking stock.

I spoke one evening with Bill Cash and Peter Butler (Milton Keynes North East); both would say 'never' to a single European currency. There was no room for compromise. I also talked with Ted Heath. He said the party might well split after the election if we did not join the European Monetary Union. If we did not join now it would – as in the past – only become more difficult later.

The Labour Party too were very uncertain of their direction but they were united in their will to win power. They had been in the wilderness for too long to let any policy differences stand in their way of achieving it. They were gaining confidence and preening themselves in anticipation of victory. They knew that, even if Blair was just a bright spark with a glint in his eye and little substance beneath, the electorate was with them and wanted a change of government.

We had all become media fodder – politicians, electors and even the media people themselves. Change is the media's nourishment: they are addicted to change and cannot live without it.

Monday, 10 February 1997

The Conservative Party has no hope of winning the next election; not a cat in hell's chance. The electorate is totally unmoved by our economic success and almost relishes the prospect of Labour uncertainty and radical constitutional change. All this points to a lack of effective leadership. A leader must carry conviction and convey it through the media to the people. John Major, alas, does not have that ability and the public's response to all the facts and arguments, which are on his side, is negative. So much for negative campaigning!

It is as if the whole country had been present at that Cabinet Committee meeting I attended shortly after he became prime minister when he dutifully consulted everyone round the table and condensed their views in his own grey matter to nothing at all. Or as if all the people had been there when David Hunt and I went to see him before the 1992 election to talk about Wales and he yawned more wearily than I have ever seen a man yawn before – a Scarfe cartoon of a yawn.

We appear to be going down in the polls when we expected to go up, which prompted Nicholas Winterton (Con., Macclesfield) to suggest that the sooner we have the election the better. My son Geraint tells me that people are abandoning Plaid Cymru to ensure a Blairite victory. I know from Enid's friend, Betty, that there are similar, seismic shifts in Greater London. 'The state we're in' (*pace* Will Hutton) is that people are determined to have a change of government come what may, for better or for worse. I fear a Labour landslide.

St David's Day, Saturday, 1 March 1997

Labour has won the Wirral West by-election with a swing of 17 per cent in a 73 per cent poll and the general election is ten weeks away at most. We are still reeling from the defeat. If the by-election swing is transferred to the general election, Labour will have a majority of 296 – the pundits say.

The Conservative Party has revealed its divisiveness in glaring style yet again. Norman Tebbit attacked Michael Heseltine in a biography review. Ted Heath has sided with Labour on devolution and the adoption of the European Social Chapter. Sir Norman Fowler attacked both Tebbit and Heath for causing dissension and pleaded for unity. Tonight's *Evening Standard* headline is 'Redwood sticks the knife in'. The PM has said: 'If opinion does not change we are going to have a Labour government and people will have to realize what a Labour government means.' He spoke of a midsummer nightmare, a new Labour Budget and rising expenditure. All this is probable. Labour have taken in the people, including many of ours whom we have neglected or alienated. We have become divided among ourselves without firm leadership. The Tories need an element of threat and fear to keep them together – as we had in Margaret's day. The consequences of defeat are alarming. The future seldom turns out as expected but we may be sure that if the country falls into New Labour's hands, their first instinct will be to consolidate their hold on it.

William Hague was in fine form in Llandudno today regurgitating much that I said in the Welsh Day debate on Thursday but in his own light-hearted and inimitable style. I am off to Cyprus tomorrow.

Tuesday, 11 March 1997

Sir George Gardiner, recently deselected at Reigate, has joined the Referendum Party. At dinner last night Archie Hamilton (Con., Epsom and Ewell) was concerned about the effect of George's defection on his own and neighbouring constituencies. George is a good publicist and a shrewd operator. He has also been an active constituency MP. Archie thought he might get 5,000 votes.

Peter Mandelson (Lab., Hartlepool) presented the best news I have heard for some time in *The Times* today. To win an overall majority of 1, Labour must have 55 gains and a swing of 4.1 per cent from Conservative to Labour. For an overall majority of 50, they must have a swing of 6 per cent. The highest swing to Labour since the war has been 3.2 per cent in 1964. I am sure the piece was meant to encourage floating voters to opt for New Labour but I found it mildly reassuring. I had to remind myself that we were in a different ball game now.

William Hague was right to say at the Unionist Club this evening that what we need is a belief in ourselves and that victory can be ours.

Wednesday, 19 March 1997

A momentous week with the announcement on Monday that the election would be on 1 May. Yesterday, I was deeply moved by a special service at St Margaret's for members leaving the House of Commons. The Speaker, Betty Boothroyd, read the lesson (Mark X: 42–5) which was all about service. It represented my credo and, I dare say, that of many others leaving the House. Enid was with me and later we attended the Speaker's farewell reception. In her short address, Betty referred to the lesson she had read and the service we had given as members. The House of Commons is all about service, she said. Our reputation is currently under a cloud but the cloud will pass.

Thursday, 20 March 1997

People ask me how I feel at the end of a parliamentary career lasting twenty-seven years. The time has gone like the wind, fast and furious, especially when I was in government. Parliament has a momentum of its own which reflects the life of the country. It is a concentrated microcosm which expresses every happening and concern of any consequence in the country at large. Not surprisingly some members can hardly bear to leave the Chamber for fear of missing something. If one stays there, the world outside, with all its stresses, feelings and emotions, comes visiting and talking spiritedly through the mouths of members. The good parliamentarian can react spontaneously and give others time to think. The media with their priesthood of questioners are no substitute for the non-stop dialogue of Parliament. Of course, I shall miss it and wish a thousand times I was there to chip in and participate, which I was prone to do in spite of a natural tendency to self-restraint and a distrust of immediate, instinctive reactions. Some parliamentarians have no such qualms and inhibitions and will speak on any subject after a few minutes only in the Chamber. But, as one dear old Labour member from the north-east used to say to me, to exonerate himself for his many silences: 'Don't forget that the whale is only harpooned when he's spouting.'

The six-week election campaign was more closely controlled from the major party political headquarters at Smith Square and Millbank than any previous contest. Candidates' glossy election addresses of high quality were centrally produced and gone were the days when candidates and their agents struggled to produce their own and printed them locally. The regional dimension, apart from broadcasting, was also much diminished.

My prime task was to supervise and check the translation of the Conservative manifesto of eighty-nine pages and 23,000 words into Welsh. Janet Davies worked all night on Monday, 24 March at her flat in Westminster and produced as perfect a professional translation as I have ever seen. We discussed some of the finer semantic points and the job was done. It occasioned personal letters of thanks from the PM and the chairman of the party.

While at Westminster, I bumped into Sir Michael Spicer (Con., Worcestershire West). He reflected the weekend newspaper comment: 'Why didn't we get rid of that dreadful man, Neil Hamilton, right at the start?' It was a question meet to be asked, as they say. Other candidates at Tatton stood down to make way for the white knight, Martin Bell, to slay the dragon.

The *Sun*'s story of Piers Merchant's (Con., Beckenham) dalliance in the bushes with seventeen-year-old, Anna Cox, coupled with Tim

Smith's (Con., Beaconsfield) enforced stand-down for lack of clear-ance in the cash for questions affair, saw the Tories up to their necks in the sleaze bog again. After the dissolution on 8 April, my wife, with her gift for malapropisms, described us all as 'dissolute MPs'.

By 14 April, the campaign seemed to be running into the sand. The big issue of Europe had been kicked into touch with promises of a referendum and free votes. But, over the following days, more and more Conservative candidates declared themselves against a single currency as they came under pressure from the Referendum Party and Paul Sykes, the Yorkshire millionaire, and his largesse. The pollsters nervously forecast a Labour landslide – they had got it wrong in 1992 – and my wife spoke of a 'hung government'.

On 30 April, I was down in Cardiff ready for an all-night television programme on the results of next day's poll. It was a beautifully sunny day with another promised for the morrow. At midday I visited the Cardiff and County Club in Westgate Street where two or three friends were praying for rain – and a low poll.

As I walked back to Llandaff along Riverside, I thought that 'time for a change' was a powerful argument when discontent abounds. Even the pigeons and the gulls on the banks of the Taff were waiting for it and the cranes, poised to gouge out the sacred turf of the Arms Park, all were waiting.

I watched John Sergeant, the BBC's political correspondent on the six o'clock news describe the expectations behind the armies of party campaigners at their respective Westminster headquarters. A Labour victory was not in doubt. Tony Blair had successfully carried conviction as the provider of an alternative government and the Conservatives had failed to dent his image. Their negative cam-paigning had not been a success. I prepared myself for the worst. Would Labour's majority be as great as Maggie's 144 in 1983 or Attlee's 146 in 1945?

By the end of the declarations of the results of 1 May, Labour had a majority of 179, including the Speaker (who in the event turned out to be my pair of many years, Michael Martin of Glasgow, Springburn). The Tory Party's representation was halved, to 165 MPs compared with 336 five years earlier. None was elected in Wales or Scotland. Britain had a new political landscape.

I have always believed in the biblical adage that, without vision, the people perish but, in a democracy, the people have a way of finding those with the best vision to lead them. Political parties are not always so fortunate and in their case, without a vision that appeals to the people, they fail and, without radical reform, become extinct.

Issues Revisited

There had been much talk off and on of my going to the House of Lords and, on Lord Cledwyn's advice, I had written to the chief whip, now Alastair Goodlad, asking that I be considered. And, when John Major wrote me a letter of thanks on 14 April 1997, I replied that I was still hopeful that he might find me 'a seat in the Other Place where the devolution issue could feature prominently in the coming months'. The Tory rout on 1 May and the defeat of so many colleagues had dimmed my prospects and, as May passed into June, I began to think of other things and a life divorced from politics.

Then at 9.20 p.m. on Wednesday, 25 June, John Major telephoned my home. John said he had been considering my inclusion for elevation to the Lords in his resignation honours list. Could I do it and be active in the House? I said that the answer to both questions was yes and then I expanded a little on the devolution issue, my concern for Wales and our total lack of representation in Parliament. I had spared him correspondence on the subject. He was grateful for that and told me he had received 80,000 letters since the election. The honours list would not be published until mid-July at the earliest and Enid and I should keep the news to ourselves until then. She was pleased that I had been given the offer after twenty-seven years in the Commons and nearly sixteen at the Welsh Office. The confirmatory letter from Prime Minister Blair that he was recommending to the Queen that I be made a life peer, did not arrive until the end of July. The public announcement came in early August. 'The irony is,' reported the *Liverpool Post*, 'that of the six Welsh Tory MPs in the last Parliament, Sir Wyn, the only one to retire voluntarily, is the only one back in Parliament.'

The arguments for and against setting up a Scottish Parliament and a Welsh Assembly had not changed much since the referendum of 1979 when the proposals of a faltering Labour government failed to gain the approval of the peoples of both countries. But, after New Labour's stunning election victory, a fresh, confident government put similar proposals at the top of its agenda. So the circumstances, in the aftermath of New Labour's triumphant tidal wave, were very different – the reverse of 1979. This time, the government proposed to hold the referendum *before* rather than after the necessary legislation had been passed by the Westminster Parliament.

I had often thought about the issue over the years when it re-surfaced time and again. The powerlessness of Labour and Plaid Cymru in Wales, except at local government level, under successive Conservative administrations, irked their MPs beyond measure. And so did the power of the nominated quangos such as the Welsh Development Agency which Labour themselves had set up before the start of the eighteen years of Conservative rule. Their frustration must have been unbearable at times. A steady stream of English secretaries of state hardly eased their pain. Rhodri Morgan and Ron Davies waxed eloquent about 'the democratic deficit' in Wales and urged a 'bonfire of the quangos'. But, now that they were in power and held 34 of the 40 seats in Wales, the democratic deficit had become a surfeit. The quangos were ready to be sanitized.

Of course, as a Welshman, I wished to see political and national self-confidence heightened in Wales; enterprise, excellence and prosperity reaching new peaks and the people flourishing as never before. But the harsh reality was that Wales was financially dependent on the rest of the United Kingdom – as was Scotland. It was a fact of life that daily confronted me as a minister when I dealt at first hand with Welsh problems. Any weakening of the umbilical chord with central government and the Treasury would be damaging to the people we served. It might be tolerable in a period of economic prosperity but the possibility of hard times had to be considered too. All the great Welshmen from Lloyd George to Nye Bevan knew only too well which side Welsh bread was buttered. Plaid's talk of Europe's becoming the main source of Welsh support was wishful thinking. Denzil Davies (Lab., Llanelli), a former chief secretary to the Treasury, and I agreed that it would be very unwise to put our trust in Europe's generosity over time. There were dangers there as well as occasional bonanzas.

Furthermore, there were enormous advantages to Wales in the English and Whitehall connection. We had easy access to the great departments of state, to their resources and their thinking. They seldom stood in our way when we wanted to 'do our own thing'.

Special provisions for Wales were increasingly common in legislation. British embassies and consulates abroad gave us superb service when required. I was also conscious of our lack of politicians of stature in all parties in Wales and the increasing eminence and power of the Scots in the government. Half the Cabinet were Scottish and the prime minister had his roots there. This was not the time to distance ourselves from Westminster and Whitehall, 'where power lay' as Nye Bevan had found.

What was on offer to us in Wales before the 1997 referendum was a glorified regional council, run by committees inclusive of all parties but dominated by the party with a majority of members in the Assembly. It struck me immediately that this was a recipe for indecision or government by secret caucus, common among Welsh Labour local authorities; so I argued vehemently for a cabinet structure with individual ministers openly accountable for their actions. Because I advocated this change before the referendum – a change eventually accepted by the government – and questioned why the Scots alone were to be asked whether they wished their Parliament to have tax-varying powers, the Assembly's more ruthless advocates hailed me as a convert to their cause. I had to deny it in a letter to the *Western Mail* (22 May 1997).

The clarity of my position was not improved by my advice to my party not to lead the anti-devolution campaign because of the stigma of failure in the general election and the temptation to electors to give the Tories another thrashing at the polls. There was a danger too that, once tarred as anti-devolutionists, we might find it difficult to get Tories elected to the Assembly if, by popular consent, it chanced to become a reality. My advice was acted upon and the Conservative opposition to the Assembly in the referendum campaign was fairly low key.

This stance also suited a party that had just endured a searing leadership contest in which Ken Clarke and John Redwood – the left and right, pro- and anti-European wings of the party – had knocked each other out, leaving the way open to the young 'unity' candidate William Hague. With others, I had supported him in a letter to *The Times* (16 June). On 12 August, I wrote a letter to the chairman of the party, Cecil Parkinson, who had been charged with reforming the party organization. The occasion was a strong complaint against the Wales Area Office in Cardiff from a keen north Wales journalist, Ivor Wynne Jones. My letter, in retrospect, was at least prescient of the referendum result.

Before long, we may well be faced with a Welsh Assembly and the need to fight elections for membership of it. My best guess at present is that in the Referendum on September 18, the Government's proposals will scrape through on a low turn out, although that is by no means certain.

In the event, the declaration of the results of the referendum in each unitary authority was a cliffhanger, the 'noes' were leading until the very last moment when Carmarthenshire turned the tables to produce a minute majority of 6,721 votes in favour – 0.6 per cent of the votes cast. Only 51.3 per cent of the electorate voted at all and since 49.7 per cent of them had voted 'No' (compared with 50.3 per cent 'Yes') it meant that only a quarter of Welsh voters were in favour while three-quarters of the electorate had not endorsed the government's proposals. I was among them and a 'No' voter. Even so, the 'Yes' vote was double that of 1979. The majority in favour, though small, had to be accepted, but it was not an auspicious beginning.

The following Saturday afternoon, Ron Davies, the secretary of state, telephoned to ask if I would join the commission being established to draw up standing orders for the new Assembly. He said the cabinet system, which I advocated and he supported, could be incorporated in standing orders and did not need to be put into legislation. Tempted to accept his invitation, I had to point out that I was likely to be the Conservative front bench spokesman for Wales in the House of Lords and therefore presenting the opposition's views on the Devolution Bill. The two roles were not reconcilable.

I was gazetted as Lord Roberts of Conwy at midnight on 1 October. I had already visited Garter Principal King of Arms, Peter Llewelyn Gwynne-Jones, at the College of Arms in Queen Victoria Street, the previous month to discuss my title. I would have liked Lord Wyn because most people called me Sir Wyn and the transition from one title to the other would have been easier for us all but Garter would not hear of it. Yes, there had been others with Christian-name titles but he did not approve. I did not insist. I appended the name of my parliamentary constituency for so many years and of Talyfan Mountain which overlooked my home in Gwynedd. William Hague telephoned to ask me to be the Conservative front bench spokesman on Welsh affairs in the Lords and all was now set for my introduction to the House on Wednesday, 22 October.

At Peers Entrance that morning, I saw the familiar face of Sir Lawrence Verney, wearing his judge's robe and wig as Recorder of

London. My mind raced back to the scene in our backyard in Anglesey in 1943 when, as a young Guards officer, he came to see me with his father and set me on my way to Harrow School. It was a timely reminder of my origins and the twists and turns of yesterday's road.

I had brought family and close friends down to Westminster for the occasion. We were joined for lunch by the two peer friends who were to introduce me – Lord Thomas of Gwydir, former secretary of state for Wales and ex-minister of state, Lord Gibson-Watt MC (and double bar). Then the three of us who were to take part in the introduction ceremony went to the robing room to don our ermine-collared red robes. (Later, my little grandson, Rhidian, was to ask why I was dressed like Santa Claus!)

After prayers at 2.30 p.m., Black Rod (General Sir Edward Jones), in black breeches with silver-buckled shoes and shouldering his wand of office, followed by Garter in hose and heraldic tabard, led the way into the Chamber. Peter Thomas followed, then myself with David Gibson-Watt bringing up the rear. At the bar of the House, we three bowed to the Lord Chancellor on the Woolsack and moved forward in single file until I presented my writ of summons to the clerk at the despatch box. He read the writ to the assembled peers and, holding a New Testament in my right hand, I took the oath in English and Welsh and signed the velum scroll.

I shall spare you the rest of the ceremony except to say that my handshake with the Lord Chancellor was the signal for the traditional, welcoming 'Hear, hear' from all sides of the House. Disrobed, I then took my place on the benches and listened to the proceedings. It was only then that I began to savour the ornate splendour of the place and the remarkable distinction of some of its occupants.

Of course, after so many years in the Commons and in government, I was familiar with the Upper House and its ways. I had trooped to the bar along with other members of the Commons to hear the Queen's Speech at the State Opening of Parliament on many occasions. As a Privy Counsellor, I had sat on the steps of the throne and listened to their lordships debate the Welsh Language Bill, for example, for which I had been primarily responsible as minister of state at the Welsh Office. The Upper House had treated the bill with the respect this novel piece of legislation deserved. I looked forward to becoming an active member. The short introduction ceremony in which I had played a part dated back to the Middle Ages when the king personally invested and introduced newly created peers. That ended with the death of Henry V but the ceremony continued until James I. He abandoned it, possibly because he had sold too many peerages (thirty-seven in two years) or was not 'ceremonious in nature' as Francis Bacon, his Keeper of the Great Seal, explained. The ceremony was restored in due course but without the personal participation of the monarch.

Black Rod, who had led us into the Chamber, is more familiar to the public as the man who knocks loudly on the door of the Commons and summons them to attend Her Majesty in the House of Peers at the State Opening of Parliament. His office too dates back to medieval times when he kept order among petitioners at Court. He is still responsible for order and security in the House of Lords. Sir Edward was every inch the part – a tall, stalwart knight worthy of the best holders of his office in any age.

Seated in the Chamber and facing the stained-glass windows and the armorial bearings on the walls – all dominated by the gilded throne – one is captivated by the grandeur of this centrepiece of the building complex, designed by Sir Charles Barry and August Pugin in the nineteenth century. It replaced the Queen's Chamber, where the Lords used to assemble, before the Old Palace was destroyed by fire in 1834. Today's House of Commons is utilitarian by comparison, a post-war construction, lacking the mystique and historical redolence of the Lords.

Over time, a new peer learns that the basic layout of the Chamber, with the raised throne dominating the Lord Chancellor's Woolsack and flanked by benches on either side, is much the same as it was depicted in Edward I's reign. Then, King Alexander of Scotland sat on Edward's right and Llywelyn, Prince of Wales, sat on his left. The bishops sat where they sit now.

Outside, in the Princes Room, are eye-catching panels portraying Henry VIII and his six wives from Catherine of Aragon to Katherine Parr. The fate of each is easily remembered by the tour guides' chant to the hordes of visiting children:

> Divorced, beheaded, died;
> Divorced, beheaded, survived.

All the other Tudor monarchs, bridging the gap between medieval and modern, look down from their magnificent niches.

The gilded Mace, carried on a stout shoulder before the Lord Chancellor when he enters the Chamber in procession, solicits a bow from each of their lordships as it passes by. The Yeoman Usher with his sword flush to his thigh, the Purse of State and the hourglasses on the clerks' table for timing divisions (with a laptop computer beside them) remind you that this place has seen many changes but is itself fundamentally unchanged. The institution it houses still survives as the second house of Parliament in spite of being abolished then restored by Oliver Cromwell and threatened time and again with radical reform.

Although part of our democratic system, the modern House of Lords is not directly elected for the simple reason that if it was it would rival the House of Commons and that might well end in conflict. 'The best Second Chamber in the world', as Lord Esher called it in the 1960s, is a product of historical evolution. 'We are fortunate,' said Esher 'to have an institution which we certainly should never have had the intelligence to create.'

The record of the House of Lords over the centuries in defending our liberties and promoting our national interests is not a bad one. It has proved its worth as an essential adjunct of our democracy. No doubt there will be changes but its essential character and integrity will remain while men and women of experience, wisdom and independent spirit attend it. But their lordships do not take themselves too seriously. As a witty outsider exaggerated 'Life in the Lords must be like life after a vasectomy – all fun and no responsibility.'

When the devolution measure, the Government of Wales Bill, came from the Commons for its second reading in the Lords on 21 April 1998, there was no great enthusiasm for it on the Conservative benches. Its only supporter was Lord Griffiths of Fforestfach – Brian Griffiths who had advised Margaret Thatcher at No. 10. Lord Howe of Aberavon told me he had spent the Easter recess ploughing through the Commons' debates and found the structure of the Assembly 'a legislative dog's breakfast and constitutional monstrosity from which much trouble is likely to flow'. Lord Crickhowell and I were equally distrustful of the government's proposals. Only the Liberal Democrats welcomed them with open arms. The contrast between what was being provided for Scotland and for Wales was there for all to see in their respective bills. Scotland was being offered a Parliament with primary legislative and limited tax-varying powers, while the Welsh Assembly was restricted to secondary legislation and had no power to raise money other than through charges and the council tax levied by local authorities. The gloved fist of the Treasury still gripped the finances of both countries; it could not be otherwise without putting the interests of the UK economy at risk.

The secretary of state, Ron Davies, proposed that he should become the Assembly's First Minister and hold both offices for an indefinite, transition period. This was centralization not devolution. It sparked a debate during the bill's later stages in the Lords in July. Nick Crickhowell and I withdrew our time-limiting amendments only when we were given a firm undertaking by the Home Office minister, the late Lord Williams of Mostyn, that the joint tenure of offices would be strictly temporary.

In October, Ron Davies had his 'moment of madness' on Clapham Common and his career as secretary of state for Wales came to an inglorious end. But he had fathered the saying that devolution was a process, not an event, and the truth of it would stay with us for a long time to come.

Loose Ends

The government's standing in the polls in early 1999 was still high and the Tories' desperately low. Tony Blair was a born populist and intelligently resilient, strongly aided by his media manipulator, Alastair Campbell, and a growing band of flexible ministers, cast in his own mould. The economy continued to flourish – as John Major had always said it would – and the government basked in its success.

Time was when governments could blame their predecessors in office for anything that went wrong for the first eighteen months or so. Thereafter, they had to shoulder the blame themselves. Not so New Labour; they carried on damning the Tories for years and got away with it. The Tories did not seem able to defend themselves. They were ashamed of their record. The opposition was so uncertain of itself, it could only play the picador to New Labour's bull. There was no brilliant matador, no Manolete, to deliver a *coup de grâce*. William Hague was a jovial antagonist to the prime minister at Questions but he did not have the killer instinct. The Tories also suffered from a terrible dearth of fresh ideas and sound minds to compose a coherent political agenda. Whenever I mentioned it, friends reached for their pagers or mobiles and excused themselves. Matthew Parris of *The Times* was not the only one who did not have 'the faintest idea' what the Conservative Party stood for. The Tories are still looking for the philosopher's stone that will turn their dross into election-winning gold.

I had always enjoyed good health but over the last year or so I had had a recurrent pain in the lower abdomen. In the morning of Wednesday, 17 February 1999, the day when I was to wind up a debate on the Severn Tunnel initiated by Nick Crickhowell, the pain was so acute that I had to visit my doctor in Great Smith Street. Armed with his painkillers, which had put me to sleep for an hour, I dragged myself into the Lords for the debate. I met Nick on the steps of the throne and told him of my condition, knowing that he had suffered from an intractable stomach ailment for years. 'Too bad!' he said. Then the two-and-a-half-hour debate began. By the end, I could barely deliver my speech but it read all right in the official record next day.

On Friday, I saw my family doctor at home. Dr Gwynfor Evans was himself a former surgeon and, having located the pain, he immediately booked me into Glan Clwyd Hospital for observation. Mr McCarthy, the consultant surgeon suspected diverticulitis – small, alien pouches on the colon – and decided to operate next day. I had to wait for a few seconds in the wings before being wheeled into the theatre. The atmosphere of mystery and the green and white robed figures reminded me of the amphitheatre at Epidaurus and the temple of Asclepius close by, where the hurt and wounded of ancient Greece came to be treated. Even the quiet reassurance of the anaesthetist as he put me under was like a stage whisper, full of mystique and magical in its effect.

I awoke on a dried riverbed of large, rounded stones, with wild horses snorting nearby. It took me some time to realize that I was in my hospital bed and that the sound of wild horses was the wind screeching outside in a very stormy night. At some stage, someone expressed concern that I was not discharging fluid properly and the pace of the saline drip attached to me somewhere was quickened. The drops became torrential. Soon, the night sister, Sharon, looked up from the receptacle below the bed and pronounced with a smile: 'You can pee for Wales now!'

I returned to the House of Lords and the see-saw of politics in the spring of 1999, eager as ever to observe but not quite as keen to participate. The Conservative Party's disarray had been exacerbated by Peter Lilley's attack on free-market principles (20 April) and Margaret herself had been drawn to express her disbelief. The parties were close in the local government elections in England on a low turnout (29 per cent) with just enough council seats passing to the Conservatives to save William Hague's skin.

It was no surprise to any of us that the nationalists did well in the Scottish Parliamentary and Welsh Assembly elections on 6 May. In Wales the Tories were relegated to third place with 9 members only compared with Plaid Cymru's 17 and Labour's 28. Of the 9 Conservatives, only one was directly elected; the rest got in on the proportional representation vote. We were no longer the Labour Party's main opposition in Wales.

Labour's failure to quell the regions with a dose of devolution and the spur it had given to the nationalists' advance was the only story that really interested the broadsheets and the media. It promised to be a serial drama with the next instalments yet to come in future elections. The Queen and Prince Philip had a rather lonely ride through Cardiff in their landau for the official opening of the Assembly at Crickhowell House. The crowds were as slim as the majority in the referendum.

But if the remnants of imperialist traditions were being abandoned in the UK they were being revived abroad in the guise of Robin Cook's ethical foreign policy, particularly in the Balkans. Tony Blair assured Parliament that the war in Kosovo was being fought 'for a moral purpose as much as a strategic interest' and it did not escape his critics that the moral purpose was to be found at home rather than in the Balkans. 'The war against the Serbs', wrote Mick Hume in *The Times*, 'is primarily about giving Mr Blair's Government an aura of moral authority and a sense of mission. It is about projecting a self image of the ethical new Britain bestriding the world. It is a crusade' (15 April 1999). In retrospect, they were ominous words. For Slobodan Milošević substitute Saddam Hussein in 2003. I was not averse to toppling him and his regime of terror in Iraq, but the effects and consequences in the Arab and Islamic worlds would be stupendous. They would haunt the world in the new century, inspire rather than defuse terrorism and sap the resources and energies of the West. The waking giant of China might stretch its arms to fulfil old ambitions. World order might become disorder on a massive scale.

In October 1999 I found a reference to our Russian telephone-tapping exploit in Vienna in 1949. It was in the defector, Oleg Gordievsky's account of the KGB from Lenin to Gorbachev. He described it as 'Operation Silver', the precursor of 'Operation Gold' in Berlin four years later, which the British traitor, Gordon Blake, had revealed to the Russians long before the plans were implemented. It was his first major betrayal. Blake was caught and sentenced to forty-two years in prison – a year for every British agent who had been executed as a result of his treachery, a journalist wrote. Blake's autobiography *No Other Choice*, written in Moscow in the late 1980s, more than twenty years after his escape from Wormwood Scrubs, contains a hearsay but recognizable account of our Vienna operation which became more extensive after I left. The mastermind behind it was Peter Lunn, head of the Vienna station of the Secret Intelligence Service. But there is no mention of its betrayal or the visitor from London of whose guilt I had become convinced over the years. Neither was there an explanation of why, having been 'blown' in Vienna, a similar but bigger operation was subsequently mounted in Berlin.

Fifty years later, I felt justified in asking the government some written questions but I drew a complete blank. 'The records of the Secret Intelligence Service are not released,' wrote the minister, Baroness Scotland, answering for the Foreign Office. The Ministry of Defence had few relevant records of the British Army in Austria and what there was had been buried at the Public Record Office at Kew. There was a hint in the correspondence that I too might conveniently bury myself there. The one thing I did find from published sources was that the culprit could have been Kim Philby. He was not posted to the US until August 1949 and he could have been our mysterious visitor earlier that summer. Oleg Gordievsky, with whom I have become friendly, tells me I may well be right. He also drew my attention to the academic David Stafford's book, *Spies Beneath Berlin*, which contains a good account of the cable tap at Smokey's in Vienna after my departure in 1949.

My diary entries for 1999 were repetitive in deploring the state of the Conservative Party. After a summer reshuffle, only William Hague and Sir George Young Bt (Con., Hampshire North West) were left in the shadow cabinet of all who had served in John Major's last Cabinet. Sir George was a true aristocrat who cycled around Westminster even as a minister. The party had been well and truly purged of its past. The trouble was that its present had no experience.

William Rees Mogg (Lord) had once suggested that Alan Clark should become Conservative leader. He had made a remarkable return to Westminster as the member for Kensington and Chelsea, but, early in September, he joined his dogs in their cemetery at his beloved Saltwood. He had become famous after the publication of his *Diaries* in 1993, spiced as they were with his amorous dalliances and waspish observations as a minister. My last recollection of Alan was of him striding fast and furious the length and breadth of a Buckingham Palace garden party. Up and down he went, without a stop. He was alone and unpopular at the time but determined to show the world he was there. He was as prominent as a stray hound lost in the countryside.

My last diary entry of the year was on Monday, 27 December 1999:

It is the end of the 1990s, the twentieth century and the second millennium and there is a general feeling of unease, which Prince

340

Charles will try to quell with a broadcast inculcating hope. The script has been leaked to the press, much to his annoyance. His theme is right for our time.

The Queen too in her Christmas broadcast tried to overcome people's fear of change. The fear belongs to the 'haves'; the 'have nots' have little to fear because they have little to lose. Change usually favours them.

What alarms me is that no one appears to be in control of any changes that may come and that we are heading for a destiny not of our choosing. We are being guided by a strange compass and there are no great principles or high values to speak of. Spin has replaced truth.

The historians are busy rewriting history. The history of the United Kingdom has become the 'story of the isles' in deference to devolution and closer union with Europe. The Welsh approach to history is also veering so as to make devolution the climax of our achievement in spite of widespread disillusionment with the performance of the Assembly and the quality of its membership. Historians are a mercurial lot, slavishly interpreting the past to please those who dominate the present. History is indeed written by the winners.

My diary continued spasmodically until the end of 2000 when I came to the end of yet another notebook. I did not begin a new one and that was the end of that. Keeping the diary had been a great help to me in digesting the meaning of events over thirty years.

Index

Abbott, Diane 322
Aberconwy 125
Aberdare 171
Aberfan 71–2
Abergele 131
Aberystwyth 8, 44, 117, 236, 245, 257, 309
Abse, Leo 82, 151
Abyssinia 4, 5, 11
Achilles 11
Acts of Union (1536, 1543) 268, 272
Adamson, Campbell 94
Adenauer, Konrad 95
Adley, Robert 246
Admiralty House 63
Advance Machine Company 216
Agar, Herbert 62–3
Aitken, Jonathan 310
Al Fayed, Mohamed 309, 310
Alexander, King of Scotland 334
Ajax 11
Akihito, Crown Princess 228
Albert, Prince 260
Alcan 146
Alexandra Palace (London) 57
Alington, Giles 42, 43, 45
All Souls, Oxford 275
Amery, John 26
Amery, Julian 26, 200
Amery, Leo 25, 26
Amis, Kingsley 144
Amlwch 143
Ammanford 309
Amsterdam 42, 43
Analects of Confucius, The 313
Ancram, Michael 201
Andrew, Prince 196
Anglesey 7, 17, 80, 116, 124, 125, 143, 144, 170, 244, 333

Anglesey, Henry, Marquis of 150, 187, 191
Anglesey, Shirley, Marchioness of 150, 191
Anglo-Irish Agreement 196
Annan Commission 129, 130, 131
Anne, Princess 224
Arab-Israeli war (1973) 92
Archer, Jeffrey 208
Argentina 152, 153, 154, 155, 156, 157, 158, 159
Argyll Field (North Sea) 304
Armstrong, Sir Robert 195, 199, 215
Arnhem 28
Ashby, David 295
Ashby, Silvana 295
Ashdown, Paddy 248
Ashmolean Museum 40
ASLEF 93
Asquith, H. H. 61
Association of Pacific Economic Communities (APEC) 283
Association of South East Asian Nations (ASEAN) 281
Athens 18
Atkins, Humphrey 80, 105, 152, 153
Attlee, Clement 111, 328
Auden, W. H. 264
Austin, Brian 285
Austin, Stephanie 285
Australia 284
Austria 32, 64
Aziz, Rafidah 280

Bacon, Francis 334
Baden-Württemberg 217, 218, 223, 312
Baghdad 254
Bagier, Gordon 109
Baglan 232
Bahrain 255

Baker, Kenneth 101, 105, 201, 219, 220, 221, 260, 261, 264
Baker, Stanley 74
Bala 268
Baldwin, Stanley 159
Balkans, the 339
Balliol College, Oxford 102
Baner ac Amserau Cymru 77
Bangor 5, 7, 53, 78, 121, 122, 125, 134, 159, 167, 170, 187, 192, 231, 232, 288
Bangor Conservative Club 121, 171
Bank of England 318
Barber, Tony 84, 85, 89
Barcelona 258, 297, 312
Barings Bank 318
Barratts 214
Barry 82
Barry, Sir Charles 334
Barton Stacey 28
Bass 214
Bassetlaw 171
Bassey, Shirley 64
Bath Festival 64
Bavaria 90, 91, 189
Bavarian Vereinsbank 190
Baverstock, Donald 57
BBC 53–8, 59, 62, 67, 71, 78, 79, 112, 120, 125, 129, 130, 131, 132, 146, 152, 153, 156, 223, 296, 319, 328
Beatles, the 65
Beaufort, Duke of 200
Beaumaris 9, 14–15, 216
Beaver Pool (River Conwy) 204, 206
Beckett, Margaret 303
Bede, Venerable 39
Bedwellty 114, 175
Beijing 292
Bell, Martin 327
Belstead, Lord 137
Benn, Tony 87, 109, 110, 151, 240
Bennett, Sir Frederic 97
Bennett, Nicholas 250, 265
Benz, Gottfried 218
Berlin 43, 70, 112, 339, 340
Bernard of Clairvaux 44
Berry, Anthony 179
Best, Keith 124, 134, 143–4, 156, 183–4, 210
Best, Robert 112
Better Tomorrow, A 87
Betws-y-Coed 121, 204
Bevan, Aneurin 61, 75–6, 113, 177, 330, 331
Biffen, John 78, 84, 129, 153, 199, 314

Birley, Mark 28, 29, 33–4, 41–2, 85
Birmingham 195
Blackpool 148, 149, 181, 288
Blackwood, Algernon 145
Blair, Ed 304
Blair, Nancy 304
Blair, Tony 299, 310, 311, 316, 318, 319, 320, 321–2, 323, 324, 325, 328, 329, 337, 339
Blake, Gordon 339
Blaker, Peter 108
Blunt, Sir Anthony 141–2, 308
Boas, 'Pip' 17, 18, 20
Bodelwyddan Castle 238
Bodysgallen Hotel 171
Boeing 283
Bolshoi 69–70
Bombay 224
Bonfire of the Vanities, The 244
Bonham Carter, Mark 61
Bonham Carter, Lady Violet 61
Bonn 116
Booth, Hartley 296
Boothroyd, Betty 326
Boscawen, Bob 254
Bosch, Robert 218
Bottomley, Virginia 291
Bournemouth 208, 322
Bowe, Colette 198
Bowen, Elfed 266
Boyd-Carpenter, John, Lord 167
Bradley, A. C. 257
Brandt, Willy 95
Brawdy 54
Brecon, Vivian Lewis, Lord 76, 113
Breconshire 77, 112, 125, 188, 193, 298
Brezhnev, Leonid 68
Bridgend 217, 228, 231, 288
Brierley, Zachry 124
Bright, Graham 293
Brighton 143, 149, 178–9
Bristol 64, 67
Bristol Evening Post 59
Britain 14, 19, 32, 91, 95, 97, 107, 174, 178, 193, 196–7, 246, 292, 298, 328, 339
see also United Kingdom
Britannia Bridge 150
British Aerospace 197, 198
British Canadian Trade Federation 244
British Columbia 115, 285
British Columbia Trade Development Corporation 284

British Council 281
British Expeditionary Force 7
British Steel Corporation 142, 175
British Telecommunications 210
Brittan, Leon 196, 197–8, 199
Brittany 90, 91
Broadbent, Richard 194
Broadcasting Bill (1980) 132, 133, 137
Broadcasting Standards Council 241
Broadwater Farm estate 261
Brooke, Henry 297
Brown, George 78
Brown, Gordon 310, 321, 323
Brown, Michael 300
Brown, Monica 46
Browns Hotel (London) 16
Brussels 217, 310
Bryant, Peter 192
BSE (bovine spongiform encephalopathy) 319, 323
Buchanan-Smith, Alick 114
Buck, Sir Anthony 152, 296
Buck, Bienvenida, Lady 296
Budgeon, Nick 274
Buenos Aires 153
Burgess, Guy 141, 308
Burman, Ben Lucien 112
Burt, Alistair 318
Burton, John Nelson 74
Burton, Richard 65–7, 215
Bush, George W. 254
Butcher, Ken 164
Butler, Chris 122, 193
Butler, Peter 324
Butler, R. A. B. 221
Butler, Sir Robin 291
Byron, Lord 67

Cabinet Office 139–40
Cadw: Welsh Historic Monuments 187
Caerleon 187
Caernarfon 6, 79, 124, 134, 202, 265
Caerphilly 271
Caine, Michael 74
Caithness, Malcolm, Lord 295
Caitlin's Pierrot Troupe 265
California 226, 229–30, 245
Callaghan, James 88, 109, 110, 111, 112, 116, 117, 118, 120, 121, 122, 123, 151–2, 155, 164, 170, 175, 200–1, 242, 253, 265
Cambridge 131, 182, 309, 317

Campaign Guide Supplement 1978 130
Campbell, Alistair 337
Campden Hill 85, 106
Canada 14, 15, 61, 244, 245, 284–7, 317
Canberra 160
Cannes Film Festival 68
Canning, George 18
Canongate (Edinburgh) 241
Capel Curig 265
Cardiff 54, 55, 57, 58, 59–60, 61, 64, 66, 70, 75, 79, 83, 88, 106, 111, 113, 122, 124, 147, 149, 151, 166, 167, 168, 171, 203, 213, 214, 217, 219, 222, 224, 228, 231, 236, 249, 250, 259, 265, 268, 269, 276, 293, 296, 299, 300, 313, 328, 339
Cardiff and County Club 328
Cardiff Arms Park 66–7, 328
Cardiff Bay 208, 284
Carlile, Alex 292
Carlisle, Joan 64–5
Carlisle, Mark 148
Carmarthenshire 63, 112, 113, 164, 332
Carr, Robert 88
Carr, Sir William 62
Carrington, Lord 125, 152, 153, 310
Cash, Bill 274, 317, 324
Castle, Barbara 88, 133
Catalan 258–9
Catalonia 217, 218, 258–9, 297, 312
Catherine of Aragon 334
Cecil, Lord David 40
Ceiriog *see* Hughes, John Ceiriog
census (1991) 269
Centre Forward Group 193
Chalker, Lynda, Baroness 195, 218, 289, 290
Champlain Industries 244
Chandler, Godfrey 101
Channel Tunnel 299
Channon, Howard 50
Channon, Paul 104
Charles, Prince 149–50, 151, 186, 269, 293, 294, 303–4, 319, 340–1
Cheltenham 240
Chequers 241, 242
Chernobyl 203, 204
Chester 231, 232
Chesterfield, Lord 208
Chiba, Kazuo 243
Chicago 244–6, 282
China 99, 101, 190, 252–3, 284, 292, 339

Chineham 300
Chittenden, Gordon 144
Chown, Mike 164, 167
Christ Church, Oxford 41
Christ in Majesty 55–6
Christino, Len 286
Chungwa/Tatung 312, 313
Churchill, Randolph 60–1
Churchill, Winston 100, 200, 310, 315
Churchill, Sir Winston L. S. 7, 12, 18,
    25–6, 88, 238, 253
Churchill Club 195, 200, 209
Cilcennin, Lord 63
City Hall (Cardiff) 147
Civil Contingencies Unit 159
Civil War 13
Clark, Alan 18, 183, 250, 272, 340
Clark, Sir Andrew 73
Clark, Lord 183
Clarke, Kenneth 311, 323, 331
Cledwyn, Lord 135, 167, 329
    see also Hughes, Cledwyn
Clegg, Sir Walter 172
Clinton, Bill 283
Clough, Arthur 49
'Club of Twelve, The' 100
Clwyd 199, 237
Clwyd County Council 142
Clwydian Hills 54
Cobbold, Sue 248
Cockeram, Eric 210
Cockpit Passage 140
Cold War 30, 68, 308
Colditz 81, 120
Coleman, Donald 163, 253
Cologne 30
Colwyn Bay 191, 228, 257
Common Market 89–91, 173
Commonwealth 114–15, 201
Commonwealth Games (Cardiff) 59–60
Communism 76, 89, 90, 225, 246
Complete Works of Oscar Wilde, The 31
Concord Pacific 284
Confederation of British Industry (CBI)
    89, 92, 94, 299
Conservative Central Council 147
Conservative Central Office 60, 299, 323
Conservative Group (in European
    Parliament) 104–5
Conservative Party 75, 76–7, 80–1, 82,
    83, 84, 85, 86, 87, 88, 89, 91, 92, 94,
    95, 96, 97, 98, 99, 100, 101–2, 104,
    113, 114, 116, 119, 121, 122, 125,
    128, 129, 130, 131, 133, 134, 135,
    137–8, 143, 148, 149, 151, 168–9,
    177, 181, 188, 196, 199, 200, 204,
    209, 211, 213, 221, 233–4, 239, 241,
    242, 246, 250–1, 252, 262, 263, 264,
    269, 274, 275–6, 277, 288, 292–3,
    295, 297, 302, 305, 310, 311, 314,
    315, 316, 317, 318, 319, 321, 322,
    323, 324, 325, 326, 327, 328, 329,
    330, 331, 332, 335, 337, 338, 340
Consolidated Fund Bill 135, 163
Conway, Derek 247, 305
Conwy 77, 78, 79, 83, 94, 98, 124, 125,
    129, 171, 173, 195, 207, 211–12,
    230, 231–2, 236, 250, 252, 260, 263,
    300, 323
Conwy Castle 261
Conwy Conservative Association 169
Conwy tunnel 163, 167, 260, 265
Conwy Valley 281, 308
Cook, Robin 308, 319, 339
Cooper, Gary 62
Cooper, Joseph 64
Cope, John 164
Cosi fan Tutte 64
Costa Méndez, Nicanor 157
Cotter, John 56
Countryside Council for Wales 276, 294
Cox, Anna 327
Cox, Michael 117
Cranmer, Thomas, Archbishop of
    Canterbury 222
Crawford Committee 129, 131
Crazy Gang 62, 65
Creutzfeldt–Jakob disease 319
Crewe 169
Crickhowell, Lord 335, 336, 337–8
    see also Edwards, Nicholas
Critchley, Julian 116, 143, 210, 236–7
Crockett, Davy 67
Cromwell, Oliver 40, 335
Crosland, Tony 109, 110
Crossman, R. H. S. 26
Crouch, David 172
Crown Buckley Brewery (Llanelli) 266
Croydon 149
Cumbria 203
Curran, Dr 51
Currie, Edwina 233
Cwmffrwdoer 222
Cyprus 52, 326

Czechoslovakia 193

Dahl, Major 29
Daily Express 52
Daily Mail 104, 124, 298, 303
Daily Mirror 62, 288
Daily Telegraph 135, 149, 208, 209, 315
Daly, Lawrence 93
Dalyell, Tam 198, 315
Daniel, Sir Goronwy 135
Dardanelles, the 6, 7
Darmstadt 190
Dartmoor 278
Darwin 159
Datsun 146
Davies, Alun Oldfield 55
Davies, Denzil 330
Davies, Elizabeth 285, 293
Davies, Howard 299
Davies, Hywel 55
Davies, Janet 327
Davies, John 92
Davies, Lorraine 67
Davies, Peter 285, 293
Davies, Ron 271, 319, 330, 332, 335–6
de Deney, Sir Geoffrey 259–60, 261
de Gaulle, General Charles 94, 95, 115, 160
de Sancha, Antonia 288
Dean, Sir Paul 172, 199
Defence Select Committee 199
Dehaene, Jean Luc 303
Delft 42
Dell, Edmund 133
Delmar, Marie Debortes 144
Delors, Jacques 303
Denbigh 82, 131
Denham, Bertie, Lord 215
Denman, Major 36, 37, 38
Denver (Colorado) 282
Depression, the 16
Derby, the 34
Derby, John, Earl of 63, 73
Development Board for Rural Wales 289, 302
devolution 112–14, 115–116, 117, 118, 120, 207, 223, 241–2, 297, 302, 311, 312, 329–32, 335–6, 339
devolution referendum
  (1979) 116, 117, 118, 120, 134, 242, 297, 329–30, 332
  (1997) 331, 332
Diana, Princess 149–51, 269–70, 303

Dickens, Charles 13, 23, 27
Dickens, Geoffrey 289
Dimbleby, Jonathan 303
Dinorwic Power Station 186
Discs a'Gogo 65
Diwaker, B. M. 37
Doldowlod 306
Dolgarrog 121
Dolwyddelan 122
Donne, John 165
Dorrell, Stephen 319
Dors, Diana 55
Douglas-Home, Sir Alec 43, 102, 113
Douglas-Home, Lady Elizabeth 43
Dow Chemicals 216
Dow Corning 216
Dresden 243, 244, 258, 286
Dromgoole, Patrick 74
du Cann, Edward 101, 102
Dublin 185, 256
Dugdale, John 165
Duncan, Alan 295
Dunkirk 14
Duncan Smith, Iain 320
Dundee 114
Düsseldorf 192
Dyfed 235
Dykes, Hugh 101

East India Company 279
Ed Sullivan Show 67
Eden, Sir Anthony 243
Eden, Sir John 171
Edgehill, Battle of 13
Education Act
  (1944) 221
  (1988) 218, 219–22, 223, 238
Edward I 129, 187, 334
Edward VIII 5
Edwards, Anne 164, 166, 173
Edwards, Huw T. 63, 75–6
Edwards, Sir Ifan ab Owen 63
Edwards, Nicholas 100, 105, 116, 117, 124, 125, 127, 129, 130, 132, 133–4, 135, 136, 137, 139, 143, 144, 147–8, 149, 152, 155, 156, 162, 163–4, 166, 168, 170, 172–3, 178, 182, 184, 186, 191, 193, 194, 195, 198, 203, 204, 207, 208–9, 212, 234, 236, 256
  see also Crickhowell, Lord
Edwards, Will 90, 124
Egger, Dr Herman 189, 190

Egton House (London) 54
Elgin family 15
Elis-Thomas, Dafydd, Lord 132, 273, 288
Elizabeth, the Queen Mother 201
Elizabeth I 222
Elizabeth II 127, 141, 182, 200, 260–1, 262, 288, 290, 329, 333, 334, 339, 342
Elrington, Christopher 40, 41, 42, 43, 187
Emanuel, Ivor 65, 74
Emerson, Ralph Waldo 230
Emery, Peter 96, 186
England 159, 170, 217, 221, 235, 241, 264, 268, 274, 290, 311, 338
English language 3, 18, 58, 125, 128, 165, 187–8, 202, 223, 258, 270, 281
Enns Bridge 31
Epsom 42
Epstein, Jacob 55–6
Esher, Lord 335
Eton 20, 28, 41, 42, 80, 272
European Commission 192
European Communities Bill 92
European Community 91, 93, 94, 102, 201, 317
European Court of Justice 320–1
European Finance Bill 310–11
European Monetary Union 324
European Single Market 224
European Social Chapter 325
European Union (EU) 246, 303
Euston 79, 80, 150, 169
Evans, Gwynfor 81, 113, 131, 132, 133, 135, 136, 137–8
Evans, Dr Gwynfor 338
Evans, Sir Hywel 127
Evans, Jonathan 291, 298
Evans, Margaret 164
Evans, Roger 272, 291, 307
Evening News 101
Evening Standard 60, 61, 167, 291, 315, 325
Everett 283
exchange rate mechanism (ERM) 237, 266–7
Excell, Oksana 284
Exeter 11
Exeter College, Oxford 44

Fabricant, Michael 273
Fade Out 74–5
Fairbairn, Sir Nicholas 258, 269–70
Falklands War, the 152–61, 163, 173

Fallon, Michael 248
Farr, John 89–90
Farr, Tommy 21, 74, 84
Fate of the Language, The (Tynged yr Iaith) 128
Fazakerley Hospital (Liverpool) 51
Fellowes, Sir Robert 260
Ferguson, Sarah 196
Ferman, Monica 141
Ferrers, Robin, Earl 270
Finance Bill (1975) 103
Finch, Harold 175
Finkelstein, Danny 323–4
Finsberg, Geoffrey 141
First World War 6, 14, 16, 63, 112, 306
Fitch, Betty 54–5, 56
Fitzgerald, Garrett 185
Flint 82, 210
Flynn, Jack 204, 205, 206, 207
Flynn, Paul 322
Fookes, Janet 168
Foot, Michael 108, 109, 110, 117, 118, 151, 165, 173, 176, 314
Ford 217, 228
Ford, Anthony 245
Ford, Lynda 245
Ford, Peter 279
Forster, E. M. 142
Four Motor regions 217, 218, 243, 258, 286, 293, 297
Fowler, Sir Norman 176, 325
France 6, 7, 14, 32, 91, 95, 217, 306
Francis, Alfred 63–4
Franco, Francisco 5
Frankfurt 217
Franks Report 163
Fraser, Hugh 103
Freight Association 299
Frostick, Michael 63
Fry, Sir Peter 314

Gadlys 8, 9, 10
Gaelic 172, 185, 219
Gaeltacht, the 185
Gaitskell, Hugh 61, 75
Galway 185
Gandhi, M. K. 230
Gardiner, Sir George 326
Garel-Jones, Tristan 247, 250, 315
Garrett, Ted 166
Gates, Bill 283
Gaudí, Antonio 297

General Belgrano 156
George V 5
George, Eddie 318
Germany 6, 7, 12, 13, 14, 75, 91, 95, 97,
    120, 137, 143, 189–91, 192–3, 215,
    217–18, 242, 243, 290, 306, 312
Ghilardottia, Dr Fiorella 297
Gibson-Watt, David, Lord 76, 80, 119,
    306, 333
Gibson-Watt, Diana, Lady 306
Gilmour, Sir Ian 148
Giovenzana, Giuseppi 258
Gladstone, W. E. 49, 232
Glan Clwyd Hospital 170
Glasgow 120
Glasgow Herald 122
Goering, Hermann 306
Goethe, Johann Wolfgang von 39–40
Goldsmith, Alec 192–3
Goldsmith, Sir James 311, 320
Goleuad, Y 3
Goodhew, Victor 167
Gooding, Alf 186, 227
Goodison, Alan 185
Goodlad, Alistair 329
Goodman, Arnold 73, 101
Goose Green 159
Gorard, Tony 74
Gorbachev, Mikhail 253, 339
Gordievsky, Oleg 339, 340
Gordon, Lord George 87
Gorman, Teresa 276, 311, 315
Gormley, Joe 89, 93
Gorseinon 216
Gouda 42
Gourlay, Harry 108
Govan shipyards 142
Government and the Governed 26
Government of Wales Act
    (1978) 117
    (1998) 332, 335
Gow, Ian 127, 147, 153–4, 165, 167,
    195–6, 242
Gower, Sir Raymond 82, 120, 233
Gowrie, Lord 146
Grace, Princess, of Monaco 270
Grade, Lew 298
Graf Spee 11
Grand Hotel (Brighton) 178
Great American Management 245
Great Orme 261
Greece 18

Green, Colin 285, 286
Greene, Graham 142
Griffith, Michael 294
Griffiths, Brian, Lord Griffiths of
    Fforestfach 221, 299, 335
Griffiths, James 112, 175
Griffiths, Mr 14–15
Grist, Ian 149, 164, 165, 166, 213–14,
    242, 249, 250, 251, 265
Growing People, The 71
Guandong 284
Guardian 87, 187, 199, 296, 309–10
Guilty Men 275
Gulf War, the 245–6, 252, 253–6, 316
Gutersloh 192
Gwent 128, 133, 222
Gwydyr House 135, 139, 166, 172, 289
Gwynedd 117, 128, 332
Gwynedd County Council 129, 202, 232
Gwynne-Jones, Peter Llewelyn 332

Haarlem 42
Hague, Ffion 276
Hague, The 42
Hague, William 276–7, 315, 326, 331,
    332, 337, 338, 340
Haig, Alexander 155
Haile Selassie 4
Hailsham, Quintin, Lord 81, 140, 200,
    237, 257
Ham-Longman, Captain 33, 34–5, 38
Hamburg 192
Hamilton, Archie 219, 221, 315, 326
Hamilton, Christine 309
Hamilton, Fred 282
Hamilton, Lord James Douglas 162–3
Hamilton, Neil 309–10, 327
Hamilton, Willie 113
Hamilton Oil 282, 304
Hannam, John 100
Hanson, James, Lord 299
Harding, Sir Peter 296
Harlech, Lord 130
Harlech Television 73, 74, 77
    see also HTV
Harman, Harriet 318, 322
Harmer Nicholls, Lord 303
Harmsworth, Vere 298
Harrassment Bill (1996) 323
Harries, Lauren 286
Harrison, Anthony 194
Harrods 309

Harrow 13–14, 15, 16, 17–20, 21–7, 29, 33, 39, 41, 53, 57, 333
Hartland-Swann, Julian 217, 218, 258
Harwich 30, 42
Hastings, Marquis of 279
Haverfordwest 54
Havers, Sir Michael 97, 142
Hawaii 229
Hawkes, Christopher 40
Heads of the Valleys road 276
Healey, Denis 102, 108, 109, 110, 151, 173
Heath, Edward 76, 78, 83, 84, 85, 86–7, 88, 89, 92–4, 95, 96, 97, 98, 99–100, 101–4, 108, 109, 113, 114, 118, 120, 126, 148, 149, 158, 169, 174, 213, 274, 292, 306, 311, 318, 324, 325
Heathcot-Amery, David 322
Heffer, Eric 88, 176
Hegel, G. W. F. 128, 218
Help Institute 281
Henry the Fourth, Part One 27
Henry V 333
Henry VIII 334
Here To-day 64
Herrick, Robert 67
Herzogenaurach 190
Heseltine, Michael 101, 148, 162, 196–7, 198, 199, 215, 236, 242, 247, 249, 250, 252, 257, 264, 272, 274, 311–12, 315, 325
Hill, Charles, Lord 73, 75
Hill, Sir James 317
Hill, John 90
Hill, William 63
Hiramatsu, Governor 259
Hirohito, Emperor 191, 227, 228
History of the Welsh in Minnesota, The 216–17
Hitler, Adolf 5, 7, 19, 20, 217
Hodge, Sir Julian 111
Hogg, Douglas 296
Holland 42–3
Holyhead 79, 124, 256, 261, 269
Hong Kong 192, 224–5, 227, 284, 292
Honolulu 229
Hook of Holland 30
Hooson, Emlyn, Lord 167, 270
Hooson, Tom 77, 188
Hope, David Michael, Bishop of London 260–1
Hopkins, Gerard Manley 65, 67
Hotel Vier Jahreszeiten (Hamburg) 192–3

Hotspot 68
Housing Bill (1979–80) 141
Howard, Michael 209
Howe, Sir Geoffrey, Lord Howe of Aberavon 104, 141, 148, 149, 157, 169, 188, 237, 246, 247, 249, 235
Howell, David 140–1, 181
Howells, Gareth 279, 281
Howells, John 267
Hoya 228
HTV 124, 129, 130, 167, 295, 303
Hughes, Cledwyn 80, 83, 91, 93, 97, 109–10, 112, 116
    see also Cledwyn, Lord
Hughes, John Ceiriog (Ceiriog) 5
Hui, Terry 284
Hulton, Sir Edward 56
Hum, Martin 243
Hume, Mick 339
Humphrys, John 71
Hunt, David 195, 238, 243, 249–50, 256, 257, 259, 264, 271, 273, 274, 275, 298, 325
Hunt, Sir John 127
Hurd, Douglas 249, 299, 311–12
Hussein, Saddam 245–6, 253, 254, 255, 339
Hutcheson, Francis 313
Hutton, Will 325
Huyton 73
Hylton, Jack 62

Ian Greer Associates 309
Imperial War Museum 36
'In Place of Strife' 88
Ina Bearings 190
Inco 286
Independent Broadcasting Authority (IBA) 130, 132, 134
Independent Television Authority (ITA) 59, 64, 72, 73
India 193, 224, 279
Industrial Relations Act (1971) 85, 88, 94, 95, 97
Industry Bill (1972) 92
Intelligence Corps 29–30
Inter-Parliamentary Union 116
International Monetary Fund (IMF) 118
Inuit art 286
Invalid Tricycle Association 66
Invest in Britain Bureau (IIB) 227
Iran 245, 253, 254

Iraq 246, 250, 253–4, 255, 318–19, 339
Irish National Liberation Army 120
Irish Republic 171, 185, 219
Irish Republican Army (IRA) 178, 179,
    185–6, 196, 236, 242
Islam 279, 281
Islwyn 177
Israel 181, 253
Italy 4, 5, 91, 97, 217, 258
ITN 123, 136
ITV 71, 73, 129, 130, 131, 165

James, Robert Rhodes 154
James I 333–4
Japan 186, 189, 191–2, 221, 224, 225–9,
    243, 259, 292
Jarrow 5
Jay, Peter 111
Jayne's Fighting Ships 152
Jeans, Alec 46, 51–2, 59
Jeans family 46
Jenkin, Patrick 197
Jenkins, Christopher 267, 272
Jenkins, Canon Claud 41, 45
Jenkins, Graham 66
Jenkins, Roy 82, 90, 91, 93, 108, 109,
    110, 151, 173, 197
Jenkins, Sheila 187, 188
Jenkins, Will 66–7
John Paul, Pope 159
Johnson, Dr Samuel 61
Jones, Alec 170–1
Jones, General Sir Edward 333, 334
Jones, Councillor Emyr Currie 203
Jones, Gwilym 265, 292
Jones, Gwyn 276
Jones, Gwyneth 64
Jones, Colonel H. 159
Jones, Huw 289
Jones, Ivor Wynne 78, 331
Jones, John Elfed 223, 235, 257
Jones, John Walter 288
Jones, Meurig 60
Jones, Mildred 170
Jones, Sam 53–4
Jones, Tom 65
Jones, Tom Idwal 112
Jones, Watkin 56
Jones-Williams, Dafydd 135
Jopling, Michael 125, 149, 164, 165, 168,
    204, 311, 319
Joseph, Sir Keith 98, 101, 102, 142, 197, 318

Joyce, William (Lord Haw Haw) 26
Julius Caesar 27
Jutland, Battle of 144

Kansai, the 227
Kapital, Das 38
Kassim, Habib 255
Kaufman, Gerald 141
Keats, John 67
Keidanren, the 227
Kemp, Walter 61
Kennedy, Joseph P. 63
Kensington Palace 289, 290
Kentucky 112
Keyes, Sarah 181–2
KGB 339
Kilbrandon Commission 100, 114
King, Martin Luther 230
King, Tom 162, 215
Kingdom, Councillor Fred 203
King's Royal Rifle Corps 28
Kinnock, Neil 114, 117, 173, 175, 176–7,
    211, 262, 263, 264
Kirk, Peter 104, 105
Kitson, Tim 99
Knight, Jill 103
Knowsley 73
Kobe 225, 226
Kohl, Helmut 191
Kosovo 316, 339
Kosygin, Alexey 68
Kuala Lumpur 278, 279–81
Kuala Lumpur St David's Society 280
Kursk 12
Kuwait 76, 245, 246, 254–6
Kuwait City 255
Kwinter, Monty 244
Kyoto 225, 228

Labour Party 75–6, 77, 78, 79–80, 81, 82,
    87, 88, 90, 91, 92, 93, 94, 96, 97,
    98–9, 108, 109, 110, 111, 112–13,
    114, 116, 117, 121, 122, 123, 124,
    125, 128, 129, 131, 134, 141, 149,
    151, 170, 171, 173, 175, 176–7, 178,
    196, 201, 207, 208, 209, 210, 211,
    214, 233, 238, 239, 240, 241, 242,
    246, 251, 262–3, 264, 271, 272, 273,
    275, 276, 296, 297, 298, 299, 302,
    303, 307–8, 310, 311, 312, 316, 317,
    318, 320, 321, 322, 323, 324, 325,
    326, 327, 328, 329–30, 331, 338, 339

Lambert, Charles 284
Lambert, Sally 284
Lamont, Norman 103, 249, 266, 267
Lamp, The 193–4
Land of Song 65, 71
Lang, Ian 260, 298, 299, 315, 319
Lankin, Francis 286
Last Days of Hitler, The 40
Latimer, Claire 289
Laugharne 56
Lawson, Dominic 242
Lawson, Nigel 181, 237, 249
le Marchant, Spencer 41, 42, 84–5
League of Nations 159
Lee, John 247
Legge, Henry 306
Legislation Committee 140
Lehrer, Tom 64
Leibing, Dr 217, 218
Lenin 71, 79, 339
Leningrad 70
Leong Chi Wayo 278
Lestor, Jim 152, 154
Leveque, Rene 115
Levin, Bernard 96
Lewis, Lloyd 68, 70
Lewis, Saunders 128, 136
Liberal Democrats 297, 317, 335
Liberal Party 61, 94, 96, 97, 99, 111, 113,
    114, 116, 118, 121, 123, 124, 135,
    151, 173, 270, 271, 292
Liddell, I. O. 18
Life of Gladstone 43
Lightbown, Sir David 291, 305, 317, 320
Lilley, Peter 289, 290, 291, 318, 338
Lillingston, Charlie 39
Lin, Dr T. S. 313–14
Lincoln, Abraham 158–9, 217
Lisbon 215
Lisburne, John, Lord 306
Lisburne, Sheila, Lady 306
Little Bible, The 13–14
Liverpool 7, 8, 16, 46–52, 82, 195
Liverpool, Lord 211
Liverpool Daily Post 10, 46, 47, 51, 59,
    329
Liverpool Echo 46, 48, 51
Llanberis 186, 265, 283
Llandaff 328
Llandaff Cathedral 55–6, 161, 167
Llanddona 13
Llandrindod 99, 100, 129

Llandudno 76, 78, 120, 121, 123, 124, 150,
    155, 171, 193, 223, 243, 265, 322, 326
Llandudno Conservative Club 121
Llanelli 112, 175, 190, 209, 266, 330
Llanelli Rugby Club 101
Llanfairfechan 124, 232–3
Llangadog 132
Llanon 244
Llanrwst 139, 223, 265
Llewelyn, David 79
Llewelyn, Sir Harry 79
Lloyd, Selwyn 78, 238
Lloyd George, David 5, 6, 8, 25, 113, 318,
    330
Lloyd George, Gwilym 76
Lloyd George, Margaret 5
Lloyd George, Lady Megan 112
Llwyd, Alun 257–8
Llyn Eigiau 159
Llyn Padarn 186
Llywelyn, Prince of Wales 334
Local Government Bill 143, 144
Local Government Reorganisation Bill
    292, 294
Local Government (Wales) Bill 297, 298,
    300, 302–3
Lockhead, George 149
Lollobrigida, Gina 57
Lombardy 217, 218, 258, 297
Lombardy Chamber of Commerce 258
London 16, 19, 20, 35, 36, 37, 46, 48, 51,
    52, 54, 55, 57, 63, 65, 106, 115, 139,
    142, 145, 159, 171, 178, 203, 214,
    215, 219, 226, 230, 281, 286, 288,
    289, 290, 297, 300, 340
Long, John 18
Long, Richard 18
Long, Viscount 18
Long, Walter 18
Longden, Gilbert 99
Lonlas 232
Lonrho 92, 309
Los Angeles 245
Lotery, Adam 106
Lotery, John 85, 106, 213
Lotery, Peta, née Hitchmough 106
Louis, Joe 21, 24
Louth 208
Luce, Richard 153
Lunn, Peter 339
Lutyens, Sir Edwin 47
Lyell, Sir Nicholas 257

Maastricht agreement 267, 271
McAdden, Sir Stephen 109, 110
MacCarthy, Desmond 27
Macdonald, Malcolm 171
Macdonald, Ramsay 171
McEvedy, Colin 17, 18, 41
McGahey, Mick 89, 93
MacGregor, Ian 174–5, 178
MacGregor, John 193, 194, 260
Mackay, Lord 257
Mackintosh, John 90
Maclean, David 299
Maclean, Donald 141, 308
Maclean, Murdo 271
MacLeod, Iain 84, 208
Macmillan, Harold 76, 81, 88, 94, 113,
    119, 177–8, 213, 322
Macmillan, Katie 306
Macmillan, Maurice 81, 306
McQuarrie, Albert 165
Madrid 215, 259
Maenan 129
Magdalen College, Oxford 41
Mahathir, Dr 280
Mahdi, the 255
Maitland, Lady Olga 311
Makarios, Archbishop 52
Malacca 279, 280
Malaysia 279–81
Malltraeth 11
Major, John 233, 237, 242, 249, 250, 251,
    252, 253–4, 257, 259, 262, 263, 264,
    265–6, 267, 269, 272, 274, 275, 276,
    288, 289, 291, 293, 294, 295–6, 297,
    298, 299, 303, 306, 307, 310, 311,
    314–15, 316, 317, 318, 320, 321,
    322, 324–5, 327, 329, 337, 340
Major, Norma 250
Manchester 17, 204
Mandelson, Peter 308, 322, 326
Mansfield, Jayne 270
Maples, John 310
Maresfield 29
Margaret, Princess 55, 63
Marlow, Anthony 276, 311, 315
Marples, Ernest 80
Marriage of Figaro, The 70
Married Love 2
Marshall, Walter, Lord 203
Marten, Neil 81
Martin, Kingsley 113
Martin, Michael 328

Marx, Karl 38
Mason, Richard 139, 147
Mates, Michael 154, 272
Mathews, Terry 286
Mathias, Eleanor 59
Mathias, Glyn 136
Maude, Francis 248
Maudling, Reginald 306
Mawby, Ray 83, 119
Mawhinney, Brian 322
Max Bell Foundation 244
Maxwell, Captain 255
Maxwell, Robert 62
Mayhew, Sir Patrick 257
Mellish, Bob 98
Mellor, David 288–9
Menai Bridge 7
Menai Straits 46, 150
Menuhin, Yehudi 64
Mercedes-Benz 218
Mercer, Chris 65
Merchant, Piers 327
Merchlyn 186
Merioneth 90
Mersey House (London) 51
Merseyside 8
Merthyr Tydfil 170, 176, 272, 292
Merton College, Oxford 191
Meyer, Sir Anthony 82, 133, 134, 199,
    210, 237
Meyer, Barbadee, Lady 82
Mezzogiorno, the 90, 91
Michelangelo 56
Michie, Bryan 62, 64
Michigan 216
Mid Wales Development 276
Midsummer Night's Dream, A 27
Mikardo, Ian 149
Milan 258, 297, 312
Millbank 327
Miller, Hal 248
Miller, Keith 62
Miller, Dr Maurice 164
Milligan, Stephen 296
Milošević, Slobodan 339
Milton Keynes 169
miners' strike
    (1973) 174, 175
    (1981) 146, 176
    (1984–5) 174–8, 179
Minnesota 216
Miskin 218

Mitchell, Austin 322
Molloy, Bill, Lord 215
Molson, Lord 171
Monmouth 82, 106, 258, 272
Monroe, Marilyn 49, 270
Montevideo 10
Montgomery, Field Marshal Bernard 29, 217
Montgomeryshire 125, 292, 298
Morecambe, Eric 62
Morgan, Archdeacon 8–9, 14
Morgan, Dr Bill 286
Morgan, Elystan 117
Morgan, Geraint 82, 131, 134
Morgan, Rhodri 276, 300, 330
Morgan, W. John 72, 74, 117, 146–7
Morgan, Bishop William 222
Morley, John 43
Morris, John 100, 117
Morris, Michael 108
Morris, Simon 202
Morrison, Herbert 75
Morrison, Peter 304
Moscow 68–71, 82, 339
Moscow Dynamos 68
Moscow Radio 69
Mossend (Lanarkshire) 313
Moynihan, Colin 304
Mudd, David 108
Munich 90, 189
Murdoch, Rupert 62
Murray, Reverend Christie 23, 24
Mussolini, Benito 5
Myers, Bob 63
Myrtle Street gang 49

Nabarro, Sir Gerald 309
Nadir, Azil 272
Nagasaki 253
Nagoya 225
Naruhito, Prince 191–2, 227–8
National Assembly for Wales 332, 335–6, 338, 339, 341
National Audit Office 276
National Broadcasting Corporation 62, 63
National Coal Board (NCB) 174, 176, 177, 178
National Curriculum 219, 234
National Eisteddfod 6, 128, 135, 187, 202, 223, 273
National Government 171
National Health Service (NHS) 291, 186

National Museum of Wales 293
National Portrait Gallery 195
National Union 104
National Union of Mineworkers (NUM) 88–9, 93, 94, 174, 175, 176, 177–8
Nature and Destiny of Man, The 28
Nazis, the 5, 32, 63, 75
Neath 163
Neave, Airey 81, 101–2, 103, 120, 121
Nellist, David 176
Neri, Rosalina 62
Neubert, Michael 272
New Labour 277, 311, 316, 322, 325, 326, 330, 337
New Statesman 27, 141, 289
New Tredegar 193
New York 51, 56, 68, 112, 208, 215–16, 230, 243–4, 245, 282
New York State 216
Newborough 16
Newbridge Electronics 286
Newman, J. H. 2
Newport 186, 193, 223, 231, 248, 306, 322
News of the World 58, 62, 63, 296
Newton, Isaac 314
Newton, Tony 269, 271, 289
Nicholas, Branwen 257
Nicholas, James 257
Nichols, Nigel 289
Nicholson, Emma 317
Niebuhr, Reinhold 28
Night Watch 43
Nightingale, Jennifer 283
1922 Committee 96, 101, 102, 114, 198, 315, 323
No Other Choice 339
Nolan, Lord 310
Nolan Report 314
Normandy 232
Norris, Steve 289, 295, 322
North Wales Weekly News 123
Northop 232
Northern Ireland 93, 97, 107, 120, 153, 196, 316, 318
Nott, John 100, 152, 156, 158, 162
Nottinghamshire 176, 177
Novello, Ivor 65
Nuremberg 189

Oakes, Gordon 108
Observer 143, 178

O'Connor, Des 64
Official Information Bill (1980) 136
Ogmore 89
Oita province (Japan) 259
Old Labour 311, 316
Oliver Twist 13
Omdurman 255
Ontario 115, 244, 259, 285–6, 293
Oppenheimer, Robert 230
Orgreave Colliery 174, 177
Orme, Stan 88
Ormett, Freddie 205–6
Ormond, John 56, 57
Osaka 225, 226–7
Oswestry 78
Othello 65
O'Toole, Paddy 171, 172, 185
Ottawa 115
Owen, Dafydd 282
Owen, David 151
Owen Glendower 67
Oxford 27, 37, 39–45, 74, 93, 317

Pacific Heights 230
Paddington 79, 186, 219, 248, 250
Padley, Walter 89
Page, Graham 104
Page, Jack 156
Paice, Jim 124
Panasonic 249
Panorama 155
Parents for Welsh Medium Education 202
Paris 34, 90
Parkinson, Ann 182
Parkinson, Cecil 181–2, 331
Parliament for Wales 112
Parochial and Plain Sermons 2
Parr, Katherine 334
Parris, Matthew 337
Path to Power, The 114
Patten, Chris 236, 242, 292
Paynter, Will 75, 175
Pearl Harbour 229
Peasants' Revolt (1381) 215
Pelham, Henry 306
Pembrokeshire 100, 124, 172, 173, 208,
     234–5, 265, 279
Pen-y-Pass 265
Pengelly, R. A. 170
Penmachno 122
Penmaenmawr 122, 123, 232–3, 288
Penrhyn Bay 123

Pérez de Cuéllar, Javier 158
Pergamon Press 62
Perth 113, 114
Philby, Kim 141, 142, 308, 340
Philip, Duke of Edinburgh 290, 339
Philip, Ed 286
Philippines, the 285
Philipps, Sir Grismond 63
Picture Post 56
Pitt, William 140, 195, 306
Plaid Cymru 76–7, 81, 111, 112, 113,
     114, 117, 118, 124, 128, 130, 131,
     134, 138, 207, 223, 242, 266, 271,
     272, 273, 325, 330, 338, 339
Plaut, Rudi 284
Poetry and Truth 39–40
poll tax 237, 238, 239–40, 241, 252, 256
Pollard, Eve 299
Pompidou, Georges 95
Pond, Bill 216
Pontyclun 189–90
Pontypool 64, 82, 151, 192
Pontypridd 202
Port Stanley 152, 159
Port Talbot 66
Porthcawl 112, 175
Portillo, Michael 248, 268, 299, 315
Portrait of the Artist as a Young Dog 66
Powell, Colin 254
Powell, Enoch 84, 92, 94, 98, 102, 109,
     116, 158, 185, 187, 195
Powys 298, 306
Prague Film Festival 68
Prescott, John 299
Preston, Peter 310
Private Eye 184
Prowse, Beverley 62
Public Accounts Committee 276, 289
Puget Sound Welsh Association 283
Pugin, August 334
Pujol, Jordi 258–9, 297, 312
Punch 50, 67
Pym, Francis, Lord 80, 89, 102, 104, 148,
     149, 152, 153, 156, 158, 167, 174,
     181, 193, 237, 311

Quebec 115
Queensland 284
Quinn, John 285
Quinn, Nancy 285

Radio Newsreel 54, 55

Radnorshire 77, 112, 125, 188, 193, 298
Rae, Bob 244, 285–6
RAF Valley 171, 266
Raffan, Keith 184
Raffles, Sir Stamford 279
Raphael, Adam 147
Rating (Caravans) Bill (1976) 108
Ray, Martha 63
Rea, Eddie 191
Reader's Digest 112
Reagan, Ronald 160
Red Wharf Bay 7
Redwood, John 271, 273, 275, 276–7, 281, 288, 291, 292, 293, 294, 295, 298, 299–300, 302, 312, 315, 323, 325, 331
Rees-Davies, Billy 103
Rees Mogg, William, Lord 340
Referendum Party 311, 320, 326, 328
Regional Employment Premium 98
Reinpell, Dr Peter 190
Reith, Lord 53, 55
Rembrandt 43
Renshaw, Keith 155
Renton, David, Lord 199
Renton, Tim 238
Return to the Rhondda 74
Reuters 51
Reveille 49
Rhineland, the 5
Rhodes, Jack 243
Rhodes, John 243
Rhodes, Sarah 243
Rhodes, William 243
Rhodesia 77, 200
Rhondda 5, 170, 214
Rhone-Alpes region 217
Rhyl 202
Rich, Colwyn 244
Rich, Geoff 244
Richards, J. J. 284
Richards, Rod 233–4, 291, 300, 302, 307, 311
Richards, Tom 55
Rickard, Don 244, 286
Riddick, Graham 304
Ridley, Nicholas 87, 181, 182, 242, 256
Rifkind, Malcolm 114, 299
Rigoletto 37
Rise and Fall of the Third Reich, The 70
Road to Opportunity 233
Roberts, Caroline 148, 165
Roberts, E. P. 2, 3–4, 5, 6, 7, 8, 13, 39, 44–5, 106, 144

Roberts, Eileen 164, 166
Roberts, Eleri 279
Roberts, Enid 57, 74, 110, 122, 125, 150, 165, 166, 167, 169, 191, 203, 206, 212, 236, 238, 241, 292, 300, 305, 307, 325, 326, 328, 329
Roberts, Frances 7
Roberts, Geraint 57, 74, 159, 179, 325
Roberts, Goronwy, Lord 79–80, 112, 132
Roberts, Hilary 164, 167
Roberts, Huw 57, 74, 167, 179, 315
Roberts, John 306
Roberts, Margaret Ann 1–2, 3, 4–5, 6, 8, 10, 12, 13, 15, 17, 18, 39, 43, 44–5
Roberts, Michael 82–3, 106, 119, 125, 126, 127, 132, 139, 147, 148, 151, 155, 156–7, 162, 163–6, 167, 168, 170–1, 250
Roberts, Owen S. 284
Roberts, Rhidian 333
Roberts, Rhys vii, 57, 74, 179, 300, 305
Roberts, Robert 7
Roberts, Wyn, Lord Roberts of Conwy
   and accepting office 105–6, 125, 126
   and agriculture 90–1, 204, 256
   and broadcasting 129–32, 133–8, 169, 218–19
   and Common Market 90–1
   and conservation 187
   and devolution 100, 112, 113, 114, 115, 117, 118, 120, 207, 223, 241–2, 297, 302, 311, 312, 329–32, 335–6, 339, 341
   and economy 90, 142, 207, 221, 223, 233, 243, 246, 282, 288
   and education 121, 200–3, 207, 218, 219–22, 234–5
   and election as MP for Conwy 76–8
   and energy 186
   and European Parliament 104–5
   and export and investment missions 189–93, 215–16, 217–18, 223, 224–9, 233, 243, 244, 255, 258–9, 278–81, 282–7, 297, 312–13
   and film 295
   and health 170, 186
   and House of Lords 239, 332–5, 337–8
   and housing 141, 186–7
   and independence for Wales 77
   and knighthood 242–3, 249
   and local government 143, 144, 274–5, 291, 294, 297, 298, 300

marriage 57
and political ambition 105, 209–10,
  211–12
a Privy Counsellor 259–61, 289–90, 333
and regionalism 217–18, 223, 298, 312
and resignation from office 290–1,
  292, 293–5, 299–301, 302, 304–5,
  307–8
and roads 186, 200, 231–3, 256, 288,
  306
and tourism 232–3
and travel 189–91, 192–3, 215–18,
  224–30, 243–5, 254–6, 258–9,
  278–81, 312–13, 326
and Welsh language 59, 121, 127–38,
  202, 212, 218, 219, 220, 221–3, 233,
  234–6, 256–8, 258, 267–9, 270–3,
  278, 288, 327, 333
Robertson, Reverend Charles 241
Robey, George 27
Robinson, Mark 193, 198, 200, 208
Roddick, Winston 223, 257
Rodgers, Bill 91, 151
Rodin, Auguste 25
Rogers, Will 112
Rolls Royce 87
Rome 90
Rommel, Erwin 217
Rommel, Manfred 217–18, 312
Romney, George 195
Roosevelt, Franklin D. 63
Roosevelt, Theodore 179
Rosenberger, Mary 283
Rowe-Beddoe, David 312–13
Rowland, Tiny 309
Rowlands, Ted 170, 272, 292
Royal Commission on the Press (1976) 108
Royal Oak 10
Royal Welch Fusiliers 261
Rugby 275
Runyon, Damon 68
Rural Enterprise Initiative 207, 256
Russell, Bertrand 284
Russia *see* USSR
Ryder, Caroline 293
Ryder, Richard 127, 215, 292, 293–4,
  299–300, 304, 305–6

St Albans 49
St Ives 100
St Mellons 291
St Oswald, Lord 99

St Stephen's Club 143
Salisbury, Lord 97, 265
Saltley 89
San Carlos (Falklands) 159
San Francisco 229, 245
Sandown 41, 42
Sandringham 289–90
Sandwich, Earl of 63
Sanyo 228
Satchell, John 260, 289
Saudi Arabia 245
Savile, Sir Jimmy 243
Savile Club 63, 85, 112, 113, 142, 144,
  145, 160, 242
Scallywag 295, 296
Scapa Flow 10
Scargill, Arthur 89, 111, 151, 174, 177,
  178, 179
Schiller, Friedrich von 218
Schmidt, Helmut 143
Schönbrunn 33, 34
Schwarzkopf, Elizabeth 37
Schwarzkopf, General Norman 254
Schwebe, R. 145
Science North Centre 286
Science World Dome 284
Scotland 112, 113–14, 115, 118, 120, 122,
  150, 159, 203, 207, 211, 221, 241,
  298, 299, 311, 312, 313, 328,
  329–30, 331, 335, 338
Scotland, Baroness 340
Scotland and Wales Bill (1976) 114, 118
Scotland Bill (1978) 115
Scott, Sir Giles Gilbert 47
Scott, Sir Kenneth 260, 290
Scott Report 318–19
Scottish Labour Party 113, 114
Scottish National Party (SNP) 114, 116,
  118, 122, 207, 211, 241, 339
Scottish Office 113
Scottish Television 61, 73
SDP–Liberal Alliance 168, 169, 173, 188,
  193, 209, 210
Seattle 115, 282–3
Second World War 6–8, 10–11, 12, 13,
  14, 19, 46–7, 63, 216, 217
Seferiantz, Vitaly 69–70
Selling of the Prime Minister, The 215
Selsden conference 87, 92, 95
Senghenydd 72
Sergeant, John 328
Sesenheim 40

Severn Bridge (Second) 182
Severn Bridges Bill 256
Severn Tunnel 67, 337–8
S4C 137, 165, 169, 219
Shaeffler 190
Shakespeare, William 26, 27, 67, 257
Share my Music 64–5
Shaw, George Bernard 88
Sheffield 262–3
Sheffield 156
Shelley, P. B. 41
Shepherd, Colin 242
Shirley, James 260, 300
Short, Clare 322
Shotton 142, 207
Siberry Report 129, 131
Sicily 12
Siemens 190
Singapore 278–9
Singapore Broadcasting Corporation 278
Singapore Economic Development Board 278
Singapore Institution 279
Singapore Radio 278
Singapore St David's Society 279
Sioux rebellion (1863) 216–17
Sir Galahad 161
Skinner, Dennis 85, 296
Slater, Jim 213
Smart, Billy 60
Smith, Adam 313
Smith, Sir Derek Walker 155
Smith, Sir Dudley 314
Smith, Ian 77
Smith, John 299, 300
Smith, Tim 327–8
Smith Square 327
Snettisham treasure 293
Snowden, Philip 171
Snowdonia 191, 203, 265
Soames, Sir Christopher 90, 148
Social Democratic Party (SDP) 91, 149, 151, 173
Socialist Workers' Party 239
Soest 192
Sony 228, 288, 313
Sorrows of the Young Werther, The 40
South Africa 101, 102
South Georgia 155
South Wales Borderers 74
South Wales Echo 244
Southall 147

Spain 5, 68, 217, 259
Spath, Lothar 217, 218
Spencer, Lady Diana *see* Diana, Princess 149–51
Spicer, Sir Michael 327
Spies Beneath Berlin 340
Splott 57
Sporting Chronicle 42
Sprick, Julius 192
Sprick, Ute 192
Sprick cycle factory 192
Spycatcher 36
Squire, Philip 202
Staedtler 189–90
Stafford, David 340
Stafford, William B. 283, 284
Stalin, Joseph 68, 79
Stanley, John 141
Stanley, Susan 141
Staying Power 213
Steamboat round the Bend 112
Steel, David 173
Steele, Mike 303
Steen, Jan 43
Steinberg, Gerry 318
Steiner, Stephen 190–1
Stephen, Olwen 244
Stephenson, Robert 46
Stevas, Norman St John 90, 148
Stewart, Donald 165
Stopes, Dr Marie 2
Strickman, Corporal 35, 36
Stuttgart 217–18, 312
Sudbury (Ontario) 286
Suez Crisis 199, 200
Sun 49, 137, 327
Sunday Express 155
Sunday Times 183, 200, 288, 295, 304, 315
Sunter, Fred 125
Swan, Bill 204–5, 206
Swansea 54, 56, 66, 79, 122, 133, 215, 232, 246
Swansea Evening Post 56
Swansea Sound 116
Sweden 285
Suzuki, Tetsuo 228
Sykes, Paul 328
System of Moral Philosophy, A 313

Taiwan 312–14
Talacre 282

Talbot, Godfrey 55
Tale of Two Cities, A 13
Tapsell, Sir Peter 314
Tatton 327
Taylor, Elizabeth 65, 66
Taylor, John 247
Taylor, Sir Teddy 81, 100–1, 314
Tebbit, Margaret 178–9
Tebbit, Norman 100, 178–9, 325
Techniquest Centre (Cardiff Bay) 284
Television Wales and the West (TWW) 58, 59–73, 75, 76
Tenby 172
Tennyson, Alfred, Lord 96
Territorial Army 6
Thackeray, W. M. 40
Thatcher, Denis 195
Thatcher, Margaret 82, 94, 95, 96, 102, 103, 104, 105, 106, 107, 108–9, 114, 116, 118, 119, 120–2, 123, 125–6, 127, 133, 140–1, 143, 146, 147, 148–9, 151, 154, 155, 156, 157, 158, 160, 162, 163, 165, 167, 168, 169, 172, 173, 174, 175–6, 177, 178, 179, 182, 193, 195, 197, 198, 199, 200, 209, 210–11, 212, 213, 214, 215, 218, 219–21, 223, 233, 234, 235, 236–7, 238, 239, 240, 241–2, 246, 247–8, 249, 250, 251, 254, 257, 262, 276, 280, 288, 291, 296, 298, 302, 305, 312, 318, 325, 328, 335, 338
Theodosian Code, the 41
Theory of Moral Sentiments, The 313
Thetis 7, 13
This World of Wales 65
Thomas, Ceri 216
Thomas, Dylan 56, 66, 67, 144–5, 216
Thomas, George 83, 105, 110, 119, 165, 166–7, 168, 169, 223
Thomas, Gwyn 67–9, 71
Thomas, Jeffrey 165
Thomas, Sir John Stradling 82, 106, 168, 172, 178, 183–4, 193, 200, 209, 241, 258
Thomas, Peter, Lord Thomas of Gwydir 77, 83, 100, 196, 333
Thomas, Dr Roger 164
Thomas, William 4
Thomas, Wynford Vaughan 53, 72, 74, 144
Thomson, Roy 61–2, 73
Thoreau, Henry 230
Thorneycroft, Peter, Lord 126, 310

Thorpe, Jeremy 96, 108, 109
Thurnham, Peter 319
Tikrit 254
Time and Chance 111
Times 27, 28, 41, 73, 92, 96, 104, 114, 165, 181, 199, 262, 315, 318, 326, 331, 337, 339
Tintern Abbey 187
Today 71
Todd, Mike 66
Tokyo 191, 227, 228, 229
Tomos, Angharad 202
Tonight 57
Tonypandy 170
Toronto 244, 284, 285–7, 293
Torrington 60, 61
Toshiba 228
Towers, Mike 59, 67
Townsend, Group Captain Peter 55
Towyn 238
Toxteth (Liverpool) 147
Toyota 233
Trade Development Alliance of Greater Seattle 283
Trades Union Congress (TUC) 86, 90, 92, 151, 177
Transport House 113
Tredegar 61
Tredinnick, David 304–5
Treffos 8
Trefriw 123
Tresilian 54
Trevor-Roper, Hugh 40
Tribune Group 108
Trimble, David 318
Troon 113
Tugendhat, Christopher 99–100
Turkey 52
Turner, Stephen 282
Twickenham 76, 317
Twickenham Studios 74
Twin Peaks 229–30
Tyler, Rodney 215
Tyler, Wat 215, 240
Tywyn Pottery 284

Ukraina Hotel (Moscow) 68, 70
Ukraine 203
Ulster Unionists 96, 318
Under Milk Wood 216
United Kingdom 53, 71, 77, 90, 112, 115, 120, 134, 137, 146, 153, 191, 203,

216, 217, 218, 219, 224, 228, 233,
    246, 259, 278, 291, 313, 318, 330,
    335, 339, 341
United Nations 158, 159, 245, 254
University College, Oxford 40, 41, 42,
    84–5
University of British Columbia 284
University of Glamorgan 281
University of Wales, Aberystwyth 281,
    309
University of Wales, Bangor 78, 124
Upper Clyde Shipbuilders 87
USA 16, 26, 32, 63, 67, 92, 95, 104, 135,
    137, 143, 155, 160, 186, 189, 190,
    196, 197, 201, 215–17, 224, 230,
    243–5, 254, 282–3, 292, 340
USSR 12, 26, 30, 31, 32, 33, 34–7, 38,
    68–71, 173, 193, 203, 242, 252, 253,
    312, 339
Utrecht 42

Vale of Glamorgan 233, 236
Valleys Initiative 207, 214, 223, 231
Vancouver 115, 284–5
Vancouver Welsh Society 285
Vaughan, Aled 74
Vaughan, Dr Gerry 106
Ventimiglia 85
Vermeer, Jan 43
Verney, Sir Edmund 13
Verney, Sir Harry 12–13, 28, 39
Verney, Sir Lawrence John 12, 13, 15,
    332–3
Verney, Lady Rachel 15
Victoria, Queen 260
Vienna 30–8, 39, 69, 141, 339–40
View of Delft 43
Villach 30, 31
VIPs 65, 67
Virginia 112
Vladivostok 70

Wagon Train 64
Waikiki 229
Wainwright, Richard 121
Wakeham, John 179, 236, 248, 289, 290
Wakeham, Roberta 179
Walden, George 319
Walder, David 101
Wales 17, 53, 55, 56, 57, 64, 65, 76, 100,
    104–6, 112–13, 114, 115, 117, 118,
    120, 125, 126, 132, 133, 137, 143,
    150, 151, 159, 170, 171, 173, 181,
    182, 183, 185, 186, 188, 189–90,
    191, 192, 193, 195, 201, 203, 207,
    209, 211, 212, 213, 214, 216, 217,
    218, 219, 221, 224–6, 227, 238, 241,
    242, 243, 246, 255, 256, 258, 259,
    264, 268, 274, 275–6, 278, 281, 283,
    286, 289, 291, 292–3, 294, 297, 298,
    299, 308, 311, 313, 315, 325, 328,
    329–32, 335, 338, 341
Wales Area Office 122, 331
Wales–Baden-Würtemberg agreement
    312
Wales Bill (1978) 115, 116
Wales in Europe 312
Wales–Ontario agreement 286
Wales West and North (Teledu Cymru)
    72, 130
Walker, Bill 315
Walker, Marianna 214
Walker, Mark Chapman 58, 60, 62, 63
Walker, Peter 114, 175, 211–12, 213–15,
    218, 221, 223, 224, 231, 232, 233,
    234, 235, 236, 238, 242, 259, 297
Walker, Tessa 213
Wallace, Billy 62–3
Walpole, Robert 306
Walters, Ira 173
Ward, Dame Irene 83
Ward, John 310, 320, 321
Wardell, Gareth 312
Warrington 151
Washington 111
Washington State 283, 284
Watkins, Alan 178
Watkins, Ronald 26–7
Watkins, Tudor 112
Watkins, Vernon 56
Weatherill, Jack 258
Webb, Steffan 202
Wella 191
Wells, Professor G. P. 'Chip' 144
Wells, H. G. 144
Welsh Books Council 128
Welsh Day 163, 326
Welsh Development Agency (WDA) 189,
    214, 258, 276, 289, 302, 312, 330
Welsh Grand Committee 80, 110, 120,
    133, 151, 251, 271, 292
Welsh Guards 161
Welsh Joint Education Committee
    (WJEC) 201–2, 203

Welsh language 3, 54, 55, 57, 58, 59, 65, 72, 112, 121, 125, 127–38, 149, 165, 171, 187–8, 202–3, 212, 218, 219, 220, 221–3, 233, 234–6, 256–8, 267–9, 270–3, 278, 283, 288, 327, 333
Welsh Language Act
  (1967) 128
  (1993) 273
Welsh Language Bill (1992–3) 257, 267–9, 270–3, 278, 333
Welsh Language Board 235, 256–7, 272, 273, 288
Welsh Language Society (Cymdeithas yr Iaith Gymraeg) 127–8, 129, 131, 187, 202, 203, 223, 227, 257–8, 273
Welsh League of Youth (Urdd Gobaith Cymru) 63, 128, 131
Welsh Medium Education Committee 202–3
Welsh National Opera Company 256
Welsh Nusery School Movement (Mudiad Ysgolion Meithrin) 128
Welsh Office 83, 100, 113, 125, 130, 135, 137, 149, 150, 162, 166, 168, 172, 187, 200, 203, 207, 208, 211, 213, 218, 222, 223, 224, 232, 235, 236, 238, 249, 256, 265, 273, 278, 285, 307, 311, 312, 329, 333
Welsh Questions 99, 184, 198, 214, 250, 297
Welsh Select Committee 312
Welsh Water 235
Western Mail 53, 72, 75, 122, 302, 331
Westland Affair 196–9, 215
Westminster, Wales and Water 208
Westward Television 60, 64
What I said about the Press 61
Wheldon, Huw 53
Whetton, Philip 297
Whetton, Roswithe 297
Whitbread 214
White Horse (Greenwich Village) 216
Whitehead, Sir John 227
Whitehead, Lady 227
Whitelaw, William 93, 102, 104, 114, 130–1, 132, 133–4, 135, 136, 137, 140, 158, 159, 167, 168–9, 181, 198, 200, 209–10, 219
Whitgift, Archbishop John 222
Who's Afraid of Virginia Woolf? 66
Wiggin, Jerry 100, 101, 108
Wigley, Dafydd 124, 134, 165, 223, 266–7, 272, 303

Wilberforce, Lord 89, 93
Wilding, Michael 66
Wilkes, John 61, 63
Wilkie, David 176
Wilkinson, John 317
Williams, Dorothy 59
Williams, Emlyn 66
Williams, Professor Glanmor 187
Williams, Gwilym, Archbishop of Wales 132, 135
Williams, Hywel 275, 293
Williams, Marcia (Lady Falkender) 97
Williams, Rhydwen 66
Williams, Shirley 121, 151
Williams of Mostyn, Lord 336
Wilson, Sir John 224
Wilson, Harold 73, 78, 82, 84, 86, 88, 90, 91, 94, 97, 98, 99, 103, 107–9, 110, 111, 113, 317
Windsor, Duke and Duchess of 308
Winn, Godfrey 62
Winter of Discontent 111, 118, 175
Winterton, Nicholas 325
Winton, Canon 167
Wise, Ernie 62
Wolfe, Tom 244
Wood, David 114
Woolton, Lord 60
Wrexham 48, 112, 228, 270
Wright, Annesley 228
Wright, Frank Lloyd 244
Wright, Peter 36
Wurtzburg, C. E. 279

Ximénes, Cardinal 293

Yeo, Tim 295
Ynys Môn 97
Young, Sir Brian 134
Young, Sir George 209, 340
Young, Hugo 183
Young, Janet, Lady 167, 181
Young Communists League 175
Younger, Diana 179
Younger, George 142, 179, 248
Ysgol John Bright 123

Zell, Sam 245
Zulu 74